AMERICAN LABOR

BY HERBERT HARRIS

NEW HAVEN · YALE UNIVERSITY PRESS

LONDON · HUMPHREY MILFORD · OXFORD UNIVERSITY PRESS

HD8072
H31

FOR EMILIE

PREFACE

THE new prominence of that labor question which Carlyle long ago characterized as the "universal great problem of the world" has of late transformed "labor" from a descriptive term into a continuing headline.

During the past few years, however, the strong upsurge of union organization in the United States has been too often treated as something only of recent origin; as if it were, indeed, almost a phenomenon of the depression itself. Hence to many people, labor's practices and personalities partake of a novel character and even seem to hold the somewhat sinister overtones of the unknown.

But labor's actions, as well as its aspirations, are neither new-born, nor menacing, nor obscure. They express the dynamics of a continuous drive toward that better life implicit in democratic government and in unionism which in this country began at about the same time.

To view the current labor movement historically, against the background of its predecessors, and thus perhaps to bring some perspective to the interpretation of its present hopes and achievements and defeats, forms the underlying purpose of this book.

The approach of the author reflects the attempt to approximate, however remotely, that spirit of free inquiry which some call liberalism and others the scientific temper.

The author wishes to give grateful acknowledgment to Professor E. Wight Bakke and Nelson Frank for valuable suggestions and criticism and for checking errors of fact; to Harold Friedman for expert aid in legal research and the compilation of an index; and to Elenore Levenson for patient assistance in gathering the scarcer items of bibliography.

Special acknowledgments are due to Rex Smith, Managing Editor of *Newsweek*, and Raymond Moley, former editor of *Today*, for permission to reproduce material prepared by the author for these magazines; to the City Club of New York for reprinting of data on union responsibility; and to Dr. William Bohn, Chief Librarian of the Rand School for Social Science, for permission to use and quote from the Debs Collection of Labor Literature, as well as to the following books and periodicals:

Bingham, Alfred M., *Insurgent America* (W. W. Norton Co.); Loeb, Harold, *The Chart of Plenty* (Viking Press); Soule, George S., *The Coming American Revolution* (Macmillan); Ware, Norman J., *Labor in Modern Industrial Society* (D. C. Heath & Co.); the *C.I.O. News, Common Sense, Current History, Dynamic America, Forum, Nation, New Republic, Survey Graphic.*

H. H.

New York City,
 November 22, 1938.

CONTENTS

Preface   v

List of Illustrations   ix

Introduction and Early History   1

From the Civil War   57

A New School of Political Economists: The United
    Mine Workers' Union of America   97

The United Brotherhood of Carpenters and Joiners   149

The American Newspaper Guild   173

The International Ladies' Garment Workers' Union:
    "The Union as a Way of Life . . ."   193

The Railroad Unions   225

Robot Revolt: The International Union of the
    United Automobile Workers of America   267

Trouble Is the Word for Textiles   305

Conclusion   351

Bibliography   433

Index   451

ILLUSTRATIONS

From the late 1820's on Labor increasingly broke into print   32

A typical lampoon of Labor's emergent political consciousness (1830)   38

Terence V. Powderly, Grand Master Workman of the Knights of Labor   80

Philip Murray and John L. Lewis   132

The Great Strike—Destruction of the Union Depot and Hotel at Pittsburgh. Drawn by Fred B. Schell.   232

Eugene V. Debs   246

William Dudley Haywood   318

Samuel Gompers   354

Unionism and the Business Cycle   359

Daniel Tobin and William Green   378

AMERICAN LABOR

Introduction and Early History

IF today you put the question, "What is unionism?" the answer you get is usually blended of passion, prejudice, and platitude in more or less equal parts. It is, you are told, just "another racket" dominated by disciples of Alphonse Capone; or, at the least, it is the vehicle for men of overweening ambition who use it to gratify their lusting after power and prestige. But really, you are assured, it is the stamping ground for the guardians of uplift and the pioneers of social progress.

Again it is an "artificial monopoly of labor," violating "natural laws of supply and demand" and hence hostile to the best interests of society. It is, on the other hand, a "normal and necessary" business device for regulating the wages and hours of work and sitting on the bulge of corporate greed. It is, clearly, a great revolutionary instrument by which capitalism may be abolished and the collectivist state ordained. It is, quite as clearly, a great stabilizing force which by helping to raise the income of wage earners tends to immobilize our institutions if only on Palmerston's principle: "If you want them conservative, give them something to conserve." It is un-American—the creation of foreign-born agitators. It is as indigenous as corn-on-the-cob. It is lawless, violent, irresponsible. It is the harbinger of industrial order, coöperation, peace.

Like any other form of collective human action, unionism has all the scope and diversity that such contradictory concepts imply. There is "business" in it, and uplift. There is revolution in it, and racketeering. For unionism, protean and complex, has its own decalogue, its own martyrs and Judases and popes and Luthers, its own splitting up of the old Catholic credo into new Protestant creeds.

In the United States today unionism and its future form
the pivot on which probably we will turn right or left or
even follow the New Deal's faltering footsteps along a new
and perhaps less miasmic "middle road."

By definition a trade union is a voluntary continuous
association of wage earners who unite to maintain and improve their working conditions. In the main they seek to
gain this goal by "collective bargaining," which means
merely that workers at a given mine or mill or store try to
fix the amount of their pay and their hours of labor by
dealing with their boss as a body, rather than on the basis
of each man for himself. The theory is simple. While the
employer can get along without any one individual worker,
he does need workers, en masse, to turn out his ships, his
shoes, his sealing wax. It is easy enough for him to discharge a single employee and replace him with another. It
is difficult, without great loss or perhaps bankruptcy, to
rid himself of his entire producing force.

Hence the metaphor of the fasces used by American
unionists since the 1790's to describe the benefits of collective bargaining. It will be recalled that the fasces were
a bundle of sticks, enclosing an ax, the whole thonged together by leather bands and carried by Roman lictors to
signify their authority. Each stick separately could easily
be broken, but the collection of sticks was strong and
could not be destroyed, at least without some cutting tool.
There was another symbolism attached to the fasces. The
bound sticks represented the essential unity of the state,
the mingling of many identities into a whole greater in
power than any of its component parts. Similarly, unionists
contend, collective bargaining, as a rule synonymous with
unionism, brings to the worker, when combined with his
fellows, a power greater than that which he might individually exercise.

The argument usually points out further that the workers need all the power they can get; for in any worker-

owner bargaining procedure, the employer starts off with a number of advantages.

He is first of all familiar with the "market," its raw materials, its credit sources, its supply of labor and technical and managerial ability, its prices for the finished commodity. Since business is conducted as a private matter, he alone really knows the inside facts of his enterprise. If a dispute as to the fairness of his wage scales arises, he can delete or pad the figures to suit his fancy and his own code of ethics. Since the turn of the century perennial Senate investigations have brought out that the books of many of our great corporations often disclose a rare capacity for mathematical acrobatics. During the NRA, moreover, government accountants with all the nascent prestige of the New Deal behind them encountered some very stubborn opposition when they asked to examine business ledgers, North, South, East, West.

Even more importantly, of course, the employer owns the plant and its machinery and the materials that feed its hoppers and its maws. Our present property relations and modes of production endow that ownership by itself with a long list of prerogatives. Bedrock in Anglo-Saxon law, and our own heritage from Blackstone, is the right of the owner of property to do with it anything he pleases. Bedrock in unionism is the challenge to this absolutism of control even though that challenge may be inversely couched in terms of "property rights" as when, for example, Homer Martin, president of the United Automobile Workers, inquires:

What more sacred property right is there in the world than the right of a man in his job? This property right involves the right to support his family, feed his children and keep starvation away from the door. This . . . is the very foundation stone of American homes . . . the most sacred, most fundamental property right in America. . . .

In this connection it is often said that today the title of ownership to the machine and its product has replaced in social might the title to land and its usufruct. The magnate who owns the assembly line is supposed to be in the same position as the lord of the manor who owned the acreage. This contention has more value as a simile for the simple than as a guide for the perplexed. For labor* in modern times has succeeded in restricting the full sway of property's prerogatives to a very appreciable extent. In this country, for example, it has used its ballot to inscribe on state and Federal statute books many laws stipulating eight hours of work per day, compensation for industrial accident, minimum wages, old-age and unemployment insurance. In 1937, with the Supreme Court's validation of the Wagner Labor Relations Act, it has been at last guaranteed the right of collective bargaining through representatives of its own choosing. By means of the strike, either walk-out, sit-down, or stay-in, along with the boycott and the closed shop, it has further encroached upon the authority of ownership and will probably circumscribe it even more in the future. Yet in all this, American labor on the whole has not so far attempted the liquidation, either gradual or abrupt, of private property,† of a profit

---

* Whether organized or not, "labor" is used here and in the following pages to designate those of the gainfully employed who derive their primary source of income from wages; and also to denote certain salaried groups which have consciously identified themselves with "labor" in its colloquial meaning, namely, the general body of wage-earners.

† This refers, of course, to wealth-producing property in both its "corporeal" and "intangible" forms when owned by private persons individually or by corporate groups: farms, stores, logging-camps, mines, factories, banks, dwellings that yield an income, commercial buildings, "service" enterprises whether advertising agency or beauty shop; and public utility property such as railroad, telephone, and electric light and power companies, etc. It refers also to the ownership of the power to create and acquire credit; and of business good will, franchises, trade-marks, patents; and of stocks and bonds, notes and mortgages and other debt-claims. It refers further to the expectancy value in undeveloped real estate and undeveloped natural resources such as forests or mineral deposits. It does not refer to the individual's personal possessions, the use-ownership of a tooth-brush or house, or the display-ownership of a star-sapphire.

and price system. Instead it has sought to adjust itself to changed and changing conditions in the production and distribution of the goods and services of an increasingly complex and interdependent society.

Prior to the War for Independence this country had no trade unions in the modern meaning of the term. In Boston, New York, Philadelphia, of course, there were various labor bodies, but they were mainly benevolent associations, their function and purpose limited to looking out for their members in times of illness and financial stress. They paid the doctor's bills and the funeral costs when the doctor's bloodlettings and leechings failed. From their treasuries they loaned small sums to members or their survivors who were in "dire and palpable need." They often assumed a dualistic role of censor. If a brother's workmanship fell below par, he was reprimanded by his fellows and urged to mind his *p's* and *q's*. If his private morals became a topic for fence-railing gossip, he was lectured on behavior "seemly for a Christian gentleman" and given advice on temperance.

In short, in a day when free clinics, poorhouses, home relief, W.P.A. projects, old-age pensions, the Elks, ward heelers, and the institutions of private charity were virtually nonexistent, such labor organizations were formed by the new town dwellers—the smiths, the wheelwrights, the cordwainers, the coopers, the hatters, the carpenters, the printers—for their mutual aid and protection against the hazards of this too mortal life. They were friendly, semi-fraternal alliances, instinct with the spirit of the "good neighbor." It is significant, moreover, that their charters and by-laws stipulated clearly that they were not to "engage" or "concern" themselves with such economic questions as wages and hours.* Nor was it necessary for them

---

* An exception to this rule was the Carpenters' Society of Philadelphia, formed in 1724. It included both masters and journeymen. From fragmentary records, it seems to have been something of a "sport" in that it was both a charitable and bargaining society. It was hazed over with secrecy as to its

to do so. Between the master employers and their work-men a sense of coöperation and give and take generally prevailed. If differences arose they were settled by talking it out over a glass at the tavern. Even though more opulent, the master was often on terms of social intercourse with his journeymen. At his establishment they faced pretty much the same problems. He often worked at a bench alongside his men. He knew what they wanted. They knew what he expected. Rules of apprenticeship and standards of per-formance were strictly observed by both. He was less an employer in the contemporary usage of the word than a master craftsman who, by extra skill or experience or good luck or all combined, had been able to call to his assistance other men in turning out a product for which he had previously gained a certain reputation.

But the surrender of Cornwallis at Yorktown changed this relationship, gave a new turn to the wheel of America's economic destiny. Before Lexington and Concord, Great Britain's policy in the Colonies had dovetailed with Jeffer-son's highest hope that Americans leave the "whirling dis-taff" to others and concentrate upon agrarian pursuits. Whereas Jefferson urged this course to confirm his con-viction that the pursuit of agriculture was the best way of life, Great Britain urged it simply to discourage the rise of any American industry which might compete with Manchester cutlery or cloth from Leeds or coal from Newcastle.

Once the cord of British control over ways of work and wealth was severed, however, Americans saw the op-portunity to establish industries on their own. Natural re-sources were not only abundant; they were seemingly limitless. The coercions of king and parliament could no longer stifle ambition or thwart initiative. The post-Revo-

---

"crafts and mysteries" as if it were a vestigial remain of some medieval guild. It imposed fines for revealing its price list to any outsider, and for "divulging the sentiments of a member."

lutionary period, however, was a time of confusion with the new nation's finance and commerce shattered and deranged by the dislocations of the war.

It was not until 1791, when the Constitution was at last ratified, that business could again be placed on a sound foundation and order restored. Under the Constitution which, from the outset, became "not a document but a stream of history," the owners of counting house and shipyard and plantation were able to found a national bank to supply themselves and their friends with credit, and also to extend it to the enterprising. A uniform currency was introduced, ending the paper money inflation which in 1787 had compelled Jefferson to spend $355.50 for three quarts of brandy. Tariff barriers between the states were abolished, ending a situation in which Massachusetts placed heavy "duties" on imports from Connecticut and New York City exacted customhouse fees for every load of firewood or dozen eggs carried by a Jersey market boat from Paulus Hook to Cortlandt Street. At the same time, negotiations for treaties and trade agreements with other nations were vigorously begun. Foreign capital was brought in, foreign credit sought out. For the alert and businessminded it was the opportunity of the world's lifetime. With domestic tranquillity assured, with ample sources of capital available, with a stupendously rich continent still mainly unexplored and entirely unexploited, with the community market becoming state wide and even national in scope, with a quickened immigration to furnish new reservoirs of labor, it seemed as if the American who wanted to carve out a business career had only to obey the mandates of *Poor Richard's Almanack* to amass if not a fortune at least a considerable pile.

At this point in our history, moreover, a special kind of businessman assumed the dominant role. He was called variously the middleman, speculator, wholesale jobber, merchant capitalist. The last designation is perhaps more correct since his function was to buy and to sell, and he had the cash and credit with which to do it. He was in fact the descendant of Marco Polo, of the trader. He was not interested in making goods but in making money. He did not as a rule either own the mill or employ artisans in a shop. He bought and he sold. He bought cheap and he sold dear. His appearance coincided with the building of waterways and roads that connected the seaboard's East with the West of an always moving frontier, widening the market, linking the producer of goods in Boston to consumers in far-off Buffalo and Baltimore.

He bought great consignments of commodities from Europe, or in the newly created United States, storing them in warehouses, and then disposing of them to local retailers who also were coming into prominence as buying needs grew more diverse, keeping pace with the country's expansion. Soon the merchant capitalist was competing with the local master employers and their journeymen. Since he was not a craftsman he was more concerned with price than quality. He operated on the principle of quick turnover, and a small "take" per item, sold in quantity lots. He wanted to keep production costs down and profits up. To depress wage levels he therefore encouraged the division of labor known as the "teamwork" or "task" system, forerunner of the sweatshop. Under this arrangement, a skilled artisan was placed in charge of each "team," but its other members had varying degrees of expertness and some none at all. The traditions, fostered by both masters and men, of solid, prideful, "well-turned" workmanship which was more expensive, gave way before the merchant capitalist's demand for more and more at less and less. The idea wasn't new, of course. William Petty, seventeenth-century economist, had long before expressed the advantages of reorganizing the craft technique of production by splitting it up into many separate operations.

"Cloth must be cheaper made," he wrote, "when one

cards, another spins, another weaves, another draws, another dresses, another presses and packs, than when all the operations were performed by the same hand."

To cut his costs even further, the merchant capitalist patronized establishments that tapped the cheapest sources of labor power—child labor, woman labor, prison labor— here and abroad. At first, from the turn of the century to the 1830's, he bought mainly from England, which was the first nation to profit by the application of stored or steampower to methods of manufacture. The barber Arkwright with his spinning jenny, the preacher Cartwright with his automatic power loom, the instrument maker James Watt with his steam engine, had enabled British manufacturers to turn out an infinite variety of goods that could not be matched elsewhere in the world at anywhere near the same price. It was not only cotton cloth and yarns but also sickles and anchors that the merchant capitalist found cheaper to "buy British" and import into the states than to get from American firms. While Washington and Hamilton, anxious to develop home industries, chided the exponents of this trend, the trader in imports flourished. He flooded local markets with goods of English make, despite the appeals of the Founding Fathers and of papers like the *Philadelphia General Advertiser* which, on its masthead, exhorted its readers:

> *Of foreign gewgaws let's be free*
> *And wear the webs of Liberty.*

The American employer hence lost his ability to fix prices in his own community, his own "sales territory." He was up against a hardhitting competition from other cities, and from other countries. To buck that competition, he had to lower his own prices or succumb.

Then, as now, labor was the most flexible factor in production costs. Other items of "overhead," interest on borrowings, salaries, rents, taxes, depreciation of plant and

equipment, et cetera, remained by and large *constant*.
But a difference of a dollar a week in a workman's wage
might for the employer mean the difference between keeping up his enterprise or having it driven to the wall by the
onslaught of an ever-fiercer and more anarchic competition. And because everything but wages was "fixed," he
had to "take it out of labor's hide" in order to undercut
his rivals—a situation that has often recurred in our business annals, sometimes from compulsion, sometimes from
sheer greed.

The merchant capitalist had thus driven a wedge between the identity of interests that had previously prevailed among employers and workmen. At first the two
groups coöperated to protect themselves against the invasion of this commercial Attila. They formulated and put
through Congress a protective tariff policy designed to
permit infant industry to grow with a new nationalism.
Both employers and workmen struggled to "increase output, improve quality." In Providence, as early as 1789, an
"Association of Mechanics and Manufacturers" was set up
"for the purpose of promoting industry and giving a just
encouragement to ingenuity." A little later, in Charleston,
shipwrights and caulkers offered prizes for labor-saving
devices. Similarly, in Boston, printers hired chemists to experiment with ink, type, paper to the end that "more merit
. . . would reside" in their product.

But the merchant capitalist, specialist in marketing, aided
by improvements in navigation and bigger and better highways, networked the nation with his distribution lines.
Caesar of the marketplace, he came, he saw, he conquered.
And more and more local employers, to survive at all, were
forced to sell their output to this middleman, matching
prices with their rivals, domestic and foreign, and often
becoming merely labor brokers who supplied workmen
on "contractor" terms. In this process of cheapening wares
for an ever-enlarging market, wages were consistently cut.

The associations of the master employers which, like those of their craftsmen, had been friendly and benevolent, were transformed into agencies for reducing journeymen's pay. They advertised in the press for less expensive help. They broke the rules of apprenticeship which called for two to six years of training and which specified the number of "learners" in a shop. By the same token, the workmen's associations cast about for ways and means of keeping wages at previous levels and retaining "work rules." They hit upon the most rudimentary and yet the most effective method. They withdrew their labor power. They went on strike.

It was in this atmosphere of incipient capital-labor antagonism that America's first trade union was born.

It was called the Federal Society of Journeymen Cordwainers.* It was organized on a sound footing in Philadelphia in 1794 after several earlier attempts had failed. It lasted for twelve turbulent years, the epitome of unionism for its day. In 1799 it conducted the first "organized" strike to resist reductions in wages that averaged from $6.00 to $11.25 per week in the shops of masters employing from three to twenty journeymen. It paid one of its members to "picket"—to make the rounds of the city's cordwaining shops and see to it that all unionists had left their work. Everything was orderly and peaceful even though this turnout was in itself very important since shoemaking was a leading industry of the country's then largest city. The union's committee presented the master employers with a list of demands, insisting that the current wage scales for "cossacks" and "fancy-top boots" and "backstraps" be retained. After nine weeks of negotiation the strikers won.

It is interesting to observe that this particular dispute had nothing directly to do with ownership of the means

* The term "cordwainer," meaning shoemaker, derives from cordwain, or Spanish leather made from goat-skin or horse-hide and used in medieval Europe for the footgear of the wealthy.

of production or with technological change. The tools were still hand tools owned by the journeymen themselves, many of whom worked at home as much as they did in the shop. It was all a simple clearcut issue between workmen's wages and employers' prices as determined by the "existing state of the market."

Six years later, however, when the journeymen cordwainers again asked for a raise in wages ($3.00 instead of $2.50 for making a pair of booties and the like) the masters refused. The workmen "stood out" once more but this time met a new and stronger kind of opposition since the employers, to put an end to this "oppression" of wage-demands and strikes, invoked the aid of the courts, setting a precedent still in vogue.

In the late autumn of 1805, therefore, an indictment of many counts was returned against the journeymen. It charged that they had combined to increase their pay and injure others and had thus violated that part of the old English common law* which forbade criminal conspiracy.

In reply the journeymen at once drafted an "Address to the Public" which was published in the November 28, 1805, edition of the Philadelphia *Aurora*, leading Jeffersonian organ, and which in part declared:

The master shoemakers, as they are called after the slavish style of Europe, but who are only the retailers of our labor, and who in truth live upon the work of our hands, are generally men of large property to whom the suspension of business, though it is a loss, is not so great a loss as the total sus-

---

* Defined by Lord Wensleydale as "a system which consisted in applying to new combinations of circumstances those rules which we derive from legal principles and judicial precedents." Its roots were found in the law reports of cases which had actually been decided. Hence Burke's remark that "to put an end to reports is to put an end to the law of England." Its tenets were not so much "set down in any written statute or ordinance" as dependent upon "immemorial usage for their support." Its doctrines relating to conspiracy in trade and employments were at that time vague. It was often alleged that a conspiracy was either a combination to gain an unlawful object by unlawful means or to obtain a lawful object by unlawful means, an elastic definition which did everything but define "lawful."

pension of the means of subsistence, is to us who obtain our income from week to week. These masters . . . have their meetings, their associations, and they pass their resolutions. . . . The name of freedom is but a shadow, if for doing, what the laws of our country authorize, we are to have taskmasters to measure out our pittance . . . if we are to be torn from our fireside for endeavoring to obtain a fair and just support for our families, and if we are to be treated as felons and murderers only for asserting the right to take or refuse what we deem an adequate reward for our labor.

At the same time an editorial writer in the *Aurora* contended that the employers' recourse to the criminal conspiracy doctrine was really an attempt "to reduce whites to slavery," and he also asked, "Was there anything in the Constitution of the United States . . . or of Pennsylvania . . . which gave one man a right to say to another what should be the price of his labor?"

Like the trial of the journeymen itself which began early in 1806 in the mayor's court with Recorder Levy presiding, this line of argument reflected the current controversy between Federalists and Democratic Republicans as to whether or not England's common law should continue to be applied in the newly liberated nation. The Federalists took the affirmative. They maintained that the common law was the incarnation of human wisdom, quoted Coke on Magna Carta, and said that the adoption of England's legal system would allay grievous dangers of anarchy. The Democratic Republicans, in dissenting, claimed that the common law merely confirmed the rule that "might makes right," and embodied the interests of the rich and powerful against the poor and weak. They quoted Jefferson on the inalienable rights of man. They said that the adoption of England's legal system would enhance the grievous dangers of monarchy.

Naturally enough the arch-Federalist, Jared Ingersoll, chief proponent of the view that the common law was already the bulwark of American institutions, represented the employers in their suit. His opposing counsel was Caesar A. Rodney, ardent Jeffersonian, a protagonist of the belief that the new nation, with new problems of its own, could do better than to swallow whole the Mother Country's methods of jurisprudence, the more especially since they placed too much emphasis upon precedent, the past, rather than the present.

When both sides had presented their cases, Recorder Levy, a Federalist who sat as judge of both fact and law, and who favored the prosecution throughout, charged the jury that:

In every point of view, this measure [the journeymen's strike] is pregnant with public mischief and private injury . . . tends to demoralize the workmen . . . destroy the trade of the city, and leaves the pockets of the whole community to the discretion of the concerned. . . . A combination of workmen to raise their wages may be considered from a two-fold point of view: one is to benefit themselves . . . the other is to injure those who do not join their society. The rule of law condemns both. . . .

If the rule be clear we are bound to conform to it—even though we do not comprehend the principle upon which it is founded. We are not to reject it because we do not see the reason for it.

In brief, the journeymen were wrong because, according to the judge, they were wrong—an outlook which had to be accepted on faith since neither existing law nor logic could sustain it. Acting upon such instructions, however, the jury found the "defendants guilty of a combination to raise their wages." The Recorder fined the journeymen eight dollars each and costs. The decision intensified the attacks of the Democratic Republicans upon the Federalist-controlled judiciary in general, giving them a new appeal.

"Shall all others," they inquired, "except only the industrious mechanics be allowed to meet and plot; merchants to determine their prices current, or settle the markets; politicians to electioneer; sportsmen for horse-racing and games . . . and yet these poor men be indicted by combining against starvation?"

Despite all this excitement, however, the journeymen were not re-hired and were very much discouraged by their Society's courtroom defeat and its consequent inability to assure them of closed-shop incomes and work rules as before. The masters who at the trial had claimed they had "no vindictive passions to gratify" and were merely "guardians of the community against imposition and rapacity" seemed bound to teach the journeymen a lesson. The latter therefore established a warehouse of their own, a kind of coöperative center for selling their shoes in order to keep their families from "abject poverty." This venture failed; and with its failure vanished The Federal Society of Journeymen Cordwainers of the City and Liberties of Philadelphia, the first among thousands of American unions to be destroyed by an adverse court decision.*

The Federal Society of Journeymen Cordwainers had been christened a "trade" union simply to indicate that journeymen in the craft of shoemaking had joined together to protect their living standards against attempts to depress them, and to guard their "competitive area" against "inter-

---

* Elsewhere the cordwainers through their unions were later involved in five other conspiracy cases: one in New York City in 1809; two in Baltimore in the same year; and two in Pittsburgh, in 1814 and 1815. They lost three trials, won a fourth (in Baltimore), and compromised a fifth (in Pittsburgh, 1815). As a whole the judges took the view that trade and manufacture would be impaired if journeymen were allowed to confederate for fixing their wages in the same way that employers were allowed to combine in fixing their prices. In this the courts merely rationalized the prevailing sentiment that the prosperity of "business" and its owners was identical with the welfare of the community and that anything which might be construed as harming the first would injure the second, a belief generally found in periods of economic expansion. It was many years before the law on conspiracy assumed definite shape. In 1827, for example, the Journeymen Tailors' Society was tried on conspiracy charges but was found guilty only of picketing, not of combination.

lopers." In general other unions of the period—cabinet makers, tailors, printers, hatters, coopers—followed the same pattern, seeking to solve the same problems, including that of the "red herring" which was early drawn across unionism's trail.

In 1825, for example, six hundred carpenters in Boston went out on strike for the ten-hour day. The response of that city's "gentlemen engaged in building" reads even to-day like an American Liberty League pamphlet. They declared that they could not believe "this project to have originated with any of the faithful and industrious sons of New England, but are compelled to consider it an evil of foreign growth" which would open "a wide door for idleness and vice . . . commuting the present condition of the mechanical classes made happy and prosperous by frugal, orderly and ancient habits for that degraded state. . . ."

The relative scarcity of skilled labor gave unions the balance of power in bargaining with employers during a span of some twenty-one years (1797–1818).

It was a balance soon shifted, however, by the depressions of a cyclic capitalism, by courts which had always been the handmaidens of ownership, by the migration from country to town of Yankee farm girls to New England's factories, and by the delayed impact of the Industrial Revolution which, by the first quarter of the nineteenth century, began to hammer furiously at the walls enclosing what was essentially a handicraft and agrarian order.

In 1820 the coruscating Sidney Smith, with all the arrogance of that day's Albion, inquired in the *Edinburgh Review:* "In the four quarters of the globe who reads an American book? . . . Who drinks out of American glasses? or eats from American plates? or wears American coats or gowns? or sleeps in American blankets?"

Yet in the same year that he put his query, Massachu-

setts reported 161 "manufactories" going at full blast, and
all New England was building cotton and woolen mills
and the working population of New York City, with its
"monstrous diversity of trades," was growing with such
wanton rapidity that "houses had tenants before they had
windows and doors" and streets were lined with dwellings
before sewers were dug, or wood laid for sidewalks, or
cobbles made for pavements. In Philadelphia more than
four thousand craftsmen were engaged in weaving alone.
Even the "frontier" settlements of Pittsburgh and Cincinnati were becoming manufacturing centers of importance,
and throughout the entire Northeast the wheels were turning at a quickening tempo and coins clinked on store counters that were piled ever higher with goods and yet more
goods.

"In 1820," says McMaster, "it was estimated that 200,-
000 persons and a capital of $75,000,000 were employed in
manufacturing. In 1825 the capital used had been expanded
to nearly nine times that amount and the number of workers to 2,000,000."

It was also during this period that unionism ramified out
into a labor movement. The distinction between the two,
and their relations to each other, are less subtle than salient. The term "labor movement" means that attitudes of
unity and coöperation among wage earners have gone beyond the confines of their own specific vocations to include the interests of their prototypes in other fields. It
means that the purely economic emphasis of unionism has
been revamped to include political action as well.

The American labor movement, then, as contrasted with
unionism proper, began in 1827 in Philadelphia—that city
which was "still the cradle of liberty" or a "hotbed of unrest, sedition and agitation," or whatever contemporary
comment you may choose. It was here that fifteen trade
societies banded together to form the "Mechanics' Union
of Trade Associations." It was the first "city central," or

alliance of workers among various occupations, in the annals of mankind. The impetus for its creation stemmed
directly from the dumping of cheaper foreign goods on
American markets after the embargo had been lifted, and
shipping freed, at the end of the Napoleonic Wars.

It was started, of course, to keep wages up and hours
down. But it soon grew a political arm, the Workingmen's
party, which was also the first organization of its kind in
world history. For there were certain needs that the unionists wanted to fill—needs which, they thought, could not
be answered by the use of the economic method alone, by
bargainings, or by strikes. Along with similar alignments in
Boston and New York, this Workingmen's party, in the
summer of 1828, therefore embarked upon what was to
become the most symbolic and significant struggle of any
labor movement in the American adventure. On its banners was inscribed a single aspiring slogan: "Equality of
citizenship."

It was, of course, the world's egalitarian age; and in
America it witnessed the "rise of the common man." In
1828 Andrew Jackson was swept into office on our first
wave of Populism, the revolt of the homespun of farm and
forge against the broadcloth of the bank and the warehouse. It was the first and most successful rebellion of the
small businessman (then for the most part the master
craftsman) and the farmer and the laborer against monopoly, against Big Ownership. It was not a protest against
employers generally, but rather against the "usurious rates
of blood-sucking money-lenders," against land speculators,
against the middleman or merchant capitalist. An editorial
in the *Mechanics Free Press*, party organ, separated the
wicked from the pure in heart. "If an employer superin-
tends his own business (still more if he works with his
hands) he is a workingman and has an interest on the side
of the remuneration of labor," the paper declared in 1829.

It must be recalled that at this time property qualifications for suffrage had been but recently removed—in 1820 in Massachusetts, for example, and two years later in New York State. The newly enfranchised worker was proud of his vote. It was not only a ballot. It was an inspiration. It was a new and wonderful tool by which he could lever himself into the better things of life. He took seriously the Declaration's words about being born free and equal, about the pursuit of happiness. He wanted to translate their grand promise into a less grubbing reality. He wanted a status of dignity in his community, and its respect. He wanted to get rid of imprisonment for debt in dank jails if he or his kind owed as little as $3 and, in one notorious case, two cents. He wanted a lien law to protect his income should his employer go suddenly bankrupt and leave him holding the bag—to the tune of a $400,000 wage loss annually in the building industry alone. He wanted, perhaps more than anything else, to have his children educated, and educated at public expense. He clamored for the reëstablishment of tax-supported schools in order to end a situation in which, as late as 1837, 250,000 children out of 400,000 of school age in the sovereign State of Pennsylvania were without any formal instruction, even in the Three R's.

Curiously enough, it has always been one of the more popular superstitions that our free school system somehow "just growed" like Topsy, or was somewhere forevisioned and blueprinted by the Founding Fathers. The more erudite may even mention something about Horace Mann and Henry Barnard. But, as a matter of fact, our free school system was almost wholly the result of unceasing agitation by the wage earners who, with the introduction of power-driven machinery, particularly in textiles, were beginning to be divorced more and more from their tools and to congregate in the mushrooming factory cities and towns.

Free schooling was then available only to the "pauper

poor," a state of affairs which, in the worker's view, knocked the catchwords of liberty and democracy into a cocked hat. His new concept of himself as a citizen who had spacious and inalienable rights didn't dovetail with the idea that his children could learn how to read and write only by means of what was really a charitable handout. "Free, equal, practical, nonsectarian, republican" education became a shibboleth around which rallied the new hosts of labor. They displayed that touching faith to which Americans as a people have been always prone: that a single reform, whether manhood suffrage, free schools, free homesteads, free silver, the single tax, may prove at long last a magical panacea.

At conventions and meetings of workingmen's parties countless resolutions were adopted, varying the theme that "equality among men results only from education"; that "the educated man is a good citizen and the uneducated an undesirable member of the body politic"; that workers were "entirely excluded from the advantages derivable from our free institutions" and had been subjected to "gross impositions" due to "want of knowledge and correct political information"; that "all history corroborates the melancholy fact that in proportion as the mass of the people become ignorant, misrule and anarchy ensue—their liberties are subverted, and tyrannic ambition has never failed to take advantage of their helpless condition"; that "there appear to exist two distinct classes, the rich and the poor; the oppressor and the oppressed; those that live by their own labor and those that live by the labor of others; the aristocratic and the democratic; the despotic and the republican . . . the one aspiring to dignified stations and offices of power; the other seeking for an equality of state and advantage"; and that, finally, "our government is republican, our education should be equally so."

The campaign to procure for all the children of the commonwealth equal education, and hence, it was believed, equal opportunity, roused many fierce factional fights. On the one hand were the "intellectuals" led by Robert Dale Owen, eldest son of Robert Owen, the English industrialist, philanthropist, utopian. Like his father, Owen *fils* was animated by a rare reforming zeal. He, too, had a Rousseau-like faith in the intrinsic goodness of man. He, too, identified himself with the cause of the earth's disinherited. He had helped his father to manage New Harmony, Indiana, a community where, it was hoped, a microcosm of the new coöperative state would be born. Its birth was long overdue—at least in the opinion of Owen the elder, who declared in 1818 that "the system of individual opposing interests," in other words the laissez-faire economics glorified by Adam Smith, had "now reached the extreme point of error and inconsistency" since "in the midst of the most ample means to create wealth, all are in poverty, or in imminent danger of the effects of poverty upon others." This self-taught draper's clerk, who read mainly in statistics and who in his twenties had become a dominant figure in Britain's cotton industry, was the first man to glimpse the immeasurable importance of the Industrial Revolution; to perceive that the application of steam or stored power to the production of goods was more crucial as a wealth-creating advance than even the domestication of animals or the discovery of the principle of the wheel. According to his own intimations of the "shape of things to come," competition for pounds and francs and dollars (capitalism) should soon be supplanted by coöperation (collectivism) in which the labor hour was to be the medium of exchange. He abhorred the economic codes and social customs then existing with all the moral fervor of the humanitarian and all the antiwaste fervor of the technologist.

I was [he once wrote] completely tired of partners who were merely trained to buy cheap and sell dear. This occupation deteriorates and often destroys the finest and best facul-

ties of our nature. . . . Under this thoroughly selfish system
. . . truth, honesty, virtue will be mere names, as they are
now and as they have ever been. It is a low vulgar ignorant
and inferior mode of conducting the affairs of society; and no
permanent general and substantial improvement can arise
until it shall be superseded by a superior mode of forming
character and creating wealth.

He was the first man to see that the unemployment
which plagued Europe after Napoleon was sentenced to
Elba had been caused by the displacements of men by machines, by the return of soldiers to their peacetime vocations, and by the collapse of the war boom's expanding
market. And at New Lanark, Scotland, where his own
mills were located, he had bossed into being an approximation of his ideal of the industrial community which, he
thought, the times demanded and from which the poverty
and degradation that marked cotton manufacture were
effectually banished. Under his management which, for
all his fine intentions, was that of benevolent despotism,
the operatives at New Lanark, drawn from the lowest
classes—drunkards and street-walkers and the shiftless,
along with children shipped in from orphan asylums—were
transformed into the best housed, best clad, best fed, best
educated, best behaved of any in all Britain. Yet when
Owen appealed to the princes of state, church, and industry to emulate his own example, he incurred the enmity of
all three. Whereas at New Lanark he had been content
merely to foster high standards of living within a community, he had from the platform attacked religion as an
obstacle to truth. He had attacked property as a form of
theft. He had attacked the family as an outworn institution. The ruling authorities began to regard him as a dangerous man and a subversive force; and his friends were
afraid to be seen with him. While denouncements of Owen
and his ideas mounted at times to fury, he decided that if
ever he were going to inaugurate his "superior order" he

required a society as yet a *tabula rasa* on which he could imprint his design. Europe, he felt, was cancerous with caste divisions and their prerogatives and "inclemencies"; still dominated by the dead hand of a feudal past.

Hence from the Rappites, a religious sect, he late in 1825 purchased New Harmony, Indiana, in the new world of America; and on July 4, 1826, he launched his "Declaration of Mental Independence" from "Private Property, Irrational Religion and Marriage," inviting the globe's "industrious and well disposed" to join this new venture. He himself returned to Scotland some months later, leaving the experiment to its own fate, which was disastrous. Like most uplifters, Owen had a fatal blind spot: he never realized that people in general were not actuated by the same desire for human betterment which, despite all his thwartings, kept burning in him. It had been his own purity of motive and his own efficiency in management that had brought success to New Lanark, and had made it less a proof of his thesis than a tribute to his intelligence and nobility of character.

In his American enterprise there were also pure motives enough, but virtually no efficiency and even less common sense. The protagonists of the New Era talked too much. They matched Platonism against Pantheism, by day and by night, opposed materialism to transcendentalism and forgot to saw wood and gather the harvest. There were naturally quite a few crackpots—the lunatic fringe that, like moths, wing toward any new light in their darkness. Then, too, there were plenty of rapscallions and ne'er-do-wells attracted by the thought of easy money and easy women. The sheer nonselectivity of Owen's invitation had allured both the salt of the earth and its scourings, and all ingredients in between. In his abiding naïveté, Owen had taken into partnership a cutthroat promoter named Taylor who by trickery soon appropriated for himself and a few dozen adherents more than a third of the colony's cattle and farming implements, and set up a false and rival Zion adjacent to New Harmony on a tract of land that Owen, in desperation, deeded to Taylor to get rid of him. Promptly Taylor and his followers built a distillery that undermined the Owenite preachments of temperance, and constructed a tannery that competed with New Harmony's own. Within three years the original colony with all its large plans for self-sufficiency, with its own granary and sawmill and slaughter house, with its own cobblers and tailors and mechanics, its own forum and school and news-paper, was but another word for chaos. In 1829 Owen sold most of the property to buyers more interested in profits than paradise, and with the tautology of reformism, which is akin to Proust's tautology of love, he repeated his efforts to regenerate mankind in England time after time.

Robert Dale Owen, however, had inherited his father's tenacity of purpose. In his opinion two mistakes had at the outset destroyed New Harmony. In the first place, he re-flected, the intellectual and cultured members of the com-munity couldn't do anything useful with their hands; in the second place, the run-of-the-mill ordinary folk had been conditioned by antisocial habits, and their inbred cupidity had been aroused by the example of the unscrupulous Taylor. It was impossible, Robert Dale Owen deduced, to move very far toward the Golden Age working with adults alone. They were either too impractical to help fashion the ideal state in miniature, or they were influenced unduly by the outlook of "me first and devil take the hindmost." Instead, he determined that it would be wiser to begin with children who were more malleable and to train them for creative living in that coöperative commonwealth which Owen the elder had envisioned. He himself had been educated at Hofwyl, Switzerland, in a school conducted as a "self-governing children's republic" by the heretical Em-manuel von Fellenburg, associate of the equally advanced, and more famous, Johann Heinrich Pestalozzi. Both men held that the purpose of education was to enable the individual to develop his latent aptitudes and to combine an appreciation of the "things of the mind and the spirit" with the exercise of some functional skill, the more manual the better. Owen's own experiences at school and at New Harmony served to confirm his view that the "practical arts and useful sciences" should be bedrock in any educational program looking toward the future of an improved humanity. At the psychological moment when the American labor movement, eager and discontented, was in a ferment of activity to gain equality of citizenship, he appeared on the scene, first in Philadelphia, and declared:

I believe in a National System of Equal, Republican, Protective, Practical Education, the sole regenerator of a profligate age and the only redeemer of our suffering country from the equal cures of chilling poverty and corrupting riches, of gnawing want and destroying debauchery, of blind ignorance and of unprincipled intrigue. By this, my creed, I will live. By my consistency with this, my professed belief, I claim to be judged. By it I will stand or fall.

At workingmen's rallies in New York and Philadelphia he preached his gospel with vigor and eloquence. He set up an "Association for the Protection of Industry and the Promotion of National Education," a propaganda and pressure organization of the first order. It refrained from forming its own political party. Rather it endorsed the candidates of the workingmen's factions, hoping by this means to "bore from within" and influence those sections of society which, in the nature of the case, seemed most susceptible to its appeal. It prepared and reprinted in circular form an "Address to the Public," and obtained the signatures of more than two thousand citizens, some of them prominent in civic and cultural affairs, to "A Memorial to the Legislature." This document described in minute detail the Owen plan by which "the State would become the guardian of all her children" and further asked the Legislature of New York for a grant of $100,000

towards the founding . . . of a Model National School somewhere in the centre of the state; such school to receive from each town and county a number of children proportioned to the population, and to support and educate them either free of charge . . . or else taxing each parent only in so moderate a yearly sum as shall not exclude even the poorest children from admission to its advantages.

The workingmen admired Owen's rhetoric, his sincerity, his learning. They were willing enough to accept his general thesis since it helped to crystallize their own groping toward that enlarged and participating citizenship promised by readier access to the tools of knowledge. The majority of them, however, rejected his specific proposal, which came to be popularly known as "state guardianship."

It must be kept in mind that Owen called for the creation of public boarding schools, no less, where children would be fed and housed and clothed and taught, regardless of social position. He had insisted also that mechanical and agricultural subjects be stressed along with the "literary" studies then in vogue. But the average workingman, with that *arriviste* attitude which, from the beginning, seems to have been imbibed with the American air, wanted for his offspring the fashionable "classicist" education with all its rotund Latin tags, the same kind of education, indeed, that the rich and well born were getting in their academies and colleges; an outlook which was but another facet of labor's economic views.

"Everything which limits individual enterprize," declared the *Mechanics Free Press* in the fall of 1830, "or tends to make the many dependent on the few, must in principle be . . . wrong. . . . Is it equal or just . . . that a few should be empowered by law to monopolize a business to themselves, to the exclusion and disadvantage of the many; certainly not."

In short, labor as a whole didn't want anything basically new or different; it wanted to share more fully in the advantages of existing commercial and industrial arrangements. It wanted for itself what the "haves" possessed. It wanted its children to rise in the world. It wanted them to be farmers with a great deal of land; or even better, perhaps, it wanted them to be merchants, shipowners, lawyers, doctors, politicians, contractors, bankers, manufacturers, to wear high starched stocks, the period's equivalent of the white collar.

Other objections to the state guardianship system were rooted in the same soil of opinion, and expressed the same fidelity to prevailing modes and mores—providing only that they be modified sufficiently to give the common man a break.

The first remonstrance was that parents would be compelled to part with their progeny, "severing the felicitous ties of home and family." Owen answered that parents would have complete freedom of choice and could send their children or not, as they pleased. The second argument was that if parents were removed from their sacred obligation to support their children, young people would thenceforth be encouraged to marry "at an immature age and impose on themselves the duties and responsibilities of parents . . . without . . . the slightest care or forethought." Owen answered that in view of this possibility, which was real enough, it might be wise to have parents pay a small fee, say $5.00 yearly, toward the upkeep of each child at school.

But it was the third objection, fostered mainly by old-time Federalist and Democratic politicians who saw in Owen a potentially strong political rival, that defeated him and his dream. These politicians claimed, and very noisily, that his entire educational scheme was an oblique method of "communizing" property, of breaking down its established and "civilized" codes, and of ultimately making the nation over in the image of New Harmony's objectives.

Against this telling accusation Owen had to contend warily, which is, as a rule, weakly, for the charge held more truth than, for the sake of expediency, he cared to admit.

Yet with his unceasing pamphleteering and agitation he managed to win quite a few converts. In New York City, for example, the painters went on record as favoring his plan; and it was also endorsed by the workingmen's political clubs in the Fourth and Tenth Wards. On the other hand, the printers, as represented by the potent Typographical Society, in a set of corrosive resolutions, berated the plan as "entirely visionary" and invited Owen to go back where he came from, namely, to Scotland, where there were "thousands daily groaning under the yoke of severe oppression" who, unlike the Americans, were without benefit of "that liberty sealed by the blood of their fathers and descended to them in all its purity."

He was also hindered more than he was helped by the aid of Frances Wright who at New Harmony had been his co-editor of the *Gazette* and with whom he had formed what the primmer historians still describe as an "intimate friendship." She was the "new woman" of the nineteenth century; but a new woman more gifted and versatile than most of her sex then or since. Born in Scotland, and of independent means, she had been brought up by Jeremy Bentham, who taught her politics; and later she became a member of the Lafayette household where her manners received a Gallic grace and polish and her mind was fructified by the hot sunlight of "liberté, égalité, fraternité." She was fiery, dynamic, handsome—a "veritable Medea," an enemy said—an advocate of free thought, of votes for women, and of their right when married to own and control property separate from that of their lords and masters. She was a dazzling lecturer who in America packed the lyceum halls, and an authoress whose *View of Society and*

Manners in America rivaled the later Harriet Martineau's "travelogues" in its acute and searching observations. And with her quick warm sympathy for the underdog's plight she was a perpetual experimentalist, always trying to "do something about it," even when her efforts were as far-fetched as her endeavor to remove the blot of slavery by inaugurating a farm colonization community in Tennessee where freed Negroes might be educated for the future's coöperative society.

After the New Harmony venture failed she removed with Robert Dale Owen to New York City and together they started the *Free Enquirer*, a weekly with more fervor than discrimination, which became the organ for almost every kind of social, religious, political, and economic extremism that appeared on the American scene.

Her association with the Workingmen's party movement soon tarred the cause with the pitch of a dual "infidelity"—since all journeymen and laborers were promptly accused of being, like herself, "free lovers and free thinkers," menacing mother, home, and country, the flag and the Constitution, beauty, goodness, and truth, and other virtues. On June 12, 1830, New York's *Commercial Advertiser* labeled the Workingmen as "poor deluded followers of a crazy atheistical woman." Previously this same paper had expressed its reaction to the entire labor movement in the tones of the decade's journalism:

Lost to society, to earth and to heaven, godless and hopeless, clothed and fed by stealing and blasphemy . . . such are the apostles who are trying to induce a number of able-bodied men in this city to follow in their own course . . . to disturb the peace of the community for a time; go to prison and have the mark of Cain impressed upon them; betake themselves to incest, robbery and murder; die like ravenous wild beasts hunted down without pity; and go to render their account before God, whose existence they believed in their miserable hearts, even while they were blaspheming him in their igno-

rant, snivelling and puerile speculations. Such is too true a
picture in all its parts of some of the leaders of the new political party, which is emerging from the slime . . . and which
is more beastly and terrible than the Egyptian Typhon.

Such attacks were extended to Philadelphia where the
editor of the *Mechanics Free Press* in a panic warned: "Let
the subject of religion alone or the death knell of our association will be sounded." Meanwhile, in addition to this
outside opposition, the workingmen's parties had to buck
all the bitter dissensions of a family row, especially in New
York City. It was here that Thomas Skidmore, self-taught
machinist, able organizer, and our first cracker-barrel
communist, emerged to take a commanding position in labor affairs and to help divide the movement into three
warring parts.

Early in 1829 events conspired to give him a fine cue.
In March of that year New York employers, hoping to
profit from an over-supply of skilled labor attracted to the
city by news of its building boom, let it be known that
they would soon require their journeymen to put in an
extra hour a day. The workers—mainly carpenters, masons, and mechanics—refused to entertain any such idea.
They had but recently won their ten-hour day. They were
going to keep it, they said, come hell, heaven, or high-
water. They were aroused and angry and not quite sure
what to do about it. Skidmore, however, was sure. As soon
as the employers' intention was bruited about, he had
formulated a plan of action; and since he had been for
years an ardent unionist, could speak with "earnestness and
conviction," and was apparently widely known and liked,
he was selected to lead New York labor's defense against
"this threat to human liberty."

Upon his advice the workers decided not to "stand out,"
that is, go on strike. Instead they held two protest meetings
near City Hall plaza, the second of which was attended by
a crowd of six thousand while thousands more spilled over

into adjacent streets under the fitful gleam of torches. And this assembly, steered adroitly by Skidmore and his chief aide, Alexander Ming, appointed a Committee of Fifty to further their cause, and to submit resolutions which would not only underline the point that "10 hours well and faithfully employed is as much as an employer ought to receive and require for a day's work . . . and as much as any artisan, labourer or mechanic ought to give" but would also examine "the nature of the tenure by which all men hold title to their property."

The purpose of this latter plunge into philosophy was to scare employers into relinquishing their eleven-hour-per-diem demand lest they set off the caps of an incipient radicalism. The stratagem was successful enough. The employers, who were called "aristocratic oppressors" by Skidmore, quickly backed down, as he predicted, thinking it more expedient not to "stir the mud at the bottom of the pool." Yet this victory in the long run proved to be pyrrhic, affixing to labor a "red and dangerous" label it did not as a whole deserve or desire, and hobbling its progress for many years to come. For Skidmore, who had drunk deeply at the founts of the three great and doubting Thomases, Paine and Spence and Jefferson, and had also steeped himself in the "agrarianism" of the French physiocrats, was less interested in preserving the ten-hour day than in inaugurating a new state of society.

On August 13, 1829, he published his *Rights of Man to Property! Being a Proposition to Make It Equal among the Adults of the Present Generation; and to Provide for its Equal Transmission to Every Individual of Each Succeeding Generation on Arriving at the Age of Maturity.* Its primary postulate was cut from the same egocentric cloth as Louis XIV's "L'état, c'est moi." It stated with cosmic simplicity that "all human society is constructed . . . radically wrong." Before the "great mass of the community" could be saved "from the evils which they now suffer," it

THE

RIGHTS OF MAN

TO PROPERTY !

BEING A PROPOSITION

TO MAKE IT EQUAL AMONG THE ADULTS

OF THE

PRESENT GENERATION:

AND TO PROVIDE FOR ITS EQUAL TRANSMISSION TO EVERY
INDIVIDUAL OF EACH SUCCEEDING GENERATION, ON
ARRIVING AT THE AGE OF MATURITY.

———

ADDRESSED TO THE

CITIZENS OF THE STATE OF NEW-YORK, PARTICULARLY, AND TO
the people of other States and Nations, generally.

———

" I hold these truths to be self-evident; that all men are created equal; that
they are endowed by their Creator, with certain unalienable rights; and that
among these are life, liberty and *property*."—Altered from Mr. Jefferson's
Declaration of American Independence.

———

BY THOMAS SKIDMORE.

New=York :
PRINTED FOR THE AUTHOR BY ALEXANDER MING, JR.
106 Beekman-street.

———

1829.

From the late 1820's on Labor increasingly broke into print.

went on, a state constitutional convention would have to be called to decree the abolition of all debts and all claims to private property. Property would thereupon be divided among all adult citizens so that everybody "may enjoy in a state of society substantially the rights which belong to him in a state of nature." Skidmore implied furthermore that a revolution might be necessary to wipe out the class distinctions between rich and poor that arose directly from the maldistribution of wealth, and of land, its chief source.

Let the poor and middling classes [he exhorted] understand that their oppressions come from overgrown wealth that exists among them, on the one hand, and from entire destitution on the other; and that as this overgrown wealth is continually augmenting its possessions at a rapid ratio, the public sufferings are continually augmenting also; and must continue . . . until the equal and inalienable rights of the people shall order them otherwise.

To a startled world the *Workingman's Advocate*, edited by George Henry Evans, a Skidmore disciple who was soon to modulate his master's voice, thus summarized what the practical application of Skidmore's program would entail:

that the title of the present owners to the whole property of each state, real and personal, lands, houses, vessels, goods and private property of every description, be at once invalidated; that the whole property of the state thus taken from those who now possess it, be put up at a national auction; that the total estimated value of the same be divided into as many portions as there are adults in the state, and that one portion (in value) be credited to each, to which amount he or she shall be allowed to purchase at the state auction.

Meanwhile the Committee of Fifty convened on October 23, 1829, to nominate a slate of 11 candidates for the state legislature in a manner that honored the great goddess, Chance. Twenty-two names of willing candidates were written on slips of paper, placed in a box, shaken around, and then 11 slips were drawn out to make up the ticket which consisted of: 2 machinists (Skidmore himself was one of them), 2 carpenters, 1 printer, 1 brass founder, 1 cooper, 1 grocer, 1 painter, 1 whitesmith, and 1 physician. Skidmore was able to persuade the committee to endorse his "general propositions." But at this juncture his ideas were being broadcast among the people, and New York's first experiment in labor politics ran smack into a storm converging upon it from three sides at once.

To begin with, the sober, responsible, "principled" sections of the populace sent wails of anguish heavenwards. Pulpit and press grew sulphurous with alarm and abuse. The Workingmen's party was termed a collection of the "barbarous dispossessed," of the "tag, rag and bobtail." It was cursed as "scum" and a body of "ring streaked and speckled rabble." And, by a natural logic, the social and religious heresies of Frances Wright and Robert Dale Owen (who was working closely with the movement) were blended with Skidmore's property subversions and shared in the condemnation of labor's political venture as compounded of "Anarchists," "Communists," and "Infidels of the Dirty Shirt."

Despite the fact that Robert Dale Owen had denounced Skidmore's scheme as "crude communism," impossible of fulfilment, both men were targets for respectable hate. Yet they strove against each other valiantly—Owen to capture the movement for his state guardianship plan and Skidmore to control it for his division of property program. From this melee of conflicting gospels a new group emerged. It was led by Noah Cook and Henry C. Guyon. They were emphatically not world saviors; nor were they, strictly speaking, labor leaders, but rather politicians adroit in backroom intrigue. They set out to rescue labor from what the hostile press called "Workeyism," and "Skidmorania." They went into the wards and built up attitudes of ridicule and resentment against the infidel Owen and the agrarian

Skidmore, and urged workingmen to cease thinking about utopias and devote themselves to "immediate demands" like the mechanics' lien law.

In spite of all this confusion and excitement, the Workingmen's party in the election of November, 1829, obtained an Assembly seat for one of its carpenter candidates, Ebenezer Ford. Three of its other candidates almost made the grade, losing by margins of 25, 26, or 31 votes. The labor press rejoiced and envisioned the "annihilation" of "freedom's enemies." Editorial raptures were short lived, however. The Cook-Guyon faction soon took over the ward organizations and at a meeting on December 29, 1829, dissolved the Committee of Fifty and passed some resolutions of its own—resolutions that excoriated any attempts to interfere with religion or with property rights. Skidmore, with a handful of followers, then set up a rival party of "the original workingmen" and in the spring of 1830 started to publish his paper, *Friend of Equal Rights,* to popularize his views. Both party and paper vanished with his death in August, 1832.

The Workingmen's party, as such, vanished even sooner. By June, 1830, the Cook-Guyon crowd had purged its ranks of all reformers and fashioned its own boss-ruled political machine. And although this new alignment sponsored "Farmers', Mechanics' and Workingmen's" parties upstate, in Albany and Syracuse, in Rochester and Batavia, the movement degenerated into a minor "politicians' revolt" within the Democratic party, as Cook and Guyon tried to use their adherents in wresting some power and patronage from the Albany Regency dominated by Martin Van Buren and W. L. Marcy.

In Philadelphia and Boston, from Maine south to the Mason-Dixon line and west to the borders of Missouri, wherever the workingmen's parties appeared, they suffered similar sidetrackings and defeats. The journeymen were political tyros. They used their ballot with all the awkwardness of a child learning to skate. They were easily scared by abuse, by the employer-hired hoodlums who broke up their meetings, by inimical public opinion. Their solidarity was undermined by the cabals of professional politicians and last-minute men who jumped the labor bandwagon only to steer it up their own alleys or to wreck it. Promises of preferment were linked with personal ambition to lure many of labor's best brains into the folds of Federalists and Democrats who, in addition, had early learned the trick of planking into their own platforms the appeals and catchwords of any third party movement which seemed as if it might make a strong bid for power.

Against this kind of opposition, the workingmen's parties contended with more energy than skill. They won only an alderman here, an assemblyman there; and in every case such victories were local and transient and costly in time and money. Street-corner campaigning, along with discussion of issues and candidates, diverted attention from keeping up union standards of hours and wages. Organization by ward and county supplanted organization by craft and trade. The most calamitous result of all this political "sturm und drang" was that the mainstay of unionism, its daily "bread and butter" tactics, was swept aside in the hope that political panaceas would decrease the necessity of a firm and aggressive stand on collective bargaining. By 1831, for example, Philadelphia's famed and powerful "Union of Mechanics" had dwindled in membership from fifteen to four affiliates and other city centrals all over the country were overcome by the same disastrous condition.

Yet while the workingmen lost as politicians, they won as wage earners. Within a decade nearly all their objectives—the abolition of imprisonment for debt, the beginnings of a free school system and the like—either had been completely gained or were being approximated in the industrial states along the Atlantic Seaboard. Labor's tumult and shouting had at long last compelled the old-line politi-

cians to take new notice of labor as an element to be con-
ciliated, to be cajoled into allegiance by democracy's technique of swapping concessions for votes.

Meantime, however, the apparent failure of the unionist
in politics inspired the editor of the *National Labourer*,
official organ of the Philadelphia General Trades Union, to
swear off, to declare "never again." "The trade unions," he
wrote, "never will be political because their members have
learned from experience that the introduction of politics
into their societies has thwarted every effort to ameliorate
their conditions." But despite this and many similar pleas
for a return to bargaining unionism, the 1840's again found
labor wooing politics with a renewed and eloquent ardor.
It was a courtship brought into being by the crash and
panic of 1837, ending eight years of hectic prosperity.

From the mid-twenties onward the completion of the
Erie, Wabash, and Ohio canals had immeasurably quickened the exchange of the West's pork, beef, grain, peltries,
and lumber for the East's dry goods, boots and shoes, hardware, fish, and countless "drugs and sundries." The ensuing
boom sent prices soaring. The effort to make wages keep
stride with this rise in living costs had attracted a great new
influx of wage earners into unionism's fold, enabling its
leaders to repair the organizational damages inflicted by
labor's essay into *realpolitik*. As always prosperity made it
easier to ask and to get more pay; and as always, too, the
wage earner could obtain more money by negotiating
through a union than by himself. And than by herself, also.
For in 1834–36 the women began to organize, the seamstresses, and the binders of books and shoes, the makers of
corsets and umbrellas and mantuas—many of whom worked
sixteen hours a day to earn from $1.25 to $2.00 a week.

The Female Improvement Society of the City and
County of Philadelphia set the pace for its sister sororities
in Lynn, Boston, and Baltimore. It appointed committees
for each trade, for millinery, for tailoring and the like, to

draw up a "ladies' wage scale" which was then submitted to the respective manufacturers and, miracle of coöperation, was accepted in every case.

By 1836 unions claimed a membership of 300,000. In Philadelphia there were 53; in New York 42; in Baltimore 23; while Newark and Boston had 16 apiece; and five of them were national in structure.

At the same time, the city central began to thrive. It expressed the necessity for the solitary locals, often too weak to cope with employers on their own, to acquire greater strength by allying themselves with other labor groups. In New York City, for example, when in the spring of 1833 the Carpenters went on strike to raise their wages from $1.37½ to $1.50 a day, the Typographical Society resolved that as "fellow mechanics engaged in the same cause" they should aid the Carpenters, raising funds for them in the honest hope that the beneficiaries would reciprocate should the need arise. The advantages apparent in this kind of coöperation fostered the idea for a General Trades' Union which would represent every "Society, Trade and Art" in the city and which was formed on August 14, 1833, by the Book-Binders, Cabinet Makers, Carpenters, Carvers, Coopers, Cordwainers, Leather Dressers and Typographers. The sponsors of the General Trades' Union were congratulated by their first president, Ely Moore, the printer and Tammany Hall leader (and, later, a congressman) for being "Pioneers in the Great Cause."

"To you, then, gentlemen," he continued, "as the *actual* representatives of the Mechanic interests . . . the eyes of thousands and thousands are turned; for should the experiment succeed here . . . other Unions of a kindred character will be formed, in every section, until their influence shall be felt and acknowledged throughout our wide and extended country."

Under Moore's guidance, the General Trades' Union

A typical lampoon of Labor's emergent political consciousness (1830).

Leslie's Weekly

was well managed, serving its components with such efficacy that it soon became the model for many imitators along the Atlantic Seaboard. It imposed strike benefit dues of 6¼ cents per month for each affiliated member. It established an excellent weekly newspaper on a coöperative basis. It lobbied through the state legislature a bill creating a prison commission. When in 1835 the Tailors walked out, the General Trades' Union assisted them to victory and then commemorated it with a grand public jubilee of speeches, torches, and parades. The New York *Journal of Commerce* complained of a "turn out operation going on," and that "the different trades are combined together in what is called a Trades' Union and each in its turn is supported by the other in striking for higher wages."

Naturally to Moore and many of his associates it seemed only logical that in the same way that craft locals received succor from city centrals, like the General Trades' Union, city centrals could be helped by a national labor organization. In March, 1834, therefore, the General Trades' Union sent out a call to every union or potential union its officers could find to attend a convention that would lay the groundwork for a national federation. In response to this summons, delegates from six eastern cities convened in City Hall in August of 1834, and designed the National Trades Union in the devout hope that it would become the third and highest manifestation of organized labor's development.*

"Labor is on the march!" exulted its press. Industry, too, of course, was on the march; and so was agriculture. Almost everybody, infected by the optimism and speculative

* The National Trades Union expired in May, 1837, in part a victim of the depression in that year, in part the victim of its own "labor at large" approach which prevented it from winning the allegiance of many strong unions which insisted on keeping their problems within the purview of their own crafts. Founders of the National Trades Union tended to devote too much time to abstractions, to debate the meaning of "political," and to prefer an educational and advisory body to a functioning federation of existing unions on the latter's own terms.

mania and boosting outlook recorded in contemporary
documents, seemed to be "on the march." The sagacious
Alexis de Tocqueville who toured the country at this time
observed that the very morale of the American people was
that of an "army on the march." Unfortunately, however,
the iron legions of economics were also on the march.

The spring of 1837 brought with it the debacle. Some ten
months before, the President, Andrew Jackson, had raised
a warning signal when he issued his "Specie Circular" or-
dering the Federal agents selling the public lands to accept
only the coin of the realm as payment. But almost everyone
else, especially the financiers and speculators, thought the
country fundamentally sound and ignored the implications
of Old Hickory's mandate.

In the public lands alone, sales had leaped from a little
less than five million acres in 1834 to nearly twenty-five
million in 1836. During this same period commodity imports exceeded exports by $111,703,519, while specie and
bullion imports outran exports to the tune of $31,575,272—
about as unhealthy and unfavorable a balance of trade as
the United States has ever experienced. Then, too, the success of the Erie Canal had inspired imitations without end,
and too often without reason, absorbing $100,000,000 of
savings and surplus into projects most of which were
worthless and, when not worthless, positively insane. To a
somewhat lesser extent the same situation prevailed in the
madcap construction of railroads.

England had invested heavily in America's industrial
development; but in the mid-thirties a panic, the result of
a glut of consumers' goods, struck the British Isles. English
creditors began to call upon debtors to meet their obligations, causing cash withdrawals that knocked the props
from under hundreds of American business ventures. And
since England was in the doldrums, Southern planters could
not sell their cotton to their main market, the textile mills
of Leeds and Lancashire. During the boom they had, more-

over, mortgaged their crops and their plantations to buy
more slaves, more cotton gins, more acreage. In the old
South the auctioneer's hammer began to fall, thudding
against the block like strokes of doom. To make American
matters worse, the Hessian fly ravaged wheat crops in
Pennsylvania, Delaware, Maryland, Virginia, and Tennessee, forcing great sections of the country to import
breadstuffs from the Mediterranean nations. In the five
stricken states, farmers were quickly bankrupted, fore-
closures were epidemic and loss of purchasing power battered down more bastions of stability.

In addition to "wild-cat" speculations in land, the "wild-
cat" credit released for all manner of dubious enterprises by
state banks which were operated more in a spirit of abandon
than of accountancy had overlaid the country with a net of
debt claims that could not be met. They were far in excess
of the nation's ability to produce in terms of actual goods
and services. And in a frenzy to replenish their liquid reserves, banks demanded payment on loans which was not
forthcoming in any degree sufficient to preserve that always
fabulous symbol called "confidence," a fiction on which
financial surety depends. The entire credit structure of the
country went into a kind of catalepsy. Within the first
eleven months of 1837, 618 banks failed. Even the glamor-
ous and impregnable Bank of the United States, "Mr. Bid-
dle's financial colossus, sir," which at that time held a position analogous to that of the present House of Morgan,
was shaken to its foundations, and somehow managed to
survive only to go under four years later as a result of this
first shock.

Everywhere prices slid from peak to valley, and wages
went tumbling after, while wheels slowed to a stop and unemployment rose. If grass didn't grow in the streets, it
merely showed a lack of ambition. In the industrial centers
it was no longer a question of how much the worker earned
on his job, but of whether he could keep or get a job at all,

at any wage—a wage that was steadily reduced to sub-subsistence levels. Unions languished for lack of members and dues and even somebody to negotiate with, for every paper headlined news of further retrenchments and closings down.

"The streets of New Bedford," said the *New York Star* of April 15, 1837, "are now thronged with seamen out of employment. Forty whale ships are lying at the wharves, but nothing doing to fit them out for sea." In Haverhill, Massachusetts, which was among the first "one-industry" towns, the shutting down of shoe factories threw virtually the entire population out of work and once proud New Englanders begged for bread at homes of the well-to-do. In New York City, from April to July, 1837, more than six thousand masons and carpenters and others in the building trades were discharged to roam the streets in "misery and idleness, not knowing where to turn."

Soon the unions—craft local, city central, the "national federations" which existed mainly on paper—were almost wholly extinguished. The few that survived were weak in men, money, and morale. The labor press disappeared—to such an extent, indeed, that the records of unionism are relatively more meager in this period than at any other time since its American inception.

Plagued by poverty and insecurity, labor joined with the nation's other "small fry" to search for cause and cure. The old antimonopoly fever broke out again. Once more the complaint arose that the "monster monopoly," the gas, coal, banking, insurance, bridge, land, railroad, and turn-pike companies, chartered by the various states, had deprived the workers, lesser employers, master mechanics, and small tradesmen of their "just and due" money-making opportunities, often driving them toward destitution.

Spokesmen for such groups pointed out that in New York State alone the number of corporations chartered had risen from twenty-three in 1815 to one hundred and seventy-three in 1836. They claimed that such institutions, with their vast funds and "perfidious" political influence, grabbed the best of everything in sight, preventing all others from gaining even a "mere and modest" livelihood.

The land monopolist, they said, through his speculations had acquired thousands of the choicer acres, robbing the common man of his chance to obtain desirable land at a price he could afford to pay and become a farmer, a prime aspiration of that day. And even if the ordinary fellow was already a farmer, the land monopolist blocked his approach to more fertile soil and greener pastures. The money monopolist or banker denied to the honest and ambitious access to that credit which properly belonged to them by virtue of their honesty and ambition. The mercantile and manufacturing monopolists, with their protective tariffs, and patents rights, and the public utility monopolists, with their franchises which permitted the public's natural resources to be preëmpted by private persons for their own profit, all similarly tended to restrict the area of economic opportunity.

All this, said labor and its allies, destroyed the free market. It forced a "pegged" or monopoly price upon the "producing classes," both in selling what they themselves made and in buying whatever else they needed.

The obvious remedy, then, was to revoke the "special privileges" of monopoly (which appeared always in the form of a corporation) and to restore free competition for everything by everybody. It was further apparent that the monopolists had secured their unfair advantages through legislative fiat and favoritism, since any corporation, to exist at all, must first receive the state's permission to be born. The thing to do, therefore, was to enter politics and put your own people into public office where they could control the state apparatus and manipulate it to your interests, as against the interests of Big Ownership. They could at least regulate monopoly, if not uproot it, and hence give elbow room and breathing space to the "little fellow," the average man.*

The belief that the chicane and connivings of rich people and the betrayal of legislators had "locked-up" the opportunities of the American people soon found a definite philosophy and a prophet. The philosophy was the "New Agrarianism." The prophet was George Henry Evans, publicist extraordinary and quondam associate of Thomas Skidmore.

Born in England in 1805, of a shabby-genteel family, Evans emigrated to the United States at fourteen, starting his labor career as a printer's devil in Ithaca, New York. He displayed a great deal of intellectual curiosity, reading constantly, if at random, in his spare time. He was early and especially influenced by Thomas Paine who made of him a confirmed and militant deist and a land reformist and after whose strong marching style he tried to pattern his own.

Like many others of the period's more-than-literate

---

* It cannot be overstressed that this general outlook has remained the animating force in the perpetual protests against monopoly, from Shays' Rebellion and the Jacksonian Revolt down through Greenbackism and Populism to Senator Borah's latest fulmination against the wickedness of our giant cartels. During the first half of the nineteenth century particularly, the dynamics of this viewpoint derived from the sense of boundless opportunity—agricultural, commercial, industrial, political—that pervaded the mechanic and artisan, the farmer and laborer, the storekeeper and smaller manufacturer. Whenever, therefore, the idea of equality of opportunity received a palpable setback, as when the "best bargains" all along the line seemed to go into the hands of the rich, the producing classes responded by assailing monopoly. Throughout American history, however, all such attacks have been vitiated by the same dichotomy. Whereas the average man wanted to curb and even destroy monopoly, he still wanted to leave "room at the top," for himself or his son, to preserve the "American right to succeed." This confusion of purpose has been best summed up by Mr. Finley Peter Dunne who ascribed to the trust-busting T. Roosevelt the following sentiments, as reported by Mr. Dooley:

"'Th' thrusts,' says he, 'are heejous monsthers built up be th' enlightened intherprize iv th' men that have done so much to advance progress in our beloved country,' he says. 'On wan hand I wud stamp thim unher fut; on th' other hand, not so fast.'"

printers, he elected himself an editor, beginning his *Work-ingman's Advocate* in New York City in 1829. He was personally very ambitious. Although he supported Skidmore, he did it with "reservations" that after a while took the form of undercover political alliances through which Evans, then more the politician than the philosopher, hoped to wrest control of New York's Workingmen's party from Skidmore.

With the panic of 1837, with the unions dissolving and the circulation of his paper, read almost exclusively by workingmen, fast approaching zero, Evans retired to a farm in New Jersey to think through his own dilemma which, he believed, was inextricably bound up with labor's own. And after three years of this rustication and self-communing, he emerged a more mature and wiser and kindlier man. He emerged also with a mission. In 1840 he published his *History of the Origin and Progress of the Working Men's Party in New York* which, he hoped, would serve a dual purpose. It would warn labor against the "ideological and tactical errors" made by its first political thrust. It would provide the foundations for his own brand of national redemption, the New Agrarianism, modeled after the free distribution of the "ager publican" attempted by the Gracchi in ancient Rome.

He felt confident that in his book he had evolved a substitute for strikes, for the closed shop, for unionism itself. At the outset he condemned by implication the rival doctrines of Fourierism, then finding an American vogue, and Owenism as "socialistic imports" from a sick and exhausted Europe. His own plan was based on individualism, not collectivism; upon the diffusion of great tracts of land still unoccupied, not upon the division of existing estates. His outlook was centered in the same natural rights theory that Paine and Jefferson had used to overthrow British rule in the Colonies. But Evans tried to forge from this theory a weapon for overcoming the "tyranny" of too great a concentration of control over the means of production. His line of argument anticipated Henry George's Single Tax and itself remains among the most arresting and neglected contributions to American economic thought.

Man's first right, said Evans, is the right to live, to *be*; a right that implies access to the sources of existence, that is, to the materials of nature. Man must breathe—he has the right to air. He must drink—he has the right to water. He must see—he has the right to sunlight. He must eat—he has the right to the soil whence food comes. Only these four rights, continued Evans, are truly "natural"; all others— liberty, capital, labor, education—are ancillary, either acquired or derived.

Here, of course, was the distinction between the "Old Agrarianism" of Skidmore and the "New Agrarianism" of Evans. Men do not have any equal right to capital, contended Evans, because capital is the result of labor, and is not a gift of nature. Whereas Skidmore wanted to divide capital and land, Evans sought only to divide the land, and to do it with regard to the special and triune character of a "natural right" which, he argued, is distinguished by three cardinal traits: equality, inalienability, and individuality.

Since every human being is a part of humanity's greater whole, Evans reasoned, he is entitled to his equal share of earth which belongs to all. And if his portion is held to be inalienable, he will be guaranteed over a span of time the benefits assured by his ownership over a span of space. In all logic, Evans insisted, nobody should be allowed to deprive himself of his natural rights, put a mortgage on them, or give title to them to someone else. The third trait, individuality, Evans stressed as a variety of separateness. Nature, he said, recognizes the individual—not the family, the tribe, the community, the nation—as the life-unit. That is the reason why the individual's natural rights must be unconditionally secured to him; else they will be usurped by the group, by corporations, by the state.*

With Evans individualism, so defined and applied, was an invincible safeguard against oppression, since every man, sure of his plot of land, could always turn to nature for subsistence. Hence private property, rather than the communizing of property, became the keystone of liberty's arch. In the Evans scheme, the individual was to be lord of his own share of creation (equality). He was to be automatically protected against dispossession of his birthright, either through fear or necessity, or the temptations of a fine bargain (inalienability). He was to be thrown upon his own resources and his well-being was to depend upon his own efforts (individuality).

From the postulates of this economic creed, Evans fashioned his political program. He began urging Congress to grant every bona-fide settler 160 acres from the public domain and to make it impossible for anyone to take it away from him, forevermore.

To thousands of people his idea seemed eminently sane and feasible. It must be remembered that, as late as 1852, congressional debates revealed that during the previous sixty years only a hundred million acres of the public lands had been sold and that 1,400,000,000 acres remained at the disposal of the Federal government. Contemporary estimates of the time required to get rid of this residue, assuming a fairly constant rate of sale, varied from four hundred to nine hundred years. That was far ahead enough for Evans; not even the most clairvoyant statesman, he thought, could ask for more. And in the columns of his revived *Workingman's Advocate* he started a propaganda cam-

* This doctrine was the first and most elaborate discussion of that philosophic anarchism which has affected many of our political metaphysicians, from Evans himself through Thoreau to the lamentations of Mr. Albert Jay Nock concerning his enemy, the state. In this regard, it is interesting to note that Evans himself conceded that in practice the family would be the unit and that children would not come into their natural rights until they reached the age of twenty-one.

paign which for sheer skill and constancy has never been outdone.

Free homesteads, he adjured Congress, meant that land-less wage earners should be furnished with implements and transportation to enable them to set themselves up as inde-pendent farmers. When a glut in the labor market occurred, he advised the trade unions, they should themselves outfit individuals and groups to stake out their land claims, drain-ing off the surplus of workers and thus boosting wages and shortening hours. To the well-to-do he pointed out that money spent for poor relief could be more profitably spent in sending the poor from the slums to the very great and open spaces where they would create new wealth and add their bit to national prosperity.

Within a year after Evans had begun his agitation, Horace Greeley, in his *New York Tribune*, endorsed the free homestead movement. Other editors fell quickly into line until, in 1849, it was estimated that out of the two thousand papers then published in the United States, six hundred favored Evans' proposal. Meantime, he had per-suaded Andrew Johnson, a Tennessee tailor who was to become Lincoln's successor, to introduce the first home-stead bill in Congress in 1845, to make life easier for the poor whites of the South's upland regions.

When the idea moved westward, settlers and pioneers supported it vigorously, seeking to increase the population of the frontier. The opposition, adorned by plain and fancy imprecations, came from the manufacturers and land-owners of the East. At first they took their stand on ethical grounds. They asserted that if workmen and "common labor" in particular were given grants of land they wouldn't know what to do with it, they would be wasteful and dis-solute and wanton and would generally distort the eternal verities of moral rectitude and the innate tendency of prop-erty to move into the hands of superior persons.

Their attacks were answered by Evans with "lead" editorials in his paper, and with pamphlets and broadsides. He wrote one appeal in particular that, even today, when political publicity has attained the status of a pseudo-science, could teach a trick or two to Charles Michelson himself. Appearing in every kind of print, on every kind of paper, this appeal was broadcast by hundreds of thousands in leaflet form in 1846.

Are you an American citizen? Then you are a joint owner of the public lands. Why not take enough of your own property to provide yourself with a home? Why not vote yourself a farm?

Are you a party follower? Then you have long enough employed your vote to benefit scheming office seekers. Use it for once to benefit yourself: Vote yourself a farm. Are you tired of slavery—of drudging for others—of poverty and its attendant miseries? Then, vote yourself a farm.

Would you free your country and the sons of toil everywhere from the heartless, irresponsible mastery of the aristocracy of avarice? . . . Then join with your neighbours to . . . limit the quantity of land that any one may henceforth monopolize or inherit . . . and . . . make the public lands free to actual settlers only. . . .

"Vote yourself a farm" became labor's war cry in the 40's in the same way that "free republican education" had been its watchword in the 20's and 30's. And even as Owen had formed his "Association for the Protection of Industry and for the Promotion of National Education" to propagate his views, Evans organized an "Agrarian League"* to herald the new day's dawn via free homesteads. Evans remembered how the brave hopes of Robert Dale Owen and Thomas Skidmore had alike been broken on the rack of partisan politics. He therefore avoided its perils. Instead of trying to build a political party around his doctrine, he at-

* The trade-union complexion of this society, along with its base in the Workingmen's party movement of 1828–36, was reflected in its first "central committee," composed of 4 printers, 2 cordwainers, 1 chairmaker, 1 carpenter, 1 blacksmith, 1 bookbinder, 1 machinist, 1 picture-frame maker, and 1 clothier.

tached his doctrine to individual politicians. He was the first labor advocate in the country to dramatize the value of a policy which would "reward your friends, and punish your enemies." His technique was simple. He taught his "Agrarian Leaguers" to exact preëlection pledges for free homesteads from candidates for public office; and then to keep reminding them (if and when elected) that they had better "deliver" before next balloting time came round.

In popularizing his views, he was helped a great deal by the German Communists, especially Herman Kriege, who had fled to the United States prior to the Revolution of 1848. A prime mover in the Bund der Gerechten (League of the Just), a secret and underground sodality founded by German workingmen in Paris, Kriege one night attended a lecture in Philadelphia on Evans' land reform and was promptly won over to its efficacy. Along with his friends he energetically set about establishing the "Social Reform Association" to do for the new Germans in the United States what Evans and his Agrarian League (later rechristened the National Reform Association) were trying to do for the native born.

Kriege was an excellent organizer and soon had formed branches of his Association in Milwaukee, Chicago, St. Louis, New York, Philadelphia, and Boston. He and his group differed, however, from the Evans faction. Whereas Evans looked upon land reform as an end in itself, the Kriege followers looked upon it as a means only, a first step toward the communist state. But Karl Marx, who controlled the old Bund der Gerechten, even though he referred to it scornfully as a "mixture of French-English socialism and German philosophy," was infuriated by Kriege's "rightist deviation" and personally expelled him from the Bund. Yet Kriege maintained to the last that he was a genuine communist who hoped that land reform in America would not so much generate the rule of Evans' individualism, through private property for everyone, as smash the domination of monopoly which, he claimed, was the primary task confronting anyone who in the United States genuinely desired a new dispensation.

Meantime, Evans kept hewing to his line. His proposal was, in a sense, merely a further and logical development of the nation's land policy. It must be pointed out that in 1796 Congress had passed a law providing for land sales at public auction at a price not less than $2.00 an acre and in a block of not less than 640 acres. It was a practice which obviously favored the rich alone since very few others could lay their hands on the necessary $1,280, or even scrape up enough cash to make a down payment which, under the later "credit system," required only a small part of the total amount due at the time of sale. By 1820 the plaints of a land-hungry populace compelled the government to change the law, to reduce the minimum price of land from $2.00 to $1.25 an acre, and the minimum amount sold to a single purchaser from 640 to 80 acres, and to abolish the credit system altogether. To Evans therefore it seemed not only practical and just but also inevitable that the next step should be to give the land away and double the amount, that is, from 80 to 160 acres.

Meantime, too, Evans—who was always the strategist— coupled his land reform with another popular crusade: the demand for the ten-hour day. For nearly a generation, American workers had been passing resolutions which excoriated the "from-sun-to-sun" hours that had been taken over from agriculture—quite as much because of cultural lag and the inertia of human habit as by the desire of employers to exploit labor unduly. And although isolated crafts—notably the masons and carpenters and cordwainers—had achieved for themselves the ten-hour-day schedule, the larger, state-wide and national attempts to legislate this working time into a "ceiling" for all labor had produced more impassioned rhetoric than concrete results. The humanitarians who in the 40's and 50's filled the woods—

Albert Brisbane and the three Channings, William E., William F., and William H., Bronson Alcott, Parke Godwin, Ralph W. Emerson, and all the other uplifters who were influenced by Fourier and helped to found "phalanxes" at Brook Farm, at Hopedale, at Sylvania—had but reiterated the earlier arguments that for reasons of brotherly love and compassion the employers should shorten hours to give workers more leisure for the cultivation of soul and mind.

Evans, however, was more realistic. He concentrated upon arguments that would enlist the employer's self-interest. He and his school tended to underscore but a single point—a point finally incorporated by New Hampshire's legislature in the first ten-hour law, which was passed in 1847: ". . . A proper reduction in the hours of labor would be found advantageous to all parties. Employers should realize a greater profit, even in less time, from labourers more vigorous and better able to work, from having had suitable time to rest." Maine and Pennsylvania soon followed suit and the parade of statutory imitation had begun, heartening Evans; for the passage of such laws seemed to prove the efficacy of his propaganda. He thereupon redoubled his efforts to "high pressure" the country into land reform. By this time, however, the idea had gone beyond him, penetrating to all parts of the country; no longer alone, he was now only another voice in a growing chorus.

During the next fourteen to fifteen years, the great American topic of conversation, next to slavery and making money and becoming a "big man" in the community, was whether free homesteads were to be or not. The question was debated endlessly—on the farm, at church, in the tavern, on the bowling green, in the halls of Congress, from the lyceum platform, across the retail counter. It broke friendships, brought dissension to the family dinner table, received the support of the spiritual Emerson and considerably less spiritual "Tammany Mike" Walsh of a Wigwam even then corrupt and tough and venal. And ironically enough a reform sponsored by Evans, spokesman for the wage earners of the East, was adopted, reshaped and finally put over by the farmers of the West; yet it was appropriate perhaps since, in essence, the plan epitomized the crude individualism of the frontier. But whereas Evans stressed equal distribution, the pioneers and settlers of the West stressed more production and population increase. While he looked toward relief for the Atlantic Seaboard's labor, they looked toward a rise in real estate values. Whereas he wanted to stop speculation, they adored it, fostered it by every means at their command. Whereas he insisted that no single person, or company, should acquire vast tracts, they favored million-acre grants to railways to help open up the country and make markets more accessible.

In the East, of course, Evans' colleagues and friends were helping to propel public opinion toward adoption of the land reform idea. The Kentucky philosopher Lewis Masquerier, Evans' most ardent disciple, had written a book— *Sociology or the Reconstruction of Society, Government and Property upon the Principles of Equality, the Perpetuity and the Individuality of the Private Ownership of Life, Person and Government, Homestead and the Whole Product of Labor, by Organizing All Nations into Self-Governed Homestead Democracy, Self-Employed in Farming and Mechanism Giving All the Liberty and Happiness to Be Found on Earth*—which was widely circulated and passionately discussed.

Moreover, the always redoubtable Greeley was breaking down the opposition of the merchant, manufacturer, and banker by striking a new and pragmatic note. He declared in the *Tribune* of August 25, 1860:

The Great West is the predestined market, not only of the imported Wares and Fabrics of the seaboard cities, but of the Iron of Pennsylvania and New Jersey, the Manufacturers of New England, the cotton and sugar of the Southwest. The faster the West can be settled and cultivated, the more independent and thrifty its settlers, the greater must be the demand for the peculiar products and merchandise of the seaboard States. A new State in the West implies new warehouses in and near lower Broadway, new streets and blocks uptown, new furnaces in Pennsylvania, new factories in New England. A new cabin on the prairies predicts and insures more work for carmen and stevedores in New York.

It took some time for this line of logic to sink in, however; and up to the very last the "lunatic and loathsome notions of Mr. Evans" were opposed by the barons of business who, at this stage, were frankly less interested in labor's ethical beatitudes than in their own bank balances.

Their mouthpiece, Representative James Allison of Pennsylvania, had declared in a House debate some years before:

By your policy, you strike down our great manufacturing interests . . . you turn thousands of our labourers out of employment. You render useless . . . millions of capital which our people have invested. . . . You depreciate value of real estate. You make a bid for our population by holding out inducements for our productive labourers to leave their old homes under the seductive promise of lands for nothing . . . thereby decreasing our population and consequently increasing the burdens of those who remain in the old states.

Yet after a while, when the leaders of finance, industry, and commerce began to realize that the politicians in Washington could very readily be persuaded to accompany grants of free homesteads to settlers with incalculably grander fiefs to railroads, even the East's plutocracy saw the light. From a madman's hallucination, land reform became a sound, even a noble, principle, instinct with patriotism. Everyone in the business community stood to gain by railroad expansion—if not by direct investment, then by the enlarged market for goods that a closer and more populous West would provide.

It was the South that fought free homesteads to the bitter end. Its Calhouns saw in the "adoption of this devilment" an unconstitutional effort of the North to prevent the westward extension of great plantations and their slaves. Many planters, their lands exhausted by stupid and careless methods of cultivation, had staked all their hopes for recoupment upon access to the fresh, fertile soils of the Southwest.

In 1860 the "ravening and radical" Republican party, with its pledge to do something quick and "complete and satisfactory" about free homesteads, and with its "backwoods baboon" as standard-bearer, was put into power by the frontiersmen of the West combined with an East where, on the question of land reform, wage earner, merchant, banker, and manufacturer at last saw eye to eye. Eleven slave-owning states of the South seceded and on April 12, 1861, the fighting broke out.

The Homestead Act, for all the ballyhoo that went with its passage, was in itself a compromise measure. It excluded, in intent and in the law's letter, the basic ideals of inalienability and limitation that had been sponsored by the original Agrarians as necessary adjuncts of the new and better life for landless labor. And George Henry Evans, who had dreamed of security and dignity and peace and proud independence for all workers, who all unconsciously had been a voice of the "manifest destiny" marking the inexorable westward push of the American economy, had done as much as any man to bring on the blood and strife of the Civil War.

From the Civil War

THE Civil War transformed legions of labor from a peacetime army producing goods into hosts of battle that did nothing but consume and destroy. Before the firing on Sumter, however, the sentiment of wage earners was definitely on the side of compromise. They regarded the impending crisis as a "politicians' plague," the result of conflicts in which, whatever the outcome, the "honest workingmen stood to gain nothing and to lose all." At this stage a black mood of pessimism mantled American labor, for the panic of 1857 had wiped out the encouraging gains made by unions in the decade before. They were gains due largely to the discovery of gold in California and the consequent business boom and vast increase in employment. And as usual in a period of prosperity, labor—and skilled labor particularly—abandoned legislative and humanitarian experiments. While the more poorly paid workers continued to chase after the will-of-the-wisps of reform, the unions, composed mainly of artisans, settled down to the cold quid-pro-quo business of getting more pay for their members by building exclusive and permanent organizations. The Typographers, the Machinists and Blacksmiths, the Stone Cutters, the Hat Finishers, and many more founded strong organizations that excluded politicians and other "friends of labor" and concentrated upon the closed shop, apprenticeship rules, ample strike funds, employment exchange offices, minimum wage and hour standards, and all the other accouterments of a "pure and simple" unionism. For the first time, moreover, such societies were formed on a national scale instead of being confined to the city or state. In this respect they merely reflected the "nationalizing of the market" which the rapid growth of railroads had encouraged.

Before 1850 water and highway traffic exceeded traffic by rail. But beginning in the spring of that year, the "hectic decade" of railroad construction swung into stride, increasing track mileage from 8,389 in 1850 to 30,373 in 1860, reversing transportation trends. "Through freight" carriers started to supplant canals like the Erie, and "turnpikes" like the old Cumberland Road, and to spread out into "trunk" lines. Soon the consolidation of "trunks" such as the combination of the New York Central with the Hudson River and Harlem in the East, and with the Lake Shore and Michigan Southern in the West, not only connected New York and Chicago directly but also paved the way for the great "transcontinental" systems of a following era. And this extension of traffic arteries from the Atlantic Seaboard to the Mississippi Valley at last widened local markets until they embraced half the continent. Stoves made in Albany were displayed in St. Louis alongside stoves made in Detroit. All this not only intensified competition but taught unionists that since business had become "national," labor must follow suit in order to function effectively. It seemed natural and obvious to labor leaders that, to preserve union norms, it would be necessary to "equalize competitive conditions" by putting a "floor" of uniform wage scales underneath the price fluctuations of a particular commodity.* Otherwise, they believed, the employer who cut his wage payrolls the most would exercise an unfair advantage over his rivals. And as union "committees of correspondence" began to flourish, informing workers in the same trade of "shop and sharp practices" throughout the country, the golden fever of the great California lodes pitted the nation's face with failures. For with incurable optimism, the merchants, speculators, financiers, manufacturers, and their countless satellites had repeated during the years 1850–57

* It is interesting to note that eighty-five years later, this same point of view is stressed by the Textile Workers' Organizing Committee in its efforts to unionize, and hence, it claims, to "stabilize" the textile industry.

the same mistakes of overexpansion that they had made from 1830 to 1837 and with the same results. And by the time Lincoln took his oath of office on March 4, 1861, the roaring pace of gold-rush affluence had been for four long years slackening to a standstill.

A genuine lack of confidence in what was going to happen next hindered business from embarking upon fresh enterprises, to recoup losses, to build anew, a fact that served only to amplify an already widespread unemployment. Meanwhile, as war came closer, labor along with the rest of the population was divided in its views of what should be done. In New England, especially in Massachusetts, workers tended to be antislavery partisans and the women and girls in the textile mills were completely abolitionist. But in New York, New Jersey, Pennsylvania, Ohio, and Illinois, many labor leaders were opposed to Lincoln and the Republican party which, they felt, was agitating the Negro issue unduly. They could not get excited over the plight of Harriet Beecher Stowe's Uncle Toms and Little Evas. Instead they accepted pretty much at face value the contention of Southern planters that the slaves on the whole were comfortably housed and well fed and taken care of in sickness and old age, whereas the wage earner, under the growing factory system, was paid next to nothing and turned out to starve in slack seasons or when he was too feeble to work. Still others, especially in border states like Kentucky, while frowning upon the "peculiar institution," didn't think it was worth a war and wanted a compromise. It was, in fact, in Louisville that workers held their first mass meeting to condemn a "resort to arms" as a solution of the slavery question or of the deeper economic discords of which it was but a part.

In St. Louis, in Cincinnati, even in Richmond, similar meetings called for "pacific measures" for reconciling the collision of interests between North and South.

And largely for the same purpose a so-called "national convention of workingmen" took place in Philadelphia on February 22, 1861. It was by far the most important labor gathering of the time, both in its leadership and in its statements of the workers' positions. It was presided over by William H. Sylvis, the "first great figure" in American labor in the trade-union, as against the reformist, sense of the term. He was the treasurer of the powerful Moulders' International Union which, depression born in 1859, lost fifty-seven of its eighty-seven locals within four years, and yet survived the "crisis of stagnation" in better shape than any other union, a tribute to Sylvis' strategic supervision of strikes, propaganda, and organizing. He was a strong-willed, tough-minded, self-educated man, a former wagon maker in his father's shop in Armagh, Pennsylvania, where he was born in 1828. In 1840 he became an apprentice in an iron foundry, was taken into partnership seven years later, and emerged in 1852 as a free-lance skilled mechanic in Philadelphia, typifying the easy shift from artisan to small master back to journeyman again that marked the period. His own experience as part proprietor of a foundry had convinced him, somewhat too plausibly, that the nation's employers

saw in the future a possibility of monopolizing almost the entire trade of the country and set themselves about doing so . . . to mark out a line of policy, which, if closely followed, would insure this result . . . the first act of the drama . . . was to reduce their margin of profits to the lowest possible standard, that they might go into market below all others. Owing to fluctuations in the price of materials, their profits would sometimes disappear entirely. This they used as an argument to their workmen, telling them that . . . they were unable to advance their selling prices, and that being unable to compete without loss they must either close up or reduce wages. . . .

They were still trying to reduce wages, against the stiff but largely useless opposition of the unions, when the delegates to the Philadelphia convention met. Yet on the floor the chief debates and discussions dealt less with unionism's own immediate concerns and more with the larger issues of the general welfare. What was probably the majority opinion of American labor in regard to the "irrepressible conflict" was embodied in such statements as:

Resolved, That we earnestly invoke zealous and energetic action at once by Congress, either by the adoption of the Crittenden,* Bigler or Guthrie amendments, or by some other full and clear recognition of the equal rights of the South in the Territories by such enactment for constitutional action as will finally remove the question of slavery therein from our National Legislature. . . .

Resolved, That our Government never can be sustained by bloodshed, but must live in the affections of the people; we are, therefore, utterly opposed to any measures that will evoke civil war, and the workingmen of Philadelphia will, by the use of all constitutional means, and with our moral and political influence, oppose any such extreme policy, or a fratricidal war thus to be inaugurated.

Yet when on April 12, 1861, the Confederate battery opened fire on Fort Sumter, the opposition to war by wage earners was drowned out by the tread of marching feet and the noise of drums. Whole unions enlisted at President Lincoln's call for volunteers; and Sylvis personally helped to recruit an entire company from among his own molders, becoming a top sergeant himself.

Meantime, the first repercussions of the war appeared to

* In essence the compromise measure introduced into the House in January, 1861, by Representative Crittenden of Kentucky proposed that in all territories acquired "now or hereafter" north of latitude 36°30', slavery was to be prohibited; but that south of this line it was to be allowed and protected as property by Congress. States formed from territory north of the line, however, were to be either slave or free as their citizens might provide in their constitutions. The Bigler and Guthrie plans were almost identical with Crittenden's.

benumb business all the more. In the beginning the people
of the North seemed too stunned and too excited to do
anything but read and talk the news of Bull Run and the
other battles of the "first campaign." The continued industrial paralysis tended to demoralize the unions, and their
numbers were further depleted by enlistments in the North
and by the loss of entire locals in the South. Even the International Union of Machinists and Blacksmiths of the
United States of America which, to the country's amaze-
ment, had been rich enough and strong enough to fight the
Baldwin Locomotive Works for four months to a stale-
mate, was finding it hard to survive. At its annual convention in Pittsburgh, in November, 1861, its national secretary, Jonathan Fincher, who shared honors with Sylvis as
a labor leader of the first rank, reported that in the six
months from April to October, 1861, membership had
dropped from 2,717 to 1,898 and that his order was "losing
more men every week." Other unions lamented that with
"panic on the one hand and patriotism on the other" it was
impossible to keep from going under.

By 1862, however, the demand for war supplies, along
with the legal tender acts of February and April which
primed the financial pump by pouring $300,000,000 of
greenbacks into circulation, lighted the fires and started
the flybelts whirring for a wartime boom. Wage earners
who for one reason or another weren't in the army found
jobs plentiful enough. In the mills of New England women
worked in double shifts. And in the next year, 1863, wholesale prices shot up 59 per cent above 1860 and advanced to
125 per cent during 1864. Yet while the middleman, the
manufacturer, the banker, and the farmer all prospered, the
worker faced new hardships. He had steady employment,
to be sure; but his real wages did not keep up with the cost
of living which mounted daily. In July, 1862, for example,
retail prices in greenbacks were 15 per cent above the 1860
level, while wages remained stationary. In July, 1863, retail

prices had risen 43 per cent and wages but 12 per cent; and in July, 1865, prices ascended to 76 per cent and wages only to 50 per cent above the 1860 base.

Once more, to protect their living standards, the workers turned toward unionism. And once more, with industry roaring to fill war orders, it was relatively easy to set up locals and persuade employers to meet demands. A labor press of no less than one hundred and twenty daily, weekly, and monthly journals appeared in the decade 1863–73, attesting to the urgency of this new national drive toward organization. Preëminent among such papers was *Fincher's Trades' Review* which has rarely been equaled and never surpassed in skill in the annals of American labor journalism. It was run by Fincher himself who, despite his fondness for purple passages, such as "Little dreamed that crew of the fearful gales they were to encounter and the terrible shipwrecks they were to witness in their eventful voyage," was a born editor. A four-page weekly (later enlarged to eight pages), it was founded on June 1, 1863, and soon attained a circulation of 11,000, reaching thirty-one of the thirty-six states, three provinces in Canada, and eight cities in England. It avoided all advertising—even the ladies' cures and patent medicines which then adorned virtually all printed matter in the United States. For Fincher was an indefatigable correspondent, and a great believer in "data" and their patient accumulation, and he wanted to crowd every stick of space with reports of labor's progress, analyses of its programs, and tables such as the following, which shows the tremendous growth of unions in the single year from December, 1863, to December, 1864:

STATE	December, 1863	December, 1864
Connecticut	2	6
Delaware	—	1
Illinois	1	10
Indiana	3	17
Kentucky	2	8

STATE	December, 1863	December, 1864
Maine	1	7
Maryland	—	1
Massachusetts	17	42
Michigan	4	9
Missouri	4	9
New Hampshire	3	5
New Jersey	4	10
New York	16	74
Ohio	4	16
Pennsylvania	15	44
Rhode Island	1	7
Tennessee	—	2
Vermont	1	—
Virginia	1	1
Wisconsin	—	1
TOTAL	79	270

And as the war continued, the demand for labor reached unprecedented heights, at times finding a shortage. Astute strategists, like R. F. Trevellick of the Ship Carpenters and Caulkers, and Thomas Phillips of the Shoemakers, and many others were all anxious to make hay while the sun was shining, to store up a reserve of union strength against the time when demobilization would bring a new glut to the labor market with the return of soldiers to civilian life. Hence among the sixty-one trade unions of the day, from cabinet makers to curriers, from tailors to tinsmiths, there was tremendous activity.

Fincher's Trades' Review for March 12, 1864, reported union effort in New York and vicinity as follows:

The Slate and Metal Roofers are organizing and it is thought they will demand $3 a day. The Segar makers are preparing to secure better wages. The Longshoremen have demanded $2.50 per day of nine hours, from the 7th inst. . . . The Piano Forte makers demand an increase of 25 per cent on former wages. . . . Wheelwrights and Blacksmiths are in council. . . . The Coopers have obtained their increase recently sought. . . . The Coach Painters and Coach Trimmers will shortly remodel their list of prices. . . .

As a matter of course the trades assemblies or combination of crafts within a city or community were infused with new vitality. First revived in 1863 in Rochester (New York), in Louisville, Philadelphia, St. Louis, and Pittsburgh, they had spread to every important industrial center when Lee yielded to Grant at Appomattox. While merely "advisory," the trade assembly exerted great power, seeking to do for local unions what the A. F. of L. and the C.I.O. are at present doing for their respective national unions. The executive board of every trade assembly was composed of the most influential labor leaders in the community, and they shaped policy with rigor and precision and without benefit of legal authority. They ordered "nonintercourse," that is, a boycott of firms that were unfair in their labor practices. They established coöperative stores, libraries, reading rooms. They appointed special agents to unionize open shops. They conceived it their bounden duty to "agitate, educate, exasperate." They lobbied with zeal and expertness. In February, 1864, for example, a bill to abolish picketing was introduced into the New York State legislature only to be smothered under the protests of trade assembly leaders.

However, the New York state trade assemblies, like others elsewhere, were less successful in promoting positive legislation on their own, especially that looking toward the eight hour day, a question then being agitated by Ira Steward. A Boston machinist who had pondered John Stuart Mill, Steward from his nineteenth year in 1850 to his death in 1883 lived only to fulfill his self-imposed mission of shortening labor's hours to eight for the reason expressed in the jingle composed by his wife:

Whether you work by the piece or work by the day,
Decreasing the Hours increases the pay

"Meet him any day," observed a writer in the *American Workman* of June 19, 1869, "as he steams along the street (like most enthusiasts he is always in a hurry) and, although he will apologize and excuse himself if you talk to him of other affairs, and say that he is sorry, that he must rush back to his shop, if you only introduce the pet topic of 'hours of labor' and show a little willingness to listen, he will stop and plead with you till night-fall."

With the spacious confidence of his kind, Steward claimed that the enactment of his single reform would improve the worker's status in every respect. He asserted that wages did not depend so much upon the prevailing supply of capital and labor, and their interaction, as upon the wants of workers as consumers. It was also obvious, he continued, that the installation of machinery had enlarged the nation's productivity to an enormous extent. The worker should therefore concentrate upon two things: on the one hand, he should urge, rather than oppose, as many did, the use of new labor-saving devices. On the other hand, he should reduce his own hours to increase his normal wants by adding to them the extra wants that leisure brings. At the same time he should insist upon higher pay to satisfy his newly expanded desires, whether for clothing or culture. Manifestly, Steward argued, the larger output of goods that the more efficient methods of manufacture could be made to release would insure to the worker a rising and proportionate share of the greater national wealth—the more especially since the employer, with better business deriving from the extension of labor's wants, and its bigger income, would be able to pay his own workers a higher wage. Steward believed, further, that the current campaign to restrict immigration, to exclude Chinese and other aliens, was quite as unimportant as efforts to bargain collectively. Once the universal eight hour law was inscribed on the statute books workers would be well on their way toward ample security and the richer life.

He convinced Wendell Phillips, the abolitionist, of the essential soundness of this approach, and Phillips contributed generously to the Labor Reform Association which Steward and his associates founded in Boston in 1864. They copied George Henry Evans' method of exacting pre-election pledges from candidates for public office; and Eight Hour Leagues were formed all over the country. The simplicity of Steward's legislative cure-all entranced many sections of American labor and emphasis upon the political began to supersede emphasis upon the economic even in union strongholds. Moreover, his candid statement that the "Labor Reform enterprise . . . expects to be served by men who at heart want nothing but position, power, honour and pay" and by "politicians in action" inspired a number of union officials to use the eight hour plan as a starting point for making a profession of politics. It was a trend constantly deprecated by strict trade unionists like Fincher who from 1863 forward kept warning that:

"Once absorbed in politics, the day passes in the workshop, with but little anxiety for aught else, save the anticipated indulgence in political scenes at night. The duties of block, ward or township committees absorb the time that should be devoted to the family and to the Trades' Union."

A few years later he was to observe caustically that, despite its absorption of labor's energies, the eight hour crusade as conducted by Steward and his followers had accomplished virtually nothing. Six states had enacted eight hour laws, to be sure, but with guile aforethought had failed to implement them effectively, making them merely gestures of appeasement. In New York state, for example, both houses had passed an eight hour measure which was signed without a qualm by Governor Fenton in 1867. But no agency was established to enforce its provisions; and when William Jessup, president of the state's workingmen's assembly, complained of this deficiency he was informed by the Governor that "every law is obligatory by its nature" and that no further steps would be taken. Jessup's reply is not recorded.

Yet the eight hour issue, for all the legislative chicanery it provoked, gave great impetus to the widely-discussed necessity for some national federation of labor through which workers in all parts of the country could act in concert to get what they wanted by means of the ballot box. The chief sponsors of this sentiment were Sylvis of the Molders and Harding of the Coachmakers, and at their instigation a meeting of the so-called National Labor Congress, later the National Labor Union, was held in Baltimore on August 20, 1866. It was attended by seventy-seven delegates from Trade Assemblies, Workingmen's Unions, Eight Hour Leagues, and Labor Organizations. Their complexion was far more political and reformist than trade unionist, though ten national unions were represented on the floor; and they debated almost every conceivable topic. They widened the breach between the politically minded of trade assembly and league and the bargaining minded of the pure trade unions by offering and quarreling over resolutions which, among other things, covered strikes, apprentice rules, Negro and women and child labor, the eight hour day, the public lands, a national labor party, education, sanitation, and alien contract labor. On the whole, however, the delegates were more concerned with monetary reform than anything else. In their *Declaration of Principles*, they used 1900 of its 3000 words in attacking the "money monopoly" as the parent of all others, urging the repeal of laws exempting government bonds and bank capital from taxation and plumping for legal tender paper money. They had cheered the address of A. C. Cameron, exponent of "Kellogism," a revolutionary forerunner of Greenbackism, whereby the government was to finance the small producer, whether farmer or wage-earner, and make him independent of middleman and banker in all his undertakings. The convention endorsed this objective; and as a first step toward it appointed a permanent committee to investigate coöperation, an up and coming movement of the time.*

The hard times which followed the end of the war as usual prompted many strikes when earnings of the workers declined. The Molders, the decade's most important union, conducted three long walkouts against members of the American National Stove Manufacturers' and Iron-Founders Association, formed on March 4, 1866, to destroy the Molders by taking in as many apprentices as plant operations would allow and by refusing to deal with the union's shop committees on questions of rules, hours and pay. Under the leadership of the redoubtable Sylvis, the Molders won the first two engagements. They lost the third, however, in Cincinnati where they were subjected to a nine months' strife that exhausted their national treasury and nearly wrecked them entirely. This defeat induced them in December, 1866, to turn off the main road of straight bargaining unionism to travel the byways of producers' coöperation which Sylvis, with his liking for panaceas, was then convinced alone could liberate labor from its new "bondage." At the September, 1868, convention of the International Molders Union he therefore recommended that its name be changed to the Iron Molders

---

* Most of the people who for the next few years attended the sessions of the National Labor Union were so engrossed in general issues of social reform that they had thrown over unionism for legislative action and various inflationary schemes to abolish the "robbery of interest rates." They neglected to set up apparatus by which their organization could receive revenues from its constituent parts, build from the bottom up, and become functional. In drafting the preamble to the constitution of the National Labor Union, Sylvis and Harding had recognized a genuine need: "Heretofore the highest form labor associations have taken is the national union of some of the trades. Between these organizations, however, there was no sympathy or systematic connection, no coöperative effort, no working for the attainment of a common end, the want of which has been experienced by every craft and calling." But they took no practical measures to fulfill this need and the National Labor Union died in 1872, in large the victim of supporters too often visionaries and theorists when not cranks.

International Coöperative and Protective Union, a suggestion approved by acclamation. In presenting his annual report, moreover, he digressed to explain his disillusionment with the everyday brand of unionism, and to stress the point that coöperatives were the only way out.

"Combination," he said, "as we have been using or applying it, makes war upon the effects [i.e., low wages, long hours, no jobs] leaving the cause undisturbed to produce, continually, like effects. The cause of all these evils is the WAGES SYSTEM. We must adopt a system which will divide the profits of labor among those who produce them. . . ."

The experience of the preceding eighteen months had in his opinion already confirmed the validity of this conclusion. Eleven coöperative foundries had been established by the Molders in Troy (2); Albany; Rochester; Chicago; Cleveland (2); Louisville; Pittsburgh;* Quincy and Somerset.

The pioneering Troy Coöperative Iron Founders Association was immediately and particularly successful. It was a corporation; but in accord with the Rochdale principle each member had but a single vote whether he held only one share or the maximum of fifty. Its very efficiency, however, created a new and paradoxical problem. The coöperators shifted quickly from a unionist to an industrialist outlook, adding their part to the proverb that in America a worker is a capitalist without money. They soon said that the fewer the stockholders the better, discouraged efforts of their fellows to "buy in." They sweated hard and long, disregarding holidays. They delivered orders in advance of their due-dates. They turned out excellent stoves at prices less than those of their "private" rivals. They featured the relative cheapness of their wares

* This was begun as the "International Foundry" to allow the president and treasurer of the union to become directors ex officio and to share authority with the management elected by the stockholders.

without giving a thought to the effect this would have on other Molders, who were not in coöperatives, and who through their union were trying to maintain wage-scales with employers forced to reduce them if they were to meet the lower prices of coöperative competition!

Along with the Coopers in Indianapolis who had established seven coöperative shops for the manufacture of flour barrels, the Troy Molders were perhaps the most thriving exemplars of a movement which had taken hold among bakers, coach-makers, coal-miners, shipwrights, printers, machinists and many more, including the powerful Order of the Knights of St. Crispin* with its 50,000 shoemakers.

Started secretly in Milwaukee, Wisconsin, on May 7, 1867, to combat the menace of "green hands" who were being used increasingly since the introduction of the McKay pegging machine five years before, the Crispins in 1870 began to perceive that theirs was a losing fight against the mechanization of their industry. In that year their Grand Scribe, Samuel Cummings, declared that "the present demand of the Crispin is steady employment and fair wages, but his future is self-employment"; and in 1871, in New York state alone, the Crispins set up 15 coöperative shoe-making shops and thirty-five stores for distributing dry goods and groceries, hardware and drugs.

During the next few years, coöperation in one form or another assumed at least a verbal importance that tended to elbow ordinary unionism aside, especially in the Northeast. The Sovereigns of Industry, for example, an indirect outgrowth of the Patrons of Husbandry in Iowa, was formed in Springfield, Massachusetts, in January, 1874, for "improving the condition and perfecting the happiness of the laboring classes of every calling." Unlike the Molders

---

* St. Crispin was a Roman shoemaker and Christian martyr beheaded for his faith in 288 A.D., according to legend. In selecting him as patron saint of their craft, the shoemakers—like the iron-puddlers who called their union the Sons of Vulcan—reflected the wage earner's fondness for a name more impressive than his occupation.

and the Crispins, the Sovereigns manufactured nothing. Rather they developed along the lines of distributors' cooperation previously introduced into the United States by Thomas Phillips, the shoemaker-reformer and English-born missionary of the Rochdale system.* In 1863 the high prices caused by the Civil War inspired him to try and transplant the Rochdale idea to Philadelphia where he organized the Union Coöperative Association which, through its store, sold necessaries and stimulated a great deal of interest in the rules of the Rochdale Equitable Pioneers Society already twenty years old in England. He was later active in the Crispins, helping to direct one of their cooperative shoe factories and still later becoming a field supervisor for the Sovereigns who in 1874 set forth their purposes:

According to their president William H. Earle, "Our order will aim to cultivate a generous sympathy among its members, and a supreme respect for the rights of others. We propose to have Purchasing Agencies through which consumers reach the producer direct, without so many needless 'middlemen' who do nothing to merchandise but *add to its cost.* 'Middlemen' not only exact a tax from every consumer but they are responsible for 'shoddy goods,' 'short weights,' and adulterations. We are determined to secure *pure goods at lower prices.* . . . In short the Order is for the hard hand-workers, the real producers of wealth, and its purpose is to enable them to control the *whole* of what they produce. . . ."

In 1876 the Sovereigns, through their "councils" or local units which paid headquarters a 20 cent per capita tax and $15.00 for a charter fee, had enrolled some 40,000 followers, 75 per cent in New England and 43 per cent in Massachusetts. They operated 45 Rochdale-like stores and

* As devised by Charles Howarth in Rochdale in 1844, it proposed neither to sell at cost nor capitalize profits but rather to charge regular market prices and accredit each member with his share of the surplus based upon the number of his purchases at the society's store. In this country the original Rochdale method was modified in many respects.

26 others that sold at cost to members, along with a number of group buying associations which had arranged for special discounts from private commercial houses. Altogether their total transactions amounted to around three million dollars a year. Their ability in many instances to provide "honest, and full measure" merchandise at prices 10 to 20 per cent below market figures allured various union locals into merging with the Sovereigns, causing consternation among trade union leaders. Their alarm over these defections was expressed in an anti-Sovereigns campaign waged by the *National Labor Tribune*, published in Pittsburgh, which contended in 1875 that "the only object of the Sovereigns is to buy cheap if they have to reduce wages to a dollar a day to do it," and said further that "the Sovereigns do not make the protection or elevation of labor's interests cardinal doctrines." In reply the Sovereigns pointed out that the majority of their members worked for wages and were therefore intimately and practically concerned with keeping them as high as possible. The Order conceded, however, that it was devoted less to collective bargaining and all it implied than to trying to "substitute coöperation, production and exchange for the present competitive system and demand for labor the entire results of its beneficial toil. . . ."

Despite the brave beginnings of the coöperative movement, whether producers as with the Molders and Coopers, or distributors as with the Sovereigns, or a combination of both as with the Crispins, its disintegration was as rapid as its rise. The newer large scale methods of production required greater capital investments than the coöperators could command—a chief reason why the National Labor Union had stressed easier credit and more currency. In addition the objective of self-employment was primarily to permit the craftsman to exercise a skill the reason for which was waning as power-driven machinery supplanted hand tools. Many of the enterprises, of whatever kind,

were inefficiently and often dishonestly managed. The
temptation to change the venture when successful into a
private undertaking was frequently irresistible to its directors. Private firms already in the field exerted every stratagem to drive this new kind of competition to the wall.
Against this array of obstacles, supplemented by the antagonism or indifference of many unions, coöperation could
make very little progress of a lasting kind; and at the decade's close it was more a memory than a movement.

Meantime, the sweep and scope of the new unionizing
campaign during the war had aroused opposition among
many groups of manufacturers. They began to establish
"employers' associations" to repel the inroads made by
unions upon the "free, white, and twenty-one" conduct of
their affairs. On July 25, 1864, in Detroit an "Employers'
General Association of Michigan" was brought into semi-
secret existence. Its governing body contained representatives from various fields of business which were subdivided
into "auxiliaries," one for the iron mongers, another for
the ship builders, a third for the sawmill proprietors, and
the like. Each auxiliary was authorized to "fix, grade, and
regulate" wages and to set minimum prices to be charged
for its own commodity. The preamble to this alliance's
constitution and by-laws attacked unions as pernicious and
dangerous because "as a natural result of this system of
general and persistent interference . . . our business is
thrown into a condition of much uncertainty. . . . Busi-
ness-like calculations and arrangements, especially such as
involve prices for work, and time of completion and delivery, are thus rendered quite impracticable. . . . If continued for any considerable time, it [unionism] must result
in wide-spread beggary, with all its attending evils—suffering, bread riots, pillage and taxation." In this same document, the employers further regretted that "well disposed
workmen" were not left to act freely but "come into contact with others of a different make and temper—uneasy

spirits, pregnant with the leaven of discontent, and whose words, constantly dropping, are full of the seeds of trouble."

The Master Mechanics of Boston (1867) and the New York Master Builders' Association (1869) followed the lead of the Michigan society in the East, reëchoing its sentiments almost phrase by phrase and setting the style for many imitators in the seaboard states.

Within a few years such paper assaults were carried into the sphere of bitter anti-union action, a result of "Jay Cooke's speculative slump" of 1873–78 which rendered competition more savage and merciless than ever before. As if in response to a given signal, employers everywhere seemed determined to rid themselves of "restrictions upon free enterprise" by smashing the unions. The lockout and blacklist were used with a bitterness new in American industrial relations. It was soon difficult to find workers willing to risk their necks by serving on committees or by participating in other union activities. In five years union membership in New York City alone dropped from 44,000 to 5,000. Many labor leaders deserted the fold, to "Go West," or to enter politics. J. H. Fehrenbach, head of the "Machinists and Blacksmiths," was elected to the Ohio State legislature in 1876. And H. J. Walls, secretary of the "Moulders," became in 1877 the first commissioner of the Buckeye state's new Bureau of Labor and Statistics. Business opportunity caused other and similar defections.

To labor's Jeremiahs it seemed as if the day of the union was "done and gone"—at least the day of the "out-in-the-open" union. Certainly it exposed its adherents to all kinds of trouble, thwarting "just and due" promotions, when not causing loss of the job. Subjected to this kind of treatment, the labor movement went underground. Its leaders met secretly. They were "hedged about," said William Davis, secretary of the Ohio Miners' Union, in a speech on July 9, 1881, "with the impenetrable veil of ritual, sign, grip, and password" so that "no spy of the boss can find his way to the lodgeroom to betray his fellows."

Out of this atmosphere emerged the Noble Order of the Knights of Labor which, founded on the theory of "One Big Union," dominated the American labor scene for the next decade.

It had been inauspiciously started in 1869 by Uriah Smith Stephens, along with some fellow garment workers in Philadelphia. Born on August 3, 1821, at Cape May, New Jersey, Stephens was educated for the Baptist ministry but never obtained a pulpit. In 1837 he was indentured to a tailor and later taught elementary school. Filled with the wanderlust of youth, he somehow contrived to travel a great deal, visiting the West Indies, Central America, Mexico, and California, whence he came East again and settled down in Philadelphia to ply his cutter's trade. He was antislavery, and pro-Lincoln. He was also a diligent "joiner"—a Mason, an Oddfellow, a "Pythian." And probably from his association with various fraternal orders, he evolved the elaborate cabalism which denoted the Knights in the public mind. To notify members of a meeting, a symbol of five stars within a circle inclosed by a triangle was chalked on sidewalks, fences, walls, scaring the rest of the population out of its wits since tales of the murderous Molly Maguires had given rise to the most sinister and fantastic rumors of labor's intentions and tactics.

The ritual of the Order set forth its principles, declaring that "open and public association having failed after a struggle of centuries to protect or advance the interests of labor, we have lawfully constituted this assembly and in using this power of organized effort and coöperation we but imitate the example of capital, for in all the multifarious branches of trade, capital has its combinations and whether intended or not it crushes the manly hopes of labor and tramples poor humanity into the dust. . . . We mean no conflict with legitimate enterprise, nor antagonism to necessary capital. . . . We mean to create a healthy public opinion on the subject of labor . . . and the justice of its receiving a full, just share of the values or capital it has created."

The Knights believed that the mechanization of American industry would soon or late erase craft distinctions and bring about a "dead level" of labor even as it was fostering vast aggregations of capital in fewer and fewer hands. They believed that only a great consolidated labor movement could successfully challenge this concentration of control over finance, industry, and commerce. They called for the welding of all workers into a single and mighty organization, regardless of trade or sex or race or religion or color or previous condition of servitude. "An injury to one is the concern of all" was their proud slogan of solidarity, their "unity in diversity."

They advocated public ownership of utilities such as railways, waterworks, gas plants; they were interested in the idea of Rochdale-plan coöperatives. They embraced the monetary panaceas of Greenbackism. They gave lip service to the ideal of the coöperative commonwealth. In fact, at one time or another, there was hardly a fad or doctrine of political economy which failed to win the endorsement of at least a part of the Knights of Labor. For much of its membership it was less a national union than a variety of religious experience. Starting with the modest "Local Assembly 1" set up by Stephens and his friends, it grew slowly. But with the disruption of unions at the very onset of the depression, the remnants of various locals in all sections of the country turned to the Knights as a rallying ground, and when Stephens died in 1881 his brain child was growing into a lusty sprawling giant that like democracy itself was chaotic and contradictory. From the beginning there were internal rows. Protestants desired to maintain the Order's secrecy. Catholics, influenced by their priests who frowned on secret societies, wanted everything to be made public. Many leaders were conservative, cautious, devotees of quiet negotiation. Others clamored for "action," for strikes. The wage earners wanted more pay, here and now. The vast array of intellectuals, socialists, utopians, and reformers who had attached themselves to the Order wanted a new society—in the future. And to cap the climax the "Grand Master Workman" of the maturing Knights, Terence V. Powderly, never quite knew what he wanted. Elected in 1879 to succeed Stephens as head of the Order, he kept his post for fourteen years, a symbol of irresolution and ineffectuality. He was born in Carbondale, Pennsylvania, in 1849, of Irish parents. At thirteen he became a railway switch tender and four years later entered its machine shop. In 1870 he joined the Scranton local of the "Machinists and Blacksmiths" union and in 1874 brought his union and himself into the Knights of Labor. His ability as a street-corner agitator was rewarded by his selection as secretary of the Order's District Assembly 5 (later 16) in 1877 and a year later he was elected Mayor of Scranton.

He was an incredible person, vague and vain. He had a neurotic inability to make up his mind. He used words as a substitute for action and platitudes as a surrogate for thought. He was full of talk about "justice" and "emancipation from wage slavery" and the "sufferings of the masses." He could sorrow for the "exploited toilers" and in the next breath complain to a friend that he had to attend a summertime union picnic and rub shoulders with a lot of noisy and sticky humanity. The Knights made their reputation by winning a series of railroad strikes, two on the Union Pacific system (1882 and 1884) and a third on Jay Gould's ten thousand miles of the "Missouri," the "Missouri, Kansas and Texas," and the "Wabash" roads. Although the capitulation of the "Wizard of Wall Street" was hailed in the press as labor's greatest victory, Powderly failed to press any of the advantages that were within his grasp. He did not insist upon any machinery for collective bargaining; he did not ask for recognition of the union or for any of the rudimentary agreements that run-of-the-mill labor leaders were daily demanding. He remained satisfied with the corporation's assurance that the Knights would not be "discriminated" against. But this ineptitude was hidden from the public which agreed with the *St. Louis Chronicle* of September 30, 1885, when it declared that "The Wabash victory is with the K. of L. . . . No such victory has ever before been secured in this or any other country."

Inspired by this seeming triumph, workers all over the country trooped into the Order's branches while membership figures mounted to 700,000 and Powderly was in a panic. He was afraid of a Frankenstein monster, of the responsibility it entailed. Despite the fact that the Order, to mollify the Catholic Church and the "phantom public," had renounced secrecy and come out into the open in 1882, press and pulpit still fumed about the dreadful power that the Knights might wield by stopping "entire industries." And Powderly, strait-laced, wanting the acclaim of the solid citizens, was alarmed lest the sheer weight of numbers would push him into some drastic action of a kind that the editors, the ministers, businessmen, and the middle class in general might not approve. He adopted a policy of "making haste slowly" which in its concrete application prevented many thousands from joining the Order.

However, the rank and file, intoxicated by the alleged conquest of Gould, went berserk. In the street, in the "workingman's club," the saloon, they were singing:

> Toiling millions now are waking—
> See them marching on;
> As the tyrants now are shaking,
> Ere their power's gone.

Chorus: Storm the Fort, ye Knights of Labor,
             Battle for your cause,
             Equal rights for every neighbor,
             Down with tyrant laws!

They also ousted many of their more conservative officers, and saluted with beer and confidence the coming of
labor's new dawn.

At the same time the four field organizers of the
Knights of Labor, who were paid on a commission basis,
were using the eight-hour day doctrine as a talking point
to sign up new prospects. The issue had been recently
revived and shorn of Ira Steward's economic theory, to
become a pragmatic "spread the work, make more leisure"
slogan, instead of a comprehensive scheme for enlarging
the nation's output of wealth. In Chicago, on May 7, 1884,
at the convention of the Federation of Organized Trades
and Labor Unions (forerunner of the A. F. of L.),
Gabriel Edmonston of the Carpenters condensed the loose
talk about the subject by proposing that, beginning on
May 1, 1886, "eight hours shall constitute a legal day's
labor." The twenty-five delegates to this meeting represented a scant fifty thousand unionists; yet with more
temerity than sense they not only approved Edmonston's
resolution but also declared themselves in favor of a
general nation-wide strike on May 1, 1886, to enforce
this demand. They further instructed their Legislative
Committee to confer with officials of the Knights of
Labor to enlist the Order's coöperation in this venture.
Actually, the Federation, which was tottering, turned toward the Knights of Labor, and hoped. Its expectations
were more than fulfilled when the idea made spontaneous
headway, and Knights of Labor organizers adopted it as
their own. In dismay Powderly tried to scotch the whole
thing by sending out a series of secret circulars, one of
which said:

Terence V. Powderly, Grand Master Workman of the Knights of Labor.

No assembly of the Knights of Labor must strike for the eight hour system on May first under the impression that they are obeying orders from headquarters, for such an order was not, and will not, be given. Neither employer nor employee are educated to the needs and necessities for the short hour plan. . . . Many are . . . in total ignorance of the movement. Out of the sixty millions of people in the United States and Canada, our Order has possibly three hundred thousand. Can we mould the sentiment of the millions in favor of the short hour plan before May first? It is nonsense to think of it. Let us learn why our hours of labor should be reduced and then teach others.

Unaware of this sabotage, the Order's rank and file, especially the unskilled and the immigrant who were thronging into its fold, looking upon it as their liberator from starvation and abuse, embraced the eight-hour cause with fervor. As during the depression of 1884-85 jobs grew scarcer and hours longer, the shorter work day with its promise to reverse both trends exercised a tonic appeal. In addition, it held all the attractiveness of an immediate demand. Unlike Powderly's supernal beatitudes such as, "Moral wealth, not wealth, is the true standard of individual and national greatness," it was something tangible. It was going to benefit the workers not in the distant future but tomorrow or the day after. It would, they felt, also enable them to flex the muscles of their new-found strength.

The eight-hour drive gained especially wide allegiance in Chicago, stronghold not only of the Knights of Labor and railroad brotherhoods and many independent unions but also of the anarchists. Despite vast differences in outlook, however, all the city's labor organizations were united in the Eight Hour Association formed by the Socialist George A. Schilling late in 1885. The Knights, of course, and the other regular unions supported the eight-hour proposal as something valuable in itself. The anarchists supported it merely as a means by which they could bore from within and disseminate their inflammatory doctrine among the unions which they regarded as the nuclei of the new social order. They were, these Chicago anarchists, romantic revolutionaries who had propounded what was known as the "Chicago Idea," blending Marxism, Nihilism, and syndicalism into a creed of violence. They believed that the "robbed class"—labor—should abandon the ballot-box for the barricade. They spurned education and collective bargaining as methods by which labor could advance its interests in a time when the American worker was being clamped into the vise of a wage system developing simultaneously from the end of the frontier's free lands, the growth of the trusts, and the expansion of machine industry.

In 1883, in Pittsburgh, Johann Most, "propagandist of the deed," anarchist extraordinary, had held a conference of the like-minded, and out of this was born the "International Working People's Association." Its program was explicit, declaring in part:

The present order of society is based upon the spoliation of the non-property by the property owners, the capitalists buy the labor of the poor for wages, at the mere cost of living, taking all the surplus. . . . Thus while the poor are increasingly deprived of the opportunities for advancement, the rich grow richer through increasing robbery. This system is unjust, insane, murderous. Therefore those who suffer under it ought to strive for its destruction. . . . Under all these circumstances, there is only one remedy left—force.

The new organization, called the Black International, drew its strength largely from dissident German socialists in Chicago. They had withdrawn from the Socialist Labor party when the split between its two factions, the followers of Marx who wanted to use the trade unions for revolution and the followers of Lassalle who wanted to use evolution for the trade unions, had produced more talk than action. They set up a Chicago branch of the Black International and through its subsidiary, the Central Labor Union, enrolled about 2,200 members chiefly from among butchers, carpenters, metal workers, and cabinet makers.*

In their strikes these craftsmen, mostly Germans, Poles, and Bohemians, had been constantly subjected to the brutality of Chicago's police. When they had gone to the polls to vote their own socialist ticket they had been attacked by the brass-knuckle and lead-pipe bruisers of the ward politicians. In self-defense they had therefore formed their own military groups, such as the *Lehr und Wehr Verein*, which drilled with rifles in cellars and woods and in theory at least was prepared to exchange bullet for bullet should the need arise.

Their own bitter experience with the forces of law and order rendered them, along with other Chicago workers, especially susceptible to the influence of the anarchists who controlled the Central Labor Union which, as a temporary tactic, vigorously endorsed the eight-hour day, and which by April of 1886 numbered twenty-two of the city's strongest unions as against the eighteen affiliated with the more conservative Amalgamated Trades and Labor assembly.

The leaders of the Black International's Central Labor Union were extremely vocal. They published five papers: *The Alarm*, in English, a bi-monthly; the *Chicagoer-Arbeiter-Zeitung*, a German daily; along with two lesser sheets, the *Fackel* and the *Vorbote*, irregularly issued; and the Bohemian *Budoucnost*.

They were also extremely able agitators. There was Albert Parsons, editor of *The Alarm*, native of Montgomery, Alabama, veteran of the Confederate army, crusader for Negro rights who had started a Chicago Local Assembly of the Knights of Labor but, impatient with

* The Central Labor Union comprised about 36 per cent of the Black International's membership in the United States.

the Order's policy, had joined the left-wing militants in 1880. He and Oscar Neebe, manager of the Beer Wagon Drivers, were the only American-born officers among the leadership of the Central Labor Union. With the exception of Samuel Fielden, a Methodist lay preacher, and an Englishman, the others—Adolph Fischer of the printers, Louis Lingg of the carpenters, George Engel, the philosophic toy-maker, August Spies and Michael Schwab who together ran the *Arbeiter-Zeitung*—had all come from Germany. They all reflected the usual desire of expatriated German intellectuals to transfer their opposition to the rigorous state of the Fatherland to American institutions which they saw through a glass darkly. They were sensitive, sincere men, energetic and extravagant in everything they said or did. In the winter of 1885, for example, depth of the bad times, on Christmas day in the morning they had organized a march of four hundred gaunt and grim-looking men and women who trudged along fashionable Prairie Avenue. One emaciated old woman held aloft a red flag to denote the coming revolution; another carried a black flag to symbolize the poverty and degradation of the unemployed. The marchers would halt before the homes of the wealthy, ring doorbells, mutter imprecations, make cat-calls. The demonstration did nothing to help the idle. It merely increased the savagery of the police toward all workers, and further scared a public already alarmed by the anarchists and their candid belief that the workers should offer "armed resistance to the capitalistic class, and capitalistic legislatures."

The wild phrases and hunger-march protests of the anarchists not only acquired for them the bogeyman name of "the menace" but were also linked with their advocacy of the eight-hour day to confuse the whole question, submerging it in the hysteria which began to pervade the whole community with the approach of May 1, date of the general strike call.

Late in April various Chicago employers, anticipating a great show of coöperation among the workers in fostering the eight-hour movement, began rigging gear and tackle to destroy it. Executives and managers of boot and shoe plants, of iron and steel foundries, of lumber-yards and box factories, met in the Hotel Sherman and agreed to brace themselves jointly against the eight-hour demand even if it would mean a temporary loss of profits and the hiring of thousands of strikebreakers. When their intention was made known, the newspapers redoubled their attacks upon the eight-hour "lunacy." The *Chicago Mail*, for example, on April 29, 1886, reminded its readers that "in addition to eight hours they [the workers] wanted everything else that the craziest socialist or the maddest anarchist could suggest." It was this kind of comment, and many others like it, that lent credence to the rumors that, on May 1, 1886, Chicago would be less a city than a convulsion, when armed thousands of workers would attempt to take over everything, from the banks and the municipal government to the livery stable down the block.

Despite all this tension the eight-hour strike in Chicago at first promised to be an almost complete success. Some thirty-eight thousand workers had left their jobs in the morning of May 1, 1886, and were joined by about twenty thousand more within the next two or three days. In the packing houses the very threat of a walkout gained the eight-hour day for thirty-five thousand workers. On the whole this first May Day failed to provide the turmoil and excitement predicted for it, and passed peaceably enough. The city had a holiday appearance as thousands of workers and their families in their Sunday best strolled the streets or "marched" in processions or listened to orators holding forth at mass meetings, some of which were broken up by police in minor riots.

Soon, however, the real trouble began. In February, 1886, Cyrus McCormick, who owned the McCormick

Reaper Works, had locked out fourteen hundred of his employees in reply to their demand that he reinstate some of their colleagues who had been discharged for strike and union activity. He had promptly hired strikebreakers to replace his regular force, and had also hired three hundred Pinkertons to guard them and plant property—a task in which the Chicago police shared with their usual enthusiasm.

On Monday afternoon, May 3, 1886, after the lockout had been in effect for three months, an open-air rally of striking lumber-shovers happened to take place on Black Road, about five hundred yards north of the McCormick plant. They were being addressed on the eight-hour day by the impassioned August Spies, the anarchist; and during his oration two hundred or more of his listeners detached themselves from the main body of his audience and tramped toward the McCormick works to heckle and beat up the strikebreakers who were just then leaving as the factory whistle shrilled the work day's end.

The resulting mêlée had hardly begun when two hundred policemen arrived on the spot. The clang of patrol-wagon gongs attracted the attention of the lumbermen who were still being talked to by Spies; and first a score and then almost his entire audience started moving toward the McCormick works, a vast straggling mass of the curious.

The police saw them coming and fired volley after volley into their ranks. The lumbermen started to run, in a frenzy to escape. The police pursued, aiming carefully, killing four of the strikers, wounding twenty more. With the vision of the dying hot in his brain, Spies hurried to the printing shop of the *Arbeiter-Zeitung* and wrote his celebrated "Revenge" circular which was printed in both English and German:

REVENGE!
WORKINGMEN, TO ARMS!!!

The masters sent out their bloodhounds—the police; they killed six of your brothers at McCormicks this afternoon. They killed the poor wretches because they, like you, had the courage to disobey the supreme will of your bosses. They killed them because they dared ask for the shortening of the hours of toil. They killed them to show you, Free American Citizens, that you must be satisfied and contented with whatever your bosses condescend to allow you, or you will get killed!

You have for years endured the most abject humiliations; you have for years suffered unmeasurable iniquities; you have worked yourself to death; you have endured the pangs of want and hunger; your Children have been sacrificed to the factory lord—in short: you have been miserable and obedient slave [sic] all these years: Why? To satisfy the insatiable greed, to fill the coffers of your lazy thieving master? When you ask them now to lessen your burdens, he sends his blood hounds out to shoot you, kill you!

If you are men, if you are the sons of your grand sires, who have shed their blood to free you, then you will rise in your might, Hercules, and destroy the hideous monster that seeks to destroy you! To arms we call you, to arms!

YOUR BROTHERS.*

He also issued a second shorter handbill which called for a protest meeting, "to denounce the latest atrocious act of the police," in Haymarket Square the next evening, Tuesday, May 4, 1886.

The Mayor of Chicago, the fat, urbane, vaguely humanitarian Carter H. Harrison, who was very much disturbed by the industrial warfare scarring his "beautiful city," granted a permit for this rally which began at eight o'clock at the old Haymarket, in the heart of Chicago's lumber-yard and packing-house district. It was attended by about three thousand men and women, including the Mayor himself. He had put in his appearance partly to show that he was the acquaintance, if not the bosom

* The grammatical errors are in the original.

friend, of the workingman; and partly to see to it personally that order was preserved. About three hundred feet away, however, at the Desplaines Street station, an extra large detail of police, equipped for riot duty, awaited developments.

The meeting was extremely quiet—especially in view of its origin. In a mood of mourning August Spies addressed the crowd on justice from a torch-lit wagon. He was followed by Albert Parsons who limited his remarks to the benefits which would go with the establishment of the eight-hour day.

Shortly after ten o'clock, Mayor Harrison, somewhat bored and vastly relieved, walked to Desplaines Street. He informed the Officer-in-Charge, John Bonfield, that the rally was tame, that "nothing is likely to occur that will require interference," and went home to bed. He had hardly left, however, when, for reasons never divulged, Bonfield—more hated by the workers than any other man in Chicago for his use of the club—ordered out the entire police detachment of two hundred men. In columns of four they marched to Haymarket Square where the assembly had dwindled to a scant five hundred. Gusts of rain fell, and a cold wind was whipping up from the lake. The meeting had been spiritless, a dreary failure. Samuel Fielden, the last speaker, was hurrying to close. Spies and Parsons had already gone.

When the police arrived they stopped in platoon formation a few paces from the crowd. Their captain brandished his sword and cried "Halt!" He stepped toward Fielden, yelling: "I command you in the name of the people to immediately and peaceably disperse!"

"But Captain," Fielden replied, "we are peaceable. . . ."

Suddenly the earth trembled with sound, and the night turned red with the flash of a terrible explosion. An unknown, perhaps an anarchist, perhaps an *agent provoca-*

teur, had thrown a bomb from the alley which abutted near the wagon serving as a speakers' stand. The smoke of the detonation blinded the police who in a panic began shooting into the crowd and among their brother officers. Some of the workers, probably from the rifle corps of the Verein, fired back. The square was a shambles; within five minutes sixty-seven policemen were wounded, seven fatally; and an estimated two hundred workers were killed or maimed.

In the hysteria which followed next day, the press of Chicago and of the nation was a shriek of horror, a cry for vengeance. It laid responsibility for the bomb on the anarchists, and almost everyone agreed. The anarchists were excoriated as serpents, as Red Ruffians, as Bomb Slingers. On May 6, the *Chicago Tribune* pointed out that they had been "nourished in the sunshine of toleration, until they have been emboldened to strike at society, at law, order and the government." Not to be outdone, the official organ of Chicago's Knights of Labor two days later declared:

Let it be understood by all the world that the Knights of Labor have no affiliation, association, sympathy or respect for the band of cowardly murderers, cutthroats and robbers, known as anarchists, who sneak through the country like midnight assassins, stirring up the passions of ignorant foreigners, unfurling the red flag of anarchy and causing riot and bloodshed. Parsons, Spies, Fielden, Most and all their followers . . . should be summarily dealt with. They are entitled to no more consideration than wild beasts. . . . Knights of Labor, boycott them. . . . Brand them as outlawed monsters . . . as human monstrosities not entitled to the sympathy or consideration of any person in the world. We are sure we voice the sentiments of the whole organization when we say that we hope Parsons, Spies, Most, Fielden and the whole gang of outlaws will be blotted from the surface of the earth.

In this atmosphere of dread and vengefulness, Spies, Fielden, Neebe, Lingg, Schwab, Engel, Fischer, and Parsons were quickly indicted by a grand jury on May 17. In the trial which followed there was no evidence against these defendants and it had to be fabricated. The police therefore discovered murder plots by the dozen, conspiracies by the score. They also kept discovering caches of guns and ammunition, bullet moulds, dirks, percussion caps, dynamite sticks and bombs, infernal machines, and pistols, displaying them all in court before a jury handpicked by the prosecution and including a cousin of a Haymarket victim. Testimony was an anti-climax. The presiding judge, Joseph E. Gary, conducted not a court of law but a witch-burning. The jury was overwhelmed by readings from the most inciting and seditious literature that the files of *The Alarm* and the *Arbeiter-Zeitung* could yield. In his summation on August 11, 1886, State's Attorney Grinnell frankly said: "Law is upon trial. Anarchy is on trial. These men have been selected, picked out by the grand jury and indicted because they were leaders. They are no more guilty than the thousands who follow them. . . . Convict these men, make examples of them, hang them, and you save our institutions. . . ."

The defense was handicapped not only by adverse court rulings but also by the refusal of the eight accused men to admit anything wrong with what they had done or said in the course of anarchist careers; and their courtroom speeches were, if anything, more of a challenge to the established order than any of their previous utterances.

On August 20 the Jury returned its expected verdict of guilty, recommending that seven of the defendants be hanged, and that Oscar Neebe, since his was merely a financial stake in the *Arbeiter-Zeitung*, be sentenced to fifteen years' imprisonment. Subsequently, after the Supreme Court of the United States claimed that it had no authority to review the trial, Schwab and Fielden* pleaded for executive clemency and their sentences were commuted to life terms. The rest asked either for liberty or death; and four of them were hanged until they were dead, on Friday, November 11, 1887. At the last moment Lingg cheated the gallows by exploding a percussion cap in his mouth.

The identification of the anarchists with the eight-hour movement demolished it utterly for the time being. Dazed and bewildered, workers on strike had trooped back to their jobs as early as May 12, unable to understand how it was that the Linggs and the Neebes had had anything in common with them. Concessions on the shorter working day were rescinded by employers to such an extent that out of the country's estimated 190,000 May 1 strikers only 15,000 either gained or retained the eight-hour objective.

Yet it was the Knights of Labor who suffered most from the Haymarket tragedy—despite the fact that Powderly refused to join a mercy plea on behalf of the condemned anarchists because it was "better that seven times seven men hang than to hang the millstone of odium around the standard of this Order in affiliating in any way with this element of destruction." He went even further. He assailed the "rampant Socialist and Anarchist" who in "canting phrase and with mock humility insinuate themselves into the good graces of men who would scorn them if they were to disclose their real feelings." But such efforts to disassociate the Knights from the Haymarket affair accomplished nothing. Parsons had been a member in good standing of Local Assembly No. 1307, which refused to expel him; and although this link of the Knights with the anarchists was slender, it was enough for many people. The confusion in the public mind as to who was who in

---

* Neebe, Schwab, and Fielden were pardoned on June 26, 1893, by Governor John Peter Altgeld on the ground that they and the other five defendants had had no semblance of a fair trial, and had been the victims of a judicial frame-up.

unionism permitted the Knights to be tarred with the terrorism which, in popular prejudice, was the hallmark of the anarchist, and the Order's membership figures plunged downward. Powderly folded his hands and prayed. Everything seemed to be going wrong. The Knights were blamed by public opinion for every flare-up of violence in strikes, for every picket line that appeared anywhere in the country. In addition the fledgling American Federation of Labor was beginning to buck the Knights in earnest. An outgrowth of a convention held by two renegade groups, the Amalgamated Labor Union and the Knights of Industry, at Terre Haute, Indiana, on August 2, 1881, the new association had begun under the name "The Federation of Organized Trades and Labor Unions of the United States of America and Canada." When it learned, however, that twenty-five independent labor bodies, composed of skilled craftsmen, were to meet in Columbus, Ohio, in December, 1886, it promptly joined its own forces with the others and the whole body emerged as the A. F. of L. The basic philosophy of its leaders was directly opposed to that of the Order. They wanted to exclude the unskilled from their unions. They wanted to abstain from any political abstractions and to concentrate solely upon collective bargaining. They refused, they said, to "sink to the level of pauper labor"; and they were determined to "protect the skilled labor of America from being reduced to beggary and to sustain the standard of American workmanship."

In vain the Knights tried to win over craft support. In 1885 they drafted a typical appeal to the Amalgamated Association of Iron and Steel Workers: "In the use of the wonderful inventions . . . your organization plays a most important part. Naturally, it embraces within its ranks a very large proportion of laborers of a high grade of skill and intelligence. With this skill of hand, guided by intelligent thought comes the right to demand that excess of compensation paid to skilled above the unskilled. . . . But the unskilled labor must receive attention, or in the hour of difficulty the employers will not hesitate to use it to depress the compensation you receive. That skilled or unskilled labor may no longer be found unorganized, we ask of you to annex your grand and powerful corps to the main army that we may fight the battle under one flag."

But such pleas, even when repeated by Powderly in person, were like sowing seeds on concrete. The A. F. of L. unions, individually and collectively, had different ideas. In the main they were the ideas of a brilliant Irishman, P. J. McGuire, secretary of the new Federation. For his model of what efficient unionism should be, he drew upon the British unions with their relatively high dues, their "benefits" in times of sickness, unemployment, death, their local autonomy. He had passed through all the radicalisms and in 1881 had taken hold of the Brotherhood of Carpenters and Joiners and built it up along the lines of pure and simple craft unionism. But he was the brain-truster rather than the administrative personality, and the executive direction of the Federation fell into the hands of a London-born, Dutch-Jewish cigar maker, named Samuel Gompers. With his allies, McGuire and Adolph Strasser, another cigar maker, he controlled the new movement from its very beginning, acting as its president from 1886 to 1924 with the exception of a single year.

From the first he insisted upon the national craft as the basis for the A. F. of L. with local unions entitled to representation only in trades where no "national" (or "international" when there were branches in Canada or Mexico) yet existed. The Executive Council, composed of the president, two vice-presidents, a secretary, and a treasurer, was charged with several vital functions. It was to keep an eye on all labor legislation and to lobby for the eight-hour day. It was to organize new local and national unions. It was to recognize "the right of each trade to manage its own affairs" yet "secure unity" among all eligible labor groups that wished to be affiliated. It was to affirm or deny the validity of boycotts instituted by its member unions. In strikes and lockouts it was to issue appeals for funds, collect them and disburse them to aid the organization so involved. Revenue was to be derived from "charter fees" and from a per capita tax of one-half a cent per month for every member in good standing. In 1887 Gompers' salary was fixed at $1,000 a year.

Although the Federation claimed membership of 316,-469 it was actually a little more than half of that and in the beginning the ties binding to it many of the prominent unions, like the Typographers, were fragile indeed since such strong organizations were reluctant to give up their own "individuality."

The A. F. of L., however, flourished, while the Knights declined, losing 300,000 members in a single year (1887). It was a triumph of leadership over logic. There was no gainsaying the Order's fundamental thesis, expressed by Powderly, that the Knights "in comparison to isolated trade unions, bears the same relation that the locomotive of today does to the stage coach of half a century ago"; or ignoring its implication that, under the new conditions of American industry, labor in the long run would have to hang together or hang separately. Nor was it the idea of One Big Union that was basically responsible for the downfall of the Knights. Rather it was Powderly, the panaceas and vagaries of utopians, and the Pinkerton Agency which, at this time, launched an adroit advertising campaign. It informed employers, more or less discreetly, that "corporations and individuals desirous of ascertaining the feeling of their employees and whether they are likely to engage in strikes or are joining any secret labor organization with a view of compelling terms from corporations or employers, can obtain, upon application . . . a detective suitable to associate with their employees and obtain this information."

What the Pinkerton Agency lacked in elegance of diction it made up in efficiency. It drew an espionage network over large sectors of American industry, causing thousands of Knights to be blacklisted and making workers think twice before joining the Order. And ironically the spy system which had given birth to the Knights of Labor battened on the society which had been formed to resist this very practice. By the early 90's, the Knights of Labor were on the downpath toward final extinction.

Meanwhile the leaders of the A. F. of L. announced that the only way to save American labor from the "over ambitious" program of the Order was to drain off the cream of labor's crop, the skilled workers, and set them up in compact, craft-conscious, exclusive organizations. They were to be the patricians of toil, and its plebeians were, as usual, to fend for themselves.

The development of this policy, with its deviations and difficulties, may be best seen perhaps by surveying the individual history of some typical unions which at present comprise a cross section of the men and women who get the wages of America's work.

A New School of Political Economists:

The United Mine Workers' Union of America

THE United Mine Workers of America, with its 580,000 members, is the largest union in the world. Its strength, however, is rooted in many things other than size. In the sphere of practical unionism, it pioneered the eight-hour day, the sliding wage scale, the "check-off." It was the keystone in the American Federation of Labor arch, from the beginning. It has served much the same function in the Committee for Industrial Organization. It has furnished a disproportionate share of present-day labor leadership. Its former secretary-treasurer, William Green, is head of the A. F. of L. The chairman of the C.I.O., John L. Lewis, remains president of the United Mine Workers, and at least twenty-five other key figures in both the A. F. of L. and the C.I.O. are graduates of this same union.

It was, furthermore, the first A. F. of L. affiliate to conduct and win an important strike. In 1898, at Virden, Illinois, a group of United Mine Workers, armed with shot guns, revolvers, and rifles, vanquished a trainload of similarly accoutered strikebreakers and company guards, with great loss of life on both sides. By means of superior marksmanship the union was granted all of its demands. And ironically, this victory was achieved with a violence that pulverized all ten tablets in the union's theology. For since its inception in 1890, it has preached and practiced "arbitration," "compromise," "mediation" to such an extent that a substantial portion of American left-wing literature is devoted to virulent attacks upon its "bargains with the bosses." In any case, with its system of "collective agreements" it has inaugurated some unique customs in capital-labor relations.

At the outset of the New Deal administration in 1933, for example, the union's economics advisor, W. Jett Lauck, and its chief counsel, Henry Warrum, collaborated with Mr. Lewis to draft what was to become the Davis-Kelly bill. This was a piece of legislation that not only gave birth to a whole brood of fair competition codes, but in essentials foreshadowed the entire NRA program. The Davis-Kelly Act, significantly for future management-labor relations, stipulated that prices could be fixed under government supervision when (a) collective bargaining was recognized, and (b) coal operators and miners, after conference, had agreed upon a set of minimum standards governing production and sale. The successors to this bill, the Guffey-Snyder Act and the Guffey-Vinson Act, likewise developed by the United Mine Workers, are similarly premised upon the assumption that a "creative" and "constructive" *entente cordiale*, based on an "identity of interests," must prevail against any dogmas of class struggle as the only answer for labor in coal.

Implicit in all this legislation is the belief that, in our complex "power-age" society, the functions of capital and labor can be performed effectively only by a new and tripartite coöperation between industry and unions and government. The evolution of this view, "stabilization by code, commission, or statute," is an American saga of horror and heroism, of conflict and coöperation among operators and miners seeking to get the most of profits and wages from the ailing unruly giant, coal. And in this process the United Mine Workers has passed from peaks of power to valleys of weakness and all gradations in between. In 1932, for example, it was virtually moribund, its membership dwindling from 432,000 to a twenty-year low of 150,000. But within a year, revived by the NRA, the union's enrollment had reached 400,000 and was growing at the rate of 75 a day. And this cyclic character of the

United Mine Workers' Union merely reflects the spectacular ups and downs of the industry itself.

In America, the words chaos and crisis—along with
funeral odes by the hundred—have been used in connection
with coal for the past half century. It has been, and remains, perhaps, our most "overdeveloped" industry. For
years it has been always on the point of dying, while oil
and hydro-electric power were to dance on its grave. In
1899, for example, bituminous coal accounted for 68
per cent, and anthracite for 22 per cent of the nonhuman energy produced in the United States. The remaining 10 per cent was more or less equally divided among
petroleum, water power, and natural gas. In 1935, however, bituminous and anthracite coal together had but 50
per cent of this total; and petroleum 31 per cent; natural
gas 9 per cent; and water power 10 per cent. Despite such
trends, however, current estimates show that about five
hundred million tons of soft coal alone will be used in
1938, an amount only a little below that of the boom year
1929, when five hundred thirty-five million net tons were
mined.

Although in 1907 W. J. Nicolls exclaimed that "the
geography of American coals is today practically a description of the United States," his observation was more
excited than precise. Soft coal deposits are scattered over
twenty-six states, with six of them—Pennsylvania, Virginia, West Virginia, Kentucky, Ohio, and Illinois—producing 70 per cent of the total, and the other 30 per cent
being largely found in Indiana, Arkansas, Colorado, Maryland, Tennessee, Alabama, Iowa, Utah, Oklahoma, Wyoming, and Montana. On the other hand, hard coal is
localized in five counties of northeastern Pennsylvania
(the only state where anthracite is found in America)
where the Wyoming, Lehigh, Schuylkill, and Susque-
hanna river valleys have yielded, during the past decade,
anywhere from forty-nine to seventy-three million tons,

averaging about one-seventh of the soft coal output. Such concentration on the part of nature paved the way for similar concentration in ownership. Giant firms like the Glen Alden Coal Company, the Philadelphia and Reading, the Lehigh Valley Coal Corporation, the Erie Railroad's "Pittston Company," and a few others, dominate the hard coal scene. Hence in recent years it has been easier for management to stabilize conditions, to fix prices, to establish labor policy, and otherwise deal with the 152,000 to 176,000 men employed. In the bituminous fields, however, there are entirely different conditions. In the first place, there are some 4,200 operators in the business, quite a few of them so-called "snowbirds and fly-by-nighters" who open up marginal mines in brisk seasons and close them down when trade slackens. Moreover, the largest concerns in soft coal, like the famous Peabody Company, each account for less than 3.25 per cent of the total production, a state of affairs which, when combined with the 503,000 men employed, tends to make competition less the life of trade than the law of the jungle. But the cutthroat competition of the bituminous industry derives from causes more fundamental than thousands of small contending units, and the vast labor force and the many wage differentials for far-separated regions. Soft coal seams vary in thickness from a few inches to twenty feet and the expense of extraction varies also, veins nearer the surface being as a rule cheaper to exploit. Since labor comprises from 65 per cent to 78 per cent of production costs in soft coal, price cutting among rivals all over the country has invariably brought wage reductions and layoffs that time and again have driven the living standards of American miners to sub-subsistence levels.

But the hazards of mining as an occupation are not confined to low pay or irregular employment. Going down to the sea in ships is safety itself when compared with going down to the mines. In the first five months of 1937, from

January to May, coal mine accidents took the lives of 521 men, 425 in bituminous and 96 in anthracite. And despite recent installations of safety devices, the death toll has not varied much in the past twenty years. The miner runs the risk of falling rock and coal, of fire, explosions, suffocation, and many other modes of injury and sudden death. In many cases the casualties could be prevented if the companies were willing to spend money to improve ventilation, to "fool-proof" signaling systems in haulage. Out of every ten thousand American coal miners, about forty-five are killed on the job during the course of the year, a fatality rate around twice that of Germany and thrice that of Britain. From 1919 to 1929, moreover, there were 22,500 miners killed during work in this country, and 1,500,000 injured seriously enough to cause a loss of working time from a day or two to many weeks.

Among the less dramatic hazards to health and well-being are the noxious fumes of "stink damp" and "rotten gas" along with the treacherous so-called "white damp," which is carbon monoxide. Daily inhalations of such gases along with coal dust induce chronic bronchial catarrh and generally tend to affect the respiratory tract to such a degree that influenza epidemics in mining communities decimate the male population. The strained, stooping positions of much digging and loading, the heavy lifting in cramped spaces, the dampness and fetidness of the atmosphere, all predispose miners to rheumatism and make them proverbially "old before their time." The lack of sanitary sewage disposal underground often fosters typhoid, dysentery, and kindred intestinal diseases.

Curiously enough, however, such dangerous work conditions have only indirectly furnished the motive power for labor organization in coal. Attempts to maintain or increase wages, to shorten hours, and to banish the company store have been the main propulsions behind the drive toward unionism which began in 1849. In that year, in the anthracite area, a John Bates formed a local union. The records of its origin and development are scanty enough. It seems, however, that it called a strike, presumably for more pay, and lost and disappeared. And though probably other and similar unions appeared at the same time, the next decade—insofar as documents are concerned—is a blank.

In the first year of the Civil War, however, some English miners of the Belleville tract in Illinois called a convention of colleagues from their own state and from Missouri. Under the leadership of the energetic Thomas Lloyd and the "silver-tongued" Daniel Weaver, the meeting—held in a St. Louis hotel—set up the "American Miners' Association," on a national scale, more or less on paper. Lloyd was elected president of the new society and Weaver was named secretary—as a tribute perhaps to his rhetorical gifts when, as orator of the occasion, he declared that the objects of the convention "are not merely pecuniary, but to mutually instruct and improve each other in knowledge, which is power, to study the laws of life, the relation of Labor to Capital, politics, municipal affairs, literature, science, or any other subject relating to the general welfare of our class.

"One of the profoundest thinkers of our day," he continued, "has said that 'All human interests, and combined human endeavors have, at certain stages of their development, required organizing, and labor—the grandest of human interests requires it now!'

"There must be," he said in a peroration that brought the delegates to their feet, applauding, "organization of labor. . . . Begin with it straight-way, proceed with it, succeed in it more and more. One of America's immortals has said, 'To me there is no East, no West, no North, no South' and I would say: 'Let there be no English, no Irish, no German, Scotch or Welsh!' "

This reference to various ethnic groups, implying conflict among them, was an early indication of the many tongues and creeds that were to make "labor in coal" a new Tower of Babel. Even today at a single colliery, say, in Scranton, Pennsylvania, it is easy enough to find Poles, Italians, Negroes, Germans, Russians, Croats, Irish, Dutch, Lithuanians, Greeks, and, in the West, Mexicans and Japanese besides.

As recently as 1910 some 48.5 per cent of coal miners were foreign born and one in seven was the American-born son of an immigrant father. In the early days of the coal industry, Welsh, English, and Scots came to this country to escape the grinding tasks of British pits. They formed the majority of the first workers in American mines. They were skilled. They readily found jobs in an industry which began to come into its own during the Civil War.

Before that time the prodigious supply of wood had hindered recognition of coal's value as fuel. But the momentum that war brings to all business turned attention upon this source of extra-human energy. Very soon coal, at first anthracite, and later bituminous, served for getting steam up under the boilers of "Mr. Fulton's strange ships," and under boilers of locomotives and textile mills, and was used to heat domestic stoves and furnaces and when "coked" employed in smelting iron ores. In a follow-the-leader stampede, during the late 60's and early 70's, the business community went coal crazy in the same way that various elements of the population had gone land crazy and gold crazy, after the fashion that has characterized too much of our economic development.

Companies were formed. Shafts were sunk. Prospectuses were issued to assure the "wise, careful, propertied" investor that the "black stones," the "black nuggets," the "black diamonds" would swing wide the gates to a new El Dorado.

And within a few years, because everybody who was more or less solvent was sure to make a fortune, and because it cost a relatively small sum ($2,500 and up) to start a mine, the groundwork had been laid for the evil that even today rides King Coal like an Old Man of the Sea: excess capacity in terms of the market.

When the war boom collapsed, the operators in a business even then overexpanded began to cut wages to meet the challenge of falling prices, of too many rivals. When the miners objected, they were quickly discharged. Thousands of others were found to take their places. For by the middle of the nineteenth century, immigration to the United States was running toward high tide, with 427,000 aliens arriving in 1854 alone.

The immigrants had been encouraged by the propaganda of land speculators who wanted settlers to enhance the worth of their holdings; by the agents of mine and mill and factory owners who wanted ample reserves of cheap and docile labor; by that "high and incomparable spirit of American idealism" which caused the day's orators to describe this country as an "asylum for the oppressed"; and by steamship companies which had cut steerage rates to the bone on the principle that mass methods of transportation would yield higher profits. The spirit of acquisition was combined with that of altruism to make Castle Garden in New York the stepping stone to sanctuary for Irish fleeing famine, for Germans fleeing the reaction and economic stringency that followed the Revolution of '48, for peoples of Central and Eastern Europe and even the Orient exchanging the poverty and the caste rigidity of Old Worlds for the splendid promise of the New.

Meanwhile, in the four states of Ohio, Indiana, Illinois, and Maryland the American Miners' Association had built its small dikes of unionism to help stem this new invasion. It was a futile effort. The best union could not combat what was early called the "menace" of anywhere from one to five foreigners waiting to take over the jobs of natives at half pay. And the antipathy which began to be attached to manual work not because it was manual but because it was

increasingly done by "poor, dirty, ignorant furriners" with
their outlandish customs, further prevented white natives
from entering the mines. In 1868 the A.M.A., hopelessly
weakened by the postwar depression, had "dwindled
away."

For the American born and for those who had been here
long enough to find their way around, the frontier still
offered the chance to acquire land for a farm. Opportunity
continued to open up for ambition in business, in the professions, in politics. In city and town a craft such as carpentry exerted the double allure of being relatively "respectable" and of being pursued above the earth's surface
instead of under it.

The pick-and-shovel occupations of digging sewers,
canals, and coal were taken over by the immigrants, and
the coal industry more than any other was built up by their
labor. They were cheated and tricked at every turn. They
therefore looked upon any unionist's talk of the betterment
that would result from organization and its *dues*, as merely
another scheme for taking advantage of them. There was
still another factor which impeded unionism's growth in
coal and elsewhere. The first desire of the newcomer was
to be assimilated, to be "Americanized." Many employers
informed them that unions, despite their American origin,
were really foreign importations, and that to deal with
them at all was a sure sign of that alien quality which the
immigrant, as a rule, was anxious to discard.

Meanwhile, various local unions kept "spotting" mine
areas, buoyed up more by the zeal of some leader than by
any actual accomplishment. Time and again efforts to gain
recognition, to improve conditions, were thwarted by the
operators. Whenever the demands of the miners as to wage
scales and collective bargaining were refused, they had but
two alternatives. They could back down. They could go
on strike. In the first case, they would be placed on the
payroll again, but in a more or less probationary sense, and

ringleaders were the first to be fired with or without excuse. If they adopted the second policy and walked out, they were equally out of luck. In Connellsville, Pennsylvania, in 1875 a group of miners went on strike and the owner, a Mr. C. M. Armstrong, "imported Italian strikebreakers, arming them with breech-loading rifles and warning them to shoot every English-speaking white man who came near them, informing them that unless they did so they would receive injury. The result was that a riot ensued, in which the Italians used their rifles, killing two men and wounding others." The Pennsylvania courts sent the Italians to the penitentiary for murder in the second degree and fined Mr. Armstrong the sum of $5.00, cash.

The story of this episode gained wide and exaggerated currency, and cooled strike ardor all over the country. Yet many strikes occurred. Their result as a rule was summed up succinctly by the Coal Statistical Register of Pottsville, Pennsylvania, which in 1878 recorded: "After a suspension of about 4 months . . . the men were starved out . . . and the organization broken up."

When the miners discovered that their use of the economic means, the strike, did them more harm than good, they turned to politics for relief. In Pennsylvania they succeeded in getting an eight-hour law passed by the state legislature in 1868. The effect of this measure was nullified, however, by a clause inserted at the operators' suggestion providing that the law would apply except in instances "where there was no agreement to the contrary." Unless miners by their own strength could arrange matters otherwise there would obviously be "agreements to the contrary" and the statute was observed more in the breach than in letter or spirit.

It was also during this period that miners hit upon the notion of "suspending" operations to relieve a glutted market, to raise prices, and advance wages. The suggestion evoked anger, surprise, and disgust among the owners. All three emotions were expressed by the "literary" Franklin P. Gowan, president of the Reading Railroad, which like most others was coming to acquire vast holdings in coal:

We who thought we understood something of the laws of trade and knew that natural causes would soon bring relief, remonstrated . . . in vain. The law of supply and demand and every sound maxim of trade . . . were thrown to the winds; and from the bowels of the earth there came swarming up a new school of political economists who professed to be able, during the leisure hours of their working day to regulate a great industry and restore it to health. . . . With the assurance of a quack, they seized upon the body of a healthy trade and have doctored it and physicked it so that it is now reduced to the ghost of a shadow of an attenuation.

Nothing daunted by this rhetorical assault, perhaps because they couldn't understand the last sentence, the "new school of political economists" pressed another claim. They wanted a sliding scale to govern wages. It was a heresy first advocated by John Siney, a lamb in behavior, a lion in talk, who had organized the Workingmen's Benevolent Association of Schuylkill County (Pennsylvania).

"We the miners," he pointed out, "have no desire to run the price of coal up too high on the market, but, on the contrary, prefer a healthy steady market which will afford to the operators and dealers fair interest on their investment and at the same time [allow] us to receive a fair day's wages for a fair day's work."

At any event Siney and others argued the Anthracite Board of Trade, comprising the chief operators, into adopting the sliding-scale arrangement in 1869. Under its provisions, wage rates per ton varied in direct ratio with the prices which the operators obtained for their coal. That is, when they received $5.00 a ton, the miner's share was $.57½. When prices dropped, however, the basic scale of, say, the $.57½ was to remain stationary. When prices rose, wages were to follow in proportion.

The operators soon tired of this innovation. They altered it, made it meaningless. They refused to "peg" a minimum wage; and without the protection of that kind of a floor, wages could decline till they reached China. As owner after owner retracted his agreement, the miners were roused to further action. They had hoped that the sliding scale was going to bring some measure of regularity and stability into their lives. They decided that it was useless to try to do anything on a local basis. Their own grievance committees, from a single community, were too weak to enforce any pacts that the employer might choose to disregard. The only solution seemed to be a national union which could negotiate in all coal regions and combat the chiselers and price cutters who were seeking unfair competitive advantages.

In 1873 the Miners' National Association of the United States of America was formed by union chieftains from Ohio, Illinois, and Pennsylvania, with Siney, the prime mover, becoming its president. At their convention they drafted a constitution which announced the new society's sixfold purpose: (1) to eliminate the causes of strikes and accept the "principle of arbitration" whenever practicable; (2) to urge all miners to become United States citizens and use their ballots to advance labor's progress; (3) to secure "true weight" of coal mined, instead of fraudulent "screenings"; (4) to shorten hours; (5) to sue for compensation when accidents resulted from employers' negligence; (6) to create a treasury of strike funds. The panic of 1873, with its vicious wage cuts, sent miners into the union as a last resort for their economic salvation. And by 1875 the Miners' National Association had 347 lodges in 13 states and a membership of some 35,000. It was a show of strength that moved press and pulpit to new vehemence. They denounced the M.N.A.'s officers as "fomenters of domestic discord" and the harbingers of "foreign strife," as "agitators" and "demagogues"—charges to which Siney

replied with the eloquence that would seem to be traditional among the leaders of labor in coal.

We have been called agitators, we have been called demagogues, because we have counseled . . . our members to try
and secure those objects [i.e., amicable settlement, better
wages, etc.]. . . . In some places even the clergy have placed
their anathema upon the society, and why? Is it wrong to
teach men to seek a higher moral standard? If so, let them
vacate their pulpits. Is it wrong to cultivate the intellect and
inculcate broader and more comprehensive views than we
now have? If so, let the newspapers close their offices or refrain from using the epithets of "ignorance" against us. Is it
wrong to advance our financial interests? If so, let those who
operate our mines and mills and all others abandon the various
enterprises in which they are engaged in the pursuit of wealth.
It appears to me . . . that that which, if advised by the
church, by the press or by the wealthy would be applauded
to the heavens, when advised by workingmen consigns them
to perdition, or ranks them in the catalogue of . . . mischief
makers.

But his voice was drowned out in the tumult of a strike
called at the Clearfield mines and approved by the Miners'
National Association. Here thirty-six union members,
Siney among them, were arrested on charges of "conspiracy and riot." They had picketed the mine. They had
persuaded a trainload of strikebreakers to leave the region
by paying their fares to wherever they desired to go. The
success of this stratagem angered the Clearfield management and the courts construed it to be a "violation of law
and order"; and thirty-five of the thirty-six were convicted and sentenced to prison terms. Siney himself was
acquitted. During the trial he had displayed a "meek as
Moses" demeanor that contrasted sharply with the fervor
of his vocabulary. He made a favorable impression on the
jury composed of leading citizens. They were perhaps also
afraid that if Siney were sent to the penitentiary, it would

only martyrize him, since he was widely known to be an apostle of gentleness and sweet reasonableness and he might, by merely languishing in prison, unloose some unpleasant repercussions.

However much the jury was influenced by Siney's mien of moderation, the miners themselves were in no mood for any counsels of temperateness. They were hungry. Their children were cranky and crying for bread. Their wives were getting gaunt and reproachful. The men had undergone wage cuts from 25 per cent to 60 per cent. Many of them had been kicked around by foremen till they had reached the breaking point of their endurance. They were mad. They were full of hate. They felt tricked, cheated, thwarted. Local after local withdrew from the Miners' National Association in a rank-and-file revolt that flared across ten states, and spurned the "methods of moderation" in favor of vigorous strike action that was mainly unsuccessful. Meanwhile, the high costs of hiring lawyers to defend the Clearfield strikers had drained the last penny from the M.N.A.'s treasury; and with its funds depleted, with its affiliates defecting daily, it had disappeared completely by the end of 1876.

But the seeds of unionism had been widely sown and kept sprouting frail and sporadic shoots. Then, in 1877–81, the Knights of Labor began to reach out into the coal fields. The Order's secrecy exercised a special blandishment upon men who had been beaten, blacklisted, demoted, discharged, and otherwise injured in efforts to gain collective bargaining. In coal, as elsewhere, the Order's "district assemblies" were "mixed." They included ministers, retailers, and bookkeepers. Meetings often generated more heat than light as professional and business views clashed with the attitude of the wage earners. The lack of a positive, clearcut program from the top added to the confusion of district assembly debate. Every once in a while, of course, Powderly, head of the Order, would utter some resounding ambiguity about "abolishing the wages system" by means of "workingmen's coöperatives" and more "education and enlightenment." The vagueness of his panaceas simply addled the thinking of many unionists who, long before the advent of Samuel Gompers, had been clamoring for "more, more, *now*."

They were asking for even less than that in Hocking Valley, Ohio, in 1884 when 4,000 miners went on strike against a reduction of from $.70 to $.50 a ton, and against the introduction of the so-called "iron clad" contracts which forbade the miners' joining a union. Although the Knights of Labor and other union groups contributed the largest strike relief fund recorded up to that time, namely, $70,333.48 in cash and more than $25,000 in food and clothing, the strikers were licked before they started. For the early 1880's was the time when immigration was at its topmost crest. In 1881, 669,431; in 1882, 788,992; in 1883, 603,322 aliens were admitted to our shores, furnishing a supply of labor willing to work anywhere for anybody for anything, hammering the stake of domestic wages to ground level. In addition to militia and mine guards, the Hocking Valley operators siphoned off a trickle of this immigrant flood, sending 3,500 "greenhorns" into the mines and breaking the strike.

There were other employers in the very same region, however, who were seeking different methods for resolving capital-labor conflict in coal and who believed, further, that the vicious competition in the industry could result only in a mutual collapse. Prominent in this group was Mr. W. P. Rend, astute, prosperous Ohio operator who in 1885 pointed out the "folly" of perpetual price-cutting, with its corollary of wage slashes:

It is said that a lower rate of mining would increase the tonnage of the Hocking Valley Region. This is only true to a limited extent as a reduction in this great coal district would be followed by like reductions throughout Ohio and neighboring states. Consequently when these various reductions would take place we would, as operators, then occupy relatively in all competitive markets the same position towards each other as at present. . . .

The American laborer is entitled to wages that will afford him not only the necessities of life but a fair share of the comforts of civilization. The operators and the railroad companies . . . have themselves to blame for the results of this false business policy. . . . As a final word I believe it would be the part of wisdom for these operators to stop this war upon their poor employees and take a fresh start in doing their business on proper and rational principles. . . .

In the same year that the Hocking Valley miners surrendered to superior forces and Mr. Rend voiced his novel and startling doctrine, the drive toward unionism went forward at a quickening pace as if it were some badly battered Anteus who nevertheless gained fresh vitality by each new contact with the earth. In that year, too, the Knights of Labor's General Executive Board, with its delicately nurtured ability to do the wrong thing, refused to permit coal miners to form a National Trade Assembly (equivalent to today's national union) out of their local and district organizations, covering the "Central Competitive Field," which includes western Pennsylvania, West Virginia, southeastern Kentucky, Ohio, Indiana, Illinois, and Iowa. Yet union leaders in this territory were convinced that "neither district nor state unions can regulate the markets to which their coal is shipped." They therefore established the National Federation of Miners and Mine Laborers of the United States (1885) to guard their "competitive area." And, late as usual, the Knights of Labor next year chartered a National Trade Assembly for coal miners, known as No. 135.

Promptly both groups, anticipating the jurisdiction rows of the present day, claimed authority over the same regions. They were, however, smart enough to coöperate in formulating an "interstate trade agreement" (the first of its kind in American history) with the mine operators led by the redoubtable Mr. Rend, at a conference held at Columbus, Ohio, in January, 1886. And to forestall friction over wage scales and hours, a board of conciliation, comprising seventeen operators and seventeen miners, was created. It appointed the mild, scholarly, diligent Chris Evans, a founder of the National Federation who was to become the official historian of the nation's coal miners, as the secretary for both factions. It was this pact, which for some years brought order into a part of the anarchy in coal, that portended in principle the collective agreements which were to find their culmination in the "price, production, and wage control" of the present Guffey-Vinson Act.

As the natural sequence of this labor unity, the National Federation, which changed its name to Progressive Miners' Union, merged with the Knights of Labor's District Assembly No. 135 in 1890 to become the United Mine Workers' Union of America. It belonged simultaneously to the Knights of Labor and the new American Federation of Labor until 1894, when the former was extinguished by its failure to combine the skilled and the unskilled, men and women, wage earners and white collarites into a body with any common discipline and direction.

The new organization, the United Mine Workers, was from the beginning set up along industrial, as against craft, lines. For to what was left of the K. of L.'s philosophy of "take in everybody" were added the special feelings of unity among the miners. The mining village, camp, or town was usually an isolated community, cut off from any very direct communication with the larger outside world. And in the complex of its social and economic relations, the "company" with its managers, its mine guards, its all-pervasive authority, was on the one side, and the workers, whether miners, engineers, firemen, machinists, blacksmiths, platemen, motormen, or "ordinary laborers," were distinctly on the other side. The shacks of the workers adjoined each other, standing row upon row in some desolate valley or clinging to the slopes of lonely ravines. Wives exchanged gossip, hung the wash on the same clotheslines. All were drawn together by the strong magnetism of having the same kind of worries, the same kind of food, the same kind of problems. Racial and religious antagonisms alone were discordant elements.

Often "the company" owned not only the mine itself but all property in its immediate environs, including the homes of its employees. In the main the miners' houses were cheap clapboard, frequently without cellars, almost always without plumbing, and roofed sometimes with tin and sometimes with heavy tarred paper. Since the company—especially in Pennsylvania, West Virginia, Illinois, and Colorado—owned these houses, it could evict obstreperous tenants and other troublemakers. Since it owned the streets, it could forbid freedom of speech and assembly. Since it often owned even the public highways leading to and from the mining center, it could prevent union organizers from entering its domain. For all practical purposes, the company also owned the mayor, the village or town council, the judge, the jury, the court-crier, and whatever press existed. It owned the company store which charged anywhere from 10 per cent to 100 per cent above the worth of groceries, drugs, working equipment, and other supplies that the miner might need for his family and himself. In Colorado, and elsewhere, the company (like the Colorado Coal and Fuel Company, controlled by the Rockefellers) leased buildings even to the brothels and the saloons.

Boys were brought into the world by the company doctor, attended the company school, listened to the sermons of the company preacher, grew into manhood and worked in the company breaker or washery, and finally were buried by the company undertaker.

The heyday of our Robber Barons witnessed the rise of this new feudalism,* unleavened by *noblesse oblige*. The unions in coal were too feeble even to begin ameliorating the time's serfdom, or to challenge the financial might behind railroads and steel that annually acquired more and more "captive" mines. From the end of the Civil War through the Gilded Age, miners kept rebelling, but like the warriors in Shaemas O'Sheal's lament, "they went forth to battle but they always fell." In the anthracite fields especially, spasms of strike fervor and revolt were not only frequent but also very dark and bloody. For it was here that the most amazing terrorist society in American annals flourished from about 1852 to 1875.

The formal name of this organization was the "Ancient Order of Hibernians." It was popularly known, and feared, as the "Molly Maguires." In theory its purpose was to

* Despite improvements of the past seventy years, however, there remain in all coal sections of the country pockets of this kind of degradation. During the first half of April, 1937, for example, Kine Hatfield, a miner employed by the Harlan-Willins Coal Company in Harlan, Kentucky, loaded ninety-one tons of coal at $.55 a ton. His earnings totaled $50.05 as shown by his pay slip submitted to the United States Senate "LaFollette" subcommittee investigating labor espionage and violations of civil liberties. But company "charges" deducted during this fifteen-day span amounted to $48.52, leaving Hatfield with $1.53. They were:

Scrip	$20.00	Hospital	$ .50	Chance	$1.00
Cash	16.50	Insurance	1.50	Social Security .	.50
Powder	4.40	Lamps	.77	State tax	.45
Smithing	.20	Burial fund	.50		
School fund	.20	Bath	.50	TOTAL CHARGES.	$48.52
Doctor	1.00	Ball club	.50	BALANCE	$1.53

The first two items were for credit and currency previously given out by the company store. The "chance" has a special significance. It seems that the company's manager, Pearl Basham, compelled all the miners to buy a one-dollar ticket in raffles for second-hand automobiles or lose their jobs. Old broken-down cars would thus fetch Mr. Basham from $750 to $800 apiece. It was further alleged, at the LaFollette hearings, that whenever Mr. Basham felt the need of more money he held a raffle—often as many as three a month. Under his supervision of company affairs, it was also said, two company doctors still receive $700 for services for which the miners are charged from $1,800 to $2,400 a month.

"promote friendship, unity and Christian charity among the members," who, under the terms of its constitution, had to be Irish and Roman Catholic. They also possessed, said that document, "the most humane feelings towards our fellow creatures in distress."

In practice the Molly Maguires were a secret association of men who killed mine superintendents, and other bosses, and "long-haired" Socialists, and "weak and corrupt" labor leaders, and wrecked trains and blew up collieries in order to get softer jobs for themselves or their friends, to retaliate for "short weight" at the tipple, to object to inadequate safeguards against entombment, and to assert their superiority over the "foreign scum" and the "dregs and scourings" of non-Irish miners who, despite their lack of Celtic grace, kept coming to America.

The society originated about 1840 in Ireland's Tipperary County where a robust and dynamic widow, Molly Maguire, set herself up as a "defender of the poor." Whenever a peasant was evicted from his land, Molly would summon a group of her boys to beat up or even murder the bailiff or process server or other hapless agent of the landlord or the crown. And for a decade, not alone in Tipperary but in Westmeath and King's and Queen's counties, too, the Molly Maguires with knives, fists, and shillalahs ruled the roost. About the middle of the nineteenth century, however, landlords finally prodded authorities into punitive action and thousands of Mollies, including (the legend says) Widow Maguire herself, came to the United States. A good many of them found jobs in the hard coal mines, especially in the Schuylkill County section of Pennsylvania. They also found it easy, under prevailing conditions, to transfer their hatred of landlords and their minions to coal operators and their subordinates.

The Molly Maguires soon discovered that they had merely exchanged one kind of poverty for another, the thatched hut for a clapboard hovel. They decided to do something about it, to better themselves; and the tactics of Tipperary were transposed to Schuylkill. By 1865 they had established at least two hundred lodges, each complete with passwords, officers and grievance committee. The last met usually in the backroom, or in the cellar, of a saloon kept by one of the faithful. And before this committee a member would cite his complaints. He had perhaps been cheated out of a supervisory job by Jones, the district manager. If discussion proved that the "brother" had been denied justice, a Molly from the neighboring region (the better to elude detection) was chosen to (a) thrash Jones or (b) murder him—in accord with the punishment he deserved. Or again it might be some "godless" Marxian agitator saying that "religion is the opiate of the people" who was thus marked down for slaughter. For the Mollies by and large were extremely devout. They were brawlers, bruisers, carousers, and killers but they regularly went to mass, although Mother Church officially and trenchantly denounced them. They frowned upon sexual impropriety. They did their best to be good providers for their wives and children. They planned murder with a prayer. They did not confess their crimes to the priest since they felt themselves to be men with a high mission, engaged in a kind of war, and hence not personally responsible for snuffing out another's life.

The revengefulness displayed by the Mollies, of course, cannot be explained by purely personal animosities or ambitions. In technique, they antedated the modern racketeer and "shake-down" artist by using the threat of death to exact tribute in the form of better jobs and safer and easier working conditions. Their murders, however, seem to have stemmed largely from their thwartings and bitterness in finding the Promised Land a place of bondage. Theirs was a barbarous protest against barbarity. It was a warning to operators who were callous to cave-ins, explosions, and other mine disasters and who gave small pay for a big ton and regarded labor as something inanimate like any other commodity.

The Molly Maguires reached their apogee in the early 70's, gaining thousands of converts throughout Pennsylvania and capturing control of the timorous and respectable "Miners and Laborers' Benevolent Association" in its stronghold of Schuylkill County. To correct brutalizing conditions of work they called the "long strike" of 1874–75. They promised to murder any local miners who returned to their jobs. Imported strikebreakers were regularly found lying in a ditch, thoroughly and "inexplicably" dead. Meantime, in a dozen communities of the anthracite area the Mollies had elected their own mayors, appointed their own judges, and controlled them as rigorously as Tammany Hall in New York controlled its own officeholders. Dazzled by their success, the Mollies prepared to extend their influence to West Virginia.

At this point, however, they encountered nemesis in the person of Franklin P. Gowan, president of the Reading Railroad, who some years before had lectured hard coal miners on the rudiments of political economy. Mining bosses in pits owned by Mr. Gowan's company were being "bumped off" on a mass production scale which lowered output and interfered with efficiency. Gowan turned his considerable talents to destroying the Mollies. He hired Pinkerton detectives of Irish descent, notably a James McParland, and instructed them to join the Mollies and find out what they could. Seven such operatives entered the society and by gruesome deeds climbed to positions of authority and trust. When they had collected sufficient evidence they testified in court against their "brethren," sending ten Mollies to the scaffold and imprisoning fourteen others for terms ranging from fifteen years to life.

The Ancient Order of Hibernians still exists.* But the Molly Maguires who for nearly a quarter of a century used murder to obtain what they felt was "social justice" (and also to pay off personal scores) ceased to function after the trials which took place in 1875.

The Molly Maguires unquestionably helped to improve working conditions by instilling fear of death into the minds of hard coal management. But they also retarded the growth of unionism to an immeasurable extent. They enabled employers to create a bogeyman myth in which *all* labor organizations and violence were held to be inseparable. The Mollies "conditioned" large portions of the public to believe the worst about labor, to be suspicious of its objectives. They were crude, ignorant men. They were depicted in cartoons and editorials as subhuman brutes. Thus they added the colors of primitivism to the composite mental picture evoked by the term "labor" in their day. And for many years after the eclipse of the Mollies, it was customary for coal operators and the Pennsylvania press to condemn as a revival of the Molly Maguire spirit almost every effort of the miners to better themselves.

The fright and the moral indignation that such descriptions aroused did much to make the advance of unionism in hard coal a contest with obloquy.

By the turn of the century the United Mine Workers had enlisted ten thousand members, largely as the result of a successful twelve-week strike in the bituminous area of the Central Competitive Field. The union had gained recognition, which by itself had stiffened its morale and widened its reputation. Its leaders felt that it was prepared to branch out by invading anthracite. But here it bucked up against a resistance as strong and stubborn as the British squares against which Napoleon's hussars spent themselves, losing Waterloo.

* It became a purely social fraternity after 1875, like a feeble "Elks." Today, however, its remaining few clubs in mining sections are rapidly disappearing.

The operators of the "anthracite monopoly"—extending over a region of five hundred square miles in eastern Pennsylvania—were few and well organized. They were also tough. Especially hardboiled was Mr. George F. Baer, president of the Reading and Philadelphia Railroad that controlled about 70 per cent of America's hard coal output and was in turn dominated by the House of Morgan. Mr. Baer was kingpin among the operators, and their most vigorous spokesman. He believed unions in general and the United Mine Workers in particular to be spawn of Satan. On the other hand, the hard coal miners who were averaging around $22.00 per month for a ten-hour day tended to look upon the union as if it were a delivering angel, shouting hosannas and surrounded by cherubim. Whereas during the previous twenty years profits and dividend slices had steadily mounted, wages had remained at 1880 levels. Resentment over this state of affairs kept piling up, year after year, until it headed a long list of grievances among which exorbitant prices for shoddy and second-rate goods at company stores also loomed large, since they affected not only the miner himself but his family as well.

For two years, 1899–1900, union organizers had sought to crystallize such discontents, pointing out that their causes could be removed only if and when unionism arrived in hard coal. Yet this vanguard of the United Mine Workers found the way rough and progress slow. There were twenty nationalities with which to deal—with all their hatreds and misunderstandings, all their "race memories" and religious differences. Many miners, moreover, suffered from the wounds of former failures to build a union. They were frightened by the prospect of reprisals against union adherents since the operators who ran anthracite had from the beginning maintained rigid and reciprocal blacklists.

Despite such obstacles, however, the union's evangelists

had brought 7,800 miners into the fold in mid-summer, 1900. Late in August, they drew up a list of demands for (*a*) an increase in wages, (*b*) abolition of company stores, (*c*) the elimination of company doctors, and (*d*) reductions in the price of powder which the miners were compelled to buy from the company at $2.75 a keg while the same keg sold for $1.10 in the open market. They formally submitted their proposals to the operators, who ignored them. On September 17 a strike was called, and three days later, despite the small membership of the union itself, more than 90 per cent of the 143,000 employees quit work.

Joyously Mr. Baer girded his loins for battle. But the cagey Mark Hanna, G.O.P. national boss, would not let him fight—at least not just then. A presidential election impended. William McKinley was running for his second term; and the Republican party, as the political appendage of Big Ownership, wanted to avoid anything that might be made into an unpleasant campaign issue—especially in Pennsylvania, a key state, where in 1896 the majority of miners had voted for William Jennings Bryan.

Hence Hanna went over the heads of the operators to J. P. Morgan himself; and at the latter's signal the operators reversed themselves with the speed of expediency and the grumblings of doubt. They yielded to the miners to the small extent of granting a 10 per cent raise in pay and cutting the price of powder 45 per cent, leaving everything else to future negotiation.

The head of the United Mine Workers, the dark and morbid-minded John Mitchell, who looked like a gypsy and acted like a banker, accepted this concession as a starting point for getting more later on, and the men returned to work.

A state of armed truce prevailed for two years thereafter. The miners were still dissatisfied and so were the operators. The former wanted more grievances remedied, notably the practice of making the miner turn out a mini-

mum of 3,190 pounds to the ton while the company sold
at the standard 2,240 pounds. The miners also were insisting, in talk among themselves, on recognition of the
union. The operators, most of them convinced that Hanna
was a damned fool interfering milk-sop, insisted on an open
shop.

The showdown came on June 2, 1902, when the operators scorned the union's ultimatum of eight hours a day
with no decrease in wages. Pumpmen, firemen, engineers
were the first to abandon their posts. Meantime the operators had made preparations to transform every colliery
into a base for military maneuvers. Within forty-eight
hours more than three thousand of the private "Coal and
Iron" police, with their shining hob-nailed boots, their
shiny holsters and revolvers, their shiny silver buttons on
blue uniforms, were hired along with one thousand "special operatives" garbed in less costly raiment, to guard
shaft and breaker and washery, which soon were surrounded with stockades and barbed-wire fences. Promptly
trains rolled in from Boston and New York, carrying
strikebreakers herded into freight cars, recruited almost
equally from new immigrants and thugs. The Lehigh Valley Coal Company began to evict all striking miners and
their families, bag and baggage, from its endless rows of
company-owned hovels.

In retaliation, the strikers in nearby cities such as Wilkes-
Barre instituted a boycott. They placed on their "unfair
lists" any business establishment that supplied the needs
of the imported strikebreakers or of local workers who refused to lay down their tools.

After the first days of the strike call, the mines for all
practical purposes were closed, mainly for lack of skilled
manpower. They were, furthermore, endangered by the
possibility of fire, explosion, and flood, since half of the
imported workers were more accustomed to find their way
around saloons, jails, brothels, and gambling dives than a

coal mine; and the other half, the "greenhorns," were still trying to find their way around the United States.

Tonnage dropped gradually to a low of 5 per cent of the total, salvaged from culm banks. For a while the operators were baffled. Then a "Citizens' Alliance," which was to have its successor in virtually every major strike up to the present day, was set up at the behest of company executives. It comprised superintendents, foremen, clerks, and various business and professional and political people who, for one reason or another, preferred to line up on the company's side. It hit out against the boycott, protesting that:

When butchers and bakers may not supply meat and bread, when the doctor may not attend the sick, the druggist may not dole out medicine and the priest may not minister either to those in health or to those at death's door; when public officers may not perform public duties, when teachers in the school may not teach or be appointed except by the consent of the strikers or their sympathizers, then, indeed, the last vestige of personal liberty has gone and society must be rebuilt upon a basis of submission to the tyranny, not necessarily of majorities, but rather of a band of men who will not hesitate to employ every means of intimidation as a lawful instrument of control.

Meantime Mitchell, who was a well-meaning man, a vice-president of the A. F. of L., and Gompers' heir apparent, kept trying to prevent a general "sympathetic strike" from spreading to the soft coal fields. To thresh out this question, 768 anthracite and 1,416 bituminous delegates attended a national convention of the United Mine Workers, held at Tomlinson Hall, Indianapolis, on July 17, 1902.

On the floor debate was vigorous and prolonged. The hard coal emissaries, along with quite a few of their soft coal brethren, contended that if the anthracite miners were licked, the operators in bituminous would seek to destroy the union in their regions, too. The advocates of this view pointed out, further, that whereas anthracite was burned mainly for household uses and bituminous for mills and factories and railroads, the one type of coal in many cases could be substituted for the other during times of shortage. On the other hand, the majority of soft coal representatives, led by Mitchell himself, insisted that they were in duty and honor bound to abide by their contracts with the operators which were to expire the following year on April 1, 1903, and which excluded strike action.

"I am firm in my conviction," said Mitchell, "that the strike in the anthracite fields can and will be won without repudiating our solemn contracts with the bituminous operators, provided the bituminous miners will rise to the occasion and do their full duty by their struggling fellow workers. . . ."

And as an afterthought he added the suggestion that if the soft coal miners weren't working either they wouldn't be able to help the strikers financially. He won. A sum of $50,000 from the national treasury was voted to be given to the anthracite locals and assessments of 10 per cent to 25 per cent were also levied to provide an extra fund.

And Mitchell's insistence that the union keep faith with the operators was but the logical application of what had already become and still essentially remains the official philosophy of the United Mine Workers: that differences between labor and management in coal should be settled by joint discussion and that the terms of the ensuing bargain should be clearly specified in a written contract which must be binding in spirit and letter upon both sides. Behind Mitchell's devotion to this creed was a good deal of practical insight. He had himself come up from the ranks. He knew from personal experience that the miners in soft coal had struggled, step by step, to stabilize employment in their industry by means of collective agreements with the employers. He knew further that to violate this variety of pact, whatever the temptation, would have injured his union immeasurably. It would have given the operators the opportunity to go to the public and say that since the United Mine Workers refused to abide by its pledges, even when set down in black and white, it was quite obviously irresponsible and untrustworthy and that therefore there was nothing to be gained by recognizing it or negotiating with it. While some Socialists berated him for his "betrayal of the working-class" it is hard to see what else he could have done, granting the circumstances and the premises of his own economic outlook which in large measure reflected the outlook of the rank and file.

Like Gompers whom he adored he was a trade unionist, pure and simple. He could write: "The average wage earner has made up his mind that he must remain a wage earner. He has given up hope of a kingdom to come where he himself will be a capitalist, and he asks that the reward for his work be given him as a working man." He accepted the implications of this doctrine—defeatist in terms of American psychology—with great calm. He also accepted capitalism, more or less *in toto*, regarding its defects as quite remediable and looking upon conflicts between employers and employed as matters to be adjusted and compromised within the framework of private ownership of the means of production. He believed that "the trade agreement is the essence of trade unionism," a view that assumed that operators and miners, for example, were really partners in a common enterprise; and that the only point of dispute was how much of the enterprise's proceeds should be allotted to the one or the other. Beyond that he did not go, dared not go. He was a very cautious man.

In the anthracite fields, in the haze of Pennsylvania's harsh July heat, most mines were idle and the strikers would not budge. Neither would the operators. The summer dragged on with the New York *Times* becoming restive, urging the companies to take a firmer stand. "The duty of the operators," it declared, "is to begin mining coal without delay." Churchmen all over the country voiced the same sentiment, embellished it. On Sunday, August 3, Father O'Reilly thus sermonized from his pulpit in the Church of the Annunciation at Shenandoah:

You should have the manhood to go back to work and defy this organization known as the United Mine Workers. It is a blood-stained organization, and it will be blood-stained until it ceases to exist. It was formed to promote crime and protect criminals. Everyone was happy and contented here until Mitchell and Fahy came and organized unions. These men are not workingmen; they are not respectable, and I wouldn't give two cents for the opinion of either of them.

Using this and similar preachments as text, the Citizens' Alliance began a campaign of hand-feeding reporters, circulating the most incredible and hair-raising tales of violence and lawlessness on the part of strikers despite the fact that they had adopted the tactics of passive resistance and would neither "work nor riot" though they were offered ample inducements to do either or both. By mid-August the strikers had sacrificed $12,700,000 in wages in what was becoming a war of attrition. Their credit had been shut off by many local retailers because the coal companies, through their New York banking connections, had "cracked down" on wholesale houses, insisting that they demand cash on the line for all merchandise shipped to stores in the strike vicinity.

Meantime a Wilkes-Barre photographer, Mr. W. F. Clark, wrote a letter to President Baer of the Philadelphia and Reading, beseeching him as a "Christian gentleman" to make at least some slight concession to the strikers, end the dispute, earn the blessing of God and the gratitude of the nation. But Mr. Baer, who in addition to other attributes had been vouchsafed a special knowledge of the Deity's will, replied in an American classic of Bourbonism:

I see you are evidently biased in your religious views in favor of the right of the working man to control a business in which he has no other interest than to secure fair wages for the work he does. I beg of you not to be discouraged. The rights and interests of the laboring man will be protected and cared for, not by the labor agitators, but by the Christian men to whom God in his infinite wisdom has given control of the property interests of the country. Pray earnestly that the right may triumph, always remembering that the Lord God Omnipotent still reigns and that his reign is one of law and order, and not of violence and crime.

By the middle of September the general public began personally to feel the repercussions of the conflict. As the supply of anthracite dwindled, profiteers boosted the price from $6.00 to $10.00 to $15.00 to $20.00 a ton. The poor who bought their coal by pail or basket paid $28.00 and $30.00 a ton.

In a final push to shatter the solidity of the strikers, the operators, through the Governor, called out the militia. Five regiments of infantry and two of cavalry patrolled Olyphant, Wilkes-Barre, Shenandoah, Lebanon. They didn't do much good. They could parade. They could stand guard. They could patronize the saloons and try to date up the girls. But they couldn't mine coal. The deadlock continued.

Meanwhile T. R. Roosevelt had succeeded the assassinated McKinley and late in August he began casting about for ways and means of ending the dispute. He summoned Morgan and then Mitchell to the White House. The latter, at least, was impressed. He had been brought up in poverty; his mother had been a washerwoman and he had had to deliver laundry baskets while the other boys were playing backlot baseball. He had developed an inferiority complex which had taken the form of trying to gain approbation and social recognition from the rich, the famous, the potent. He listened in rapture to the President, who appealed to him in the role that Mitchell had assumed as his own, that of the diplomatic polished gentleman who mingled at ease with the social world, or at least with Mark Hanna. Roosevelt submitted to him the proposal that Morgan and his ace brain-truster, Robert Bacon, had fashioned. They recommended that a commission be appointed by the President to settle the question. While the commission was investigating, however, the miners were to return to their jobs; and both sides were to accept the commission's awards as binding for three years. There was a joker. The commission was to include an army or navy engineer, a mining engineer, an eminent sociologist, and a Federal judge from the eastern Pennsylvania district. No labor representative was to be allowed—a proviso that expressed Morgan's seignorial view that serfs should be seen but not heard.

To remedy this lack of labor representation, Mitchell urged that a priest be added to the commission since most of the miners were Catholic and might by this method be induced to accept a body that otherwise was a surrogate for "the propertied classes." T.R. approved and selected Bishop John Spalding of Illinois.

Trailing clouds of vicarious glory, Mitchell returned to Wilkes-Barre to offer this arbitration scheme to delegates of the anthracite miners. They didn't like it. They were angry that no labor spokesman was to sit with the commission. They distrusted E. E. Clark, Chief of the Order of Railway Conductors, who out of the bedlam of T.R.'s mind had been named as the "eminent sociologist" despite his record of strike-breaking during the Pullman walkout.

In addition, the tentative outline of the agreement with the operators did not provide for the more than five thousand firemen, engineers, and pumpmen who had really begun the strike, had had the least to gain and the most to lose, and whose posts had been taken over by nonunion men. Mitchell replied that he was very sorry about it and while "it may be true that some will be sacrificed, and much as we shall regret that, I desire to say that no battle was ever won that didn't carry with it some victims."

After two days of similar argument, Mitchell persuaded the men to accept the Morgan-Bacon truce. On October 23 they returned to the mines and next day the commission began its hearings.

It examined 558 witnesses, in Scranton, in Philadelphia. And on March 18, 1903, it delivered its verdict which specified: (a) a 10 per cent increase in the rates paid contract miners, retroactive to November 1, 1902; (b) an eight-hour day for engineers, pumpmen, and firemen and a nine-hour day for all others; (c) a sliding wage scale with a one per cent increase for each five-cent advance in the selling price of coal at New York City over $4.50 a ton F.O.B. It established an arbitration board comprising six persons, three to be chosen by the operators and three by the miners, to iron out difficulties that might arise under the terms of the new pact. Yet the commission dodged the issue of union recognition by quibbling the point that Mitchell in negotiations had not represented the United Mine Workers *in toto* but only the anthracite miners, a conclusion that was more jesuitical than just.

The miners felt betrayed. They had struggled for five months. They had undergone incredible privations with that sullen and proud tenacity notable among men who work in the pit. They had lost $25,000,000 in wages. They had received no assurance that a miner still wouldn't be fired for joining a union. They had saved Mitchell's face, causing him to be praised in the press as the most "enlightened and progressive labor leader of this generation." They did not think that such praise was worth their suffering. They looked forward to the expiration of the agreement in 1906 when, they promised themselves, "we'll build a real union and make it stick." But to do that they had to wait a long time.

In 1920 Warren Gamaliel Harding was elected President of the United States and John L. Lewis was elected president of the United Mine Workers' Union of America. In terms of the future, the latter was the more important event.

For some years Lewis, as vice-president of the union, had functioned as its chief in fact, if not in name, since its official head, Frank J. Hayes, divided his time almost equally between getting drunk and going to sanatoria seeking by means of Keeley cures to vanquish a dipsomania as tragic as it was invincible.

His successor was forty years old. Even then he looked like a cross between a ham Shakespearian actor and an idealized statue of labor's might. He was six feet tall, of vast bulk, with wild and wiry black hair and beetling eyebrows. His chin was a crag of flesh, and his eyes held the gaze of the miner who toils in the pit toward the sun. His voice was resonant with all the treble-to-thunder range of a Wurlitzer organ. He was immensely intelligent; his energy was inexhaustible, his intellectual curiosity endless; and he was animated by the implacable conviction that he was chosen of destiny to hew great ends.

He was well qualified for his new post. He knew mining and miners. He had started out digging coal in Lucas, Iowa, at the age of seventeen. He had risen by quick stages from committee head of his local to its representative at union conventions. In 1911 he had been picked out by Gompers as a man of singular promise and appointed Field and Legislative Representative for the A. F. of L. He was hence enabled to travel around the country a great deal, observing much at first hand, peddling the wares of unionism in steel, in glass, in lumber, and in copper for five and a half years. Impressed by his minute knowledge of the coal industry which Lewis studied by day and by night, John P. White, then president of the United Mine Workers, named him as the union's statistician in 1916. But Lewis

had more than a gift for figures. He was also eloquent—
not only from the rostrum but in more intimate gatherings.
His advancement within his union was as swift as it was
merited by exceptional talents. When he became its president, moreover, he inherited an extremely prosperous and
going concern—esteemed by its fellow unions within the
A. F. of L. as well as by the public outside.

For from America's very entry into the World War, the
union had displayed a keen patriotism. More than 20,000 of
its members had enlisted in addition to thousands more who
had been drafted. It had held strictly by the provisions of
the Lever Act, which, under the guidance of the War
Labor Board, had prevented strikes for the "duration."
Along with most of organized labor, the United Mine
Workers had benefited from wartime prosperity. Wages
had risen to $6.00 and $7.00 a day and even more in some
instances, employment was steady, and hours had been reduced by government mandate to eight a day.

Some five months after the Armistice was signed, however, the union held a convention on September 11, 1919,
in Cleveland, Ohio, where two thousand delegates, with
Lewis presiding as acting president, voted for a 60 per
cent increase in pay, a six-hour day and a five-day week.
They justified this rather sudden and startling maneuver
by saying in effect that the profiteers—among whom coal
operators were particularly prominent—had made millions
from the carnage which had kept American mines at capacity production. It was time, said the union, that the
miners' right to a share in such enormous gains should be
recognized.

When the triune demand was placed before the coal
operators, however, they rejected it with what amounted
to oral apoplexy. In reply, union officials convening on
October 23 announced that a strike covering both soft
and hard coal fields would be called on November 1.

From his sickbed President Wilson protested that "it

[the forthcoming strike] is not only unjustifiable but is unlawful. The law will be enforced and means found to protect the public interest in any emergency that may arise." Other government officials pointed out that the Lever Act, though enacted as a war measure, was technically still in effect. It was an argument which Lewis countered by reminding them that the "Hindenburg line has been in Germany for a year." He also attacked President Wilson's "attitude" as being "the climax of a long series of attempted usurpations of executive power."

Mr. Wilson responded by speeding through Congress a set of sharp resolutions supporting his position. In turn Lewis accused him and the United States Cabinet of allying themselves with sinister Wall Street influences in the attempt to "deny justice to labor and to precipitate our country into industrial turmoil."

Meantime the newspapers had whipped up the public into a frenzy of alarm over the prospects of a coal shortage, here and abroad. The projected strike was in fact going to set off world-wide repercussions. While the President and Mr. Lewis were exchanging their "you're another" quotes for the headlines, cables from Vienna carried news that the Austrian government, in view of the many deaths caused by fuel shortage which had also slowed rail traffic to a standstill, was planning to buy a vast quantity of American coal. Moreover, in France, the German invasion had destroyed coal mines with such rigor and precision that experts declared it would take from six to nine years to restore them to effective operation, and hence Paris began to clamor for American coal. In the Fatherland itself trains had been stalled for ten days without coal to fire locomotive boilers, along the Rhine the intense cold prevented the sitting of Weimar courts, and Berlin also wanted to order American coal. Government officials in Rome announced that Italy's coal supply would last only three or four weeks, and they likewise intended to pur-

Philip Murray and John L. Lewis.

chase American coal. The American public followed suit, leaving their orders urgently and early with dealers, and enterprising farmers began to chop down their trees. In spite of all domestic and foreign pressures, the strike was called on schedule, picks were stacked and work whistles blew in vain. The next day, November 2, eight hundred Federal troops entrained from Camp Taylor, Ohio, for duty in West Virginia coal fields. The Governors of Utah and Wyoming called out the National Guard. After the first week the coal stoppage (save for nonunion and marginal mines which were reopened by the hundred) was almost complete. It had forced nine Chicago factories to shut down, throwing twenty-five thousand men out of work. In nearby Gary, Indiana, the great steel plants were closed and in Kansas City, Missouri, schools were discontinued.

On November 8, Mr. T. T. Brewster, spokesman for the coal operators, made an appalling discovery. The strike, he announced, had been directly inspired by the Bolsheviks Lenin and Trotsky and financed by Moscow gold. Lewis denied that he had received even a ruble. He asked for proof and Brewster backed down with a celerity unnoticed by the papers which had played up the story for three days.

The Federal government, through Attorney-General Palmer, had prevailed upon United States Justice A. B. Anderson in Indianapolis to issue a restraining order against United Mines Workers officials, forbidding them to go ahead with their widespread walkout. The American Federation of Labor, after a few days in which to become properly aghast, joined the war of words by thundering that "the government injunction is so autocratic as to be staggering."

Editorial writers compared the situation with the memorable anthracite strike of 1902. They reminded their readers that then the operators had been distinctly at fault and that an "aroused public opinion" had finally brought them to book. It was further argued that in the current conflict the union was plainly at fault, defying the government and disregarding the general welfare. And this view, repeated in metropolitan daily and village weekly all over the country, became a rapier thrust that union fencers found it hard to parry.

They could with reason put the onus of the strike upon the collective "greed and callousness" of the operators and denounce them further for artificially restricting coal output to raise prices and for arranging scandalous rebates from railroads with which the coal companies were financially linked. Yet to risk any further extension of the fast-mounting public antagonism and government hostility toward the union was a course suited only to the romantics of the barricade school.

On December 7, therefore, Lewis—accompanied by the union's plump, urbane, and very hard-working secretary-treasurer, William Green—conferred with President Wilson in the White House study which had been the scene of a similar meeting with the operators the day before. That night a strike settlement was announced. Its terms called for an immediate 14 per cent increase in wages and left other questions to the judgment of an impartial commission to be established at once.

William Green said afterwards:

The fight resolved itself into one against the government and not against the operators. We could have whipped the coal operators but we could not if we had wanted to, whip the strongest government on earth. . . . If we had not accepted President Wilson's proposal the powers of the Federal government would have been turned loose against us with greater ferocity than anything we have ever seen. We knew we had reached the limit.

But the union's troubles, despite the moral lift of this victory and the setting up of the new Coal Commission (forerunner of many, many more), had only just begun. The war of words which had beclouded basic strike issues was soon replaced by a battle of "facts and figures" which has continued up to the present and which has tended to make the coal industry a statisticians' paradise during the past two decades. By 1920, of course, the idea of an advance agreement had been well implanted in the minds of operators and the union alike, the former looking upon it as an inescapable evil which could be perhaps circumvented and the latter regarding it as the beginning of wisdom. In any event, to achieve a basis for negotiations, each side invoked the high gods of correlation analysis. The subjective quality of mathematics has never been more apparent. Despite such bickerings, however, the contest for power had been shifted, during the 1920's, from the tipple to the conference table; and the result of this newer kind of bargaining was embodied in contracts of law. The importance of such pacts, hoped for by Siney, rigorously maintained by Mitchell, was reiterated by Lewis in a magazine article that he contributed to *The Survey* magazine's symposium on the high price of coal:

The mine workers are now working under a scale of wages fixed by the United States Bituminous Coal Commission. . . . Those wage schedules were written into an agreement between miners and operators which will not terminate until March 31, 1922. There can be no modification or abrogation of this agreement in any coal producing district without disturbing the integrity of the contract throughout the entire nation. The United Mine Workers will resist any attempts to disturb the equanimity of its present contractual relations!

Yet the union's equanimity was very definitely disturbed by many long bitter strikes which occurred not only when operators refused to renew wage-scale agreements but also when miners in unorganized areas sought concessions, objected to cuts in pay. For in the roaring 20's coal remained the sick giant among the titans of American industry.

Water power and oil in supplying extraneous energy encroached more and more upon coal's domain. The incredible inefficiency of a good deal of mine management, antiquated methods, refusal to install technological improvements which the union, with great foresight, recommended even at the risk of displacing manpower, combined with the old evils of overdevelopment to infect the United Mine Workers with the same ailment that kept the doctors hovering anxiously around the bedside of King Coal.

During this same period, moreover, coal capital like that for textiles went south. Hundreds of new nonunion mines were being opened up below the Mason-Dixon line where Lincoln's abolition of Negro slavery had only paved the way for a new industrial peonage of both black and white. In Alabama, in Tennessee, in Kentucky employers were notoriously and ruthlessly "open shop." Union organizers seeking to invade such areas were murdered, beaten, ridden on rails, tarred and feathered, and otherwise treated to fine old Southern hospitality. In West Virginia the companies employed the same tactics of tyranny with such rigor that union membership in that state dwindled from 10,000 in 1920 to less than 600 in 1929.

Everywhere operators were more or less candidly voicing the belief that if they were going to make profits at all they would be compelled to "take it out of labor's hide."

The very agreements which Lewis cherished almost wrecked his career and often split the union into warring factions and also bound some sheaves for Communist harvesting. For such pacts presented a double dilemma.

Along with other top officials in the United Mine Workers like its vice-president Philip Murray, Lewis honestly tried to organize all labor in coal. But when union missionaries were slain or railroaded out of mining communities where free speech was only a phrase, nothing much could be done but safeguard strongholds already built up in union territory and await a more propitious turn of events. Nonunion miners going out on strike would insist that Lewis call out all the other workers in coal, whether covered by a contract with the owners or not. The theory was that only a major coal stoppage could focus enough attention upon the cause of the original strikers to force the operators to meet with them and come to terms. Obviously if union mines continued to produce while nonunion mines were closed, there would be no general coal shortage, no big headlines, no investigations, no intervention by the Federal government.

Quite as obviously, Lewis believed, if he called a strike in violation of the contract signed with an operator who was living up to its provisions, the job of ultimately obtaining this kind of an agreement for the whole industry would be immeasurably impeded, if not made impossible. He was, after all, a "business" unionist who prided himself upon his realism. But neither this line of reasoning nor the strategy it entailed impressed miners who were virtually starving in nonunion pits. Even in his own union there were "outlaw" or unauthorized strikes while Communists like William Z. Foster sought to convert all this dissatisfaction among the rank and file into rival organizations or movements to oust Lewis from his "despotic and autocratic" rule. In response he indulged in some of the most vicious and vitriolic red-baiting that this whole period of anti-Bolshevik hysteria records. Everyone who fought him was excoriated as a minion of Moscow and in meeting after meeting parliamentary procedure was flattened out by the steam-roller of the Lewis machine.

His own progressive lieutenants like John Brophy and Powers Hapgood, who were respectively to become director of the C.I.O. and head of the United Shoe Workers, a C.I.O. affiliate, openly accused him of "betraying" seventy-five thousand miners working in pits owned by the United States Steel Corporation when he refused to send funds or organizers to aid this great nonunionized group. In Illinois Frank Farrington, and in Kansas Alexander Howatt were intriguing to seize his sceptre for themselves, or bestow it upon another.

In the mid-twenties, with his vexations mounting daily, he took time off to write a book—perhaps to take stock of himself and his union by putting things down on paper. It was a revealing book, as significant in what it omitted as in what it said. In economics it showed its author to be an advocate of laissez faire, still loyal to the thesis that under a system of free enterprise the ultimate prosperity of all is to be assured by the utmost efforts of everyone to better his own condition. The volume, named the *Miners Fight for American Standards*, was better in its treatment of concrete problems than of abstractions. His statement concerning the check-off, for example, remains the best explanation of its origins:

The system [the check-off] is the traditional way for the miner to pay any debt he owes. It started with the operators who checked off money for rent, insurance, house coal, taxes, the company store bill, hospital charges, compressed air, carbide, oil, squibs, detonators, medicines, powder, dynamite, batteries, and even Red Cross contributions.

Yet, ironically, though Lewis in both theory and fact knew more about the coal industry than any other man in the United States, it was a knowledge almost without power. He and his union were unable to cope with the new growth of holding company and interlocking directorate which, through the House of Morgan and others, fused steel, motors, railroads, and mines into a single financial empire that, among other things, furnished its own coal and favored the open shop. And as the rest of American business moved swiftly toward the debacle of Black October, 1929, coal was already disintegrating as competition with other fuels and between operators kept lowering profits, wages, and morale. Even the famous "Jacksonville Agreement" in 1927, hailed as ushering in another "new era," soon had a host of chiselers who looked upon their "contractual obligations" as scraps of paper. Miners in many places were receiving $3.00 a day for a two- or three-day week; and although in 1924 the union had reached an all-time high in membership, having on its rolls 497,000 of the 700,000 men employed, the prolonged depression in coal, intensified in 1925–26–27, provoked countless defections.

Palpably the dual strategy of the union—(1) to stabilize the central soft coal areas by strict adherence to contract and (2) to organize the Southern and Western mines to prevent the undercuttings of nonunion operators—had failed on both counts. In desperation Lewis and other officials took the attitude that the interplay of "natural forces" would drive inefficient, uneconomic mines out of the industry, would force superfluous labor into other occupations. The underlying belief was that "laws of supply and demand" and the "survival of the fittest" would soon or late cause something nice to happen in coal. But both Adam Smith and Charles Darwin failed Lewis and the United Mine Workers.

And as a result of this "do nothing" policy, Lewis became a much hated man among the rank and file. They wanted him to "do something." But he seemed at this time to be quite as bewildered and thwarted as they were themselves. He assailed the operator-retailer conniving to cheat the consuming public by short-grading coal. He denounced the Muscovite, domestic, foreign, and imaginary with great fervor and flourish. But the miners were still dissatisfied with their low pay and little work. They began to mutter about his thousand-dollar-a-month salary. They complained about his Cadillac and his chauffeur, both of which would have done credit to a Park Avenue dowager. And Lewis' wiry black hair was getting grayer when in 1932 the union, to maintain its voting strength in the A. F. of

L., paid a per capita tax on 300,000 members although really its rolls had shrunken to a scant 150,000.

Then came Roosevelt and the early days of the New Deal. Summoned by brain-truster Raymond Moley to help draft recovery legislation, Lewis submitted the Davis-Kelly bill; for from an apostle of "let us alone" he had become an advocate of "give us a plan."

When the thesis of government aid to unionism was written into NRA's Section 7a, Lewis saw his chance to do or die. He did. He did very effectively. He gambled the last $75,000 in the union's treasury upon a bold, brilliant organizing campaign, so successfully planned and executed that after a meeting in Williamson, West Virginia, 4,200 newly inspirited miners signed up within two hours. He drove himself to the uttermost limits of his gargantuan strength. Cars and trucks, banners and flares, slogans and prayers of rejoicing were hurled with an inspired corps of organizers into the coal fields, North, South, East, West. "The law is on our side," they chanted. "The government's with us," they cried. "John L. and the President are buddies, I'm telling you." Within twelve months the United Mine Workers was bigger and more powerful than ever before, with more than 515,000 dues-paying members watching moves at Washington with a newborn interest, and with high hope.

And with this single magnificent stroke, John L. Lewis had redeemed himself, recovered a lost prestige. At fifty-three a new career had opened up for him and for his union. Both were ready to play a larger role on a greater stage.

The NRA did not fulfill the great expectations of unionists in general and the United Mine Workers in particular. That famous "Magna Carta of American Labor," Section 7a, quickly became but a paper right. It envisaged "code" labor provisions as the product of conference between employer and employee. But the former in many instances simply contrived labor provisions out of his own head, without even "courtesy consultation" with his workers.

Hence Section 7a conferred a privilege which was meaningless until it could again be made real by labor's resort to its own chief weapon, its own collective bargaining strength. Under the NRA, "industrial self-government" was government of, by, and for industrialists (and their financial backers), and the interests of labor and the consumer were less than secondary.

In the Bituminous Coal Code, moreover, this kind of self-government, instead of fostering a "let's get together on price pegging" procedure as in other industries, provoked a collapse of the price structure and renewed an old-time anarchy. The operators were unable to reach or maintain agreements among themselves. They knifed each other with reckless stupidity.

Meantime the leaders of the United Mine Workers were taking a realistic inventory. They looked back upon the history of their union. They saw vast expenditures of time, funds, energy. They saw sacrifice and devotion that had often attained the heroic. They saw the strands of the preceding forty-five years woven into a single pattern: the attempt to improve wage and work conditions within an industry racked by internal rivalry, and its profits increasingly threatened by competition with other fuels.

They recalled that previous efforts to stabilize coal's production and sale, and thus strengthen its competing position as against oil and water power, had time and again been wrecked. They recalled, too, the 56 per cent of the inside workers in American coal mines who, when not totally unemployed, earned less than $1,000 per year. Perhaps Lewis himself particularly remembered the implications of a scathing resolution passed in March, 1930, at a rump convention of United Mine Workers called by his "socialist" opponents, John Brophy and Powers Hapgood:

The history of the United Mine Workers of America under the regime of John L. Lewis has been an unbroken series of defeats . . . has thrown hundreds of thousands of our members and their families into the depths of poverty and destitution. Election stealing, convention packing and slugging of delegates have reduced the old-time democracy of the union to a ghastly farce.

In any case, beginning with the first days of the New Deal, Lewis and his chief aides displayed great willingness to proceed on the assumption that times were changing, that new needs demanded new answers. And after a good deal of soul-searching, and a good deal of disgust with the way the NRA was letting labor down, they concluded that more vigorous and direct government intervention would be the only way out for their own union.

Thus while the Bituminous Coal Code was creating competitive havoc and near collapse, the United Mine Workers were devising the National Coal Conservation bill, better known as the Guffey-Snyder (later the Guffey-Vinson) bill. In the main it was a constructive proposal, supporting the contention of many economists that efficiency and coöperation among American businessmen have often been the result of labor's good sense and good will. In this instance, of course, the United Mine Workers divorced laissez faire only to marry a perhaps more unpredictable variant of state capitalism.

In essentials the Guffey-Vinson Act, passed after stormy debate, established (under the Department of the Interior) a National Bituminous Coal Commission of five "neutral" members appointed by the President. Among other things, the Act authorized coöperative marketing agencies; created a Coal Labor Board to settle differences between operators and miners; empowered the Commission to determine fair and feasible prices; stressed the necessity for collective bargaining; imposed an excise tax of 15 per cent with a refund or drawback of 90 per cent for producers who comply with the Act's intent; and set up an independent consumer counsel's division to represent the public interest.

The congressional hearings on the Act, condemned as the "Guffey abortion" by railroad executives and manufacturers and others who want to keep coal costs down, revealed a new mood of coöperation between operators and unionists. They also showed that both groups welcomed the government as an active guardian. And whatever happens to the Coal Commission, whatever mistakes have been made in selecting its personnel from among an unduly "political" and pro-producer panel, this miniature experiment in planned economy is probably the forerunner of many more to come.*

In any event the United Mine Workers is currently committed to the idea that, in addition to fair practice codes for industry and unions strong enough to enforce collective bargaining, Federal agencies of price and production control must be created to achieve a new and more lasting kind of prosperity, "planned" to improve labor's lot as well as to increase profits. And to prove the efficacy of this approach, the United Mine Workers had to try to build equally potent industrial unions in natural resource and mass production fields alike. Its leaders perceived that concentration of control over American industry has been centered in small financial cliques. By means of the holding company, a handful of men not only hold sway over American banking and credit facilities but also, by sitting on the directorates of major corporations, help to determine their operating and labor policies. The implications of this far-reaching and vertical power over

* Recent rulings of the Commission which have sent soft coal prices up by 16 per cent prompt the question as to whether or not it really promotes the public welfare to plan for a single industry unless that industry is part of a nationally planned economy. It is a fundamental question which the United Mine Workers, along with other unions and the rest of the populace, will soon have to face.

the wages of work had been hammered home to the United Mine Workers by the great United States Steel Corporation which owns "captive" nonunion coal mines. By sweating its labor it was for years able to sell to itself at prices which inspired others to break their contracts with the union in order to meet "competition" by slashing wages.*

In the third year of the New Deal, United Mine Workers officials decided that if they were to keep coal unionized, once and for all, they would have to organize steel. Yet the same people who wielded great influence in coal and steel exercised similar prerogatives in motors and chemicals. It became apparent that, in the long run, to save his own union, and to advance its new philosophy, John L. Lewis would have virtually to unionize the nonagrarian, non-entrepreneurial population in the United States. In the final analysis it was a question of challenging and curbing the monolithic might of the "Big Money" by mobilizing great masses of men and welding them into political and economic unity.

The thesis of the United Mine Workers that government-aided unionism and government-coded industry alone could attain equilibrium of our economic forces and save capitalism from its most implacable foes, the Bourbons who would rather break than bend, had to be backed up by labor's voting strength. But before workers could be made ballot-conscious and politically potent, they first had to be made economically potent, unionized, taught how to bargain collectively, and when, and why.

It was the necessity for this kind of dual or reciprocal strategy which coincided with other and similar American labor dynamics to give birth to the Committee for Industrial Organization. In short, the drive toward industrial unionism in which the United Mine Workers took the initiative, with John L. Lewis as the spark-plug, is only

* In 1936 the United Mine Workers faced a strike situation over this very issue.

incidentally the result of that "great personal ambition" with which successful labor leaders are accused of being peculiarly accursed—as if successful financiers, industrialists, politicians, editorial writers, and publishers were immune to any such weakness.

In considerable measure, therefore, the Committee for Industrial Organization is a logical outgrowth of the seventy-five-year-old effort of the nation's coal miners to achieve "American standards of living." The descendants of men once derided as "a new school of political economists who emerged from the bowels of the earth" to do their unorthodox thinking, have of late accomplished crucial changes in our economic methods, our political modes, our social mores.

In addition to questions of a planned economy for coal, and perhaps for the nation, the union's future will be plagued more and more by the problems of an advancing technology. In this respect, during the past fifteen years, the chief trend has been toward the reduction of hand labor, especially hand shoveling, which as late as 1923 engaged 490,000 men of the industry's 700,000. In the automatic shovel alone dipper capacity has been enlarged from about four cubic yards in 1914 to thirty-two in 1937. Ingenious machines have been perfected for driving entries, for loading in rooms, for almost everything else. Some pick or push the coal onto an elevating conveyor. Others with a lobster-like motion gather it up into the embrace of huge claw-like "arms." Still another, the underground power shovel, noses its scoop into a pile of broken coal, swings around, jettisons its load into the waiting mine car. Loading, of course, has always been the hardest part of the miner's job. In order to throw coal into his car, he must lift it vertically from two to five feet and horizontally from six to twelve feet. Whereas the machine relieves him of this burden, it tends also to relieve him of his employment.

Similar changes have occurred in cutting and cleaning.

Lying on his side, the old-time miner undercut a slot or "kerf" some two or three feet long, under the bottom of the seam so that, once loosened, it would fall. The danger of this task stimulated inventors to trying to get rid of it. Even in the late 80's practical cutting machines were manufactured and the proportion used has jumped from 5 per cent in 1891 to about 86 per cent in 1936, the while their speed, size, and mobility have been increased threefold. Formerly, too, the miner was supposed to keep an eye peeled for pieces of slate and "bony" coal, throw them back into the waste as he worked. Lately, however, "shaking" tables, moving currents of water and air, have been increasingly employed to separate coal from its slightly heavier impurities. In bituminous the tonnage mechanically cleaned has risen from 3.8 per cent in 1906 to nearly 13 per cent in 1936 with a vast extension now pending; and the amount of coal mechanically loaded has risen from 1,500,000 tons in 1923 (first year of the statistical record) to 47,000,000 tons in 1935 and now approximates about 14.5 per cent of all underground production. In Wyoming some 90 per cent, in Indiana about 62 per cent, and in Illinois about 56 per cent of soft coal is now automatically loaded, and the desire of operators to cut wage costs may be counted on to accentuate this tendency.

Such trends plow deep furrows in the soil of the human equation. The miner historically has been strong in body and proud in spirit. He is also an individualist. As compared with auto workers along an assembly line, for example, he is under a minimum of supervision; and in matters of judgment he is his own boss, on the job. He often takes the attitude that each ton of coal he mines is an obstacle personally overcome, a test of strength and guile between himself and nature. In developing his own work habits he often tends to bring a sense of animism to the problems of the pit.

But the machine's advent in coal is gradually changing

all that. Instead of the "going it alone" isolation of a single miner, or a pair or trio, the machine requires the synchronizing of many men, in gangs and crews, under more and more direction. It exacts, besides, a "quick-reaction" time, a direct reversal of the miner's traditionally slow and dogged ways. It calls, too, for the ability to adapt promptly, and a knack with bolts and screws becomes more valuable than the skill with pick and shovel acquired patiently after many arduous years.

The short-run effects of this new mechanizing of coal mines are tragic. Perhaps because of the very challenges and hazards of their occupation and the manual and mental dexterity it entails, miners are notably fond of their work. They are very reluctant to try anything else, even when the opportunity presents itself. Currently, of course, when they are discharged and seek to get jobs elsewhere the cards are stacked against them. They rarely possess other than mining experience and are hence thrust into the glutted market of unskilled labor. A few may obtain employment in new fields and succeed in orienting themselves to new pursuits. The rest are due for the relief rolls— which all too often form a halfway station along the route to America's own lower depths, the sphere of the "unemployables" who, sodden with despair, beaten into apathy, have ceased to be anything else than sleepers conjuring up dead dreams.

On the other hand, the long-run effects of mechanization* may prove a boon to the working force which is retained. Mechanization lightens the miner's physical tasks to an appreciable extent and increases his productivity, even though the machine offers perils of its own. It also helps to bring about higher wage scales by bettering the industry's competitive position in relation to other fuels—

* To cushion the shock of a too rapid mechanization, the union has employed the eminent consulting engineer, Dr. Walter N. Polakov, author of *The Power Age*, to help devise ways and means for "staggering" the introduction of labor-saving devices.

always providing, of course, that the kind of government participation which the union has trenchantly fostered will not end up either in direct government ownership or in a democratic collectivism where the anarchy of old-time competition will be once and for all extinguished.

The United Brotherhood of Carpenters and Joiners

I

THE building industry, a congeries of many diverse trades, is in many ways less a business than a form of speculation. On the one hand it is balance-wheel and barometer of American prosperity. It is a chief market for steel, stone, brick, wood, paint, glass. New buildings for factory, store, office, home immensely widen the demand for fan-belts, showcases, filing cabinets, and the almost endless array of commodities that come under the heading of household wares. In "good times" it employs about 2,165,000 workers annually. Millions of other wage earners depend upon its highs, lows, and medians. It is the largest single disburser of wages in the United States. Its leading firms, in their complete service from the architect's first smudgy "rough" to the completed skyscraper that challenges the wind, lightning, and rain, epitomize America's power-age efficiency.

On the other hand, the building industry is a symbol of what happens to men, money, morals, materials, and machines when competition to achieve monopoly control becomes unbridled and gallops away down the road of racketeering. An unholy alliance between the corrupt and corrupting contractor, the boss in the backroom, and the union business agent still accounts for hundreds of schools, hospitals, courthouses, along with private structures, that give a new meaning to the word "jerry-built," and that have enriched the underworld's argot with the term "get a contract," used to describe every mode of living, as if all Americans were a race of pirates existing on extortion.

Whereas many participants in the building industry re-

main men of honor and probity, its unsavory practices
have for two generations done much to lower business
ethics by the easy expedient of removing their foundation
of simple honesty. The unions within that industry reflect
a similar departure from the rules of virtue. Nowhere else,
in fact, is there to be found so cogent a proof of the axiom
that unionism in America is merely the other side of capitalism's coin. It is the same coin. It is not a token of any
other minting.

In general, five indigenous conditions keep the building industry in a state of turbulence and allow the doctrines
of laissez faire to reach a final ferocity. It is carried on out-
of-doors. It resorts to that systemless system known as
"sub-contracting." It is changeable. It is closely linked with
graft in politics. It endows the union's business agent with
the powers of a despot.

It differs from manufacturing, for example, in that the
latter is usually conducted within a plant, its location fixed,
its labor force relatively stable. A factory, moreover, has
ample storage space for materials to meet emergencies,
either for shutting down or for quickening operations.
The sheer bulkiness of building materials means that they
have to be used promptly, especially in an urban area. They
also have to be delivered on the site to "jibe" with the
arrival of the thousand and one other ingredients that the
modern edifice requires. Weather hazards of rain, sleet or
high winds can slow down the process of erection to an
appreciable extent, often stopping it entirely—a serious risk
since most building has to be completed within a specified
date on penalty of forfeit. If, for instance, a contractor fails
to have an apartment house ready for the renting season, he
faces great loss, perhaps bankruptcy. Moreover, his need
to obtain building permits, and to conform with fire, sanitation, zoning, and other regulations, as a rule requires him
to get and remain in the good graces of the political party
in power; and to help keep it there by one means or an-

other; and frequently it is futile for him even to bid on public buildings, national, state, or municipal, unless he is himself "one of the boys" or willing to "cut them in."

And as if to confound confusion all the more, the task of putting up a building is only technically in the hands of a single contractor. He is, of course, legally responsible for fulfilling the terms of his accepted bid as to size and the time of completion. Yet he is usually a broker, parceling out portions of the work to a myriad of subcontracting specialists in structural steel skeletons, in bricklaying, in decoration, and the like. Too often he is merely a shoe-string speculator, animated more by hope and nerve than by knowledge, and properly belonging to the company of the faro wheel or the roulette table. Moreover, the contractor often travels from city to city whenever an old job is finished and a new job is beginning, and his labor force is almost as migratory. Its interests are not tied up with a single employer but with many. In 1921 the Hoover Committee on Waste in Industry found that "one man, in the course of five and one-half years, worked for 76 different contractors, and was hired 108 times."

Yet the urgent necessity for maintaining a steady competent labor supply remains the chief cause of the contractor's vexations. He is, after all, always working against a deadline and speed is the essence of his effort. The passage of time, the fads and customs of renting and moving, and "doing-the-house-over" seasons all conspire to give the workers a bargaining advantage that they seldom enjoy elsewhere. Refusal to meet the wage and hour demands of his employees may make the contractor lose his shirt, since a strike in his particular industry is not so much a work-stoppage as a calamity. It expunges precious hours and days from a calendar that almost always is too short. If he fails to satisfy his workers, they lay down their tools with dispatch and watch the clock tick him into terms. If he tries to hold out against union claims, his only recourse is to hire strikebreakers, who are usually wasteful and inefficient and who are in imminent danger of receiving a sock on the chin from some union-hired thug. In this regard the contractors have only themselves to blame for the introduction of strong-arm methods. Around the turn of the century in New York, Chicago, and San Francisco, they began to employ toughs and gunmen to beat up recalcitrant labor officials who insisted that union standards, such as the closed shop, be enforced. In retaliation, unionists engaged the services of "gorillas" to slug "scabs" or to dynamite a half-completed structure if a contractor wouldn't recognize the validity of union rules. Long before Prohibition raised gangsterism to its highest glory, employers and unionists in the building trades had done more than any other groups in the country to smooth the path for the shakedown artist who provides "protection" on a weekly fee, and for other racketeers.

Naturally the immense influence wielded by the building trades unions has endowed its labor officials with a power often abused. The exercise of that power centers chiefly in the person of the union's "business agent." Three definite union needs presided over his birth in the early 1880's and his evolution has coincided, step by step, with the development of the industry from a handicraft to a "technologically tenuous" pursuit. In the epoch of bustles and bicycles-built-for-two, every union as it grew in membership and strength began to require a full-time official to represent it in its relations with the employer and with other unions, and to guide its internal affairs. Previously this function had been assigned to the traditional "job steward," as old as unionism itself. He examined "union cards," collected dues, kept nonunionists off the premises, saw to it that apprenticeship and other working rules were minded. And so long as the association between worker and employer remained in essentials that of the master journeyman and craftsmen, the "job steward" sufficed.

When, however, around the end of the nineteenth century, progress in science and invention changed construction methods from handwork to mechanized processes, and added to the "primary" brick and wood of the mason and carpenter a score of new materials and a score of new crafts, the situation became too complex for the "job steward" to handle in addition to his own task. He was, after all, an employee. If he paid more attention to union routine than to his own work, the employer would seek to get even by "riding" him, by giving him more arduous assignments since, as a union member, he was immune from discharge for "union activity."

With the growth of subcontracting, moreover, infractions of union regulations were more frequent and the unions had to have someone who could be always on the lookout to safeguard their interests. Hence the "business agent," in taking over the duties of the job steward and amplifying them, rapidly rose to dominance in the union's affairs. Since he was hired by the union he could talk back to the boss with impunity. Since he could devote his whole day to union problems, he gradually took into his own hands a manifold array of functions. He visited the job to reconcile any disagreements that might have occurred, to thwart violation of various and sundry union "rights, claims and priorities."

Today he also often serves as employment agent, treasurer, overseer, and organizer, with many prerogatives. His offices bring him tremendous influence, and often an even more tremendous revenue. He "gets around a lot." He knows where the "best," i.e. the longer-lasting, jobs are to be found and how they are to be dispensed.

The employer, of course, realizes that the "good will" of the business agent is not only valuable but vital. For the latter appears for the union in arranging wage scales and working rules and can penalize the contractor for ignoring either or both. The business agent is also his union's spokesman in central labor councils, where he meets agents from other unions and can lay plans for "sympathetic" walkouts.

But the business agent's ace-in-the-hole is his power to call strikes. The speed with which building construction is conducted makes the reference of disagreements to a union meeting or an "arbitration board" virtually impossible. Disputes have to be settled on the spot, and at once. The business agent, as union leader, is therefore judge, jury, clerk, and court-crier. He decides. Since he usually has "understandings" with the business agents of other unions, he can not only call for a strike for his own members but also often obtain "a sympathetic strike" involving all other workers on the job, enabling him to paralyze the most gigantic project within fifteen or twenty minutes.

The temptations to exploit all this influence for personal gain are always present, and largely irresistible. The contractor, of every degree and kind, is willing to pay for freedom from strikes, and to pay through the nose. In New York City, for example, the notorious "labor czar," Robert P. Brindell, was a kind of "super business agent" who took all the city's building trades for his province. Ignorant, ruthless, by turns dockhand and druggist's clerk, he had clawed his way up from the bottom until in 1913 he dominated the Pier and Dock Carpenters' Union mainly with the aid of his own strong-arm committee of former stevedores and wharf rats who displayed equal facility in the use of lead pipe or brass knuckles. In 1916, Brindell by making a deal with William Hutcheson, president of the United Brotherhood of Carpenters and Joiners, united his own union with the Brotherhood to enable him to operate under the mantle of relatively greater respectability. He also used this merger as the entering wedge for gaining a foothold, and later control, of all the city's Building Trades Unions. Within three years he had bargained and blustered his way into an absolute rule of the Board of Business Agents which late in 1919 he transformed into the Building Trades Council, getting it chartered as an official part of the A. F. of L. and preparing to hoist his Black Flag.

It was his ambition to create, through the Council, a monopoly of labor supply in the same way that the Building Trades Employers' Association, by collusive agreements among its member contractors and manufacturers, had monopolized the metropolitan market for electrical equipment, metal lathing, sand, marble, cement, plumbing fixtures, and the like. The Employers' Association discovered in Brindell a servant willing and eager to assist them in their efforts to extinguish all "independent" competitors outside the Association, and by thus "stabilizing" the industry leave all the pickings for their own group alone.

Hence on December 17, 1919, the Building Trades Employers' Association arranged with Brindell's Building Trades Council to hire only Council-approved workers who, in reciprocation, were to use their skills exclusively for members of the Association. The 115,000 craftsmen represented on the Building Trades Council by their business agents had to pay Brindell $1.00 a month for the privilege of being on his "O.K." list. Otherwise, as his assistant explained to them, "youse ain't going to get nothing."

But such dues for being allowed to work were only a part of Brindell's income. Wielding the power to assign or withdraw carpenters, electricians, bricklayers, wood, wire, and metal lathers, hod carriers, tile and marble setters and many more, on any kind of construction, he demanded his "cut" from everything and everybody, from a hot-dog stand on Coney Island to a skyscraper in midtown Manhattan.

He euphemistically referred to his bribes as "strike insurance" since his receipt of a "premium," ranging anywhere from $500 to $50,000, alone could guarantee a contractor the uninterrupted flow of labor energy on his working premises.

Even potent and renowned firms like Thompson, Starrett and Company, the George A. Fuller Construction Company, and Todd, Iron and Robertson* were unable to buck Brindell and had either to award their contracts to concerns he designated or pay him directly to avoid "labor trouble."

The Building Trades Council, under Brindell's reign, was more than ever before a subdivision of Tammany Hall to whose ward heelers he gave business agents' jobs at $75.00 to $150.00 a week. Furthermore, he never failed to split his "insurance premiums" with the sachems and sagamores who, in exchange, saw to it that the numerous complaints against Brindell's activities merely gathered dust in the files of the District Attorney's office, and that "Red Mike" Hylan, Mayor of New York, recognized his unselfish devotion to the public good by appointing him a member of the city housing commission.

Under such circumstances, employers and business agents were rendered even more cynical and hardboiled than before. They determined to "get theirs." Scruples vanished as the quest for easy money supplanted the desire to build. As not infrequently happens in the case of a government tax, or a raise in the wage scale, employers doubled and tripled the cost to them of the Brindell holdups, adding it on as "preliminary expenses" to their cost-plus estimates and bills.

Yet this triple alliance of corruption—employers, Brindell, and the bosses in the backroom—killed the goose that laid the golden eggs. During the four years of Brindell's ascendency (1919-22) New York City's construction costs zoomed 200 to 300 per cent, inducing an acute housing crisis which caused the state legislature to set up

---

* Mr. Hugh Robertson, executive vice-president of this company, has testified that he had personally handed over about $33,000 to Brindell upon the latter's promise to "keep things going quiet and smooth" on the $40,-000,000 Cunard Line Dock project which was being constructed by Mr. Robertson's firm.

its Lockwood Committee, with Samuel Untermyer as counsel, to investigate the reasons why single dwellings, apartment houses, hotels, theaters, and all manner of buildings, public and private, cost so much.

The Lockwood Committee lifted the lid over this cesspool of graft. It stirred up a considerable amount of public indignation and was subjected to a great deal of vituperation as the "enemy of the laboring man." It succeeded in sending Brindell to Sing Sing along with several of his aides. It failed, however, to stop Brindell tactics which, not only in New York City but throughout the country, remain (in somewhat less spectacular form) as some verification of the axiom that: "Behind every crooked labor leader is a crooked employer."

As a whole building trade unionists are indifferent or resigned to this sort of shakedown. The business agent controls the political setup within the union and to dislodge him would entail years of stubborn uphill struggle by rank and filers who would have no guarantee whatsoever that his successor would be any better. The majority regard the business agent's extortions as a "sideline" and since this money comes from the boss they are not unduly grieved. What they expect the business agent to do, however, is to "deliver the goods." If he has enforced rules, obtained wage increases, promoted greater "job security" they are fairly content. The graft, they think, is nothing out of their own pockets.

The contractor, of course, is the man who forks over. The heads of our most reputable concerns condone this practice or oppose it half-heartedly. Often unless the contractor "comes through" as requested, the support of the business agent is transferred to a competitor who has fewer scruples. And this "support" is significant. If a contractor named Phineas Peabody, let us say, refuses to be "swindled by a low-down racketeer," the word goes round that Peabody is a Simon Legree and a chiseler who would cheat the honest son of toil out of his last dime and is always having "labor trouble" and it would be best for all concerned if someone else were awarded the contract for, say, carpentry, or tiling, or plumbing, or electric wiring, or whatever.

In many cases the contractor merely succumbs to the policy of paying graft, since in the long run it may be cheaper to pay it than to live up to union rules, thus improving his competitive position. The business agent who receives an extra $100 or $200 or more per week as a token of the contractor's undying esteem and affection often looks the other way when nonunion materials are used and nonunion men are hired. In addition, the business agent is often presented with a "bonus" to prevent rival contractors from "muscling in" on territory preëmpted by the business agent's considerate friends.

The "cost-plus" methods prevailing in building construction make it easy for the contractor to pass on the overhead of tribute to the building owners or investors who, as a rule, prefer to blink at such customs rather than to have the completion of their project indefinitely postponed. And though many contractors deem it "good business" to buy insurance against labor difficulty from the business agent, the question remains, "good business" for whom?

II

AMONG the 2,165,000 workers engaged in building erection, with their 18 national unions and their 52 crafts, some 696,000 are carpenters, and about 300,000 of them are organized into the United Brotherhood of Carpenters and Joiners of America.*

---

* In 1937, the thirty-first annual report of the A. F. of L.'s Building and Construction Trades department listed by 150,000 carpenters in "good standing," a term which means merely that they have paid their dues, refrained from becoming public nuisances, and proclaimed their distaste for the C.I.O. and all its ways.

At the moment the Brotherhood is usually held to be the biggest affiliate of the A. F. of L.* and it has practiced, since its beginnings, the laissez-faire preachment of "What we can get, that's ours. Otherwise, leave us alone." It has been embroiled in more jurisdictional† rows than any other ten unions combined. It has sought to command allegiance from every group of workers in the field of construction that a flexible imagination could conjure up. For nearly sixty years of unbroken strife it has battled to win control over timber and sawmill workers, coopers, machinists, longshoremen, metal "lathers," and many more besides. Its credo of survival, fashioned in 1891, still remains "Once wood, it is always the right of the carpenter to install it no matter what the material now used may happen to be." And this "principle of substitution," by which it lays claim to any new process that has replaced an older one, is a steady war cry.

For all practical purposes, the Brotherhood ignores the implications of the doctrine voiced in 1935 by Dr. George Otis Smith, Director of the United States Geological Survey, that: "the entire framework of our civilization is being changed from wood to minerals as the end of our forest reserves comes into view and as modern machinery makes it possible to build more durably of sand and stone and clay of which there is no end. . . ." Nor has the Brotherhood been perturbed by the same authority's recipe for an office building: "Take by weight 60 parts of gravel, sand and crushed stone; 58 parts of tile and brick; 27 parts of building stone; 19 parts of cement and 16 parts of steel, with such other ingredients as copper and glass and asbestos, and paint to suit one's taste."

* Latterly this has been disputed by the Teamsters who claim 154,000 members, and assert that the 1936 secession of a vast number of lumber and sawmill workers from the Carpenters left the Teamsters the numerically strongest affiliate of the Federation.

† In union circles, the word "exclusive" is added to the dictionary's definition of jurisdiction as the "lawful right to exercise official authority, whether executive, legislative or judicial."

Rather, by means of a leadership that has tenaciously clung to the gospel of "once wood, it belongs to us," the Brotherhood has been consistently effective within the limits of its somewhat narrow objectives. It has also been extremely cautious and conservative. Only once has it hearkened to the gongs of political revolt. It is the archetype of "pure and simple" business unionism, its ambitions confined to the plain formula of "more pay for less work."

Less than fifty years ago, almost everything needed for building a home was made by the carpenter, right on the premises. He fashioned the newel post, as well as window frames and doors. Using ax and adze he cut pillars and beams. At present, however, an ever-larger portion of this work is done by machinery in the mill. It is then shipped "prefabricated" ready to be put into place. And this trend has transformed the carpenter from the skilled and versatile artisan of a generation ago into a modern "assembler" in a dozen different operations. His old-time insignia of handsaw and handplane are being supplanted by their power-driven descendants that bevel and true edges, rip beams, mold and mortise with nonhuman speed and precision—in much the same way, indeed, that the automatic hoist is replacing the hod, and the pneumatic drill the pick.

Way back in 1894, P. J. McGuire, Gompers' right-hand man and then secretary of the Brotherhood, was complaining that "year after year work is becoming less plentiful owing to the recent innovations of architectural construction. With the introduction of iron and steel frames in the larger buildings, with iron and stone staircases, tile floors . . . metal wainscoting, with cornices . . . in many cases of material other than wood . . . the increase and perfection of wood-working machinery, the chances of steady employment of carpenters are extremely uncertain."

At first, to combat the threat of such "recent innovations," the Brotherhood, ruled by the eloquent McGuire, a pseudo-Socialist, made its first, last, and only foray into the realm of reform. It assumed, vaguely enough, that by arresting the growth of the "trusts" which controlled and profited from the use of these new materials and labor-saving devices, it could somehow help to improve general economic conditions and thus create more jobs for its members, at better pay. It joined up with the Populist movement, dominated by farmers who in their "Granges" and "Alliances" were complaining of "10 per cent mortgages, and 10 cent corn," and invoking the great American cure-all of "more and easier money."

"The government of the United States," thundered McGuire at the Brotherhood's 1893 convention, "is great enough to issue an American paper currency of its own, without interest, direct to the people as a full legal tender for all debts. . . ." And a year later, he and the Brotherhood were helping to prepare the way for William Jennings Bryan's "You shall not press down upon the brow of labor this crown of thorns, you shall not crucify mankind upon a cross of gold." Barnstorming the country, McGuire exhorted the Brotherhood locals and other unions that: ". . . organized labor everywhere should insist on a bi-metallic standard of currency and the maintenance of silver on a parity with gold. We cannot permit the debasement of any part of our legal currency to suit the whims of the non-metallists . . . that they may depreciate values, undermine labor, reduce wages and at the same time . . . collect . . . every dollar of bonded indebtedness on mortgages that they hold against the industrial classes of the country."

But with Bryan's defeat in 1896, and the collapse of the period's anti-gold, anti-Wall Street crusade, the Brotherhood turned its back, once and for all, upon salvation by the state. Instead it concentrated upon more immediate goals such as obtaining the eight-hour day. It had, moreover, two difficult organization obstacles to overcome. It had to protect the bargaining strength of its members by excluding "green hands," by creating for itself a monopoly position, an exclusive franchise to certain types of construction activity. It had also to eliminate rival or "dual" unions seeking hegemony in the Brotherhood's own territory; and in pursuing this policy it locked horns early in its career with the Woodworkers' Union in what was to become the most costly and bitter quarrel over jurisdiction in American labor history.

In the late 80's woodworking machinery began to produce standard parts in quantity, depriving the outside carpenter of much work he had formerly done. It also opened the way for the scorned "saw and hatchet" fellow, that is, an unskilled "handyman." The Brotherhood promptly put forward the claim that the woodworkers in a factory belonged to the carpenters alone. They quickly revised their constitution to extend their authority, adding to their former categories of "carpenters, joiners, stair-builders and cabinet makers" three new spheres of influence: "millwright, planing-mill hand, or any journeyman running woodworking machinery."

As a sop to its competitor, the Brotherhood after a while granted to the Woodworkers complete control over all common "mill hands" and some furniture makers. It soon appeared, however, that this concession was enabling the Woodworkers to expand appreciably until in 1898 it seemed as if it would enroll 50,000 or more members. The Brotherhood didn't like it; and the Carpenters brazenly revoked their agreement with the Woodworkers, while the latter, angry and bellicose, appealed to the A. F. of L., asking for "full and sole jurisdiction over all factory woodworkers." After endless conferences, the A. F. of L. awarded jurisdiction rights to the Woodworkers' Union, pointing out that the Brotherhood had itself conceded such priority in a number of written pacts. The Brotherhood, however, balked. It refused to relinquish the dues and allegiance of its more than 30,000 woodworking adherents. It proceeded on the assumption that the A. F. of L. ruling didn't exist. It "raided" the membership of the Wood-workers, made trouble with their employers by refusing to touch products created by its rival, and generally raised havoc. It bribed, cajoled, plotted its way to supremacy in woodworking with such success that in 1907 the Wood-workers' Union had but a remnant of 7,000 of a 45,000 membership and "two thirds of these," lamented its last secretary, "are desirous of joining the Brotherhood of Carpenters because they realize the hopelessness of their condition."

In 1908 the A. F. of L., admitting the inevitable, reversed itself entirely, ordered the Woodworkers to amalgamate with the Brotherhood, and in 1912 Gompers himself pre-sided over the ceremony that united the contending fac-tions. In rendering a decision of this kind, however, the A. F. of L. established a precedent that has plagued it ever since. It had gone on record that "might makes right," and by letting the Carpenters "get away with it" encouraged other unions to imitate the Brotherhood's example. From that time on, the Brotherhood's behavior has often been in-defensible. In countless cases it has simply appropriated the jurisdiction rights of other unions. It has agreed to arbitrate differences, to accept as final the findings and recommenda-tions of various A. F. of L. boards as to jurisdictional claims and counterclaims. Yet on every occasion when the award of such agencies went against it, the Brotherhood threat-ened to resign from the A. F. of L. and ignored what, in union circles, is tantamount to a court order. In short, it has desperately held to the policy "heads we win, tails you lose."

In his struggle for existence, in his efforts to offset and outwit the results of technological change, the carpenter, through the Brotherhood, has acted on the belief that as a skilled craftsman he retains a special right to his job for which he has served a four-year apprenticeship, and in which he has acquired a special facility of hand and eye. He looks upon his functional ability as a vested interest, an unchanging property right, and he wants to prevent others from trespassing upon his own domain.

Of course, the desire to win control over a certain economic area is hardly confined to the carpenter, or any other unionist. Every businessman seeks to enlarge the sphere of his activity; and in the building industry itself, the architect and engineer often engage in jurisdictional feuds of their own about tasks that overlap. The contractor often ignores them both, drawing his own sketches, making his own calculations of stresses and strains, and dispensing with the services of a subcontracting specialist, say, in tiles. But since there are few effective organizations to enforce "working rules" among professional men and employers their quarrels rarely make the headlines.

The Brotherhood, however, keeps an Argus-eye on all similar matters. It prohibits, for example, the use of a journeyman's tools by "helpers" to strip forms from concrete, although they can do it quite as capably as the full-fledged $1.25 or $1.50 per hour carpenter. The Brotherhood justifies its work restrictions and its high hourly wage on much the same grounds. It points out that even in a boom year, like 1927, when more than six billion dollars were spent in building construction, its members averaged but 174 work days out of a potential 308. It argues that the seasonal character of the industry is hardly its own fault, and that the carpenter has to live and support his family the year round on what he can earn in the short and busy "peak period." Hence anything that will give him more employment, or stretch out the employment he has, is in his own mind warranted by the harsh laws of economic necessity.

Today the Brotherhood remains the bulwark of conservatism within the American Federation of Labor. It is run autocratically by "Big Bill" Hutcheson who at sixty-four still weighs three hundred pounds and stands six feet three inches. The Brotherhood's constitution which he amends at his own pleasure, together with his determined personality, have combined to centralize all power over union affairs in his hands. He presides over all conventions, calling them whenever the spirit moves him, letting a period of eight years (1928-36) elapse between convoking one national meeting of the Brotherhood and another. He appoints all committees. He issues and revokes all charters—with the consent of the executive board which he utterly dominates. He selects all the Brotherhood's $75.00 to $100.00 a week organizers and business agents. He pays himself $200.00 a week, plus substantial "expenses." He prefers to "raid" the membership of unions already formed rather than spend the Brotherhood's own funds for effective recruiting "on its own." He has conducted unceasing jurisdictional warfare upon painters, cement finishers, plasterers, asbestos workers and others, winning more often than he lost. He could see a carpenter in a steel robot, providing it could pay dues. That he has remained president of the Brotherhood since 1915 testifies in part to the timidity and inertia and cynicism of its rank and file, in part to Mr. Hutcheson himself.

In 1916, when he had been head of the Brotherhood for only eleven months, seventeen thousand New York City carpenters, in a series of special meetings, voted four to one to obtain a fifty-cent daily increase in their wages which had been unchanged since 1907. In accord with A. F. of L. practice they asked and received permission from their national officers to make this demand. After detailed negotiations with many different employers, the New York carpenters succeeded in signing contracts for this raise, covering however only fourteen thousand of their number. To extend the same benefit to the remaining three thousand, local chieftains planned to bring them out on strike on May 1. Portents of victory were propitious in view of a building boom that was starting.

Suddenly, inexplicably, Hutcheson ordered the strike to be canceled. He simply gave his command, without explanation. In any event it was too late. On the date specified the three thousand walked out. Then from Indianapolis, national headquarters of the Brotherhood, Hutcheson hurried to New York, went into occult sessions with various groups of employers. He emerged only after he had signed a new pact which stipulated that the three thousand strikers were to continue work at the old wage scale, and which nullified the fifty-cent advance already attained by the fourteen thousand others. He called a meeting attended mainly by seven hundred pro-Brindell men, told them what he had done, caught a train West.

As soon as the New York City carpenters recovered from their astonishment they passed a referendum which, by a vote of 11,745 to 119, rejected Hutcheson's "act of perfidy," while New York State's Council of Carpenters denounced his action as "a betrayal of the carpenters of New York, and a violation of the principles of the labor movement." Only Brindell's followers endorsed Hutcheson's mystic maneuver.

In a rage at this insurgency, Hutcheson expelled sixty-five New York locals which, in protest against this "corrupt bargain," went vigorously on strike. Again Hutcheson hastened to New York; and together with his ally, Brindell, began to line up strikebreakers to assist the employers in smashing this "unauthorized" rebellion. His reward was the even closer intimacy of Brindell* and, it is alleged, a 50 per cent share of the $85,000 which the employers paid out for their joint services. Despite Hutcheson's valiant efforts, however, the New York carpenters won their strike; and

* In 1922 Hutcheson narrowly escaped being sent to prison along with Brindell. In that year, Samuel Untermyer wired the A. F. of L. convention in Denver that, in his opinion, the "Federation will be . . . exceptionally fortunate if the Carpenters' Union can rid itself of Brindell's crony, Hutcheson, who has been an evil influence," but the Federation did nothing about it.

by appealing to the courts forced him to reinstate them all as "members in good standing."

In Chicago, eight years later, Hutcheson by similar tactics again aroused a large branch of the Brotherhood to violent protest, this time futile. Along with his assistant, Harry Jensen, he again met secretly with key groups of employers; again signed an agreement which, in this instance, embodied the essential provisions of the open-shop Landis Award against which Chicago carpenters, two years before, had waged a contest that bled them white. In this situation, too, opposition was greeted with prompt expulsion—a practice which Hutcheson has also regularly observed in Detroit, Philadelphia, Los Angeles, Boston, wherever and whenever dissenters raise their voices.

Today, as during the past twenty-three years, his opponents within the Brotherhood seem to have little chance of unseating him by internal changes. They are unorganized; they largely lack sufficient funds to take their grievances to court; and an attitude of resignation which is best expressed by the frequent statement that "It's all a racket, anyway—somebody else might be even worse," subverts the attempts (among the younger carpenters in particular) to oust him. Practically, moreover, he controls, through his business agents, all "work cards" which are as important to the building trades unionist as badge, uniform, and Civil Service rating to a policeman. Finally, Hutcheson's favorite habit of not counting votes cast against his policies complicates any appeal to balloting.

As the epitome of "business" unionism, modeled mainly after the abuses of a "business" society, the Brotherhood's concessions to altruism are characteristically few. It maintains a home for retired carpenters in Lakeland, Florida, pays death and disability benefits ranging from $25.00 to $400.00, and grants pensions to members who have paid dues for a minimum of thirty years. It also publishes a monthly magazine, *The Carpenter*, which exudes a quaint,

Victorian aroma. It is edited by the white-haired Frank
Duffy, Hutcheson's friend, secretary of the Brotherhood,
and an unconscious ironist. For in addition to diagram lessons on, for instance, roof sheathing for wood shingles and
correct methods for gluing wood turnings, *The Carpenter*
contains quotations such as may be culled from the Golden
Treasury of Great Thinkers, e.g., "Our reach must exceed
our grasp" (Browning); or "If the people can obtain a fair
compensation for their labor, they will have good homes,
good clothing, and good food. . . . The great interest of
this country is labor" (Daniel Webster). Every issue also
features inspirational "poetry" like these beginning lines:

> Help a fellow forward, man,
> Help a fellow all you can,
> When he's out of step and slow,
> Courage gone and can't say "No" . . .

Such communings with the Muses are mingled with
news items like the following: "Local 559 of Paducah,
Kentucky, writes that work is very scarce in that vicinity
and advises traveling brothers to stay away"; with reprints
from magazines and newspaper editorials assailing the
C.I.O. and all its ways; and still more reprints of William
Green's statements to the press, radio broadcasts, telegrams
to Congress. *The Carpenter's* "In Memoriam" department
recaptures the folksy flavor of a bygone day in its sanguine
caption:

> Not lost to those that love them,
> Not dead, just gone before;
> They still live in our memory,
> And will forevermore,

and in announcements such as: "Brother Jackie Davis,
charter member of Local Union 436, New Albany, Indiana, died recently of heart trouble while at work. The
New Albany charter was issued in 1900.

"Brother Davis was a faithful member of his local, always taking an active part in the local's activities. He served as Chairman, trustee and delegate to the Falls City Carpenters District Council."

On its blue cover *The Carpenter* proudly displays the Brotherhood's motto, "Labor Omnia Vincit." In 1924 when the Federation's executive council endorsed, tepidly enough, the candidacy of Senator Robert M. La Follette for President of the United States, Hutcheson campaigned for Coolidge. In 1932 he was chairman of Hoover's labor committee and was presumably promised the post of Secretary of Labor in the event of a G.O.P. victory. In 1936 he performed a similar function for John D. Hamilton and Governor Alfred M. Landon, and received the blessing of the American Liberty League as the beau idéal of a sane progressive labor leader when he resigned his place on the Federation's executive council to proclaim his hostility to its pro-Roosevelt resolutions.

He is devoutly the kind of Republican who hears the creak and clatter of the tumbrils every time anything is done to help the common man, especially "common" unskilled labor. At the 1924 convention of the Brotherhood he declared: "Every member of our organization should remember that it is a trade union . . . and that if any time any member advocates anything that pertains to Industrialism, or Communism, or any other ism that has for its purpose . . . the putting into effect of what might be termed industrial organization, there is no place . . . for that kind of man. . . . There are only two isms that should enter into our organization—that is, unionism and Americanism."

Indeed his antipathy to industrial unionism amounts to a kind of neurosis. In 1935 at the Atlantic City convention of the Federation John L. Lewis was pressing the question of industrial organization from the floor of what was to be a historic session. Hutcheson was furious. He kept shouting "Point of order!" to persuade the chairman, William Green, to cut short Lewis' plea of the moment: that the delegates of the rubber union, proponents of the industrial idea, had the right to be heard. At the first few interruptions, Lewis merely scowled, then remarked that Hutcheson's interjections were "pretty small potatoes." At this juncture, Hutcheson stood up, replied that he had been "raised on that kind of potato," which explained his size. He called Lewis a bastard, lumbered toward him with the gait of an angry bear, swung a haymaker at his chin. He missed, Lewis landed with a hard right to the face, and they both went down, grappling in a clumsy clinch, amid the crash of chairs and pandemonium.

The experience did little to minimize Hutcheson's hatred of the "industrial idea." He is currently the most powerful single force, both as a symbol and as an individual, standing in the path of unity between labor's warring factions. Whereas he himself is no longer a member of the Federation's executive council, he manages—through Frank Duffy—to retain a strong influence in its deliberations. William Green admires him, and fears him, views shared by most of the Federation's high command.* When the United Mine Workers and the International Ladies' Garment Workers "withdrew" from the Federation to form the C.I.O., the Brotherhood became the A. F. of L.'s biggest affiliate, and consequently the biggest per capita tax contributor to its treasury. Very conscious of the trump-card this situation gives him, Hutcheson is profane and adamant when peace proposals are broached on any but "craft by craft" terms. He announced in 1936 that if ever "the American Federation of Labor should accept the plan of the Committee for Industrial Organization— namely to organize all workers on an industrial basis, the only solution for our Brotherhood would be to sever our affiliation with the Federation."

* Green has described Hutcheson as "A strong personality, an outstanding character, a forceful man."

Recently, however, he has had to face what may soon in the future be his jurisdictional Waterloo. For in 1936 more than seventy-five thousand lumber, sawmill, cooperage, veneer, and furniture workers in the Northwest seceded from the Brotherhood on a double count. They claimed that Brotherhood organizers had been inefficient, if not corrupt, in leading the series of strikes that swept through the timberland of Washington and Oregon in late 1935 and early 1936. They were, they said, "fed up" with paying their "federal union" dues of twenty-five cents a month to the Brotherhood without being allowed to speak or "vote" at its conventions, or have any voice in shaping its policy. They therefore fashioned the International Woodworkers of America and on July 20, 1937, were chartered by the C.I.O. Hutcheson's reaction was a promise of "the sweetest little fight you've ever seen." He kept his word. He promptly persuaded Dave Beck, ruler of the Pacific Coast's "Teamsters," to prevent his men from trucking any "C.I.O." lumber, with the result that hundreds of camps and mills were shut down and thousands of lumberjacks and mill hands thrown out of work. There were bloody ax-handle rows injuring more than a thousand men seriously enough to require hospital attention, as adherents of the A. F. of L. Teamsters and the C.I.O. Woodworkers sought to settle the controversy in the traditional roughneck fashion of the Northwest.

For his own part, Hutcheson has forbidden Brotherhood carpenters to drive a single nail into "C.I.O. wood." In a special emergency circular, released in March, 1938, to the "officers and members of all Local Unions, District, State and Provincial Councils" of the Brotherhood, Hutcheson again emphatically warned his adherents that "they must not handle any lumber or millwork manufactured by any operator who employs C.I.O. or those who hold membership in an organization dual to our Brotherhood." He further instructed them "to appoint a committee to inform your employers and dealers that our members will refuse to touch C.I.O. products," and "Let your watchword be 'No C.I.O. lumber or millwork in your district' and let them know it."

Some time thereafter, the *Oregon Voter*, a conservative weekly, observed that "In Portland, the C.I.O. lumber workers are being starved into submission." They had been informed that, to get on the payrolls again, they must relinquish the Woodworkers for the Carpenters, since the Brotherhood's boycott has already threatened many prominent firms with bankruptcy.

Whereas Hutcheson, in this situation, will probably be able to impose his will once more, the implacable hatreds for him and the Brotherhood generated by this conflict have all the ingredients of a slow fuse and dynamite.

The American Newspaper Guild

SIRED in Walter Murray's basement bar in Cleveland, nursed in Heywood Broun's New York penthouse, and finally baptized in Washington's National Press Club, on December 13, 1933, the American Newspaper Guild is a bread-and-butter trade union, despite the still widespread belief that it is like the medical and bar associations. Collective bargaining is the Guild's reason for being; and by this means it seeks to raise pay, shorten hours, achieve greater job-security, and otherwise improve working conditions for its 16,797 members* in some three hundred newspaper and newsweekly plants throughout the country.

The idea of unionizing editorial employees is neither new nor startling. It has been talked about over the beer of America's Fourth Estate since the early 1890's. In Europe, of course, journalistic unions have existed for more than forty years. Denmark has three, the eldest of which, known as "Journalist-Foreningen," provides retirement pensions for its members while the other two, the "Copenhagen" and the "Provincial," defend professional interests, ethical and economic. France has thirteen of them, which in diversity resemble the Chamber itself, although the largest, the "Syndicat des journalistes," is strictly trade union in aims and methods and includes about 77 per cent of Parisian journalists or about thirteen hundred men. In Great Britain, the famous "National Union," founded in Fleet Street in 1907, is not only allied with the Printing and Kindred Trades Federation, but also displays an aggressive "labor consciousness" and numbers about 4,900 adherents or half of all England's newspaper writers.

But in the United States, until the past five years, the

* 13,505 "editorial," 3,292 "commercial."

frequent efforts to organize the "working press" ended in futility, with some few exceptions—notably in Milwaukee, Wisconsin, and Scranton, Pennsylvania, where newswriters' locals were chartered by the International Typographical Union in 1899 and 1907, respectively, and still are flourishing. In other communities, however, where the strong pro-labor atmosphere of Scranton and Milwaukee was lacking, the I.T.U. found the going so difficult that in 1923 it threw up the sponge and relinquished its jurisdiction over newsmen and women.

As a rule, such failures to organize American journalists resulted from inexperience on the part of the organizers; from the threatening or flattering attitudes of publishers who often seemed willing to replace veterans with youngsters; from the newswriter's feeling that "I can get a job elsewhere—there's always room for a good man"; and from apathy, general and specific. But probably more important than anything else was the ruling concept that the journalist was not a "workingman" in the customary and manual meaning of that term. He was rather regarded as a professional, like a surgeon; or as a craftsman, like an expert cabinet maker; or even something like the creative artist vaguely skirting the circle of belles lettres.

He had to write, and writing is a gift or at least a special aptitude. His function was cerebral, for he had to fashion coherency from a corner of life's chaos. His product was assumed to be qualitative and individualistic, as compared with the quantitative and standardized output of, say, a linotyper. Hence there was the possibility of immense variation between what he could do and what his associates in the same category might accomplish. He was, in short, supposed to be a free and self-expressing soul and the alleged Bohemianism of his way of life added luster to the legend of his "liberty." His composite portrait, as currently painted by the cinema and popular fiction, is still that of a Richard Harding Davis whose alter ego is Sherlock

Holmes, while shades of Don Juan and Horace Greeley hover in the background. By-line glory and the glamour of his job were held to compensate for a comparatively meager salary.

Today, however, the Guild advances a diametrically opposed view. Jonathan Eddy, its executive secretary and a moving spirit in its founding, says of it:

Our interests are identical with the interests of all those who have to work for a living. They are the same as any other wage or salary earners such as miners, carpenters, and musicians. Although the late Marlen Pew in *Editor and Publisher* once characterized us as being "red as the Kremlin's walls," we're really a white-collar labor union.

Of course we have special capacities, training, and wide variations in ability. But the same argument, that difference in merit argument, has been used by employers against everybody—retail clerks, or adding machine operators, or men along a conveyor belt whenever they attempted to better their conditions by forming a union. It's pertinent, isn't it, that actors, both stage and screen, with variations as wide—if not wider—than journalists are solidly organized . . . that Robert Montgomery, Joan Crawford, James Cagney, Fredric March and other leaders in the Screen Actors Guild who can't be compared with extras still fight to maintain extras' wage scales just the same. Take Leopold Stokowski. He's an ardent union member. He canceled a performance at a Pittsburgh theatre because the proprietors weren't meeting the obligations of their union contract.

Certainly Heywood Broun, president of the Guild since its founding, who receives $35,000 a year for his widely syndicated "It Seems to Me," along with other revenues from writing, reveals even greater union zeal than the famous film stars or the conductor of the Philadelphia Symphony Orchestra. From a philosopher who could be equally rapturous about poker, horses, and his own avocational painting, he has in recent years become a vigorous proponent of unionism and all it signifies, especially as it may be a way out for middle-class groups who own only their own talents and abilities. A genial open-handed giant of a man, fond of good drink and good food and their accouterments, he was born in Brooklyn in 1888 of socially prominent parents. He attended Harvard where his failure to pass an examination in French I prevented him from getting his diploma. After his non-graduation, he began to run the gamut of newspaper work, moving from reporter to re-write man to sports editor to dramatic critic to columnist, a category in which he often displayed a deep sympathy with the plight of the underdog. In 1917 as war correspondent with the American Expeditionary Forces his pungent satire on the ineptitudes of brass-hats angered George Creel, head of America's "Bureau of Public Information," who recalled Broun from scenes of battle.

During the postwar period of anti-labor hysterics, when Attorney General Mitchell Palmer was seeing Bolsheviki in his soup and Grand Kleagle Howard Stephenson was recruiting members for the Ku Klux Klan, Broun scourged their intolerance in words like steel whips.

Then, in 1927, when it appeared that the Anarchists Nicola Sacco and Bartolomeo Vanzetti were to be executed by the Commonwealth of Massachusetts for their profession of a creed, rather than the commission of any crime, Broun's protests in the *New York World* attained the eloquence of Zola's "J'accuse," created a great public stir, but aroused the resentment of the Pulitzer sons, owners of the paper, who refused to allow two of his columns to get into print. He resigned, only to reinstate himself at the turn of the year and then to be discharged four months later for his plaint in *The Nation* that New York City lacked any genuinely liberal newspaper—a direct hit at the *World*.

It is said that this experience shocked him into the perception that, despite his fame, his wide following, his personal friendship with the Pulitzers, he was merely another hired hand when he sought in all honesty to deal with issues in a manner that violated the social and economic outlook of his employers. It was this realization which perhaps prompted him to join the Socialist party, running for Congress on its ticket in 1930. Meantime, however, he had obtained his present post as columnist for the Scripps-Howard newspaper chain where, by the terms of his contract, he is permitted to express his opinions regardless of the company's editorial policy. Since Roy Howard, Chairman of the Scripps-Howard Board of Directors, is a foe of the Guild and all it represents, Broun's exercise of his contractual right to promote pro-Guild and pro-union sentiments has recently created a situation analogous to that which he faced with the Pulitzers and the old *World*. In any case, Broun's position as president of the Guild has served to integrate his random urges toward social usefulness into a definite philosophy that may be described as "the rest of us against the owning few."

He is, however, considered to be far to the "left" of the majority of Guildsmen. On the whole, they admire and respect him as a human being and as a journalist; and they also appreciate his hard spade-work in getting their union established; but they are less enthusiastic about his present political philosophy. It is often alleged, of course, that he is a "Communist tool," or a "fellow-traveler," or even a party member, albeit secretly. In recent years his not infrequent support of the party's official "line" has given currency to the quip that nowadays if you read Broun regularly you no longer have to buy the *Daily Worker*. Yet for all this apparent coöperation with the party, his own radicalism appears to be more firmly rooted in the moral righteousness tradition of the Whittiers and the Garrisons, the Channings and the Cobbs, than in the gospel according to Saint Karl. Like any other great polemicist, his need to exercise a high capacity for indignation has perhaps above anything else led him to sympathize with a political view that, whatever its other attributes, fulfills this need in copious measure. In any event he has identified himself completely with the aspirations of that new "labor" which includes insurance salesmen as well as iron puddler, and for $1.50 a week he currently conducts a column in the *C.I.O. News*, edited by the shrewd, sardonic Len DeCaux.

Broun shares the belief of many other observers that American publishers have only themselves and their own obduracy "to blame" for the Guild's formation. Beginning in 1931, for example, a wave of salary slashes engulfed the nation's city rooms. In altogether too many cases, publishers used the depression merely as an excuse for pay reductions ranging from 10 to 40 per cent, while dividends remained comparatively good. Often they explained that they hated to do it, but that reporters and copy and desk men, along with the clerical forces, were the only employees whose incomes could be curtailed since the printing craft unions of compositors, photoengravers, pressmen, stereotypers, mailers, and the like would resist wage cuts by strike action and perhaps throw everybody out on the street.

As a consolation prize, this argument, which became a publishing cliché, provoked unexpected repercussions. It turned thoughts toward unionism as a defense against insecurity, talk over the beer grew louder, and the question "If they [the printing trades craftsmen] can do it, why can't we?" was put with a new belligerency. Meanwhile, under the NRA, the newspaper code was a dead letter though able administrators tried to bring it to life. Resentments burned hot and high among the country's working press when their claims and suggestions were ignored day after day by the code's do-nothing grievance board.

A rallying point for this umbrage, the Guild, brain child of four Cleveland newsmen, gradually got under way, and at the outset executed a telling bit of strategy.

It conducted a nation-wide survey that disclosed that the average income of a reporter after twenty years of experience was $38.00 a week whereas minimum pay for mechanical workers on newspapers who were unionized averaged from $50.00 to $70.00 a week after four or five years of service. Furthermore, it appeared that but 10 per cent of America's 24,000 editorial employees earned $50.00 or more a week; that 26.5 per cent made between $32.00 and $49.00 a week; that 47.5 per cent received less than $32.00 a week; and that 27 per cent had to work for $20.00, or less, a week.

The results of this investigation were broadcast far and wide; and in response to the realism of such statistics, newsmen and women very soon began to sign on the Guild's dotted lines, pledging to pay into the Guild treasury $.75 a month if they earned up to $25.00 weekly; $1.40 up to $40.00; $1.75 up to $75.00; $2.00 up to $100.00; and $2.50 for any income more than $100.00 a week.

The Guild's quick growth (it had enrolled about six thousand members by January, 1936) stirred American publishers to a renewed solicitude for freedom of expression which, they said, the very existence of the Guild would endanger. In reply Guild spokesmen, especially its wry, knowing secretary, Mr. Eddy, denied that "we wish to control or influence editorial policies" and pointed out that the Guild had time and again gone on record as opposing any propaganda in news sources.

The American Newspaper Publishers Association, along with other similar alliances, was not convinced. Its general counsel, Mr. Elisha Hanson, who was later retained by the Associated Press to war simultaneously against the Guild's objectives and the constitutionality of the National Labor Relations Act, assured interviewers that "affiliation of newspaper reporters or editorial writers with an organization which can demand or command . . .

support of any particular program affecting broad public interest ". . . cannot be countenanced by a publisher who wishes to preserve the integrity of his news columns."

The issue found its cause célèbre in the case of Morris Watson, an Associated Press writer who was discharged for his Guild activity with the phrase that he would "be happier elsewhere." After several hearings the National Labor Relations Board sustained Watson's contention that he had been dismissed because of his devotion to the Guild and ordered his reinstatement. But Associated Press officials, along with many members of the American Newspaper Publishers Association, objected to this ruling. They insisted that it be threshed out in the courts. They asserted that even if Watson had been fired for Guild activity the National Labor Relations Board had no right to intervene and so violate freedom of the press. The brief filed by their attorney, Mr. Hanson, among other things expressed their fear that "they [their employees] may organize to destroy their employer; to tear down the government; to support the government; to aid a political party or oppose it; to indulge in national or international controversy; to control the source of news and flow of information to influence public opinion."

To Guildsmen this mode of reasoning seemed to stem from either ignorance or hypocrisy. They argued that publishers have consistently done most of the very things which, in the Watson case, they viewed with alarm, namely, "to aid a political party or oppose it" (in New York City, for example, the *Herald-Tribune* is as rabidly Republican as the *Post* is pro-"Third" New Deal); "to indulge in national or international controversy" (William Randolph Hearst virtually started the Spanish-American War by his brand of yellow and jingo journalism); "to control the source of news and flow of information to influence public opinion" (methods of "subscriber-control" over the great press services, the "A.P." and the "U.P.," enable the publisher to set the "tone" of news dispatches; almost every owner of every news organ in the United States has his own list of "Sacred Cows" about whom nothing uncomplimentary can be written, and his own group of advertisers who must not be alienated by news or views that might impair their profits and who may also have their publicity releases, disguised as bona-fide news, printed at regular intervals).

Implicit in the Hanson line of argument is the assumption that publishing is a very special business, occupying so unique a niche in society and rendering so vital a service that it cannot by its very nature permit the unionizing of its editorial departments or come under the purview of a government which may seek to regulate conditions of employment.

The Guild replies that ever since the NRA an incredible amount of Pecksniffian piety has been put forward by publishers concerning that very serious question, freedom of the press. Often to forestall government rulings about wages and hours, publishers have advanced the thesis that they should be exempt from any such interference* since "the American newspaper has always been an institution affected by the public interest."

That is correct. But, the Guild maintains, so are electric light and power companies "affected by the public interest" and in essentially the same manner. After all, the Guild view holds, a newspaper owner is engaged in producing a commodity for public consumption. He is doing it for profit. He is doing it at his own risk. The character of his undertaking does not by itself make him a savior of humanity, nor yet the kind of altruist who is indifferent to red ink on his ledger, nor is he expected to be either one or the other. He is a businessman. His is distinctly a private enterprise. Unlike the public utility corporation, he doesn't

---

* There is no record, however, of any American publisher refusing "government interference" in the form of specially reduced post-office rates and other subsidy-like services.

even have to obtain a franchise from the government of the community he serves. Under the Constitution, he may advocate monarchy, Mohammedanism, or mock-turtle soup as a cure for nervous debility.

His function, however, since he owns a *news*paper, is (as the Guild sees it) to gather and disseminate news facts and information and opinions that will please his own variety of readers. For it is upon the basis of circulation gained by his special kind of editorial content, and the reader-interest he develops, that advertisers buy his space; and the sale of space is the chief source of his revenue and of his profits, since usually the 2 or 3 cents for a newspaper, or the 5 or 15 or 25 cents for a magazine, don't begin to cover the costs of production.*

From this point of view, if the newspaper owner instructs his editors to dilute or distort the reasonable reportorial accuracy of an event, he is simply in the same category as a baker who puts alum in a loaf of bread. In brief, the Guild believes, a publisher's obligation to the public welfare is no more and no less than that of any other businessman who is guided by simple honesty and seeks to purvey his article at a profitable price. In no other respect does the publisher "owe" anything to the public; and in turn the public owes him nothing, nor can its agencies of government in all logic be expected to owe him immunities not granted to other business.

Since in a democracy, however, ready access to reliable news is a vital necessity, there has properly grown up that proudest tradition of American journalism: the separation of news columns from editorial pages. Despite notorious exceptions, this practice has been frequently

* As a result, the American press has been and largely remains, strongly anti-union. It isn't only that labor unions don't advertise, but that the commercial, industrial, and financial firms which do advertise rarely welcome the unionization of their employees. In this respect, the publisher believes that unless he defers to the feelings of his advertisers they will withdraw their patronage of his pages.

maintained by responsible publishers, out of pride in their product, and also from a sense of moral obligation. And it is on this point of the purity of news sources that Guild opponents continue to concentrate their fire.

Early in 1937, in Flint, Michigan, Mr. Russell B. Porter, correspondent for the New York *Times*, was denied admission to Fisher Body Plant No. 1, held by sit-down strikers, because he lacked a Guild card, while another reporter who showed Guild credentials was allowed inside and shown courteously around.

It must be pointed out that Mr. Porter's predicament was not directly the result of anything said or done by the Guild, but was rather due to a decision of a local strike committee which, it appears, acted upon the assumption that union men must not only stick together but are also more to be trusted. The implications of this incident are obvious enough.

On the other hand, it should be recalled that the very creation of the Guild has done much to improve the dependability of reports on labor conditions if only because Guild members have been permitted to observe meetings and conferences from which all reporters were previously barred. In former times, for example, in New York, Detroit, or San Francisco, a reporter often would try to cover a meeting of one of the maritime unions, say, but only at the risk of contusions. He might get as far as the secretary, who would begin to explain the situation, when a couple of the rougher brethren would inquire who the stranger was and upon being informed of his identity would usually give him a minute or less in which to make his exit unaided. This behavior merely reflected the attitude, still pervasive in American labor, that newspapers are invariably on the employer's side and that therefore the reporter was somewhat of a stool pigeon who put in an appearance not to get a story but to "get something on them," or invent it.

The Guild, however, has accomplished a great deal in modifying, if not overcoming, this atmosphere of distrust. Its own members have broken the ice of entrance into labor circles for the profession as a whole. It has in this way helped, rather than hampered, other non-Guild journalists to replace second-hand accounts by their personal observation.

In this regard, the Guild—with its emphasis upon high standards of professional conduct—points out that it is doing service in bolstering faith in newspaper veracity and perhaps helping to save certain publishers from themselves, from the penalties of their own excesses. It was no accident, Guild members say, that one of Huey Long's most cogent appeals to the "common man" consisted of references to "them lyin' newspapers." The point merely confirmed the experience of millions of wage earners who had seen reports of their routine unionizing efforts blown up into implications of "subversive" action, as if their demand for decent living standards were somehow un-American. Their tendency to suspect the validity of the news has been considerably arrested by the Guild, through its insistence upon a "favor the facts" approach.

Notwithstanding all this, the attorney for the Associated Press, in his appeal* to the Supreme Court in the Watson case, contended that Mr. Watson in the course of his allegiance to the Guild tended to favor labor's cause and that if he were reëmployed his pro-labor prejudices would filter through his work, since the author and his creation are "one and inseparable"; and that this circumstance would undermine that "freedom of expression" which must be "jealously protected."

In rebuttal, Mr. Morris Ernst, representing the Guild as a "friend of the court," maintained that any such premise

* *Associated Press* v. *National Labor Relations Board*, included 301 U.S. 1-147 (1937) as one of the five famous decisions in which the Supreme Court upheld the National Labor Relations Board and validated the Act which gave it being.

in itself "confuses freedom of the press with integrity of the news; that the Constitution does not guarantee the objectivity of the press, nor is objectivity obtainable in a subjective world; and that the question . . . really raised is not whether news shall be unprejudiced but rather whose prejudices shall color the news." He further said, in effect, that under the National Labor Relations Act the newspaper proprietor is still boss of his business and has the final word in formulating its policy. No matter how many of his editorial employees are organized, he still retains the "ultimate blue pencil"; and if a writer's work is displeasing by virtue of any bias, the publisher may reject his copy, change it, or discharge its author as he may see fit.

Of course, this whole question of the objectivity of the news contains the vestigial remains of the ancient quest for absolutes. Many centuries ago the Greeks agreed that only the gods were impartial. Of late there is very little evidence to show that either they or their impartiality inhabit the corporeal forms of publishers, reporters, or anyone else.

While the battle still rages along this free-press front, the Guild is successfully trying to enlarge its present enrollment of about 48 per cent of the editorial and 2.5 per cent of the commercial newspaper employees in the United States. For its jurisdiction, which originally included only newswriters and others connected with news-handling such as photographers, artists, layout men, retouchers, editorial secretaries, copy boys, and the like, has been recently extended to members of accounting, advertising, and circulation departments—everyone, in fact, who has anything to do with a newspaper, except executives, and the printing trades craftsmen who are already unionized.

In almost all the larger cities, such as New York, Chicago, Philadelphia, Boston, Detroit, Cleveland, and San Francisco, the Guild has enlisted a majority of the working press on dailies and on the news associations—the Associated Press, the United Press, etc. It has forty-seven signed contracts, including sixteen papers of the Scripps-Howard chain, along with working agreements with most of the Hearst press.*

In 1936 it joined the American Federation of Labor, but a year later, at its national convention, voted to affiliate with the Committee for Industrial Organization.† It is concentrating at present upon "vertical rather than horizontal spread into new territory." There are, after all, 2,666 daily and 12,165 weekly newspapers in the United States which not only have an estimated circulation of 38,962,000 but also contain innumerable smaller units, scattered from coast to coast, rendering travel costs to many of them prohibitive for the trio of organizers, which is all the Guild can currently afford.

Its emphasis upon increasing gains already achieved in various plants is therefore making a virtue of necessity, especially in view of the frequent difficulty in collecting dues. For the fiscal year 1937-38, Guild auditors reported an operating deficit of $13,000, outcome of the laxity of the locals in getting and remitting assessments and per capita payments to meet a very businesslike budget drawn up to balance with seemingly certain revenues.

But whatever its financial standing at the moment, the symbolic significance of the Guild can hardly be over-stressed. It represents a new awareness among a white-collar, native-born, exceptionally well-educated group, imbued with a middle-class psychology, that its own economic status is neither more secure than nor superior to that of the "common laborer" in overalls or dungaree.

It also helps to underscore the vast changes that have

---

* It has flourished particularly in New York City where it is recognized as exclusive bargaining agent by the *World-Telegram*, the *Post*, the *Daily News*, and the *Mirror*.

† This vote of delegates was contested by various Guildsmen but a referendum among the entire membership upheld the decision by a 2 to 1 majority.

accompanied the development of the American newspapers as a democratic institution during the past 125 years.
From the times of Benjamin Franklin's *Pennsylvania
Gazette* up through the days of James Gordon Bennett's
Herald, the journalist was usually a graduate printer, often
as absorbed in the mechanical problems of his calling as
in its editorial practice. Contemporary writers, mindful
of his printing craftsman origins, referred to his occupation as the "newspaper trade." The journalist needed but
little capital since he could start his paper "with a shirtful
of type and a cheese press." Up until the 1880's, in fact,
an ambitious compositor could often beg or borrow funds
and establish his own newspaper in, say, a county seat. As
editor-proprietor who had a hand in every phase of his
enterprise, he was answerable to himself alone. His income
in general derived directly from the sale of his papers, plus
some little advertising by local merchants and some occa-
sional "national" advertising of toiletries, especially soap,
and patent medicines. There was no Ford Motor Company, no Standard Oil, no General Foods, no Iron and
Steel Institute to solicit his "favorable views toward business" by allocating to him a due portion of million-dollar-
a-year advertising appropriations. He was the free and
fighting journalist of an earlier pioneering tradition, the
"poor man's advocate" and the "people's friend." He was
looked upon as a "professional" like the minister or the
doctor rather than as a "businessman."

By the beginning of the World War, however, technological advances in getting and distributing the news,
the constant increase in literacy, and the tendency of merchants and manufacturers to use the newspaper more and
more as a medium for selling their wares, required the
installation of rotary presses, linotypes, stereotyping and
other expensive machinery if the newspaper proprietor
was to "keep up with the times." At present the physical
plant investment for even a "country" newspaper, serving

a community of from ten to a hundred thousand, costs about $10.00 per unit of population. Hence the trade (printer-journalist) which had turned into a profession (editor-proprietor) has today become a business (publishing)—in certain respects a very big business, indeed. When in 1879, for example, Robert Wylis Scripps started the *Penny Press* (now the Cleveland *Press*), his borrowed few thousands sufficed. Today it would cost about $100,000,-000 to duplicate the plant facilities and connected real estate owned by the Scripps-Howard chain which he founded.

Graduates of modern "schools of journalism" thus rarely dream of buying or starting a newspaper of their own. The capital outlays—a minimum of $100,000 for a town of 10,000 inhabitants, $1,000,000 for a city of 100,000—preclude any such possibility, save in the rarest instances. Instead, they sell their services to someone else who owns the physical equipment.

According to William Allen White:

Merchandising of the news for a long while to come will be affected as it is now with a strong property interest. It will require machinery to assemble the news. It will require capital to distribute the news. And capital, today or tomorrow, always has a lively sense of its own advantage . . . is instinctively . . . class-conscious. It is that class consciousness which is discrediting the press of the world today, especially in the English-speaking democracies. Any newspaper in any American town represents a considerable lot of capital for the size of the town. The owners of newspaper investments, whether they be bankers, or stockholders of a corporation, or individuals, feel a rather keen sense of financial responsibility, and they pass their anxiety along to newspaper operatives whether these operatives be superintendents known as managing editors, foremen known as city editors, or mere wage-earners known as editorial writers, copy-desk men, reporters or what not. This sense of property goes thrilling down the line. It produces . . . a bias that in time becomes—unconsciously and probably in all honesty—a prejudice against any man, or any thing or any cause that seriously affects the right, title or interest of all other capital, however invested.

In short it is this loyalty to existing property stakes, transmitted by publishers to their newswriters and others, that explains much of the hostility of the American press toward unionism which, by its nature, seeks to modify the absolute exercise of "property rights." Newspaper owners are therefore apt to resent the new identification of their editorial staffs with the "ordinary wage earner" by way of the Guild.

When at its 1936 convention the Guild recommended "independent political action by labor" and urged its officers and branches to coöperate with other union groups for that purpose, the officials of New York City's *World-Telegram* singled out this decision for special attack:

It is along this line that minority pressure groups have proceeded in Italy, Russia and Germany with a resultant destruction of free and independent journalism. In each of these countries the entire national press is committed to the support of a single political faith, and in each the first requirement for holding a newspaper job is adherence to that faith. The Guild formula today is the Farmer-Labor party. Tomorrow it may be Communism, Fascism, Republican, Democratic—or any other political dogma that appeals to its leadership. This paper can have nothing whatever to do with such an intellectual regimentation in the newspaper profession.

In Section 4a of its constitution, however, the Guild expressly stipulates that "no eligible person shall be barred from membership, suspended, fined, expelled or discriminated against by reason of sex, race or religious or political convictions or because of anything he writes for publication"—a doctrine that is hardly endorsed by the dictator-ridden countries mentioned by the *World-Telegram* management which, after protracted negotiations, signed a pact with the Guild, granting a forty-five hour week, seniority ratings, and other demands.

However, the Guild's "preferential shop," a special feature of its contract, still arouses almost as much publisher antagonism as its official sympathy with the political aims of labor in other spheres. Recently a conference of representatives from eleven different newspaper associations condemned the Guild's kind of contract on the ground that "a closed shop means a closed editorial mind"—a somewhat extraneous pronouncement from the Guild's point of view since it is not supposed to concern itself with editorial policy, but only with bettering the salaries, hours and general job-security of its members. Under the terms of the "preferential shop" agreement, the publisher, should he desire to add to his staff, first asks the Guild to furnish qualified candidates for any jobs he may want to have filled. If within thirty days the Guild is unable to supply satisfactory personnel, the publisher chooses anyone he pleases "provided however" that "no such person shall be given employment if he has been expelled or suspended from the American Newspaper Guild . . . and has not been reinstated." Furthermore, the publisher, if he hires someone outside of Guild ranks, must require his new man to affiliate himself with the Guild, also within a thirty-day interval. In addition, the Guild has introduced into its contracts a "dismissal indemnity" clause to buffer the blow of being thrown out of work. Thus, whenever an employee is for any reason laid off, the publisher must pay him a sum equal to one month's pay for each year of employment; and in computing the amount of this dismissal indemnity the base rate used must always be the highest income received by the employee within six months prior to the date of separation.

The growing identity in structure, methods, and outlook between the Guild and other unions will perhaps produce some drastic changes in the American labor movement itself—despite the fact that the very name "Guild" was chosen to placate various potential adherents who in the beginning objected to unionism as such. It is not alone that the Guild has adopted "typically union tactics," finding out what it means to picket, and conducting several successful strikes, notably in the *Seattle Post-Intelligencer*. For as Guildsmen take their places in various labor councils, they are brought into more intimate contact with labor's problems and its increasing tendency to look toward their political solution. It may therefore be that the Guild will henceforth supply a caliber of intellectual assistance that American labor, with few exceptions, has regularly spurned. It is no disrespect to the "honest workingman" to say that the average journalist as a rule is more articulate than the plasterer, or brakeman, or quiller and has a larger grasp of social and economic issues than they. Journalists, moreover, are inclined to think in terms of political action, since it is linked closely with word-power. They also have little awe of legislators, government officials, or lobbyists. They have seen too many of them at close range. And it must be recalled that the journalists of London, Leeds, and Manchester, following Shaw and Wells and the Webbs, helped largely to incubate the British Labor party. Their American colleagues may play a similar role here; and though this whole trend is still incipient, it is certain to be one of the most crucial aspects of the Guild's future.

The International Ladies' Garment Workers' Union

"The Union as a Way of Life . . ."

THE International Ladies' Garment Workers is far more than a trade union. It is also a welfare agency, an educational institution, a philanthropic society, and a kind of experimental station for the amicable adjustment of industrial disputes.

It was formed on June 3, 1900, at a "national convention" held in New York City's "Labor Lyceum" on East Fourth Street and attended by eleven delegates. They represented the dubious but eager two thousand members of seven different cloakmakers' and pressers' unions located in Manhattan, Newark, Philadelphia, and Baltimore. The founders were able to raise thirty dollars in cash which covered the cost of the charter and seals that signified the International's affiliation with the A. F. of L. and left enough over for the general secretary to buy a ledger, a bottle of ink, pen and nibs, and stationery, which he transferred to his two rooms in a Lower East Side tenement, first "office" of the union.

Today the International has five million dollars in its treasury reserves, invested chiefly in Federal, state, and municipal bonds. It has 262,000 members, 70 per cent women, 30 per cent men, many of whom display an almost religious devotion to their union, its aims, its policies, and its leadership.

They pay dues ranging from 25 to 35 to 50 cents a week, or about a penny for every dollar they earn.* Certainly they get an amazing lot for their money—more perhaps than the adherents of any other union in the world.

* Dues income of all affiliates for 1937 amounted to $3,700,116, of which the International's central office received $1,441,000 as its "per capita" of 15 cents a week for each member.

In the thirty-eight years of its existence, the International has reduced their hours from 70 to 60 to 56 to 48 to 40 to 35 and, beginning in 1939, to 32½ per week. It has similarly helped to raise their real wages to a very appreciable extent, and to eliminate many and diverse health hazards. Yet its significance in the American labor movement is that it has gone beyond these manifestations of intelligent unionism. Propelled by the special conditions of women's garment making and by the aspirations of its polyglot membership, it has evolved a philosophy of responsibility to industry and to the community at large that in itself forms a "case study" of socialistic aims and ideals as adjusted to and modified by the American environment.

Up until about 1870 "ready-made" dresses and gowns and hoopskirts, capes and cloaks and coats, mantillas and mantuas were made mostly by native-born women of Welsh, Scotch, and Irish ancestry in the shops of the merchant who specialized in "Ladies' Furnishings and Notions" and who sold either by the yard or the garment. It was a trade largely dominated by German Jews whose forbears in Berlin, Munich, and Frankfort had for generations conducted most of the clothing commerce in the First Reich.

In America such merchants, or merchant-manufacturers, allotted a space in store or warehouse to the work of women who plied needle and thread and pedaled at Mr. Howe's "most marvelous and intricate" machine, and were as a rule presided over by an "imported" French tailoress who saw to it that the results of all the sewing, cutting, pressing, pleating, basting, and fitting at least approximated the fashions decreed by Paris.

Within the quarter of a century between 1870 and 1895, however, three crucial changes occurred in the industry. The first was technological. In 1876 the heavy steel cutting knife was patented and put on the market. It enabled the operator to cut several folds at once, even of thick velvets and woolens and brocades, but considerable strength was required to wield it and men began to replace women in doing the job. The second change was in the division of labor—quickened by an expanding market and improvements in the sewing machine which together fostered the "contracting system" with its sweatshop evils. As business grew, the merchant-manufacturers were reluctant to crowd their shops with garment makers who occupied space better devoted to the still brisk trade in piece goods and finished apparel. Gradually, in Boston, New York, Philadelphia, Chicago, and Baltimore, such dealers began to "let out" first portions and then nearly all the manufacture of the cheaper "ready-to-wear" goods to "outside" shops, the owners of which guaranteed to furnish clothing made up to specifications.

At the same time the growth of railroads extended the demand for "boughten" raiment even to rural areas, while in the cities the élite and their imitators were beginning to give up their seamstresses, permanent or traveling, and to patronize the custom shops.

In the single decade 1880 to 1890, the industry enlarged the value of its output from $32,000,000 to $68,000,000 annually; its invested capital rose from $8,000,000 to more than $21,000,000; the number of its establishments increased from 562 to 1,224, and the number of its workers from 25,192 to 39,149.

It was obviously a "coming" business. What was more, it was relatively easy to enter. If you could obtain a "contract" or "bundles" from the larger merchant-manufacturer, you could set up an outside shop of your own for as little as $50.00. The sewing machine was cheap and could be bought on the installment plan or rented on a monthly basis. It was small and several could be installed in a fair-sized room. Motive power was supplied by the operator's own foot-action on the treadle. The process of production itself was easy to learn, and its more elaborate phases could be picked up with a few weeks of training.

To meet orders that often swamped their facilities, the merchant-manufacturers—some of whom were becoming wholesalers and retailers only—thought it easier and cheaper to place upon the outside contractor the task of breaking in new labor and getting out the finished goods. They believed that otherwise they could never carry on their business since "the number employed . . . in making the garments . . . is so vast that it would be next to impossible to furnish sufficient workrooms for their accommodations in the same buildings where merchandise is sold."

By 1893 this practice had fastened itself upon the industry to such an extent that the New York State Bureau of Labor reported in that year that in Manhattan out of "a hundred wholesale-cloak houses" only "half a dozen now provide their own factories and workshops." Such firms as Oppenheim, Collins in New York City, Marshall Field in Chicago, and Day, Callaghan in Boston each had as many as twenty-five or thirty "outside shops" turning out women's wear for their counters.

Together with such developments, and marking the industry's third great change, was the vast new influx of Jews from Russia, Poland, and Rumania, comprising 10.7 of the total immigration to the United States from 1891 to 1900. They came to escape pogroms and every other kind of social, political, and economic restriction. They came to see if the tales awesomely told in the Ghetto about the "golden land," "Columbus' country," were really true; if America was a place where a man could worship as he pleased and by the exercise of mind and muscle "work himself up" in the world.

By and large they were divided into three groups. First were the artisans, blacksmiths, carpenters, shoemakers; but the majority were tailors, a fact which predisposed them to seek employment in the needle trades. The second group consisted of the more prosperous moneylenders, dealers in grain, and storekeepers seeking to escape the persecution of the bureaucrat who insisted on a "shakedown" under threat of depriving them of their licenses and hence of their livelihood. They usually brought a little capital with them to this country; and the small amount required to buy an interest in an outside shop or start one of their own suited their purpose admirably.

In the third group were the "intellectuals." Whereas the others had traveled to the Land of Promise motivated largely by the more ordinary religious and economic reasons, the intellectuals were animated by an idealism that found expression in such movements as the "Am Oilom," or "Eternal People." It was a "back-to-the-land" society which in 1882 raised funds in Kiev, Vilna, and Riga to send immigrants to this country and establish agricultural settlements in Louisiana, South Dakota, Kansas, and Oregon. The ferment released by such forces as Darwin, Comte, Marx, and Bakunin, along with accounts of Robert Owen's ventures, which had been discussed a good deal in German, then the language of the educated Jew, had also instilled into many of the intellectuals the ambition to build a new social order. One especially fervid group set up a communist colony, "New Odessa," in Oregon, which, like most of its predecessors, whether Fourierite phalanstery or Brook Farm, failed to regenerate mankind and lasted but a few short years.

When they arrived in America most of the intellectuals were unable to earn a living as sons of the soil, as scholars, as philosophers, or as the engineers of the new coöperative commonwealth. They had to take what work they could get. They therefore labored alongside of other immigrants who, with the assistance of the various "Jewish Aid" organizations, had been placed in jobs with their coreligionists, living among their countrymen—who had preceded them here—to gain some surety and guidance in a strange new world. For the most part unable to speak English, desperately poor, willing to work for anything, they were absorbed by the thousands into the contracting shops that almost hourly were opening up in the cities of the Eastern Seaboard. Agents from such concerns—mainly mere "holes-in-the-wall"—would meet incoming boats at Ellis Island and mingle with the steerage passengers, trying to spot tailors and offering them jobs, and keeping an eye peeled, too, for husky blacksmiths or droshky drivers who could be trained to run the heavy, hot irons over the pressing boards.

The majority of these newcomers to the American garment industry found Gehenna instead of Canaan. Sweatshops were at this time moving toward their meridian of horror and degradation. Many hundreds of them were located in tenement house fire-traps where in fetid, dim-lighted rooms, full of vermin, workers crowded upon one another and in fair weather spilled out onto the roofs, still stitching doggedly away since they were paid on a piece-rate basis.

The laconic report of an Illinois factory inspector describes a cross-sectional shop at 159 West Taylor Street, Chicago:

This is in rear of lot, over stable; entrance by narrow passage between houses in front; low-ceiled and dirty; bare brick walls; sink in room gives out bad smells; gasoline used in pressing; odors from alley and stable coming up combine to make stench unbearable; no separate closet for women; employs seven men, three women.

And another at 549 West Nineteenth Street:

Home shop, in basement of tenement house, low, dark and filthy; dimensions of work room were 14 x 14 x 17½; two windows; room contained four sewing machines; stove with fire in it; and four men and three women working; air intolerably bad; folding doors were open between this shop room and the living room in which Darwut (the owner) and his wife eat and cook and keep boarders; the boarders (two) slept in a low room off shop, unlighted and unventilated.

In New York City, chief center of the garment trade, conditions were worse, if possible. Plumbing in the shops that clotted the Lower East Side was still of the Chic Sale variety. The workers often had to pay for the privilege of getting a job "to learn" and for keeping it once it was mastered. They were ridiculed as "greenhorns" for clinging to old-country habits. Their ignorance was exploited on every side. They were fined for being a few minutes late. They had to buy their own needles and thread from the proprietor (often a person who had preceded them here by a few years), yielding him 300 to 500 per cent profit on package or spool. Whether reefer, presser, cloaker, skirt-maker, all had to work sixteen and seventeen hours a day. Many of the single men slept on their bundles in the shop, to "save rent" and "to borrow a couple of hours tomorrow." They often carried their own foot-treadle machines on their backs, going from job to job. Average wages were $7.00 and $8.00 and $11.00 for a seventy-hour week and were often held up until an entire shop had finished an "immediate delivery" order. "Mistakes" in payment which were made by check were frequent and enraging, but argument about it could mean instant dismissal. Dust from cloth piled high on tables and floors promoted the whole catalog of pulmonary ailments. Sometimes whole families, especially "learners," labored from sunup to midnight to earn $15.00 a week.

Battered and bewildered by the rigors of this new life, many of them turned with freshened ardor to the synagogue for solace in prayer, in kissings of the Torah, in the hair-splittings of Talmudic dispute.

The intellectuals, however, had been attracted to such groups as the "Arbeiter Verein," branch of the Socialist Labor party, and to the "Pioneers of Freedom," an anarchist fraternity, and they were sure that they had discovered quicker and better paths to redemption. They tended to regard themselves as a collective Moses destined to lead their people out of bondage. They tried to convert their co-religionists to more inflammatory creeds. For Isaiah they offered Karl Marx, and Kropotkin in exchange for the Ecclesiastes. Their efforts were rebuffed with fear and hostility. Many of the "greenhorns" believed that the intellectuals, with their scorn of religion, were but Christians in disguise, determined to subvert the Jewish faith.

The intellectuals therefore changed their tactics. Instead of indulging in abstract argument they tried to help the workers with their immediate everyday problems, to transform their apathy and dejection into more militant moods. As early as 1886 they had organized an "Anti-Sweating League" and in the German and Yiddish press and by word of mouth campaigned against the sweatshop. They urged the workers to study, to read, to learn English, to "orient" themselves to their new environment, and to dare to stand up against the most hardboiled proprietor. Gradually the workers grew accustomed to the idea that the intellectuals were the only people to offer aid when they were in trouble. But in spite of this the intellectuals gained few active followers. Whereas the workers were grateful for succor in times of crisis they did not, as a whole, accept the political and economic views of their benefactors. Only a small minority was won over, forsaking the traditions of "Chedar" and "Schule" for the Social Revolution which, as every enlightened person knew, was just around the corner.

Yet the intellectuals and their handful of the rank and file wielded an influence far out of proportion to their numbers. They were certain that their cause was "right, just and invincible." They were willing to take upon themselves the most onerous tasks in calling strikes and seeing them through; and in the early days of unionism in the needle trades they often assumed commanding roles.

During the 80's a few unions had been formed, notably the Dress and Cloak Makers in New York City, who had waged the industry's first significant strike in 1883.* Their revolt spot-lighted the triangular nature of the trade with its special relations between manufacturer, contractor, and labor, for in this instance the contractors tended to side, morally at least, with the workers against the bigger businessmen who allied themselves into the first Cloak Manufacturers Association to repel the "foolish and misguided" attacks of their newly joined adversaries.

The walkout attracted a good deal of attention as the "Immigrants' Strike," and the union, aided by the sob-sisters of the daily press (who suddenly discovered that starvation, even among foreigners, had its picturesque side) and by the Knights of Labor, gained its goal of a $2.50 minimum for a day that began at 8 A.M. and ended at 6 P.M. It was soon chartered as a Knights of Labor local assembly, but its immigrant members didn't quite know what that meant. To them a union was a device for getting enough to eat. They were unprepared for the grandiose Mumbo Jumbo by which the Noble Order, through its ritual, expressed the yearnings of that day's workingman for a greater personal dignity, a sense of "being somebody" other than a very "common laborer" at the bottom of the heap.

In his *Memoirs*, Abraham Rosenberg, who was to become first president of the International, depicts the astonishment that marked their first encounter with the Knights:

I still retain a vivid picture of the scene which took place when the District Master Workman and his deputies, all Irish, came to perform the ceremony of installing us. We were all new in America and we did not understand a word of what

* The late Joseph Barondess, known as the humanitarian, and the idol of his own cloakmakers and other needle trades workers, was the leader of this strike and others which followed it.

was said. We could only see how one of them took a piece of chalk and drew a large circle on the floor and told us to stand on the circle. Then another deputy placed a small sword on the table and a globe was hung on the side of the door of the meeting-hall. . . . Many of us on seeing the sword were not sure whether we were all going to be slaughtered or drafted into the army. . . . Only later, did some explain . . . that if any one of us broke the oath and became untrue to the interests of Labor, he would be pursued by the sword and would be unable to escape because the Knights were strong the world over.

Other groups, from reefers to corset-makers in the variegated industry, were heartened by the success of their dress and cloak colleagues and began to set up unions of their own. All of them ran into trouble. Among other things, many of the workers looked upon their jobs merely as stopgaps until they could enter more alluring occupations or perhaps become bosses themselves, and thought "what good will this union do me then?" Many of the women in the industry looked upon their jobs as a prelude to marriage and maternity, often working at home for "pin-money" for their hope chests, driving wages down by their willingness to do a batch of sewing or what not for next to nothing.

In addition, extremist factions warred constantly for the allegiance of the unions. In the mid-eighties, Johann Most, fiery disciple of Bakunin's new Nihilism, established headquarters in New York City and published a little booklet entitled *Science of Revolutionary Warfare—A Manual of Instruction in the Use and Preparation of Nitroglycerine, Dynamite, Gun-Cotton, Fulminating Mercury, Bombs, Fuses, Poisons, Etc. Etc.* He was an eloquent man with black flowing hair and a black bushy beard and his slogan was "Extirpate the miserable brood!" (the capitalists). His appearance and activities first gave American cartoonists that stock character which has survived to the present day, bearing the label of every "subversive element." He was the idol of revolutionary clubs in New York and especially in Chicago where August Spies, Louis Lingg, Michael Schwab and the other anarchists who were accused of hurling the Haymarket Bomb on May 4, 1886, at a labor rally in Haymarket Square, so improved upon his lessons that a jury sent them to the gallows. In his pamphlets like the *Beast of Property* he preached "the creative joy of destruction," called upon workers to drill rifle corps, to exterminate "the race of parasites." He prided himself upon being a "propagandist of the deed" like a terrorist under the Czar. He had founded the International Working People's Association in the belief that only by the adroit use of percussion-caps could the workers, whether in his native Germany or in the United States, liberate themselves from the "shackles" of "capitalist blood-suckers." Whenever possible Most and his lieutenants would try to bore from within the feeble unions in the garment trades and usually smashed them because their lurid talk frightened almost everyone away.

At the same time the Socialist Labor party, guided by the handsome and brilliant orator, Daniel DeLeon, told the workers that they should join only the trade union branches of the S.L.P. which itself kept splitting off into splinter groups.*

Simultaneously, the A. F. of L. was berating the "blunders" of the Knights of Labor which retorted in kind, while both sought the fidelity of the newly organizing workers. Agents from the Industrial Workers of the World traveled to the Atlantic Seaboard to infuse the Eastern wage slaves with Western derring-do and to denounce the A. F. of L. as the "American Fakiration of Labor" and "The American Separation of Labor." They labeled Gompers a "traitor to the working-class" and tried to convince the bewildered

* One of them became the present Socialist party which itself is now divided between the Thomas "leftists" and the right-wing Social Democratic Federation, led by Algernon Lee, James Oneal, Louis Waldman.

garment workers that their salvation depended on the adoption of the I.W.W. platform.

All such conflicting claims were in a sense but reflections of the larger shapes of the depression which in the early 90's descended upon the country "like a plague of Chinese locusts." Unemployment, intensified by a vast rise in immigration, hit a new high of four million. Gaunt, desperate men and women milled in the streets of a dozen great cities in futile parades of protests, listening to "agitators who gave them visions," retreating before police who "gave them clubs," and in snow and sleet and the hot sunshine standing for hours in breadline and soup-kitchen queues for handouts. In New York City there were bread-riots, while at the old Waldorf-Astoria a party was held for a prize-winning black and tan dog that wore a $15,000 diamond collar.

A few months before the panic depths of 1893 Senator John J. Ingalls declared in the United States Senate:

We cannot disguise the truth that we are on the verge of revolution. . . . Labor, starving and sullen in the cities, aims to overthrow a system under which the rich are growing richer and the poor are growing poorer, a system [that] gives to a Vanderbilt and a Gould wealth beyond the dreams of avarice . . . condemns the poor to poverty from which there is no escape or refuge but the grave. . . . The laborers of this country asking for employment are treated like . . . mendicants begging for bread.

Despite the general depression, or because of it, the women's garment industry continued to grow, for "ready-mades" were getting cheaper and cheaper and women still had to have "something to wear." From 1890 to 1900 the number of establishments increased from 1,224 to 2,701, or 120 per cent, and the number of workers from 34,149 to 83,759, or 114 per cent. At the same time, moreover, that organizing efforts of the American Federation of Labor, the Knights of Labor, the Industrial Workers of the World, the Socialist Labor party, and the Most Anarchists who had fused syndicalism to their terrorist creed, served to keep the garment worker's head spinning, vast alterations in his own trade dizzied him all the more.

Still further refinements in the sewing machine and in the steam pressing machine combined with more complex and intricate marketing methods to subdivide his function into the "specialized" routines of mass production. Instead of being made by four or five workers, a garment now would pass through thirty or forty different hands before completion. Hence "subcontracting" within a shop began to keep stride with this new diversity.

The owner, for example, would hire two or three pressers who would contract to take care of all the pressing and who would in turn hire two or three or four of their own "subpressers" or "helpers" at $6.00 or $7.00 a week to do most of the work. A skirt-contractor would engage a dozen men, who in turn would hire five or six assistants, each of whom had two or three "sub-assistants," until an arrangement of "sub-sub-sub-contracting" ensued. It created a hierarchy of its own, an endless chain of bantam-weight bosses, light-weight bosses, welter-weight bosses and heavy-weight bosses, all of them interested in keeping wages down.

The International—from its beginnings in 1900—therefore faced an uphill journey to achieve the primary objectives of unionism, "a living wage," "shorter hours," and "decent conditions." Its official philosophy was in theory colored by its many Socialist sympathizers, and its first constitution in its preamble endorsed the "class struggle" and all its implications.

The International's practice, however, was the pure pragmatism of Gompers: "All you can get, here and now." In fact it reflected the official A. F. of L. creed in almost every respect. It urged high dues to build a strong strike and out-of-work benefits treasury. It pinned great hopes on the use of the union label and the effectiveness of the boycott. It discouraged strikes, save as the last resort, and counseled mediation instead. At conventions it regularly passed Socialist resolutions and quite as regularly filed them away. Yet there was one vital difference between the International and other A. F. of L. constituents.

At that time all the A. F. of L. unions except the United Mine Workers were "craft" in structure, their members recruited from occupations like carpentry where a modicum of skill was needed. For such unions, the strict observance of apprenticeship and shop rules, the permit-card method of parceling out job assignments, the maintenance of jurisdiction over all workers within its special "skill area," endowed the skill-possessing group with superior bargaining power that derived from its "corner" on the labor market. In the women's garment trade, however, virtually all operations—that of the cutter was and remains the single exception—required no lengthy training period, and could be picked up within a few days. The more skilled and the less skilled were in much the same position. Immigration and hard times alike rendered it impossible to curtail competition from "outsiders" and to safeguard wage scales unless all workers within the industry, well-paid cutter to pittance-paid "helper," were welded into a single body. Acting on the assumption that skilled and unskilled have a unity of interests that transcends the limit of occupation, the International from its beginnings has been a combination of both the craft and the industrial types of unionism. It has also fashioned a successful technique for reconciling inter-union disputes over jurisdiction by setting up "Joint Boards" on which workers from every classification, within a given territory, receive "proportional representation."*

Despite such feelings of mutual aid, of "one for all, and

* In this regard it is interesting to note that in peace talks between the A. F. of L. and C.I.O. factions, the International in its structural form has been often mentioned as furnishing, in microcosm, the model which organized labor in America may eventually adopt.

all for one," however, the International in 1910, after a
decade of effort, found itself unable to modify effectively
the evils of a trade which was thriving upon the cheapness
of its human labor. Union strategists at last concluded that
the only way to correct abuses which were particularly
vicious in New York City would be a strike which would
close up every shop in the city "tight as a drum" and bring
the employers to book altogether and all at once. Experience had convinced the International's leadership that when
an employer did recognize the union, with its higher wage
scales, he was placed more or less at the mercy of rivals who
kept an open shop and who could cut prices at will, under-
selling his unionized competitor.

By talking up this future Great Event as a quick, bold
stroke that would improve conditions all along the line,
union officials roused workers from their resignation, result
of many previous setbacks, to a desire for action. And at the
tenth convention of the International, sixty-five delegates
by a 55 to 10 vote authorized the General Executive Board
to sound the "call" whenever "advisable."

It was a do or die decision. Advance preparations in their
scope resembled a major military offensive. Weeks before
the strike summons was issued, halls were hired for meetings, lawyers hired to fight court action, and bookkeepers
hired to supervise and allocate funds. To test the temper
of the workers, the first labor rally ever to be held in Madi-
son Square Garden was arranged by the union's leaders for
June 28, 1910. The response was overwhelming, the enthusiasm hysterical, as thousands unable to enter the Garden overflowed to nearby streets to be harangued by
"step-ladder" speakers.

Suddenly, at two o'clock in the afternoon of July 7,
1910, peak of the season, 60,000 garment workers quit.
A half hour later the 92 per cent of the industry centered
in New York was utterly paralyzed. It was the greatest and
most startling withdrawal of labor power in American his-

tory; for caught up by the excitement of the occasion, non-union workers had also joined the marching multitude that surged toward meeting halls on lower Fifth Avenue, snarling traffic for block after block, north and west, south and east of the Union Square area. Many of them cheered, lifting their shears, their knives, their measuring chalk like banners. Others wept, and still others called upon the "just God." A contingent of about five hundred women, converging in front of a loft building at West Twenty-third Street near Eighth Avenue, recalled the prayer which had begun the "uprising of the twenty thousand" shirt and waist and dressmakers the year before, and again started to chant the awesome oath, "If I turn traitor to the cause I now pledge, may this hand wither from the arm I now raise, if I turn traitor . . . ," as they moved steadily along, their voices challenging all the clangors of the street.

It was a brave beginning, planned with a fine sense of the curtain. The day before (July 6) the International's high command—Rosenberg, Dyche, Polakoff—had convened a secret session of the General Strike Committee of forty-five who approved of the date proposed by Rosenberg and themselves set the hour. They also ordered the presses to run all night to print special editions of the *New Post*, union paper, which in English, Yiddish, and Italian told International members that the zero hour had come. Up at dawn, picked squadrons thrust copies of the *New Post* into the hands of workers as they entered their lofts.

Despite the daring and the drama of this strategy, the combat became bitter and grim and long and nearly ruined both sides. The quarter of a million dollars raised by the International, by the *Vorwarts*, and the New York *Call*, and by socially minded sympathizers such as Frieda Kirchwey and Fola LaFollette, and philanthropists like Jacob Schiff was still insufficient to buy enough food for out-of-work strikers and their families. Many workers suffered from semistarvation as scanty reserves vanished and the union allowance often permitted but one slice of black bread and one cup of tea for breakfast, dinner, and supper.

On August 27, Justice Goff of the New York State Supreme Court granted an injunction against the International, alleging that the strike was for the "closed shop" and was thus illegal and that even peaceful picketing could no longer be allowed. It was an opinion which the New York *Times* declared the "strongest decision ever handed down against labor." To the workers it climaxed a series of disappointments, especially the constant bogging down of negotiations between the International and the Cloak, Suit and Shirt Manufacturers Protective Association over such questions as to whether a buttonhole maker should receive $.90 or $1.00 per hundred Grade A buttonholes. Meantime, employers were losing millions as retailers beseeched them for goods they could not deliver. The few firms which had signed with the union, and other firms which had hired strikebreakers, could not begin to meet the demands of the market. After nine weeks, when both owners and workers had reached a state of exhaustion, a settlement at last was reached between the International and the Employers' Association.

It was called the "Protocol of Peace." Despite its grand name, with its Eastern European flavor, it was really a species of collective agreement, yet something of a unique specimen. At the request of A. Lincoln Filene, Boston dry-goods merchant and leader in the Civic Federation of New England, who was both morally and financially disturbed by the causes and consequences of the strike, Louis Dembitz Brandeis acted as impartial chairman for the negotiations, and he injected into the settlement a new spirit of industrial relations.

The "protocol"—while specifying wages, hours, and "shop rules"—otherwise differed from any similar pact.* It

---

* This was the first collective agreement between a union and an association of employers since the United Mine Workers' pact in 1902.

had no time limit, and could be terminated by either side simply by "giving notice." It was a "treaty of peace" founded purely upon the good will of its signatories. It created a brand new body in American industrial life, a "Joint Board" of sanitary control, composed of both unionists and employers, to abolish threats to health, such as improper ventilation, and threats to safety such as inadequate fire escapes. It set up a Committee of Grievances to handle minor frictions and a Board of Arbitration to settle major disputes, to "consist of one nominee of the manufacturers, one of the unions, and one of the public."

The features of this last proposal were the "invention" of Brandeis, who affirmed that industrial conflict could be better resolved by brain power than by force and who also introduced the idea of the "public" as both victim or beneficiary in the processes of production, their smooth flow or their stoppage.

Both manufacturers and workers accepted this viewpoint with reservations of their own. The former adopted the protocol mainly as a mechanism for equalizing labor costs and making competition less cutthroat. The latter ratified it only as a compromise when their resources had been drained to the last dime and they knew that they could hold out no longer. Union sachems, like Rosenberg, then president of the International, were conditioned by Marxist thinking and were reluctant to swallow the thought of "common interests" and "coöperation" between employer and employee, to have "class collaboration" supplant "the class struggle."

Many on both sides regarded the protocol as a makeshift, and at first it almost failed to function. Like foremen in motor plants of a later day, the petty bosses in the garment trade could not get used to the thought that they could no longer hire and fire at will. The workers, still influenced by the idea that unionism was somehow synonymous with strike action, were angry that under the terms of the protocol they had given up the right to strike and were compelled to abide by rulings of the Board of Arbitration as "final and conclusive."

Yet the protocol, despite countless moves to call the whole thing off, and sabotaging by both employer and worker, finally justified itself. It worked. Like a piece of new elaborate machinery it creaked at times, needed lubrication, and many adjustments, but in the long run performed the function for which it had been designed. It was hailed as a "beacon light" for union-management relations in other industries as its conference procedures replaced the arbitrary exercise of authority on the owner's part and retaliation by the worker. The essential principles of this protocol, despite many variations in detail and even more temporary setbacks, have remained to dominate the union's attitude to the present day.

Before the efficacy of this approach was vindicated, however, the International was subjected to a vicious internal strife that almost destroyed it. In August, 1920, various Communist factions and fragments from seventeen nations gathered in Moscow, organizing themselves into the Communist International. Out of this meeting sprang the Red Labor Union with the avowed purpose of "taking over" the labor movements of the Western world. Its twenty-one-point program declared that it would at once "be necessary to establish Communist nuclei" in all labor bodies. In the United States, the Trade Union Educational League, founded by William Z. Foster in 1921, was the instrument through which the Communists sought to gain control of A. F. of L. unions. At the outset of this campaign, the units of the I.L.G.W.U. were chosen as the most fertile fields for sowing discontent, since their ranks were full of Russian and Polish Jews who were ecstatic over the abolition of czardom and who would be, it was thought, "emotionally receptive" to salvation by the Soviet.

Meantime, the I.L.G.W.U. had been riding high. It was

at a new top of power and prestige, with 3,900 agreements covering 160,000 members, mainly as the result of the World War boom. At its convention in the summer of 1920, there was much exuberant talk about a greater "voice in management," about "industrial democracy," about the "new role of the worker." It was the bright day before the cyclone's coming. The post-armistice depression, beginning in the fall of 1920, destroyed business activity much as a twister levels a Kansas town. In the women's garment trade hundreds of firms folded up as retailers canceled orders by wire, telephone, and special delivery. Other employers tried to save themselves by slashing wages to keep their share of a dwindling market. Agreements with I.L.G.W.U. locals were revised, tacitly ignored, openly abrogated. In the retrenchments of panic, thousands of garment workers were laid off. In New York, Chicago, Boston, Cleveland, Baltimore, Toledo, and Toronto, from 1921 to 1924 great strikes to maintain operating pacts with management proved mainly unsuccessful. The workers were baffled and discouraged by an experience the more demoralizing for its contrast with the halcyon days of a few short years before.

At this juncture, Mr. Foster and his aides made an entrance onto the I.L.G.W.U. stage, an appearance exquisitely timed to the cue of the workers' mounting resentment. Foster was, and is, perhaps the most gifted organizer, per se, in the United States. And for three years, as the depression deepened, he exploited his talents to such good effect that in 1925 the Communists ruled the important locals of the Joint Board of the Cloak Makers Union and had made appreciable inroads elsewhere. That same year Foster concentrated all his forces in New York City for a final thrust.

With the return of all the old "sweating" evils to an industry virtually at a standstill, with jobs "scarcer than diamonds," with fears of future want making them despondent and desperate, many I.L.G.W.U. workers succumbed to Foster's promises of a "new day" in a better-than-nothing mood. He captured local after local, including the famous No. 2, No. 9, and No. 35, each with its thousands of members.

The only local that, like a Praetorian Guard, stood out against this Communist invasion was the powerful Cutters Union No. 10, oldest in the I.L.G.W.U. It was managed by a dynamic resourceful Polish-born Jew, David Dubinsky. He argued that Foster was more interested in promoting the Communist party as a political force than in restoring the I.L.G.W.U. to its former strength; that the doctrines and tactics of Communism were unsuited to the American scene; and that the I.L.G.W.U. workers would have to evolve more indigenous methods of meeting the menace of unemployment, and of short pay for long hours. Dubinsky was promptly subjected to some unexcelled abuse. The Fosterites charged him, among other things, with "inciting cutters against operators, Italians against Jews, making secret horse deals with the bosses, 'fixing' union elections . . . using thugs against opponents, expelling them at his pleasure . . . so . . . that he and his gangsters can make the union a gold mine for themselves."

In reply he appealed to his record, accused Foster of misleading the workers with "pie-in-the-sky" fantasies, and the war of words and the clash of loyalties continued as Foster called for "class struggle" and Dubinsky for "constructive collaboration" between managers and workers.

To people who had known Dubinsky in the old country his anti-Communist activity seemed very much like a *volte face*; for from his early youth he had been a firebrand in Poland's trade-union branch of the "Bund," a kind of Jewish Sinn Fein.

He was born in Brest-Litovsk, Russian Poland, in 1892, and three years later was moved by his parents to Lodz where his father set up a bakery, employing many hands. Dubinsky attended the local Jewish Academy where he received the equivalent of a grammar-school education along with some religious history and Hebrew. Upon his graduation at the age of thirteen he served a three-year apprenticeship in the paternal shop and at sixteen was made a master baker. Despite his youth he was also made assistant secretary of the Lodz Bakers Union, for here as elsewhere the bakers were the most illiterate and the most bellicose of unionists, and Dubinsky could read and write, precious accomplishments, and could also debate with the best of them. So zealous was he indeed that he personally conducted a strike against his father, demanding an extra two zlotys a week for the men who tended the great ovens. In the same year he was banished to Cheliabiask, Siberia, for making an "incendiary" speech. Since neither the climate nor the Czar's hospitality attracted him, he cut his stay to a few weeks by the simple expedient of starting to walk toward European Russia and not turning back. Although his family, upon his return, greeted him in a manner befitting the prodigal son, differences in economic views disturbed the dinner-table gatherings to such an extent that he embarked for the United States, arriving in New York City in 1911. He obtained a job in a knee-pants shop on the lower East Side, studied English by night, and decided to become a "cutter" not only to earn more money but also because the cutters were the "front pew" men, the "aristocrats" of the industry. Their skill with knife and shears was the crucial factor in turning out a good or bad garment, or saving a piece of spoiled cloth from ruin. He was often consulted by the employer to help estimate costs in creating a new style and this dealing with management also enhanced his prestige. Then, too, the cutting room was physically separated from the rest of the establishment, and its occupants were always a smaller, more select group than the others in the shop, a circumstance which contributed to the general feeling that a cutter was a personage indeed.

Moreover, from the 1890's, the Cutters' Union—especially its New York Local No. 10—was one of the few labor organizations to maintain its strength and its discipline even though with the years its original Welsh and Scotch founders gave way to Jews and later to Italians and Slavs. To this union, which he joined six months after his arrival, Dubinsky at first brought the radical ardor of his Bundist days. He was very soon "Americanized," however, concluding from his own observation and his omnivorous reading of American history that unions in this country, by the very nature of American society, couldn't get very far by relying upon Marxist syllogisms.

Fluent, a good mixer, able to speak Russian, Polish, Yiddish, and English with varying degrees of accuracy, he soon acquired a key position in the Cutters' Union by the tactics of the typical go-getter, proving to be an excellent organizer, an even better executive. He is today in fact less a labor leader in the customary usage of the term than an efficiency expert. As manager-secretary of the Cutters No. 10—a post to which he ascended in 1921—he handled its finances with what amounted to a kind of wizardry. If he couldn't raise enough money through dues, he would invent special drives for "Old Age Funds" and the like to keep his union's coffers full against a rainy day. Colleagues derided him humorously as the "miser" and "Mr. Morgan" but forked over for the varieties of special assessments that his ingenuity devised. By such means he has built up a credit standing that is rare, if not unique, among American labor leaders. From his earliest days as a union chieftain he could always swing a substantial loan with no other collateral than his reputation for being able to get "money out of the air."

It has been his financial acumen, above anything else, that explains his rapid rise to vice-president, general secretary-treasurer, and finally president of the I.L.G.W.U., a post to which he was elected by acclamation in 1932. For when in 1926 the Communists under Foster, preferring "militancy" to "arbitration," called a strike of thirty-five thousand workers that ended in a shattering defeat for the I.L.G.W.U., in wage losses of $3,500,000 and otherwise, the only local that was solvent was Dubinsky's No. 10. He transformed it into a kind of first-aid society, helping other I.L.G.W.U. affiliates to get back on their feet, to maintain offices and morale. He and his cutters who had supported the strike with funds and pickets on a "labor unity" basis, while condemning it as a foolhardy maneuver, became an anti-Communist brigade, making the rounds to steam up antagonism against a leadership which in their own phrase "had used the workers as a catspaw for Moscow politics," and ousting Foster's surrogates from positions of influence and trust.

Today in his own career Dubinsky typifies the new "working philosophy" that is the dynamic behind the I.L.G.W.U. He explains it:

As our union grew and acquired a greater measure of influence over work-conditions we began increasingly to stress participation in the conduct of industry. . . . Side by side with our demands to the employers to assume greater responsibility for work conditions, we came to realize our own responsibility to industry. . . . Uniformity of labor costs, equal opportunities in all markets, elimination of unfair practices . . . even the organizing of employers into trade associations has become an integral part of our program as a union. . . .

When the Supreme Court nullified the NRA codes in 1935, the I.L.G.W.U., which had benefited greatly from the stabilizing effect of the Blue Eagle, "changed it into a Phoenix and then raised it from the dead." In conjunction with his chief lieutenant, the brainy, ebullient Isadore Nagler, Manager of the New York Cloak Joint Board, Dubinsky worked for weeks with cloak and suit employers to devise an inter-industry "voluntary code," the only one of its kind. It is an elaborate, delicately balanced system of mutual agreements that has, at its hub, a "Recovery Board" which enforces fair-trade practices and sponsors uniform labor conditions in every market. It covers all but 4 per cent of the entire field and has established a "Consumers Protection Label" sewn into 96 per cent of all women's coats and suits made in the United States.

Under Dubinsky's leadership of labor in the nation's fifth industry, with its annual production of $1,325,000,-000 worth of women's wear, the I.L.G.W.U. has 8,640 agreements with firms in the United States and Canada, 7,320 of which are covered by contracts with 62 employers' associations and 1,320 by independent pacts with individual concerns; this accomplishment is all the more astonishing in view of the industry's seasonal shifts in production and other indigenous traits which tend toward general disorganization and disruption of employer-employee relationships.

The women's garment trade is peculiarly sensitive to the cycles of climate, and in addition holiday occasions—not only the new Easter bonnet tradition but also school commencements, summer vacations, and all the social activity that reaches its apogee between Thanksgiving Day and New Year's—all do their part to create peaks and valleys in consumer demand. The mutations of style, moreover, keep manufacturer, jobber, contractor in a frenzy to get out "the latest thing" before another "latest thing" supplants the "hot" number sponsored, as a rule, by one firm and quickly copied by the others. Production schedules are therefore apt to be more hand-to-mouth affairs than long-range programs. The effect of all this upon jobs is illustrated by the fact that in 1935, in New York City's cloak and suit branch of the industry, sixty thousand operators were employed during the "peak" three months and only twenty thousand during the "slack" three months of the year.

To the transient whims of style, as aggravated by fashion experts and advertisers, is added intense competition among producers, prompting them to create a vast variety of styles to draw outlets away from each other. They offer many different "newest" things all at the same time, as if novelty itself were the highest good. A basic style shift often induces bankruptcy and widespread unemployment, as in the 1920's, for example, when the popularity of the knee-length one-piece dress ruined many once prosperous blouse and skirt divisions in the trade.

Furthermore, the jobber-contractor system, with its so-called "outside" shops, still hangs like a sword over the industry's head.* Whereas in most industries commodity production is intimately linked with wholesale and retail distribution, in the women's wear field manufacture is often divorced from merchandising. Unlike the jobber in other business spheres, who is merely a middleman, buying finished articles in large quantities and selling in small, the garment-trade jobber selects the fabrics, designs the fashions, and maintains showrooms, complete with more or less ravishing models, to display his wares to prospective purchasers. He assigns the mechanics of turning out his brassières, or ensembles or swim-suits or whatever, to the contractor, providing him with the materials and specifications, and driving sharp bargains to gain the lowest possible price.

It is a process which often calls forth suicidal rivalry as contractors cut their profit margins to obtain the jobber's

---

* There are, of course, many manufacturers who exemplify the "inside" system in that they themselves have styles designed, buy the raw materials, have the garments made up in their own factories, and arrange for sales. Yet there is no Big Business in the sense of industrial concentration; the six largest firms together employ but 3.7 of the workers. On the other hand, contracting shops account for 25 per cent of the total output in cotton dresses, 50 per cent in infants' and children's wear, 54.7 per cent in cloaks and suits, and 71 per cent in silk dresses.

patronage and to keep it. Wages, which comprise only 15 per cent of total production costs, are constantly "chipped at" to reduce the contractor's overhead and to improve his competing position.

The I.L.G.W.U. has checked this "jungle" competition to an appreciable extent by stipulating in its contracts that the jobber, instead of shopping around all over the place, may use only as many contractors as he may legitimately require and may not dispense with their services in an "indiscriminate" manner or otherwise indulge in "unfair trade practices." By means of this and similar devices the union coöperates constantly with employers to police an anarchic industry, trying—among other things—to prevent style piracy, a prevalent evil, by joining with the Fashion Originators' Guild to discover and penalize offenders who copy designs that others have paid large fees to procure.

If a contractor should attempt to "run away from the union" and set up shop in some remote New England hamlet, for example, where he can obtain $4.00 and $5.00 a week labor,* I.L.G.W.U. organizers pursue him like a nemesis, spending much time and money and energy to bring him to terms since "the unionized shop owner finds it impossible to compete with the chiseler who pays a pauper's wage." When in 1935 the Blue Dale Dress Company moved its plant from New York City to evade union wage scales in violation of its agreement with the I.L.G.W.U., the latter sued and the New York State Supreme Court upheld its contention that this firm was legally and morally bound to return to Manhattan. Justice McCook, who rendered the decision, affirmed that "the logic of the situation calls for application of strong measures" when unscrupulous employers are tempted "to play one community off against another."

At present, out of a maximum potential membership of

* Before the Federal Wages and Hour Act became effective.

345,000 in the United States and Canada, the I.L.G.W.U. now has 262,000 members, divided as follows:

Per Cent Unionized	Branch of Industry*	Average Number of Workers per Shop
90	Blouses	28.5
80	Children's Outerwear	35.0
97	Coats, Suits, and Separate Skirts	19.0
95	Dresses	37.8
97	Corsets and Allied Garments	64.9
80	Infants' Wear	25.3
50	Knitted Outerwear	48.8
50	Knitted Underwear	187.8
75	Underwear and Nightwear	47.7
40	Cotton Garments	128.4

At Dubinsky's insistence, fifteen certified public accountants travel the year round out of national headquarters, going from local to local in fifty-two cities and towns to keep track of just where the dues money goes and why, and otherwise to improve the quality of the union's arithmetic.

Work or no work, dues have to be paid. And except for 4 per cent in mining districts where the traditions of the check-off are tenacious, all International members pay on a voluntary basis, a technique employed to stress the idea that "it's up to them" to share in the burdens and benefits of the union. And to increase further their sense of personal participation, the International's press is edited to and for them by the brilliant union publicist Max D. Danish, who has largely helped to mold the favorable public opinion the union now enjoys.

The official bi-monthly, *Justice*, printed in English, is read by 170,000 members who subscribe to it in preference to other language publications such as the Yiddish journal *Gerechtigkeit*, read by 35,000, the Italian *Giustizia* with a

* About 73.2 of the entire industry is located in New York State, chiefly in New York City; 4.3 in Illinois, mainly in Chicago; 4.5 in Pennsylvania; and the remaining 18.0 is scattered widely among 38 other states.

circulation of 45,000, and a Spanish and French edition of *Justice* read by 10,000 apiece.

The I.L.G.W.U.'s racial composition is of course constantly changing, and in many respects it records the succeeding waves of immigration to the United States with the accuracy of a hydrographic chart. It was mainly Jewish in 1900*; but in that year began the large influx of Italians into the industry. Within a decade they had formed their powerful Dressmakers Local No. 89, choosing that number in memory of 1789, year of the French Revolution, and adopting as their slogan *Pane e Rose* ("Bread and Roses") to signify they would not be satisfied with "crumbs from the loaf" but would also insist upon "liberty and leisure" as well. They are currently led by Luigi Antonini, vice-president of the International, a robust, picturesque figure in flowing black tie, black hat, and ample Capuan cloak. He is an ardent anti-Fascist with a gift for polemics and *realpolitik*, and has been chairman of New York State's American Labor party since its founding in 1936.

Today in New York City's dress trade men and women of Italian descent comprise 51 per cent of the labor force, while Jews are but 32 per cent, Negroes 5 per cent, Spaniards and Latin-Americans 2½ per cent; and the remaining 9½ per cent presents the apotheosis of the "melting pot" and contains, among others, Irish, Turks, Germans, Poles, Hindus, Armenians, Chinese, and French. In San Francisco, in a similar dressmaking group, Spanish-Americans form 27.2 per cent, Italians 20.2 per cent, Russians 17.4 per cent, and Jews but 10.2 per cent. In the smaller communities I.L.G.W.U. members are almost exclusively native-born whites, many of them of the fourth and fifth generation, and quite a few of them people who have lost their own farms or stores.

To preserve its unity of purpose amid all this ethnic di-

* Today it is 75 per cent non-Jewish.

versity the International spends a great deal of its time and energy in "extra-curricular" activities that tend to make its own brand of unionism less a bargaining agency than a "way of life."

Its educational department, for example, with its cultural and recreational divisions, is far and away the best of its kind in the United States. It is the pet project of the thoughtful, handsome Julius Hochman, a vice-president of the International, who assures this enterprise of its funds.

Under the exceptionally able and imaginative direction of Mark Starr, veteran of the British Labor movement, and Fannia M. Cohn, famed anti-sweatshop crusader, the department conducts study classes in English, Public Speaking, Parliamentary Law, American History, Labor Problems, Training for Union Service, and Current Events. Lecturers of national repute address its forums. It has a varied athletic program of baseball, basketball, bowling, and soccer with teams drawn from all of its affiliated locals. It gives instruction in music and has set up forty of its own bands, orchestras, and choral societies. It teaches dancing, "tap," "ballroom," and "interpretative." It presents operas like *Aïda* with its own cast. It gives free showings to members of movies like "Zola," the French "Carnival in Flanders," the Russian "Baltic Deputy." On its own Labor Stage in New York City it produces plays like John Wexley's *Steel* and musical revues like the very successful *Pins and Needles*. It arranges exhibits for the paintings of both WPA and private artists. It schedules picnics and outings and hikes in the country for members and their children, and dances in the winter for adults only. Its "handbooks" and manuals of union tactics and songs have been adopted, with slight changes, by the newer unions in motors, rubber, steel. It grants scholarships to promising students at Bryn Mawr, at the University of Wisconsin.

The International also concerns itself with the physical well-being of its members. In 1913 it organized the Union Health Center in New York City, the biggest clinic of its sort in the country, staffed by sixteen doctors and four dentists. Some of them, like Dr. George M. Price, Director, have done notable research on the relation of working conditions to the chief ailments of women's wear workers: tuberculosis, defective eyesight, blood infections, and nervous strain resulting from the effort to keep pace with the new "speed-up" devices such as snap-fastening and blind-stitching machines. About ninety thousand I.L.G.W.U. members use the Union Health Clinic annually for everything from curing a cold to getting a cardiograph, and receive excellent medical care at about one-quarter of the cost* elsewhere, since the union underwrites whatever budget the Health Center needs.

Some years ago the International invested $500,000 in the thousand-acre estate of a New York multimillionaire in the Pocono Hills, Forest Park, Pennsylvania. The union has transformed this property into a vacation resort for its members and the members of other labor groups. The main buildings and adjoining cottages accommodate one thousand guests. For $19.00 a week, and a union card, it is possible to spend as much time as one pleases at this "Unity House," play tennis, go boating, swim, ride horseback, and so on; rooms are on the luxurious side and the food of a quality rarely encountered for $19.00 a week.

In addition to "taking care of its own," the International —under Dubinsky—has evolved the outlook that labor, instead of being at any time an object of charity, should stand on its own feet, be able to contribute to the welfare of others, thus increasing its own self-respect and fulfilling its obligations to the community at large. Hence, among I.L.G.W.U. disbursements are such items as "American Red Cross for Drought and Flood Victims, $10,000"; an annual contribution of $10,000 to the Los Angeles Sanitarium in addition to the construction of the Hillquit Memorial Hospital for its own afflicted members on the

* They pay 50 cents for a general examination.

sanitarium grounds in Duarte, California; and among its investments are $100,000 worth of bonds in New York's World's Fair Corporation to help underwrite this enterprise.

In the present A. F. of L.-C.I.O. war the International has lined up with the latter and contributed hundreds of thousands of dollars to C.I.O. drives in textiles and steel. Yet Dubinsky, as spokesman for his union, wants harmony, the sooner the better, and he has waved the olive branch on every possible occasion. A stout barrel-chested man, less than five feet six inches in height, with sharp brown eyes, black hair whitening at the temples, and a brisk nervous manner, Dubinsky has pounded the table and champed his cigar at a score of conferences looking toward labor peace, insisting that if "the will to peace really exists, the way can be readily found."

For he believes that only a unified labor movement can help to create that new political alignment which will carry forward the implications of the New Deal. Any such party, he affirms, must be built up "from the grass roots of a state-wide basis first." It must not be a strictly "labor" or class party, but must make "ample room for all liberal and progressive groups, wage-earners along with white collar people of our middle classes and . . . all other gainfully employed citizens . . . to achieve a common program for the rational production and distribution of our national wealth."

Yet he is daily working to achieve a united labor movement for what is perhaps a more immediately important reason. He is convinced that the "wide participation in the aims and objectives of industry by responsible, constructive unions" alone can insure greater stability to American society as it moves inexorably toward a future "democratic collectivism" which, he thinks, may even "place the unions in a position of leadership alongside of management," with government helping both.

The Railroad Unions

DESPITE the increasing competition of pipe-lines, trucks, buses, passenger cars, and planes, along with the more traditional boats and barges, our railroads remain the key industry in the American system of transport. Their grand total capitalization amounts to $18,885,941,857—a legendary sum still needing an Einstein with the hands of a Gargantua to squeeze out the water. In 1936–37 such carriers employed about a million men and paid out nearly two billions in wages and salaries. And during the past few years, while the C.I.O.'s strong surges toward industrial unionism continue to inspire furious controversy about the "labor problem," the union-management relations of our railroads have been constantly held up as an ideal toward which other unions and other management might well aspire.

The situation is not without irony. Some fifty years ago when Gould and Vanderbilt were dealing in railroads and Rockefeller was turning their secret rebates into a formidable racket, the New York *Times*, in a single issue of July 26, 1877, referred to striking engineers, firemen, brakemen, and others as "hoodlums, rabble, bummers, looters, blacklegs, thieves, tramps, ruffians, incendiaries, enemies of society, brigands, rapscallions, riff raff, felons and idiots."

They were, of course, nothing of the kind. They were simply workers who wanted to earn enough to keep themselves and their families in food, shelter, and clothing. They also wanted to retain, without the retaliations of blacklisting, their feeble and feckless organizations which then were not even trade unions, in the sense that they sought or practiced collective bargaining, but were merely mutual insurance and fraternal groups. For during the last half of the nineteenth century railroading as an occupation held such high hazards that insurance companies refused to consider men in the engine cab, or atop the freight cars, or in the yard, as "acceptable risks." To safeguard the welfare of their families in case of injury or death, such workers formed their own "Brotherhoods" and "Orders" as insurance benefit societies to which they regularly paid "premiums" while other unionists in other spheres paid "dues."

In March of 1863, for example, twelve locomotive engineers, meeting in Detroit, between runs that were constantly extending beyond the confines of Michigan, founded Division No. 1 of the Brotherhood of the Footboard.* They were, at that time, primarily interested in shortening their unduly long hours at the throttle, the result of the fusing of separate roads into "trunk" lines; yet as soon as their organization got under way their thoughts turned toward "post-mortem security" and within four years the Brotherhood established its subsidiary, The Mutual Life Insurance Association, which enabled Brotherhood members to carry life and accident indemnity insurance, chief reason for the society's quick growth. Similarly in 1868 half a dozen conductors of the Illinois Central formed in Chicago the union now known as the Order of Railway Conductors, which in its origins had the object of furnishing "material aid . . . from a fund attained upon the assessment plan, to disabled members . . . and their widows, children and heirs." In 1873 the Brotherhood of Locomotive Firemen† grew out of a meeting of eleven furnace-feeders who had gathered in an old shed in Port Jervis, New York, to discuss the collection of funds for the family of a colleague killed the day before in a boiler explosion on the Erie Railroad. Among their num-

* The name was later changed to the current Grand International Brotherhood of Locomotive Engineers.
† The present-day "and Enginemen" was tacked on in 1906 to recognize the many members who upon graduation to engineering posts nevertheless preferred to retain affiliation with the Firemen.

ber was an earnest cracker-barrel philosopher named
Joshua A. Leach. He used the occasion to impress upon
his associates the need for arranging mutual protection
against the dangers of their calling. He pointed out
that voluntary contributions were, at best, inadequate
and pitifully small and that they furthermore tended to
fluctuate in amount because of unemployment, perhaps,
or the deceased's lack of popularity. In this respect, Leach
held that a dead man's wife and children should not be
penalized for his failure to be a good mixer. He convinced
his auditors and prodded them to action until from this
Port Jervis group stemmed the first Lodge of the Brotherhood of Railroad Firemen which within a year held its
first national convention attended by delegates from twelve
branches in five states: New York, New Jersey, Pennsylvania, Ohio, and Indiana.

Similar circumstances accompanied the birth of the
Brotherhood of Railroad Brakemen of the Western Hemi-
sphere (changed in 1899 to the Brotherhood of Railroad
Trainmen) when eight yard and train employees of the
Delaware and Hudson Railroad met in a caboose on a summer evening in 1883 and over their corn-cobs and beer decided to create a benefit society that would pay $7.50 a
week to members who became sick or were injured in the
course of duty. They were promptly joined by a like-
minded group from Oneonta, New York. Like its predecessors, this "union" of the Trainmen was more concerned,
in its first years, with insurance than with independence on
the job. It soon started to develop a legal-reserve-plan insurance business, embracing not only total and permanent
disability but also straight life and endowment policies.

Significantly, the constitutions of the early transportation Brotherhoods—now the "Big Four"—contained no
clause calling for collective bargaining, no mention of demands for improved working conditions, nothing indeed
save pious aspirations toward raising the social, moral, and

intellectual standards of their membership, and equally pious hopes that harmony and amity would mark all dealing between their employers and themselves. In such charters the details of the insurance features alone were paid the compliment of definite phrasing.

Yet even such perquisites to family welfare and self-respect were denied to their employees by the railroad dynasts of that day, who feared that the Brotherhoods, despite their timidity, might yet conceal the germs of a genuine wages-and-hours unionism. The railroad magnates were probably the most anti-social, irresponsible crew ever to appear on the American scene, their archetype Gould boasting that "I can hire one half the working class to kill the other half."

These Fisks and Cookes and Goulds and Vanderbilts were "promoters" in the worse sense of the term. They were committed to the doctrine that labor is less the energy of human beings applied to the creation of wealth, than a commodity, its price to be fixed purely by the current speculative needs of proprietors. Their roads were not built so much as swindled and bribed into being by means of fake companies, fake bonds, even fake fraud. Their dividends, paid on monstrously inflated stock, were still continued in the midst of the panic which their devious financial maneuvers helped largely to fasten on the country in the decade 1875–85.

In 1877 they discovered that, in order to maintain their credit and to keep up dividend payments threatened by their own excesses of paper manipulation, they had to lower expenses. Then, as now, labor comprised about 63 per cent of operating costs. Hence in June and July of 1877, the Pennsylvania, the New York Central and Hudson, the Erie, the Michigan and Southern, and other lines announced a 10 per cent wage cut, a policy which, on the Baltimore and Ohio, affected all wages of more than $1.00 a day.

Such slashes were the signal for spontaneous strikes that ricocheted like a crazy billiard ball over the surface of the country, sweeping west from the Atlantic Seaboard to Illinois, and thence south to Missouri, ending finally in California. At railroad termini in thirty cities and towns locomotives were silenced and train movements stopped.

As a whole the populace was at first on the side of the strikers. Almost everyone had been mulcted, one way or another, by the railroad buccaneers. Western settlers had found the choicer acres preëmpted by railroads which through government grants had acquired "right of way" over 312,000 square miles of land—an area three times the size of the six New England states. Farmers had been compelled to fork over "all the traffic will bear" rates for hauling their grain, their livestock, their dairy products. Merchants and manufacturers had also been forced to pay through the nose for shipping their goods. The widows and orphans and other small investors had seen their investments crumble after the appearance of new shares created through a pen stroke. Even the militia summoned by West Virginia's Governor Matthews to put down disorder along the B. & O. line refused, after a first short skirmish, to fire upon the strikers, mingling with them instead.

In its edition of July 22, 1877, the Baltimore *Sun* editorialized:

There is no disguising the fact that the strikers in all their lawful acts have the fullest sympathy of the community. The 10 per cent reduction after two previous reductions was ill-advised. The company for years has boasted of its great earnings and paid enormous dividends. All that it could save of the reduction upon the wages of the 300 men, averaging about $6.00 a week, would be less than $10,000 a year. . . . The losses of the company [on account of the strike] have been estimated at $100,000. The firemen have evidently worked hard and suffered much on very small pay. They are chiefly old employees, married, and having families. . . .

The more intelligent seem content to appeal to the public, and ask if wages that do not now permit over $5.00 to go to . . . a family are more than sufficient as a remuneration for experienced labor, full of danger and responsibility. The singular part of the disturbance is in the very active part taken by the women, who are the wives and mothers of the firemen. They look famished and wild, and declare for starvation rather than have their people work for reduced wages. Better to starve outright, say they, than to die by slow starvation.

It was only when Federal troops, called out for the first time in American history to settle a labor dispute, were kept moving in trains along the B. & O. route that "law and order" was at last restored—by the expedient of firing volleys into crowds of strikers and sympathizers, at various station stops, killing and wounding an undetermined number.*

In Pittsburgh the slaughter became a summer's blood bath. Since local militia tended to fraternize with the workers, Governor Hartranft imported a thousand Philadelphia Hussars, very proud of their uniforms, to help the Pennsylvania Railroad "clean out" the Smoky City. The resentment of strikers against wage cuts had acted like a percussion cap, setting off the pent-up fury of the hungry and homeless against panic conditions and causing them to riot and loot. When the Hussars arrived on their special trains they were met by hostile crowds which surrounded the company roundhouse and rammed an oil-soaked flaming box-car into it. The besieged militia had to shoot their way out, killing twenty-one, wounding twenty-nine, among them women and children, and losing several of their own number.

Elsewhere similar scenes of violence occurred as the ordnance and rifles of Federal troops and militia, aided often by vigilantes, "shot the strike to pieces." The work-

* It is a matter of record, however, that in Reading, Pennsylvania, on the night of July 23, ten people were killed and forty wounded by the soldiers.

ers were starved into impotence and railroad magnates steadily refused to meet with their leaders and talk. Toward the end of July, when the blockade in the East and Mid-West had rendered the tie-up of rail traffic almost complete, and railroad boards of directors were beginning to think they might have to negotiate or give way a little, Rutherford B. Hayes, President of the United States, saved them the humiliation. He decided that interference with train movements was not only an assault upon property rights but also rebellion against the national government. He stated his intention of declaring martial law and sending soldiers to every strike center. His threat did much to dishearten the workers, awed by the prospect of trying to fight what would have been practically the entire United States army, with its artillery, and its Gatling guns. His pronouncement, climaxing other difficulties, was the coup de grace to the body of their morale. By August America's first great general strike movement had collapsed, amid press shudderings that the tactics of the Paris Commune had been transferred to the land of opportunity by wild-eyed and dirty foreigners who failed to appreciate, in the words of the Reverend Henry Ward Beecher, that "persons have the right to work when or where they please, as long as they please, and for what they please, and any attempt to infringe upon this right and to put good workmen on a level with poor workmen—any such attempt to regiment labor is preposterous."

For a time the railroad owners, the "James Boys in frock coats," walked in fear and trembling. They had been thoroughly frightened and still anticipated repercussions, perhaps a new upsurge of revolt. When nothing happened, and when the mutterings of the beaten multitude subsided, they began to persuade legislatures to appropriate tax-payers' money for building state armories where, it was hoped, National Guardsmen could be trained to put down "labor violence" with more dispatch and better discipline than they had previously displayed. The railroad captains also hired detectives to ferret out the ringleaders of the strike movement in order that they might be discharged, blacklisted, prosecuted for "malicious conspiracy"; while thousands of the rank and file, before they were allowed to resume their jobs, had to pledge that they would never again look at a labor union, including even the innocuous Brotherhoods, and of course the secret, and until then scarcely known Knights of Labor, which in many places had been the spearhead for strike action.

In 1894, moreover, after seventeen years of comparative peace, the great Pullman strike obliquely enabled railroad officials in particular, and employers in general, to test on a large scale an anti-labor weapon more potent by far than blacklist or troops; namely, the blanket or "omnibus" injunction.

In 1880, in Pullman, Illinois, just south of Chicago, George M. Pullman, inventor of "comfort cars," had been inspired by Krupp in Germany and Sir Titus Salt in England to establish a "model town," a home-and-work center for turning out his "traveling palaces." The pamphlet, *The Story of Pullman*, prepared by a public relations staff, described this community as surrounded by "bright beds of flowers, and green velvety stretches of lawn, shaded with trees, dotted with parks, and pretty water vistas and glimpses here and there of artistic sweeps of landscape gardening . . . a town, in a word, where all that is ugly and discordant and demoralizing is eliminated and all that which inspires self-respect is generously provided." It was, in short, a utopia which "has illustrated the helpful combination of Capital and Labor without strife or stultification."

The facts, however, hardly coincided with this advertising writer's idyll. Many of the five thousand workers employed by the Pullman Company to make and repair its cars which were used on about three-quarters of the nation's railway lines, claimed that the "flower beds" and

The Great Strike—Destruction of the Union Depot and Hotel at Pittsburgh.
Drawn by Fred B. Schell for *Harper's Weekly*.

the "artistic sweep of landscape gardening" did more to
impress visitors than assist their own comfort. As in coal-
mining communities, the "company" owned all property,
not only the foundry and steel mill and factory but also
the streets and the public utilities and the dwellings of the
workers. "Living on each other's laps" in tenements that
had no bathtubs and one faucet to every five families, they
had to pay rent to their employer who was also their landlord, and at rates 25 per cent higher than for virtually
identical accommodations in nearby Kensington. They had
further to buy his gas and his water, place their savings
in his bank, use his library at 25 cents per month, and also
consult his physicians who were myopic to any "large"
compensation claims for injury or death from work at
Pullman lathe or forge.

In addition, Mr. Pullman's hostility toward unionism
was akin to the righteous rage of that medieval baron when
the commoner suggested that serfs were also people. Yet
despite this atmosphere of antagonism nineteen locals of
the American Railway Union had been quietly organized
among 3,700 Pullman workers, an immediate result of
wage cuts ranging from 25 to 40 per cent between September, 1893, and May 1, 1894. Whereas in the preceding
year adverse conditions had caused all but 900 of them
to be laid off, they realized that business was beginning
to pick up again and that their decreased incomes represented the company's effort to equate its losses by "taking
it out of their hides" now that more employment had come
again and orders were piling up. They were further angered by the fact that, even in the depths of the depression
when 75 per cent of their number were virtually without
income, Pullman had continued to pay 8 per cent dividends
on watered stock that in 1894 reached a total capitalization
of $36,000,000; and that during the whole retrenchment
program no company officer, superintendent, or manager
had had his salary reduced.

They were aroused even more perhaps by the inability of Pullman, employer, to identify himself with Pullman, landlord, who refused to lower rents despite the 25 to 40 per cent diminution in income that Pullman, employer, had decreed for his "one big happy family." His workers, living always on subsistence margins, began to starve with their wives and children, and the aesthetics of their environment did little to allay the pangs of hunger.

In denouncing the "inhumanity" of this kind of wage-cutting program the Reverend W. H. Carwardine, for two years minister of the Pullman Methodist-Episcopal Church, pointed out that, under this regimen,

. . . after deducting rent the men invariably had only from one to six dollars or so on which to live for two weeks. One man has a pay-check in his possession of two cents after paying rent. He has never cashed it, preferring to keep it as a memento. He has it framed. Another I saw the other day, for seven cents. It was dated September, '93. The man had worked as a skilled mechanic at ten hours a day for twelve days, and earned $9.07. He keeps a widowed mother, and pays the rent, the house being in his name. His half month's rent amounted to $9.00. The seven cents was his, but he never claimed it.

In May of 1894, after a winter of deprivation, a grievance committee of workers conferred with Mr. Pullman. He pleaded poverty, insisted that philanthropy, rather than hard-headed business considerations, had induced him to cut wages, just to keep going, give the men something, and perhaps enable him to compete for new contracts. It was an argument which would have been more convincing if the company's surplus of $4,006,448 hadn't been so well known; and if the advantages of keeping his equipment in good condition, to forestall depreciation, hadn't been so obvious; and if the upswing in his own orders hadn't been so widely advertised.

Nevertheless, the workers—upon his assurance that certain complaints (excluding the question of rent reduction;

he couldn't go into that) would be investigated further—retired with the feeling that maybe the "Big Boss" was right, and things were bad and just couldn't be helped, and they would have to take their medicine until times improved.

Their philosophic resignation was shattered, however, when within forty-eight hours of this interview three moving spirits of the grievance committee were laid off, for no reason other than their daring to cite troubles in paradise, and despite Mr. Pullman's personal pledge that none of the grievance committee would be "discriminated against in any way." The violation of this promise in a few hours accomplished what months of suffering and hardship had failed to do. The workers called a strike, a decision quickened by local officers of the American Railway Union who in turn looked toward their national leaders for aid and guidance.

Unique among the period's labor groups, the American Railway Union was a precursor of the vertical, as against the craft, style of organization, profiting by the "One Big Union" mistakes of the Knights of Labor. The A.R.U. had been founded on June 20, 1893, by Eugene Victor Debs, who in his later years was to become the most worshiped and vilified exponent of an "Americanized" Socialism in the United States. A tall gaunt man, with a literary turn of mind, an altruist who was practically ambitious for the welfare of others, he was born in Terre Haute, Indiana, the son of Alsatian immigrants of exceptional culture. Despite his own desire for better education, he had to start work at fourteen, scraped paint from railroad cars, tried his hand at clerking in a grocery store, only to return to the yards where at twenty he was elected secretary of the local lodge of the Brotherhood of Locomotive Firemen. In 1880 he was named national secretary-treasurer of the Brotherhood and within twelve years built it up from near bankruptcy into a flourishing concern. At thirty-four he was acclaimed a great success, his future was secure in the labor world, he "had everything." Yet in 1892 he resigned his $4,000 a year post with the Brotherhood in protest against its refusal to support the strike of the Switchmen's Union in Buffalo early that year. To Debs this lack of coöperation among railroad workers as epitomized by the Brotherhood's behavior was not only ethically monstrous but in the long run a form of hara-kiri.

He had for years preached federation of existing railroad unions to prevent their "scabbing" upon each other and upon unorganized workers, and to achieve solidarity in aim and action. Finally he was convinced that his own Brotherhood, like that of the three others, concerned itself overmuch with high dues for insurance benefits and with ceremonials and mystic hand-clasps, and not enough with concrete measures to improve the status of railroad labor, whether of high or low degree, whether on trains, in the yards, or along the "right-of-way." After many wrestlings with the angel of his doubts, he decided to dedicate himself to the mission of uniting railroad men into a single, all-embracing union, a goal toward which he was inexorably urged by his own wide reading, his observations, and the inner springs of his personality. Gentle in manner, with a deep compassion for the lowly, he attracted people by his eloquence and his nobility of character. He was, indeed, the most trusted and most popular labor leader in the United States when in 1893 he launched his American Railway Union, for the presidency of which he received $75.00 a month when he got it.

The astonishing growth of the American Railway Union was among the most discussed phenomena of the day and derived jointly from the industrial method of organization and the admiration and affection in which Debs was held. Moreover, his sure-handed guidance of the spontaneous strike against James J. Hill's Great Northern in April, 1894, had magnified the importance of his new organization. Within eleven months it had established 465 different lodges, with a total enrollment of 150,000 as compared with all four of the Brotherhoods which together had about 140,000, the American Federation of Labor which had then about 275,000, and the declining Knights of Labor which claimed about 168,000 after anywhere from a dozen to twenty-five years of organizational activity on the part of each of them. Assailed by both business and labor organs for his temerity and his crazy notions, Debs —in accord with the principles of industrial unionism— had chartered branches among Pullman employees who, technically, were not railroad workers although they did manufacture and repair Pullman cars and also refurbished the rolling stock of other firms.

The leaders of the Pullman locals of the American Railway Union had often beseeched Debs and his lieutenant, George W. Howard, to call them out on strike to remedy intolerable abuses. Yet Debs, with the pragmatism of a working idealist, wanted to delay any such maneuver until the American Railway Union was older, more experienced, more powerful.

The Pullman workers, however, dumped their walkout into his lap. Almost before Debs knew what was happening they had set up their Central Strike Committee, stationed a cordon of pickets to guard company property, warned against violence, asked the company to negotiate and iron out grievances, and had received the now classic response of the obdurate employer, "There is nothing to arbitrate." Debs felt that, despite the unpromising situation —for the strike could not have come at a worse time, with the slack employment in the Pullman shops—he couldn't let the workers down. He and Howard assumed command, issued orders that the American Railway Union's policy of moderation and conciliation must be followed at all hazards, and assessed members of the union 3 cents a day toward support of the Pullman employees. In line with

the pacific spirit of the American Railway Union's constitution—"differences . . . adjusted, harmonious relations
. . . maintained" without the necessity for "strike and
lockout, boycott or blacklist"—Debs refused to sanction
sympathetic strikes planned in other Pullman plants in St.
Louis, Missouri; Wilmington, Delaware; Ludlow, Kentucky. For three weeks nothing very much transpired at
Pullman, Illinois. The workers were passive, sent their
delegates to request the company to arbitrate. The company, in turn, through its vice-president Wickes, denied
that any part of its industrial relations needed discussion,
either between workers and company officers, or by "outside parties" that were offering their services to settle the
dispute.

Finally, as a last resort to force Pullman into a gesture
of mediation, the American Railway Union on June 21,
1894, ordered its members not to handle Pullman cars if
the company after five days continued to spurn the workers' attempts to arbitrate.

The ultimatum had no effect on the company and on
June 26 the boycott began.

Whereas the boycott involved the railroads only indirectly, the Pullman Company promptly found an ardent
ally in the General Managers Association, an unincorpo-
rated body formed to study traffic and other problems
and drawn from the executives of twenty-four railroads
with termini in Chicago. These men controlled 40,000
miles of road, 220,000 employees, and two billion dollars.
The very day that Pullman cars became "untouchables"
the Association ordered the immediate discharge of any
worker who refused to switch them, an act which transformed the boycott into a strike; every time a switchman
was fired for "cutting out" a Pullman car, his colleagues
on the crew would quit in protest, until within four days
all "Pullmans" were "dead" in Chicago and eleven rail-

road lines were at a standstill as the result of ancillary walkouts.

At this juncture, Debs made his famous appeal to "The Railway Employes of America" saying that "the struggle . . . has developed into a contest between the producing classes and the money power of the country. We stand upon the ground that the workingmen are entitled to a just proportion of the proceeds of their labor. This the Pullman Company denied them. . . ." He pointed out that "the fight was between the American Railway Union and the Pullman Company" until "the railway corporations, through the General Managers Association, came to the rescue [of Pullman] and in a series of whereases declared to the world that they would go into partnership with Pullman, so to speak, and stand by him in . . . starving his employes to death. . . ."

He further insisted that the strikers remain passive in their resistance, and refrain from any word or deed that could be construed as a threat to property. At first they obeyed this fiat with the discipline of a Prussian regiment. The Association and Pullman soon perceived that such pacific measures would probably insure a victory for Debs, and the American Railway Union. They therefore imported two thousand strikebreakers from Canada, instructed them to rip up tracks, and destroy signal towers, while secret *agents provocateurs* set fire to freight cars marooned on Chicago sidings. All this enabled the Association to accuse the strikers of violence and arson. Since such tactics failed to whip up enough public frenzy, the Association resorted to its most cunning move. It caused strikebreakers to attach mail cars to trains made up exclusively of Pullmans, in order to place the strikers in the position of interfering with the United States mails. Naturally, when the strikers "cut out" Pullmans they at the same time hampered the movement of the mails.

In this respect the Association outsmarted Debs; it soon

wept in anguish over the desecration of this Holy of
Holies, the conveyance of mails, and its lamentations were
echoed in the press which praised the Association's appeal
to Attorney-General Olney for 3,400 deputies who were
sworn in by U. S. Marshal Arnold. They were chosen,
these deputies, by a man named Egan, publicity director
for the Association, and were paid by the Association,
thus performing the dual function of government officials
and agents of private enterprise. They had a few minor
clashes with groups of strikers, stones were hurled, bricks
heaved, and names called, and no real damage was done,
except that on one occasion Marshal Arnold himself was
pleasantly rolled in the dust.

The Association, however, seized upon his discomfiture
as proof that "uncontrollable outbreaks of violence" had
occurred, and wired President Cleveland for Federal
troops. In violation of all existing law relating to the separation of state and Federal powers, Cleveland on July 4
commanded four companies of the Fifteenth U.S. Infantry
to march to Chicago./Governor John P. Altgeld of Illinois, as soon as he learned that Federal troops had been
ordered to "occupy" Chicago, protested to President
Cleveland:

I am advised that you have ordered Federal troops to go
into service in the State of Illinois. Surely the facts have not
been correctly presented to you in this case . . . or you
would not have taken this step, for it is entirely unnecessary,
and, it seems to me, unjustifiable. . . . Local officials have
been able to handle the situation. . . . The Federal government has been applied to by men who had political and selfish
motives for wanting to ignore the State government. At present some of our railroads are paralyzed, not by reason of obstructions, but because they cannot get men to operate their
trains. . . . The newspapers' accounts have in many cases
been pure fabrications. . . . You have been imposed on in
this matter, but, even if, by a forced construction, it were

held that the conditions here came within the letter of the statute, then I submit that local self-government is a fundamental principle of our Constitution. . . . As Governor of the State of Illinois, I protest against this, and ask the immediate withdrawal of Federal troops from active duty in this State.

A short exchange of telegrams between the President and the Governor ended in the former's triumph, to the delight of all the "respectable portions" of society who looked upon Altgeld as the spawn of Satan since he had, in the preceding year, pardoned three anarchists, Neebe, Schwab, and Fielden, who had been imprisoned for alleged complicity in the Haymarket Bomb. Association members were particularly pleased because they had been fearful that Altgeld would station state militia around their property to protect it even from the maraudings of their own strikebreakers—which was the last thing they wanted.

The Association was pleased with itself for other reasons; for when on July 6 Federal troops began to move trains crammed with Swift and Company meats from the Union Stock Yards, violence, genuine and grim, flared up with a frenzy long suppressed. Men who, aching in head and heart over the plight of their famished families, had yet tried to remain loyal to "Gene's" preachments of peace, with the appearance of the regulars could stand it no longer and ran amok. In response to the request of an alarmed Mayor Hopkins in Chicago, Governor Altgeld dispatched company after company of militia to aid local police and Federal troops in restraining the mob spirit that swept over the Windy City. Street fighting began and crowds collected in front of trains moving out of yards, a wall of angry flesh that sought to arrest the progress of great engines steaming slowly from roundhouse and siding. And yet Debs still was trumping the Association's ace. The ranks of the strikers held firm while fourteen thousand soldiers clanked, in full accouterment, over the cobblestones of Chicago. On July 6 the Associated Press correspondent filing his story pointed out that "despite the presence of United States troops and the mobilization of five regiments of state militia; despite threats of martial law and bullet and bayonet, the great strike inaugurated by the American Railway Union holds three fourths of the roads running out of Chicago in its strong fetters, and last night traffic was more fully paralyzed than at any time since the inception of the tie up."

Meanwhile, in North Dakota, Colorado, California, Idaho, Montana, and in many Eastern states, occurred sympathetic walkouts by engineers, firemen, repairmen, signalmen, yardmasters, telegraph operators and many more. Officials of the Brotherhoods were scared and furious. They expelled any member who joined in this "lunatic insurgency." The strike was condemned by Grand Chief Clark of the Conductors, by Grand Master Wilkinson of the Trainmen; but the rank and file believed in Debs and were sure he was right, and many lodges withdrew from the Brotherhoods to affiliate themselves with the American Railway Union. In the model town of Pullman, Illinois, all shops and plants were silent and the strikers, to the amusement of the country, used bicycles to keep their picket lines.

Meanwhile, too, the Association was carefully preparing its court campaign against the American Railway Union, hoping to demolish it with a single blow from the bench. At the request of Association officials, Attorney-General Olney obligingly named Edwin Walker as special counsel to represent the government in the Association's attempt to obtain an omnibus injunction against the strikers. Despite the fact that Walker for twenty-four years had been attorney for the Chicago, Milwaukee and St. Paul Railroad, a line particularly affected by the strike, he was nevertheless considered to be sufficiently objective to represent his old clients and their friends and an impartial government, at the same time, and also to be on both private and public payrolls for rendering his patriotic services. In his every step Walker was advised by Olney, an implacable foe of unionism, a "right-thinking, upstanding" person who saw the milling mobs of revolution every time anything was done for the non-owning man. And it was Olney who, among other things, instructed Walker not to depend upon warrants issued under statutes against individuals guilty of criminal behavior, but to use the injunction as a device to thwart *anticipated* criminal action.

Hence with the connivance of a United States Attorney-General, and on the initiative of his Department of Justice, the most sweeping anti-labor injunction in American history was issued by Judge Grosscup of the United States court in Chicago on July 2. It restrained Debs, Howard, and the entire membership of the American Railway Union from any interference with the mails, or with interstate commerce, or with the business affairs of the twenty-four railroads involved in the strike and it further prevented oral efforts to persuade workers to join the walkout, since it expressly prohibited "compelling or inducing . . . any of the employees of any of the said railroads to refuse or fail to perform any of their duties . . . or to leave the service of such railroads."

Under the terms of this injunction the very act of picketing was itself rendered a crime, while the right of trial by jury was abrogated; and the same judge who issued the injunction was empowered to enforce it. The Association, by this feat, shattered the morale of the strikers and overthrew the "Debs rebellion." For if the workers submitted to the injunction and abandoned all strike activity until a court test, they would be certain to lose, in the interval, all they had previously gained. If on the other hand they flouted the injunction, they faced arrest and imprisonment on contempt of court charges.

In a last desperate counteroffensive to regain ground lost, Debs sought to hurry pending plans for a general strike. It was his somewhat grandiose scheme to call out first workers in the Chicago area and proceed from city to city until a national paralysis of industry would be the challenge of the "producing classes" to the might of the "money men."

Although some bakers and cigar makers and machinists and teamsters sporadically responded to this idea, the A. F. of L. leaders, especially Samuel Gompers, opposed the whole plan as "unwise and inexpedient." The Brotherhood chieftains not only opposed it but sabotaged the current strike by assisting the Association to find engineers and firemen and dispatchers skilled enough to replace those who had quit or had been locked out.

Retreating slowly, Debs again proposed, through Mayor Hopkins of Chicago, that the strike and boycott would be both called off, providing only that the Association and Pullman would agree to reinstate all strikers, without discrimination, except those "convicted" of "crime"; but both the Association and Pullman ignored this offer of a truce, letting it be known that they could not "recognize anarchism."

While all this was happening, Judge Grosscup had summoned a special Federal jury which assembled on July 10 to determine whether a state of insurrection against the United States government then prevailed. It was obvious that, in the judge's own opinion, insurrection, along with related abominations, not only existed but would submerge American civilization unless the special grand jury found that if "two or more persons corruptly or wrongfully agreed with each other that the employees of the several railroads carrying the mails and interstate commerce should quit and their successors should, by threats, intimidation or violence, be prevented from taking their places, such would constitute a conspiracy. . . ."

Thus instructed by Judge Grosscup as to what its decision should be, the jury returned indictments against Debs as president, Howard as vice-president, Keliher as secretary, and Rogers as chief organizer of the American Railway Union on the counts which had been lucidly indicated. On the same day, July 10, that the jury declared Debs and the others guilty, they were arrested, and the offices of their union raided and papers and books seized by Federal agents. Released on bail on the conspiracy charge, Debs and his three aides were again arrested on contempt of court charges for "disobeying" the cease and desist orders of the injunction issued on July 3. They went to jail to force a test by trial, which was postponed time and again and finally began in the fall with Clarence Darrow among the attorneys for the defense.

The prosecution, led by Walker, who still represented both the Association and the government and who was still coached by Olney from the sidelines, contended that the American Railway Union, by directing workers to go on strike, had "conspired" to restrain trade among the states. The union's lawyers countered with the argument that the American Railway Union was a voluntary association, that its adherents had by acclamation voted of their own free will to walk out and that therefore "conspiracy" was irrelevant to the whole situation since union members merely were exercising their legal right to strike, a right guaranteed to them for generations.

In December, after Pullman had refused to testify and had run off to a hiding place in New York City, and after the records of the General Managers Association, which clearly showed conspiracy on the part of the railroads, were not admitted as evidence although all documents of the American Railway Union were freely introduced, the United States Circuit Court, invoking the Sherman Anti-Trust Law which, ironically, had been passed with labor support to curb the collusions of monopoly among the new great cartels, determined that Debs and his colleagues were guilty as charged. Debs was sentenced to six months in the county jail at Woodstock, Illinois, and the others received terms of three months apiece.

The following spring the Supreme Court unanimously upheld this decision. To many observers, however, it appeared that the tortuous explanations which accompanied this verdict of the high tribunal formed an excellent example of rationalization. For to keep this particular injunction legal, the court was forced to validate two extremely vague and far-fetched principles. In the first place, it had to prove that a certain contemplated act would inflict great damage to property unless forestalled by a restraining order of the court, a difficult hurdle to take since the injunction was normally issued to prevent picketing, and the boycott in instances where no actual property was endangered. The Supreme Court therefore invented the concept that the "expectancies" which derive from the exchange relationships between a merchant and his customers, and from the "for services rendered" relationship between employer and employee by themselves comprised "property." Hence, it was deduced, a strike with its picketing tends to injure the employer's "expectancy" of retaining his labor force or getting a substitute personnel, and the boycott likewise tends to undermine the merchant's "expectancy" of keeping his patrons and obtaining new ones, an "expectancy" embodied in the imponderables of "good will."

Of course, the "injury-to-property-of-expectancy" thesis could not alone justify the injunction, for under American law there can be no recovery for losses sustained as the result of a person, or a group, exercising their legal rights. If therefore the strike and picketing and the boycott were legal, nothing could be done to prevent their use from impairing "the expectancy" of an employer. It was thus imperative to show that the injunction came under the pur-

Eugene V. Debs.

view of "equity" or extraordinary justice, and that strike, picketing, and boycott alike comprised a "conspiracy" against the complainant (that is, the Association).

Since Olney had contrived to change the anti-monopoly intent of the Sherman Anti-Trust Act into an anti-labor activity ruling (linking with it the thought that interstate commerce had been disrupted by the Debs uprising), the Supreme Court found it easy to follow his mode of logic. It decided that when workers sought to interfere with an employer's "probable expectancies" by using the strike, picketing, and boycott, or any or all, a court order could thwart all three types of action on the basis of "malicious conspiracy" looking toward economic detriment.

When Debs, brooding in his cell at Woodstock, learned of the Supreme Court's expedition into the realm of "class metaphysics," he embraced Socialism, rededicating himself to a new and larger crusade: the abolition of a system which, in his view, permitted the President of the United States, its Attorney-General, its Army, its Circuit and Supreme Courts to align themselves with a Pullman and the General Managers Association to beat American wage earners back into a new hopeless serfdom, to break their unions, and leave them with the choice of "work for what we want to give you, or starve."

During the decade which preceded the Debs revolt, the frequency of strikes, the resentment of workers against fourteen- and fifteen-hour days, against being on call at any time of the day or night, against the insecurity of a three- to five-day work week, against the refusal of the roads to install rudimentary safety appliances—all were linked with spasms of agrarian antagonism toward excessive and discriminatory rates, and the financial sway held by Eastern railroad capital over the markets and mortgages of the West. The Populist movement in itself was in large part an uprising against the might of the "octopi," the American railroad empires.

The American people, with their ingrained tendency to curtail too great power of any kind as soon as it assumes obvious proportions, began to think that the "Robber Barons" were getting away with altogether too much. Propelled by granger and labor agitation, supported by large parts of the public, the famous Act to Regulate Commerce was passed by Congress in 1888. Among other things, it set up a five-man commission to prevent unjust discriminations among shippers. It has been almost annually followed by legislation seeking to limit still further the private control over rail carriers. In 1893 the Safety Act, in 1898 the Erdman Act, in 1903 the Elkins Act, in 1907 the Hours of Service Act, in 1908 the Ash-Pan Act, in 1909 the Transportation of Explosives Act, in 1910 the Safety Appliance Act, in 1911 the Boiler Inspection Act, in 1913 the Valuation Act, in 1916 the Adamson Law, in 1920 the Transportation Act, in 1926 the Railway Labor Act, in 1933 the Emergency Railroad Transportation Act, and in 1934 the Amendment to the Railway Labor Act, especially in its sections creating the three-man National Mediation Board—all have signified the attempt of the American public, through its government, to determine fair and reasonable returns on investments by fixing rates and trying to substitute orderly methods of adjusting employer-employee differences for the strife and friction of lockout and strike.

The public, of course, has a very special and direct stake in the safe and uninterrupted operation of what Senator Sorghum used to call the "glorious arteries of our national commerce." The theory behind gifts of land to them and loans that were often gifts was that they performed a function that was a public trust. Certainly in our "technologically tenuous" economy, with the railroads still carrying about 69 per cent of our freight, a cessation of train service into, say, New York City, would within twenty-four hours cause food shortages that, if continued, could bring starvation in their wake.

Certainly, too, in more recent times, especially during the past dozen years, a newer spirit of coöperation and good will, of joint allegiance to the job of "running our railroad," has in many instances begun to supplant what was once a savage antagonism between management and men. It is an evolution of attitude which has accompanied, almost step by step, the development of the air-conditioned aluminum alloy hundred-mile-an-hour streamlined "Zephyr" from the old iron monster with boilers that "went out" (i.e., blew up) with dreadful regularity.[*]

Today there are 128 subdivisions of American railroad labor, divided into seven broad categories. Executives, officials, and various staff assistants comprise 1.1 per cent; professional, clerical, and general, 15.7 per cent; maintenance of way and structures, 21 per cent; equipment and stores, 27.8 per cent; while the remaining 34.4 per cent come under the heading of "transportation" in both its stationary and moving aspects.

Out of a total of some 1,065,000 employees, more than half belong to unions that are organized almost exclusively on a craft basis. There are now twenty altogether, five of which—with a membership total of about 134,000—are affiliated with the A. F. of L. Among the larger "independents" are the American Federation of Railroad Workers and the Brotherhood of Signalmen with 20,000 and 12,000 members respectively. The celebrated "Big Four"— the Brotherhoods of Locomotive Engineers (59,108), Firemen and Enginemen (60,886), Trainmen (116,274), and the Order of Railway Conductors (49,953)—have steadily remained outside of any larger labor alignment. Since the turn of the century they have become distinctly more aggressive, a trend which started in the mid-nineties

[*] Between 1888 and 1892, for example, 316 persons were killed and 2,582 injured in train accidents, a large proportion of which were due to defective locomotive boilers.

after the defeat of the American Railway Union had warned them that they would have to be more aware of collective bargaining and tougher if they hoped to wring any concessions whatsoever from their hard-bitten employers. Often acting in concert, and still confident of their superior status, since their members comprise the aristocracy of railroad labor, they have preserved their own autonomy and rights of self-determination despite the pleas of Gompers, Green, and latterly of various C.I.O. leaders to link fortunes at least on some paper or "joint council" basis.

The insurance features of the Big Four through the years have fostered the accumulation of vast sums, enabling them to become heavy investors in many spheres of American enterprise. With very few exceptions, they have managed their funds with foresight and integrity, and have regularly paid a long list of benefits to the survivors of thousands of their former members. In 1922, the "Engineers," then particularly prosperous, were able to build their own skyscraper in Cleveland, Ohio, at a cost of $1,250,000. They also own the Coal River Collieries in West Virginia where, as employers, they twice clashed with John L. Lewis and the United Mine Workers over the question of unionizing a union-owned mine!

The Big Four, counting among their number thousands of the highest paid workers in the country, and being in a sense "men of property" who collectively own millions in securities, have been for years noted for their conservatism and taunted about it by the more liberal factions in the American labor movement. Anxious to keep their funds intact, in order to meet their insurance dividends, they have been understandably reluctant to go on strike since nothing else depletes a union's treasury reserves with such disheartening speed. Instead they have tended to rely on arbitration, and to exploit the fact that the interlocking of their four-ply congeries of skills renders them indispensable if trains are to be kept running. They prefer to invoke government aid to gain wages, hours, and other demands whenever possible. In 1916, for example, the Adamson Law, making the eight-hour day mandatory on the nation's railroads, was rammed through Congress by President Wilson to avert a strike threatened by the Brotherhoods, in conjunction with other unions, unless this working-time minimum were granted.

When the United States entered the World War the Federal government took over the railroads. Perhaps more nonsense has been printed about this subject than about anything else in recent American history. In the first place, the only reason why the government assumed control was that such carriers, conditioned to bitter and unceasing competition with each other, seemed unable to visualize the unitary nature of the transportation problem in time of war. Faced by the exigencies of moving vast masses of men, munitions, and other war materials over a great continental area, the government soon found that the intense rivalry among the railroads rendered it inexpedient to depend upon either their efficiency or their patriotism. A central coordinating body, implemented by the ultimate powers of government, was required to enforce order and coöperation, the fusing of many diverse parts into a smoothly functioning whole. Hence in 1917 Congress created the Federal Railroad Administration to direct the nation's traffic on rails. By and large it turned in an excellent job, modernizing railroad equipment, which as usual was behind the times, to the tune of $400,000,000 and returning it to private hands in better shape than it had ever been before.

Government operation during 1917-20 was the best break that American railroad labor ever had. The Federal Railroad Administration had inherited a force dissatisfied with its failure to keep its income in step with fast-rising costs of living and angered by executive rebuff of efforts to raise its real wages. The labor turnover was surprisingly high in view of the expertness required of large sections of the personnel; and the workers' loyalty was at low ebb. The first thing that the F.R.A. did was to raise rates of pay after conducting some very searching studies into real earnings as compared with prevailing prices. But its most valuable and long-lasting contribution was the creation of machinery which, like other new mechanisms, was creaky at first and needed a lot of lubrication, but which did manage to resolve controversies between management and labor without engendering the bad blood of other days. The various Railway Adjustment Boards, with their equal representation from both sides, with government sitting in as party of the third part, decided thousands of cases in which conflicts were discussed and new procedures adopted often by unanimous vote.*

Moreover, the various bureaus and commissions of the Federal Railroad Administration were catholic in their views. They recognized the existence of the "common" unorganized laborer, the "shack-dwellers," outside the pale of the Big Four's "Brahmins," and granted them sizable raises.

When the war ended and the A.E.F. was carried home to civilian life, the government prepared to hand the railroads back to their private owners. The workers, however, found no rapture in this prospect. They had been given decent and humane treatment. It was a brand new experience for many thousands of them, and few among the then nearly two million railroad workers wanted to relinquish it. Although wage boosts had not fulfilled their first high hopes, the "atmosphere," the whole new complex of relations engendered by government control,

---

* In this connection, it is interesting to note that Commissioner Joseph B. Eastman, Federal Coördinator of Transportation, in referring to these boards, has said, "I find, notwithstanding the government was then in control of the railroads, that the decisions in favor of the carriers exceeded those in favor of the employees."

had been distinctly pleasant. For the first time many of
them had been at least regarded as men, as people of dignity and importance in the scheme of winning the war.

The drive for continued government operation was in-
itially sponsored by the Brotherhoods, taken up by other
railroad labor, aided and abetted by unions in every trade
throughout the country. The idea was cheered and cussed
in congressional corridors. It brought the cold sweat of
panic to various Wall Street groups which quickly dispatched one of the most expensive lobbies of modern times
to Washington to scotch this "pernicious and subversive"
doctrine.

The sentiment for government ownership was crystallized in the Plumb Plan, named for its author, Glenn E.
Plumb, able general counsel for the organized railroad employees. It proposed, in brief, a form of guild socialism
under which the government was to buy, through a bond-
issue, all basic railroad properties, after putting their valua-
tions "through the wringer," and then to lease them as a
national nonprofit corporation. Earnings were to be used
for paying interest and operating expenses and for retiring
bonds within fifty years. Savings over and above such outlays were to be divided between the government and all
employees, from chief executive to track-walker, in accord
with an elaborate pro-rata scheme.

To "push, popularize, publicize" this scheme a Plumb
Plan League was formed with Samuel Gompers doing the
honors as president and Warren S. Stone, Grand Chief of
the Engineers, doing the work. The organization, with
more zeal than precision, claimed a following of six million
people, drawn from railroad labor in general, the A. F. of
L., the Non-Partisan League, the Farmers National Council, and other sodalities of agrarian discontent. The League
established headquarters in Washington and an energetic
lobby of its own. It button-holed Senators, pushed Representatives into a listening corner, and created a weekly

newspaper *Labor** as the Big Bertha in its educational battery.

Yet the Plumb Plan's proponents were beaten before they started. It was not alone the Bolshevik menace which the press discovered as the motive behind its backers. Nor yet was it entirely the pressures exerted upon Congress by railroad financiers nor their adroit propaganda about the "notorious inefficiency" of government and its "wastefulness and red-tape" as compared with the diametrically opposed attributes of private business. Government control of railroads had been, after all, an emergency, a war measure. And soon after the Armistice was signed, the American people, as if with a shudder of revulsion, turned away from anything identified with the war and started to squander their whipped-up hates upon such domestic "foes" as radicals and reformers and others who violated the canons of a new and more parochial nationalism.

By the time Croix de Guerre Medals began to be displayed in pawn-shop windows—and very cheap they were, even then—the nation's deepest desire was that return to normalcy which Warren G. Harding talked about.

After six days of hearings, of cross-examining Plumb Plan advocates, the House Committee on Interstate and Foreign Commerce tossed the plan out of the window with the statement that it "was more firmly convinced than ever that government ownership is not, and ought not to be, the solution of the problem" and that "the so-called Plumb Plan is impossible."

To allay employer-employee tensions already evoked by the impending return of the roads to private operation, Congress in 1920 passed the Transportation Act,† part of

---

* The publication survived the purpose of its founding and today shares with *The New Leader* the reputation of being the "best" labor journal in the United States.

† In many quarters, the Act was assailed as "a gigantic fraud," and "reckless robbery." Opponents asked why, after being ten months in committee, it had been rushed through both Senate and House within seventy-two hours after it was reported out. Denouncing its passage, Congressman

which called for the establishment of a Railway Labor
Board, precursor of the present-day apparatus for railroad
amity. It had nine members appointed by the President
with the Senate's consent. Carriers, labor, and the public
each had three representatives. No similar body in American annals ever faced a more complex and troublous task.
The Board was charged with the obligation of fixing "just"
wage scales and working rules for 1,950,000 railroad employees of extremely diverse occupation. It had to meet
the issue of wage increases that had been postponed through
eighteen months of dickering. It had to begin its job amid
the turmoil of postwar readjustments when forecasting
the economic future, even over the short run, was any
crystal-gazer's guess. It had to conciliate workers smarting
under the summary rejection of the Plumb Plan by the
House Committee. It had, finally, to adjudicate differences
between management and labor when all other moves for
mediation had failed.

From its first day it encountered the intractability of
muddle. Almost immediately, for example, it had to define
and rule upon the question of a "living wage." During the
war while wages in other industries, like building and steel
and motors, had been keeping pace with rising prices, the
income of railroad workers, in terms of buying power, had

Huddleston declared: "So far as I know it is not claimed by anyone that the
Transportation Act originated in Congress. Its real origin was in banks,
railroad lawyers and other lobbyists. . . . By the . . . Act, the Treasury
was opened to the railroads. Under Section 202, $200,000,000 was appropri-
ated to pay their claims. Under Section 209 . . . $631,000,000 of government
gifts to the railroads are already in sight . . . will probably reach $800,000,-
000. Under Section 210, $300,000,000 were placed at the disposition of the
railroads as loans. These vast sums must come . . . out of the taxpayers'
money. To them must be added the provision of the Act upon which the
rates were increased so as to yield 6 per cent upon railroad stock, water,
fraudulent capitalization, and all, aggregating $18,900,000,000 whereas . . .
the value of all stocks and bonds and other railroad securities . . . aggre-
gated only $8,000,000. Under the increase of rates made in 1920 it was esti-
mated that over $1,500,000,000 would be taken directly from the pockets of
consumers and . . . in the end would increase the cost of living and doing
business $6,000,000,000 annually."

steadily declined. Yet they had been genuinely patriotic, carrying out their duties in letter and spirit. They had refrained from capitalizing on their crucially important position to make more money by going on strike.

As soon as the Railway Labor Board was set up, however, they looked to it to make up for their losses. The Board was bombarded with statistics by the brainy and diligent W. Jett Lauck, then consulting economist for the unions. His compilations showed that, in view of the period's inflationary prices, an annual wage of $1,700 for example would have to be boosted to about $2,100 to render pay envelopes "real." His figures marched like a Roman legion over the long road of testimony stretching before the Board. His estimates were countered by accountants and statisticians for the railroads who declared the roads would be bankrupted if they granted any such increases which, in sum, amounted to a billion dollars.

After weighing the pros and cons of perhaps the most exhaustive arguments about the "living wage" ever heard, the Board handed down its decision of a $558,000,000 general raise. Even so, nobody was particularly pleased, although union leaders acknowledged that at least the Board had tried to do the "right thing." "While the decision," said President Carter of the Locomotive Firemen and Enginemen, "of the labor board did not come up to our desires, or our expectations, yet I cannot recall a single instance where a wage . . . settlement of any kind proved to be absolutely satisfactory to everyone concerned; and just as long as we have wage bargaining I feel confident that the same situation will exist. . . ."

In part, of course, such opinions were voiced to counteract in advance any move by employers to reduce payrolls. Yet that move was made almost at once. In the summer of 1920 the pale sun of postwar prosperity suffered a sudden eclipse. Retrenchment in business generally reacted quickly and unfavorably upon railroad revenues. Instead of earning the 5 ½ per cent intended by the Transportation Act, returns were cut to 3 ½ per cent. The ratio of operating expenses to income mounted to 94.37 for the fiscal year, the highest on record. By January, 1921, Class I railroads alone were in the red for $958,399,000. Only three alternatives seemed open to officials for restoring profits.

They could raise freight and passenger rates. But this was inexpedient since the railroads, to meet the higher wage bills of the Board's recent award, had passed the cost on to their customers by already boosting all rates from 25 per cent to 40 per cent. The shipping public was inclined to believe that such excessively high charges were partially responsible for the business recession. The second possibility was to increase the volume of traffic—a feat that would cure the collapse itself. The third course was to cut expenses; and since labor still constituted about 63 per cent of all operating outlays, the railroads assumed the role of Indian giver. They went before the Board and in effect demanded that they be returned the wage raises they had but a short time before allowed.

Their employees were maddened by what they called "Trojan horse trickery." They had seen the roads gain inordinate profits and they felt that they themselves—having just obtained some remote approximation of their proper due—were once more being compelled to "take the rap" for the new decline in earnings. They inveighed against the Board's personnel, alleged that the surrogates of the "public" had been "reached" by Wall Street, and attacked the whole thesis of "ability to pay" returns on investment since, they claimed, the accounting methods used by the railroads did more to confuse than to reveal the facts. After many tumultuous sessions the Board determined that the railroads had just cause for lowering wages. It therefore decreed pay reductions all along the line—reductions that in many instances canceled the gains that labor had recently achieved. The dissenting minority opinion of the

Board's labor representatives flayed this procedure and maintained that

the wages fixed by the majority decision are such as to condemn these railway workers to lives of extreme poverty. . . . It may be asking too much to urge that human life is in no class by itself, not to be listed indifferently among the costs of transportation.

. . . The wages most recently determined are in some cases 50 per cent of the amount needed for a fair standard of living. Maintenance and expansion costs of the railways must be paid, and with the "cordial" and "patriotic" co-operation of the workers; the "maintenance costs" of the workers are considered to be "theoretical" when they are considered at all. Such is the basis for the series of wage decisions now being made.

In rendering this "cut-wages" verdict, the Board dug its own grave and then expired of "labor complaint" in the form of the Big Strike of 1922. At the instigation of officials of the New York Central and Pennsylvania railroads, the Board's award was used by the Association of Railway Executives as a first salvo in a new union-breaking campaign which, among other objectives, tried to substitute "company" unions for the bona-fide kind.

Moreover, the reductions ordered by the Board proved especially drastic for men in the repair shops, who were further angered by the railroads' reversion to the old evil of "farming out" repairs, that is, taking them away from their own plants and assigning them to independent contractors. It was a process that cost twice as much, but, in the railroads' opinion, was double the pleasure; for by farming out repairs unionists were deprived of work, and their unions of dues, a condition which, it was thought, would make it easier to introduce company or employee representation "unions" which, generically, "will do anything for labor except help get employers off its back."

On July 1, 1922, in protest against wage cuts and the

company union program of the railroads, 400,000 members of the Blacksmiths, the Sheet and Metal Workers, the Boilermakers, the Railway Carmen, the Machinists and the Electrical Workers, comprising the Federated Shop Crafts, put down their tools. Within two days they were joined by a cross section of other railroad workers, oilers, plumbers, signalmen, freight handlers, and many more, bringing the total on strike to more than a half million men. Despite the lapse of twenty-eight years, and as if to verify Spengler's axiom concerning the "eternal recurrence of the similar," the 1922 walkout duplicated in its essentials the Debs uprising, except that no single great leader of labor emerged, and fatalities were relatively fewer. Service was crippled, all over the country, and strikebreakers hired by the thousands. The New York *Times* correspondent reported:

The down and outers and the professionally unemployed are now working for the railroads. When the call went out for strike-breakers, these classes came a-running. . . . Train load after train load of [such] recruits have been dumped into a railroad town to have the company officials discover that they harbored and paid a precious crew of thugs, gunmen and sharks, second-story men and ex-bootleggers. Many of them were just resting up after a stretch in prison. . . . With them came the honest, good-for-nothing bum . . . who a year ago panhandled his way from park to park and into one jug after another, at the expense of the city's gullibles, has for the past few months become a personage.

Sought after and welcomed by all the rival strikebreaking agencies, fly-by-night detective, and fake industrial bureaus, he has been depended upon to help break the strike and keep it broken. . . . If he travels at night Pullman accommodations are included in the bill. . . . Throughout the length and breadth of the land the hoboes and the toughs are enjoying the hospitality of the railroads. Instead of dodging fly-cops they are under their protection. East and West the ancient

habit of gun-toting has been revived, virtually all the new employees carrying weapons. . . .

President Harding, however, in pursuing his career as
professional dupe, commended these strikebreakers as "fine
loyal workers" and "upstanding citizens." In addition to
paying the agencies $25.00 a head for supplying such
patriots, the Class I railroads alone, for the month of July,
spent $6,000,000 for "special officers." In Massachusetts,
Governor Cox mobilized the State Constabulary; two artillery companies were rushed to Concord, New Hampshire; fake bombs were planted by United States Marshals
on Santa Fe property in San Bernardino, California; and
Attorney-General Daugherty, through Judge Wilkinson,
fabricated a far-reaching injunction which confirmed his
own promise that "I will use the power of the Government within my control to prevent the labor unions from
destroying the Open Shop. . . ."

On July 31, President Harding proposed to Dewitt
Cuyler, chairman of the Association of Railway Executives, a peace formula drafted by Secretary of Commerce
Herbert Hoover. Under its terms, "Railway managers and
workmen" were "to agree to recognize the validity of all
decisions of the Railroad Board," "the carriers to withdraw
all lawsuits growing out of the strike," and "all employees
on strike" were "to be returned to work and to their former positions, with seniority and other rights unimpaired."
On August 3 the strikers signified their willingness to
accept this offer at least as a basis for negotiations. Two
days earlier, however, Herbert Hoover had spent a very
unhappy afternoon sitting in at a conference of railroad
financiers, attended by Charles E. Mitchell, President of
the National City Bank; Steward Prosser, President of the
Bankers Trust Company; Benjamin Strong, Governor of
the Federal Reserve Bank in New York; Edward R. Stet-
tinius of J. P. Morgan & Company; and several others.

Hoover was unable to persuade them to accept his peace program and in turn was informed that the bankers would not permit their railroad managements to consider a settlement unless the strikers would relinquish their seniority rights, time-and-a-half pay for overtime and holidays, and similar privileges achieved over many years.

On August 7 President Harding indirectly transmitted this message to the strikers, who rejected it. Meantime, since skilled shop mechanics were, and are, key men in keeping engines and cars in condition for service, delays and accidents resulting from defective repairs and inspection mounted daily. The "Big Four," which as usual steered clear of scenes of battle despite the urgings of their membership to support the walkout by vigorous action, kept trying to arrange an agreement between the Association of Railway Executives and the Federated Shop Crafts. All such attempts collapsed against the opposition of employers like Samuel M. Vauclain, President of the Baldwin Locomotive Works, who later declared in a speech delivered before the New Orleans Association of Commerce, early in 1923:

I have got 25,000 men working for me in a little foundry back east. I'd like to see any union labor leader start something among them. Why, when the railroad strike was starting, a bunch of labor delegates came around the plant. In twenty minutes I had every damned one of them in jail. I was told I had no right to put them in jail. I said: "But they are in jail, aren't they? Now go and get them out." You've got to act quick when you are facing a crisis.

When in the middle of September the workers had been worn down and the railroads had lost astronomical sums in revenues,* individual carriers and individual unions

* The tie-up in many places had dramatized the efficacy of motor-trucks for transporting goods, especially for the shorter hauls, and the railroads thus lost a large amount of business they never regained.

began gradually to patch up their differences, both sides seeming pretty sick about the whole affair.

Only seven of the then sixteen railroad unions had gone on strike, a circumstance applauded by the *Wall Street Journal* which affirmed on October 17: "It is no paradox to say their inability to stand shoulder to shoulder thruout the strike was the most fortunate thing that could have happened, first for the country at large and eventually for the investors in railroads."

Fortunate or not, the events of this strike had generated an "unhealthy" bitterness, as pointed out by Whiting Williams in *Collier's* magazine:

In the past nine weeks the most disturbing thing has been the spirit of such statements as these: "Seems like they ain't no government for us working class people" or "It started with me the day my father wheeled all our household stuff in a couple of baby carriages out of a mine town up in the hills into the snow; evicted we was then. Same now. I thought us . . . had got by all that."

This belief in working class persecution is the most outstanding and serious result of the labor wars of 1922. In some degree it always follows industrial conflict, but in no other strike of recent times have the workers felt that the railway management and the public hit them unfairly with the fist of the non-partisan courts. The so-called Daugherty injunction has done more than anything else in a generation to arouse in the minds of hundreds of thousands of workers a growing doubt as to whether our Government can be trusted to play fair.

Despite such attitudes, and the sad fate of the first Railroad Labor Board, the principle of government as arbiter in railroad industrial relations was thought by all interested parties to be too important to be abandoned. On May 20, 1926, President Coolidge signed the new Railway Labor Act, designed to cure the defects of previous legislation. This Act was amended in 1934 to enlarge the scope of "government meddling" by laying upon the industry the legal obligation to arbitrate and confer out disagreements between management and men.

Currently the National Mediation Board (set up as a tripartite labor-capital-government body by the modified Railway Labor Act*) enters the stage whenever a road and its employees, or several roads and a single union or group of unions, are unable to get together on wages, hours, work conditions. The Board's various adjustment branches particularly seek to iron out obstacles when, for example, railroad executives interpret an existing contract to mean one thing and union officials construe it to mean something else again, usually the opposite. Furthermore, as its trump-card the Board can fall back upon a special clause in the law creating it which calls for a second "emergency" board to be appointed by the President if and when the regular machinery of mediation breaks down.

The compulsory provisions of this recently changed Railway Labor Act bring up the question as to whether or not it is far-seeing national policy for an industry, its labor, and the Federal government to be so bound by the gyves of legal restrictions that if labor should seek relief from intolerable inequities by going on strike, its action might be construed as a flouting of public authority.† Whereas under this Act labor is assured freedom of behavior, it is a freedom curtailed by the necessity of adhering to a single and specific method in settling disputes. Some years ago British railway employees rejected a similar arrangement on the ground that it tended to impair their crucial right, namely, the right to strike. In this country, Mr. Leslie Craven, the gifted counsel to the Federal Coördinator of Transportation and author of "A Plan for

* Its personnel was reduced to three members since the National Railroad Adjustment Board and its regional subdivisions deal with grievances formerly handled by the old (1926) Board of Mediation with which the creation of adjustment bodies was optional, not mandatory, as in the existing statute.

† The reverse, of course, is similarly a moot point.

New Railroad Legislation," takes the view that "the same conclusion should be reached" in the United States:

Labor prefers to deal at arm's length. It can strike harder if it is not too close. It seems to be regarded as a certainty that the labor representatives upon these boards would not be able to retain the confidence of their constituency, the labor unions not having reached the place where such representatives can retain the confidence of the unions if they do not secure the results the unions want.

In any event, the National Mediation Board and its adjustment corollaries have functioned with notable success during the past four years. Their very existence, furthermore, does much to encourage railroad officials and union spokesmen to argue out their controversies by themselves; for the prospect of "having to go through it all again" is seldom alluring.

It should not be assumed, however, that because the adjustment boards have on the whole proved satisfactory to all concerned, their techniques could be imposed upon other industries with equally felicitous results. Railroading, like other enterprise, has its own attributes and its own problems. Since 1888 it has been increasingly subject to government regulation. Its labor, until very recently, has had comparatively steady jobs, safeguarded in most instances by seniority rules and ratings. On the other hand, the underlying premises upon which the railroad boards rest provide at least a starting point for objective inquiry into the amicable resolution of industrial conflicts in other spheres.

Moreover, while the debate as to the value of the railroad boards still continues, its very ingredients may soon be mixed in quite another crucible. The present plight of the railroads, their well-nigh universal bankruptcy and receivership, the anachronistic character of much of their financing and equipment, and the growing tendency of railroad unions to act in a more concerted fashion* have all combined in recent years to quicken the trend toward greater government intervention in railroad affairs—to such an extent, indeed, that government ownership and operation may occur somewhat sooner than is generally believed.

* In this regard, the pooling of knowledge and ideas among the Railway Labor Executives Association, which contains such astute and resourceful labor leaders as George Harrison of the Railway Clerks and A. F. Whitney of the Brotherhood of Railway Trainmen, is extremely significant. The Association's members have coöperated effectively, for example, in establishing an excellent system of unemployment compensation for the nation's railroad workers. Talk of some modern adaptation of the Plumb Plan has been revived and is frequently heard. More immediately important, perhaps, is the general conviction in such circles that should a strike situation occur in the future, it will find, for the first time, a virtually complete unity among all railroad labor organizations.

Robot Revolt: The International Union of the United Automobile Workers of America

I

THE mass production of automobiles for a long time has been the platitudinous symbol of American "progress," a word which is almost always associated with mobility alone.

Until the beginning of 1937, however, there was very little which resembled progress in the management-labor relations of our four-billion-dollar motor industry. The 433,000 men and 18,000 women employed in making passenger cars, trucks, hearses, tanks, station wagons, tractors, buses, taxicabs, and ambulances faced, and in part still face, conditions more medieval than modern.

Despite the widely publicized five-and-six-dollar-a-day minima, and hourly rates which, for a few, reached highs of $1.09, annual earnings of auto workers averaged less than $1,300 in the prosperity year of 1926 and less than $1,000 in the depression year of 1935. Early in 1930, Helen Hall, one of the country's foremost social investigators, interviewed a cross section of Detroit's auto workers and found, among others, such archetypes as: "William Powers, 30, two years at the Chevrolet plant. $1053.52 earned in 1929. He has seven children under 11 years of age"; and "Benjamin Desuka, at Dodge Brothers for nine years. His income for 1929 was $934.50. He is 33, his wife 30, and they have five small children"; and "Ralph Brenda, ten years . . . in the industry; 41 years old. His earnings for 1927 were $621.77; for 1928, $708.50; for 1929, $903."

The feeling of insecurity generated by such incomes and by the irregular employment they reveal was described by an Italian "punch-press" operator, named Rizzo, with an economy of means that would seem to mark him as an unconscious disciple of Walter Pater:

I worka six years with this job, but all that time eight months is the longest I ever go steady in one year. For more than one year I only worka two or three days a week. Everybody say here, "Why don't you save when you worka?" But how can you save when you no worka steady? If I could get $5 a day all year, I could put this little pieca for the coal, this little pieca for the rent, this little pieca for the electric and maybe then I can putta this away for to save and know where I go. But now you work, you make something; you stop. You spend what you got save. You getta the debts. Then you get a job. You pay the debts. You save a little. You stop. And now I stop too long this time. Me, I don't drink. I stay home nights with the keeds.

Even so, the wages in motors are relatively good when compared with those paid elsewhere. On the other hand it takes all the makeshifts of a poverty more shabby than genteel to stretch them over the seasonal layoffs to which the industry, by its own promotion of gadget consciousness and the annual model fetish, and its acute sensitivity to any rise or decline in national purchasing power, has become particularly prone.

However, it was not against the size of the pay envelope, per se, that General Motors workers staged a series of sit-downs at the end of 1936. The cause for this spectacular strike, which lasted forty-four days, involving 40,000 workers directly and 110,000 indirectly, and paralyzed sixty plants of a giant corporation in fourteen different states, went deeper into the secret places of the psyche than the question of so much cash return for so much work done.

It expressed the pent-up resentments of men in revolt against being de-humanized, against being only a badge, a number, a robot in thrall to a vast and intricate succubus of machinery, draining them of energy, threatening to cast them on the scrap heap after a few short years. It reflected a long-simmering rebellion against humiliations inflicted by the impersonality of a great corporation which, no more callous than its rivals, sapped the health and vitality of its workers and then turned them over to the government to support as soon as approaching middle age began to diminish their usefulness.

The conveyor-belt system as developed by Taylor, blessed by Bedaux, and applied by all motorcar manufacturers is sometimes hailed as the highest triumph of American technology. In terms of the blueprint, in the measurement of fatigue toxins, and stop-watch studies to determine and direct the most efficient expenditure of energy at a mechanized task, it probably deserves this praise. In terms of human beings, however, its efficacy is quite generally abused. It is not the paper planning of scientific management which is at fault, but rather the violation of its findings that has made the names Taylor and Bedaux hated. Speeds recommended by installation engineers, for example, as assuring "peak efficiency" for both human and machine participation in a given process are often stepped up, forcing workers to draw upon the uttermost limits of their strength and endurance to keep in rhythm with a mechanical pace-setter. After all, foremen, superintendents, plant managers as a rule receive their "hay-in-front-of-a-donkey" bonuses only when they are able to enlarge "standard" output by getting more units produced with "normal" equipment, and getting more work out of the same number of men.

The inventor of scientific management, Frederick W. Taylor, had envisioned different results. When he formulated his standard piece-work methods, his differential rates, his whole schemata of making production conform with the laws of the physical sciences, he had hoped to eliminate discord between capital and labor by increasing the net output of industry to such a degree that both employer and worker would benefit from this national enlargement of real wealth. In any event he was sure that the latter, under the dispensations of his industrial design, would be guaranteed a "living" wage. Many of the companies which adopted his principles, however, did so only to the extent that they tried to quicken and amplify production without paying any attention to what it did to labor, and without giving it any remotely proportional share of the profits which accrued from applying the techniques of Taylorism.*

Today, for instance, motorcar manufacturers still lack, toward their workers, even that rudimentary sense of responsibility which prompts any dirt farmer to pasture a faithful horse; they remain indifferent to how fast the men wear out as long as there are others to replace them, and appear equally indifferent to the inadequacy of their buying power—all of which would make Taylor turn in his grave. For he had, in the beginning, devised ways to conserve the individual's energy over the span of years; and he was convinced that mass markets alone could sustain and justify mass production.

Inside vast oblong buildings of brick, glass, and stone, under the hot glare of arc-lights, amid the whir and chug-chump of wheels, the automobile workers stand alongside great belt lines which move in front of them inexorably at the touch of a distant control button.

In the interior of a "body" plant, for example, at the far end of the belt, a new frame, a metal skeleton, bolt-sinewed, begins its journey. It reaches the first man who puts on a rim, goes to another who sets a fender, while underneath, men on their backs on little roller carts tighten axle bolts, each man doing the same thing, eyes fixed on the chassis, sweat rolling from his face, jaws clamped, lift, turn, screw, liftturnscrew, with the tempo often imperceptibly quickened, unable to leave the line to go to the

* A substantial number of advanced industrialists, of course, not only have tried to realize Taylor's vision with considerable success, but have also improved upon his methods. Their efforts, to some observers, justify the hope that American industry can yet find ways to adjust modern machine production to the needs and wants of the population; and by raising national living standards to much higher levels infuse present-day capitalism with a new ability to survive.

toilet, to get a drink of water, hour on hour, with the straw boss warning step lively, you're slipping fella, with the fear of losing the job if you don't keep up, making you strain tired muscles till your own body is a single throbbing ache while the belt, detached as a river coursing between its banks, flows smoothly on.

In other departments, even in the assembly of standardized units for crank cases, radiators, cushions, such scenes constantly occur, especially at times of peak production, and are virtually the same whether the individual plant is owned by Ford, General Motors, or Chrysler, who between them control 93 per cent of the domestic business, or by independents like Nash, Hudson, Packard, Studebaker, and Graham who divide the remaining 7 per cent of American auto sales.

When the shift is over the workers tumble half-dead with fatigue into buses, trolleys, or their own cars, mainly second-hand. Some acquire nervous twitchings popularly called "the shakes." They get home "too tired to do anything but eat and go to bed."* They are too all in even to read the paper, or take in a movie with the wife, or shoot a game of pool with the boys, or play cards with friends.

"It takes your guts out, that line," and "The speed-up, that's the trouble," form the dual refrain of auto workers in Detroit, Flint, Hamtramck, Saginaw, Pontiac, and other Michigan communities which together form the center of

---

* During the Flint sit-downs a group of women were interviewed at Cook's restaurant, commissary for the strikers. A dumpy, motherly woman of German descent, with straw-colored hair and pale-blue eyes, declared, "I'd like to shout from the housetops what the company's doing to our men. My husband, he's a torch solderer; they call 'em welders, but that's not what he is; he solders. You should see him come home at night, him and the rest of the men in the buses. So tired like they was dead, and irritable. My John's not like that. He's a good, kind man. But the children don't dare go near him, he's so nervous and his temper's bad. And then at night in bed, he shakes, his whole body, he shakes."

"Yes," chimed in her companion, a sharp-faced brunette, "they're not men any more if you know what I mean. They're not men. My husband he's only thirty, but to look at him you'd think he was fifty and all played out. And unless we have the union things will get worse."

the world's motorcar universe. The report of the NRA's Research and Planning Division says:

The grievance . . . mentioned most frequently and . . . uppermost in the minds of those who testified is the stretch out. Everywhere workers indicated that they were being forced to work harder and harder, to put out more and more products in the same amount of time and with less workers doing the job. There was a tendency to excuse the automobile manufacturer for the lack of steady work . . . but when it comes to increasing their work loads they are vigorous in denouncing the management as slave drivers, and worse. If there is any one cause for conflagration in the Automobile Industry, it is this one.

In recent years the auto workers have been increasingly recruited from the hills of Tennessee and Kentucky and from the farms of Michigan and Ohio. Beginning in 1922 and tapering off in 1930, the migration of these men to Detroit and other towns accounted for forty-seven out of every one hundred automobile employees. During the same period an appreciable influx of Negroes from the South reached its apex in 1926 when nearly 10 per cent of all Ford employees were colored and assigned to the harder, heavier tasks such as "sanding" and "foundry work." Many of the workers, of course, are transients comprising the so-called "suitcase battalions" and "bundle brigades" who rush in at the first rumors of a busy season and largely vanish at the first signs of slackening schedules. The nearness of the Detroit area to the Dominion has also attracted a considerable number of Canadians and Britishers who with the Poles, Belgians, Irish, Mexicans, Germans, and Hungarians add their polyglot part to a labor force which, however, remains predominantly native born.*

The young backwoods men and women who flocked to

* It is interesting that less than 1 per cent of the workers in Detroit motor plants are natives of that city.

motordom's Mecca were lured by visions of what, by agricultural standards, was a Big Money paradise. Mainly of "good American stock," they tended to be as parochial as they were healthy and strong. They knew nothing of unionism, often regarded their jobs as temporary, as a means of "getting some money saved" and then buying a farm or opening a little business on their own. They were also unskilled, nor did they have to be otherwise. With the mounting mechanization of the industry, about 45 per cent of its jobs can be learned within two or three days; about 35 per cent within a week; some 7 per cent within two weeks, and the remaining 13 per cent within a month to a year or longer.

The old-time craftsman's sense of creative satisfaction in the work of his hands is therefore a lost emotion for the majority of the industry's workers. They rarely see, or can recognize, the finished product to which they have contributed their own minute and regimented share. Often they handle only a part of a part of another part; for in this sphere the division of labor has attained a degree of specialization that is at once an engineering feat of a high order and an object lesson in how the technics of a civilization outstrip its ethics and its social values.

During the past two decades the industry's emphasis upon youth, with its greater speed and endurance, has kept displacing older employees at an ever-accelerating rate. In the Detroit region small loan firms refuse to consider auto workers over forty as acceptable risks, despite the beatitudes of Mr. Walter B. Pitkin; and also despite the amazing number of hair-dyeing specialists who flourish in the vicinity; for to the auto worker the discovery of the first "silver threads" is perhaps even more tragic than the same discovery by the professional beauty.

But this disregard of seniority rights—rights which mean simply that the man longest on the job has a prior claim to it, especially at a time of rehiring after a slack season—is only one among many grievances plaguing the industry's labor since the end of the World War. Others include the "incentive" or bonus plan by which a group of workers, geared to the human metronome of the fastest among them, receive extra money for extra "lump" output. In this operation calculations for figuring the return of each worker are so abstruse that often they have no way of finding out how much they earn.

But more injurious to individual self-esteem on the job is the practice of espionage. In this the motor manufacturers were among the most conspicuous offenders until revelations of the LaFollette Senate subcommittee, investigating civil liberties, caused cancellation of many contracts with such private detective firms as the Pinkerton Agency to which General Motors, over a period of three years, paid $419,850, or Corporations Auxiliary which cost Chrysler $72,611 for 1935 alone.*

Henry Ford, supreme individualist, who does his own financing and owns his own steel, cement, electric power and light, and assembly plants, his own coke ovens, and the like, also "rolls his own" in matters of espionage. He has hired Harry Bennett, an ex-sailor, ex-pugilist, to establish a spying and stool-pigeon system which works in the plant and also in large measure dominates the police and politics in Dearborn, Michigan. The favorite pursuit of Bennett and his boys is ganging up on union organizers, trying literally to beat them down, and otherwise forestall the coming of collective bargaining to Ford's.

---

* There are 228 other detective agencies dispensing what is euphemistically named "industrial service." It is, of course, nice work if you can get it as the $50,000 and $60,000 a year salaries of executives in such concerns attest. Among certain legal theorists, the fact that American corporations have spent as much as $80,000,000 a year for this espionage activity would seem to call into question their right to remain incorporated under the laws of any state in the union. All the states—along with the Federal government—guarantee civil liberties, which have rarely been so flagrantly violated as in this setting of men to spy upon workers and "report" their efforts to form a union of their choice by exercising their constitutional rights of freedom of speech and of conscience.

On May 26, 1937, for example, Walter Reuther and Richard Frankensteen, top officials of the United Automobile Workers, who had secured a city permit to distribute union leaflets to Ford workers as they changed shifts, took their places atop a street overpass debouching from one of the gates of the great River Rouge plant. Newsmen and photographers who had learned of their intention chatted with them for a moment and shot a few pictures. Suddenly Frankensteen and Reuther and their companions observed that a crowd of some one hundred and fifty men had converged on an adjacent platform, and were lounging about. They had seemed to materialize as if in response to a signal. They definitely didn't appear to be workers, for, as Reuther later testified at a National Labor Relations Board hearing,

. . . they had no lunch baskets and wore no badges. . . . After the pictures were taken we were approached by some of these men on all sides. . . . One called out that we were on private property and to get the hell off of there. Frankensteen and I turned to get off the bridge in obedience to the command. I had hardly taken three steps when I was slugged on the back of the head. I tried to shield my face by crossing my arms. They pounded me over the head and body. . . . I was knocked to the ground and beaten. . . .

They picked me up and threw me bodily on the concrete floor of the platform. Then they kicked me again and again. They tried to tear my legs apart. Seven times they raised me off the concrete and threw me down on it. They pinned my arms and shot . . . jabs to my face. I was dragged to the stairway. I grabbed the railing and they wrenched me loose. I was thrown down the first flight of iron steps. Then they kicked me down the other two flights. . . .

Frankensteen was given a similar "work out" and one of his aides had his "innards smashed."

Whereas Ford's public-relations staff strove mightily to convey the impression that Frankensteen and Reuther had been repulsed by "loyal employees" incensed by union efforts to convert them, the testimony given by reporters and cameramen, along with Dr. Sanford of the Chicago Federation of Churches who happened to be on the scene, revealed that "thugs, hoodlums" and "brass-knuckle-men" of Bennett's "Ford Service" organization were responsible for this vicious attack.

Moreover, despite the fact that a Grand Jury has indicted the Ford Motor Company and members of Bennett's strong-arm squad for wilful intent to do bodily harm, Bennett still retains his post as "personnel director" of the company and still boasts that if a Ford worker joins a union, he knows the particulars within twenty-four hours and has arranged for the man's discharge within forty-eight.

The general knowledge among auto workers that the man next to them on the line may be a secret agent, eager to amplify a kind word about unionism into a plot to "take over the factory" and impelled to make up lies out of whole cloth to justify his pay, freezes the warmth of normal human intercourse among men sharing a common enterprise. Everyone keeps a buttoned lip, does his stint silently in an atmosphere of mutual distrust. Even casual references to the political situation have been construed, by labor spies, if it suited their purposes, as "subversive" doctrine, as agitation, as trouble-making. Save among proven friends the talk of auto workers is talk of sports and equally innocuous subjects.*

Furthermore, under the division of executive authority that prevails in the industry, the foreman, who is management's surrogate, right on the job, exerts a tremendous power. He sometimes exacts tribute from the workers, allowing them to keep their jobs by kicking in so much a week, or "selling" the less strenuous assignments. In his

---

* As indicated in later pages, the creation of the United Automobile Workers Union has done much to rectify many of these and related abuses.

little world he is, more often than not, the petty tyrant personified. He can "reward his friends, punish his enemies" with a vengeance. His opinions are pontifical, his jokes hilarious.

Against such conditions—lack of seniority rules, irregular employment, the speed-up, the despotisms of the foreman or straw boss, elaborate methods of payment—the auto workers inveighed in vain for years. Detroit's own Chamber of Commerce proudly proclaimed that the city was "open shop," and an exemplar of the "American Plan."

From the industry's infancy, however, workers time and again tried to build unions. In the early days, when the pace of manufacture, carried on in small shops, was relatively slow, skill was somewhat at a premium and labor was recruited from the ranks of carriage and wagon builders, steamboat engine mechanics, machinists, carpenters, painters, furniture and metal workers. In 1891 the International Union of Carriage and Wagon Workers was founded to embrace all horseless-carriage labor and was charted by the A. F. of L. as an industrial union, an act which in itself acknowledged the incipient mass-production character of the industry.

The onrushing mechanization of motor factories with the years naturally lowered the importance of the more skilled craftsmen, transferring them to the routine tasks. Yet even while the special aptitudes represented by the International were declining, "raiding expeditions" on the part of the Blacksmiths and the Painters, who respectively claimed as their own anyone who handled metal or wielded a brush, fostered so many jurisdictional rows that the International was expelled from the Federation in 1918 for its refusal to abide by the "he's mine" contentions of various craft-union captains. In the same year, however, officers of the International rechristened their union the United Automobile, Aircraft and Vehicle

Workers, a title which, it was thought, nicely anticipated
all future contingencies. The new group gained considerable momentum in the "body" plants especially, enrolling
about 39,000 members within two years. In 1921, however, it called a strike for which it was improperly prepared, and promptly exploded. A few of its fragments
were captured by a Communist boring-from-within contingent which also soon expired. The disintegration of
the U.A.A.V. had been hastened of course by the discharge and blacklisting of its more active spirits whose
names were forwarded to company managers by men
planted for that purpose—a reflection, in part, of the anti-
union sentiments stimulated at that time by Attorney-
General Daugherty's anti-labor drive.

The same motif was to repeat itself monotonously for
the next decade, like the theme of Ravel's "Bolero."

In 1926, however, the A. F. of L. decided that the time
was ripe for unionizing the nearly half-million auto workers, almost totally unorganized except for a handful of
pattern makers, machinists, and painters. The Federation
in that year held its annual convention in Detroit and
William Green announced that jurisdictional claims would
be soon suspended since the repetitive nature of conveyor-
belt production and the sub-assembly of the parts it carried tended to blur craft lines. Somewhat gingerly certain
General Motors executives let it be known that they might
look with favor upon the creation of unions in their major
plants as an experiment in management-labor coöperation,
an attitude in contrast to the declaration of the Automobile
Chamber of Commerce which condemned the whole idea
of unionizing motors as an "un-American undertaking."

Feelers were put out to arrange a meeting of minds
between William Green and Henry Ford, but the latter
was too busy dismantling his Model T machinery at the
time to discuss anything quite so esoteric. As a matter of
fact, the A. F. of L. proposed to launch a unionizing cam-

paign in motors by the dubiously astute strategy of getting
the employers to help start it. In grandly vague style, the
Federation's directorate talked about the "social wage"
and the identity of interests between ownership and labor
in that "mass production needs mass markets." It was an
approach which, despite the ambiguity of A. F. of L. presentation, still has great potential merit and deserves more
objective study and honest evaluation than it is likely to
receive. But the A. F. of L. failed to spot-light the issue
with either showmanship or common sense. Its high command was too feeble to inspire the respect of employers or
to win the allegiance of the workers.

Besides, the local heads of the Federation's affiliates in
the Detroit area were up to their ears in municipal politics.
They were "doing all right" for themselves. And with the
exception of Detroit branches of Arthur O. Wharton's
Machinists, they didn't relish the prospect of bestirring
themselves, re-arranging dues, favors, and personnel, and
otherwise undertaking the difficult spade-work of arousing
a "bunch of ignorant hill-billies" to union consciousness.
Within a few months the very concept of bringing unionism to motors had become in A. F. of L. circles a hope so
half-hearted that it soon ceased to exist.

Early in 1933, however, goaded by wage cuts, layoffs,
inhuman resort to the speed-up, workers began to walk
out in a congeries of minor, infra-department strikes that
were yet portents of more to come. On September 22, the
Mechanics Educational Society, an independent union
which had enrolled nearly all of the industry's highly
skilled tool and die makers, pulled out hundreds of its
adherents in protest against incomes which had shrunk
from an average of $2,717 in 1929 to $1,300 in 1933. In
the Detroit region such "aristocrats" of labor, accompanied by many commoners, walked out at Buick, Chevrolet, A. and C. Spark Plug, Fisher Body, Cadillac, Dodge,
Hudson, Plymouth, Packard, and extended their strike to

Ford at Edgewater, New Jersey, and to Nash at Kenosha, Wisconsin.

Meantime the NRA codes for the motor industry were being formulated in the summer of 1933. The weather was hot, the atmosphere electric and the codes displayed both characteristics. They were transparently pro-employer—to such an extent, indeed, that it was the auto workers who first rechristened the NRA the "National Run Around."

The manufacturers wrote their own ticket, and punched it. They already had their association which, despite the absence of Mr. Ford, enabled members to get together in maintaining uniform labor and price-fixing policies. They did not need the NRA's sanction to indulge in such forms of intra-industry collaboration. Acting in customary concert, they inserted in the auto codes an "averaging clause" which was to govern hours of work and which was obscurely phrased. What lucidity it had was based on the assumption that only *average* hours per week could be limited. That is, five forty-eight-hour weeks, plus a forty-eight-hour week of lay-off, were to equal six forty-hour weeks. There was also the slick "merit clause," a Philadelphia lawyer's way of violating the spirit of the famed Section 7a which, among other things, forbade discrimination against unionists. Since merit or competence is judged always by the employer, any worker who favored unionism by word or deed could suddenly be found to have lost his ability and could be fired on some trumped-up charge.*

Angered by this trickery, the auto workers cast about for guidance toward unionism's goal. They had a confusion of choices. The I.W.W., the Socialist party, the Communist party, the American Industrial Association all entered the arena with at least paper organizations eager

---

* Ironically, in view of later developments, the only other industry to obtain this same concession from the National Recovery Administration was that of chemicals which, like General Motors, is also dominated by the duPont family.

to enlist members. At last the A. F. of L. itself yawned out of its somnolence, stretched, and stumbled into activity.

Its organizers, however, were largely men who had been graduated from the Brown Derby, "I'm tough, see, have a cigar, leave it all to me, boys," school of the old-time pot-bellied walking delegate. They were also hobbled at every step by the jurisdictional jealousies of the various crafts. Despite such handicaps, however, an estimated 210,-000 auto workers more or less quietly joined the Federation's "federal unions."*

But the new unionists were bewildered. They couldn't get their questions answered. They asked if they were going to become a nationwide industrial union, or whether they were to be kept waiting until the membership was subdivided into craft groups. Nobody seemed to know, least of all the field organizers. The A. F. of L. didn't know either. It was marking time, its most costly and colossal luxury from its earliest days.

Meanwhile, to forestall the growth of any genuine unionism and to comply with the letter, and not the intent, of the collective bargaining provisions in the NRA codes, the employers started to fashion "company" unions, often forcing men to join them on pain of forfeiting their jobs. Meanwhile, too, as the speed-up and longer hours for but slightly increased pay continued, the A. F. of L., prodded by rank-and-file insistence, set March, 1934, as the date on which auto workers all over the country were to go on strike and with a single bold stroke end company unions and all the fraud and chicane they implied.

---

* A union structure developed by Gompers at the turn of the century to enroll the unskilled under the A. F. of L. banner. The federal union, members of which usually pay dues of 35 cents a month, or $4.20 a year, is looked upon by A. F. of L. officialdom as a "feeder" from which the skilled will be soon or late drained off and allocated to various craft unions in accord with jurisdictional rules. For more than thirty years, however, federal union spokesmen have complained that they pay dues but receive neither voice nor vote in shaping Federation policy.

At President Roosevelt's request, however, this "threat to returning prosperity" was averted by Federation leaders and many long days of muddled mediation ensued. Out of the final settlement were hatched two new eggs of the Blue Eagle, both of them, in the view of most auto workers, rotten. The first was the Automobile Board which was to prevent company reprisals against unionists, and to guarantee collective bargaining rights. It was presided over by Dr. Leo Wolman, a brilliant statistician but far less gifted in promoting harmony. With the impassivity of a brass Buddha, the Board for nine months listened to a recital of workers' woes but did little or nothing toward action of any ameliorative kind.

The second egg was the proposal for proportional representation by which the company unions, along with the genuine variety, whether A. F. of L. or otherwise, were to be heard equally in all negotiations between managers and men. Soon three warring groups—the company unions, the A. F. of L., and non-Federation unions—were at loggerheads, demonstrating that the industry's employers had been very wise in once more applying the doctrine of "divide and rule." In the long run they outsmarted themselves, especially with their emphasis on company unions which, formed always on a plant-wide basis, were but prologues to a drama of industrial unionism soon to be played. For a time, however, the inertia of the Automobile Labor Board, the craft squabbles within the A. F. of L., the organization conflicts outside of it, provoked an estimated 75,000 unionists into turning in or tearing up their union cards.

The elections held early in 1935 under the Board's auspices clearly reflected the prevailing temper of the nation's auto workers. Out of a total of 154,780 ballots cast, 111,878 workers voted for "unaffiliated representation." In other words, the majority were so fed up with the clamors of competition for their allegiance that they didn't

want any of the existing unions to act as their agents. Only
14,057 voted for the A. F. of L., 7,071 for other legitimate
unions, and 21,774 for the company-run kind. Hundreds
of thousands of workers refrained from thus registering
their will, apparently in their discouragement believing
even this gesture a waste of time.

Yet the deep desire to be unionized swirled like a strong
current temporarily dammed up. The A. F. of L.'s federal
locals had meanwhile begun banding together in what was,
at first, a loose alliance under the name of the United Automobile Workers. It was directed by Francis J. Dillon, an
A. F. of L. veteran business agent hand-picked by William
Green against the majority votes of delegates to the
U.A.W.'s convention at Detroit in August of 1935. The
convention reluctantly agreed to permit Dillon to remain
at the helm until an appeal citing his unfitness could be
considered by the Executive Council of the A. F. of L.
which was scheduled to convene at the Federation's own
annual sessions in Atlantic City two months later.

But this appeal somehow was sidetracked in the tumult
that surrounded the withdrawal of John L. Lewis and
Company from the A. F. of L. to form their Committee
for Industrial Organization. In any event Green insisted on
keeping Dillon in command of the United Automobile
Workers, a tactical blunder of the first magnitude. For
Dillon epitomized the old-fashioned approach to unionism
adhered to by the more Victorian-minded craft leaders.
On the other hand, the United Automobile Workers were
more and more convinced that unionizing techniques devised for the nineteenth century were not applicable to the
twentieth. In one of its earliest pamphlets, addressed to the
worker, it declared, ". . . No man today is alone an automobile maker. You join with thousands of others in a collective productive effort. Does the manufacturer hire you,
put you at a bench or forge, give you a heap of iron ore,
a pile of cloth, a supply of raw rubber and a few sheets of

glass, and then tell you to get to work and make automobiles individually? . . ."

Animated by this outlook, the auto workers in general were heartened by the creation of the C.I.O., founded as it was on the premise that either mass-production workers were to be organized, and speedily, or that "labor's voice" would soon be modulated down from at best a mild forte to a very soft and plaintive pianissimo, if it were to be heard at all.

Various other unions, such as the Coughlin-sponsored Automobile Industrial Workers Association and the Associated Automobile Workers of America, called the "Greer bunch" after the name of its principal, shared the affection of the U.A.W. for the industrial idea. All three groups began to talk about a fusion of forces, looking to the C.I.O. for guidance. They didn't get it, at first. The C.I.O. was already embroiled in fifty-seven different varieties of controversy and had to feel its way cautiously for some six or seven months. By the time Roosevelt was reëlected, however, it was sending scouts and advisers into Detroit to assist the U.A.W. in ousting Dillon and hence to shatter A. F. of L. prestige and influence for many miles around.

To get rid of Dillon, of course, required no Machiavellian genius. His action to thwart strike efforts in nearby Toledo's Auto-Lite and Chevrolet plants had lashed the members of his own union into bitter antagonism. In the spring of 1936 the U.A.W. supplanted him by electing Homer S. Martin as its president. He was then thirty-four years old, a former minister emotionally identified with the underdog. A graduate of William Jewel, a "freshwater" college at Liberty, Missouri, he had won the national hop-skip-and-jump championship and combined a study of sociology with his preparation for the cloth. In 1932 he was named pastor of the Baptist Church in Leeds, Missouri, a Kansas City suburb.

His congregation consisted in part of auto workers and he was moved by their plight to sermonize upon the theme that the "man who pays workers less than a living wage . . . and takes advantage of the depression to drive down living standards and then comes to church on Sunday is no Christian but a . . . pious hypocrite." He also remarked upon the difficulty of trying to save men's souls when their bodies were undernourished, suggesting that before there would be the brotherhood of man there would have to be bread. A few more homilies upon this general theme found him a preacher without a pulpit, the church deacons observing that such views were more subversive than supernal.

Martin then took a job in a Kansas City Chevrolet factory where he embraced the gospels of unionism devoutly and articulately. Immediately he was out again. He was classed as a "trouble-maker." He began to organize in earnest, becoming head of a federal local, and then vice-president of the U.A.W. under Dillon whom he detested, and who cordially returned the sentiment. Boyish and wholesome-looking, Martin resembles in appearance and manner the beau ideal of a Y.M.C.A. secretary, radiating good will and go-getting pep. His talents are primarily evangelical and he transformed open-air rallies and assembly-hall meetings of the union into something pretty close to good old-fashioned "revivals."

Late in December, 1936, after a vigorous organizing campaign during which Martin hit a new sawdust trail five and seven times a day, the U.A.W. sent a letter to Mr. William S. Knudsen, then executive vice-president of General Motors, asking for a conference on the general subject of collective bargaining. The letter enumerated the auto workers' complaints and pointed out that local attempts to settle questions of wages, hours, and work conditions with branch officials had always arrived nowhere.

The company replied, through Mr. Knudsen, that it could not talk, and suggested that Martin and his followers seek adjustment of grievances with local plant managers. This was, in Martin's view, nonsense. The corporation's industrial relations policy was explicitly determined at the top and local administrators merely carried out the orders of their superiors.

"It's the merry run-around again," muttered U.A.W. members and in exasperation many of them spontaneously sat down in the Fisher Body Plant at Cleveland, Ohio, on December 28, 1936—ringing up the curtain upon the most spectacular and significant capital-labor drama of the post-crash period.

Next day the sit-down was extended to Fisher Body Plant No. 2 in Flint, Michigan, where the U.A.W. had submitted a sample contract to the plant manager with the request that he ponder its terms as the basis for future discussion. In reply he discharged five staunch unionists. Enraged by this "sock in the teeth," U.A.W. members and others also sat down. Next morning workers in Fisher Body Plant No. 1, also in Flint, heard the rumor that the company had begun to remove necessary tools and dies to weaker union places, to Pontiac, Michigan, and even to Atlanta, Georgia, to forestall production stoppages and to have the workers in these places break the Flint strike. In protest U.A.W. men and their well-wishers sat down in Fisher Body Plant No. 1 with a gaiety that was later transformed into a grim tenacity of purpose, while the movement caromed to Anderson, Indiana, to Kansas City, Missouri, to Norwood, Ohio, and to Atlanta, Georgia, spreading from one General Motors plant to another throughout the country.

The high command of the C.I.O. which had recently annexed the United Automobile Workers was surprised and shaken by the suddenness of this sit-down epidemic and would have preferred smallpox or something simple instead. From the standpoint of John L. Lewis and his aides, the timing of this strike in motors couldn't have been more maladroit. At the moment the C.I.O. was hurling nearly all of its new might in money and men into the Steel Workers Organizing Committee's drive on steel, proceeding on the theory that if this "most impregnable fortress of the open-shop" could be made to yield to the C.I.O.'s assault, the whole industrial salient could be more readily conquered. To Lewis, as to his Marshal Ney, ca-canny, Scotch-born Philip Murray, success or failure in unionizing steel was to be Austerlitz or Waterloo. They hadn't reckoned on any new major engagements on a new front.

Yet they were duty bound to send succor to Homer Martin and the U.A.W., which as a union was still very young. Its leaders were honest and intelligent but they by and large lacked experience in all the multifarious activity, from publicity releases to maintenance of morale, that any big strike entails. With misgivings, Lewis dispatched John Brophy, Director of Organization for the C.I.O., to U.A.W. headquarters in the Hoffman Building in Detroit as the herald of more reinforcements and supplies to come, and later wired the Flint sit-downers that the C.I.O. and its affiliates "pledge you complete and unanimous support in the conduct of the strike. . . . You men are undoubtedly carrying on through one of the most heroic battles that has ever been undertaken by strikers in an industrial dispute. The attention of the entire American public is focussed upon you. . . ."

With the stubborn and desperate courage of men carrying the banners of a new crusade, the Flint sit-downers refused to be dislodged for weeks that stirred headline writers to new heights, editorial writers, columnists, and radio commentators to new hysterias, provoked bitter debates in the Senate and House, and divided most of the population into two emotionally overstrung camps, warring over the subject of the strikers' favorite song:

When they tie a can to a union man,
  Sit-down! Sit-down!
When they give him the sack, they'll take him back
  Sit-down! Sit-down!

When the speed-up comes, just twiddle your thumbs,
  Sit-down! Sit-down!
When the boss won't talk, don't take a walk,
  Sit-down! Sit-down!

II

THE "sit-down" which between September 1, 1936, and June 1, 1937, involved 484,711 American workers not only in motors but in rubber, steel, textiles, ship-building, subways, oil-refining, shoes, newspaper publishing, baking, aircraft, and countless other manufacturing service and retailing spheres, is a strike of a very special kind. Whereas in the everyday variety employees leave mill or mine or store or factory to picket outside their place of business, in the sit-down they remain inside at or near their usual posts but do no work. They just sit or stretch out on the floor or benches or loll around on their feet. And if a sit-down lasts long enough —dozens of them in mass-production plants last only a few minutes or a few hours—it becomes a stay-in, properly speaking, though the term sit-down is already a colloquialism used to describe this technique, per se, whatever its duration.

Its advantages are obvious. Police and militia can more easily disperse a picket line in the open than an "occupied" plant where windows may be barricaded and gates barred. "You can't ride a horse through a brick wall," remarked a grizzled old unionist in Detroit during the General Motors stay-ins. "With the sit-down today the boys don't have to put up with that, anyway."

Sit-down psychology differs profoundly from that of any other strike tactic. In the first place, the men stay together all the time instead of meeting irregularly at a hall or union headquarters or in the street. They talk, become better acquainted, generate feelings of unity and coöperation, "one for all, and all for one." In the second place, the sit-down gives the individual worker a new and rare sense of power—especially in highly mechanized industries where relatively few men can literally "tie up the works." To William Smith, the anonymous, one of thousands, the very fact that "Alec and me and the rest of the boys did that" can prove as intoxicating as mulled wine. And unlike the walkout, when he is away from the job, the sit-down enables him to see and hear the results of his active inaction. Gongs go bonging, phones shrill, straw bosses storm, managers get flurried and mad and machinery is idle—all because of what he and his companions have done. His behavior opens up to him new vistas of self-importance and of labor's importance in the producing scheme. For the time being, anyway, he is another Chico who lifts up the manhole cover from underneath, breathes new air, and declares to the world, "I'm a very remarkable fellow." In conjunction with others, with all the fun of teamwork, he has wrought his will over something big and powerful and significant; and by this means he has at least partially purged himself of various thwartings and grievances. Over and above immediate stimuli, therefore, the sit-down is often a method by which the worker may transform his particular conveyor belt or loom or pit or lathe or counter into a whipping post on which to vent his dissatisfactions with his job, with his whole way of life.

In the briefer type of sit-down, often called "quickies," and usually invoked to slow down the speed of the "line," the men conduct the entire affair themselves. It's their show, with no red tape, such as asking the approval of union officials, if any.* In the more extensive stay-in, of course, the whole performance is likely to be carefully stage-managed by union officials many days in advance, down to the last props of arranging for food, sleeping facilities, and entertainment.

To the worker the sit-down is frequently high excitement. The humdrum nature of much modern mechanized work renders it a welcome diversion, despite loss of pay. It is thrilling—a relief from monotony. And one of its dangers, of course, is that like all forms of power it may be easily abused. It is quite possible for a group of "natural agitators" or neurotics or even practical jokers to turn a plant topsy turvy by sitting down for no good reason. Hence labor leaders urge their members to go slow on sit-downs, and always to consult with local union heads in or out of the establishment before participation. In their opinion it is far too effective a weapon to be blunted by too much use.

Contrary to popular impression, the sit-down is not an instrument designed and patented by the C.I.O., although its widespread use in this country happened to coincide with the high spots of the C.I.O.'s organizing campaign during 1936 and 1937 especially.

Len DeCaux, editor of the *Union News Service*, the movement's official news bureau, declared:

As a matter of fact the first experience of the C.I.O. with sit-downs was in discouraging them. This was in the Akron rubber industry, after the Goodyear strike. C.I.O. representatives cautioned . . . the new unionists against sit-downs on the ground that they should use such channels for negotiating grievances as the agreement provided.

The attitude of the C.I.O. towards sit-downs has from the

* The "skippy" is still another variant of the species and consists of, say, skipping every tenth fender as it travels along the belt, to reduce the number of units to be handled within a specified time. It is as a rule used only in the more extreme instances when the speed of the line has been "notched up" 10 or 20 per cent, causing almost unendurable exertion.

first been consistently that of all responsible union officials to any form of strike. When employers refuse to bargain with the union of their employees, and threaten, spy upon, and repress them in many illegal ways, the workers are driven to protect their rights with such means as are at their disposal. Union leaders worthy of the name . . . then lay the blame for such industrial conflict where it belongs, squarely on the shoulders of those who provoke it by refusing the workers their rights.

But when collective bargaining is fully accepted, union recognition accorded and an agreement reached, C.I.O. unionists accept full responsibility for carrying out their side of it in a disciplined fashion, and oppose sit-downs or any other strike action while it is in force.

And in supporting this general approach, John L. Lewis at about the same time announced that "the C.I.O. stands for punctilious observance of contracts, but we are not losing any sleep about strikes where employers refuse to recognize well-defined principles of collective bargaining. A C.I.O. contract is adequate protection against sit-downs, lie-downs, or any other kind of strike."

Despite William Green's statement that "both personally and officially I disavow the sitdown strike as a part of the economic or organization policy of the A. F. of L.," numerous Federation unions, notably electricians, hotel and restaurant, theatrical and building service employees engaged in sit-downs to protect their wage scales and for other reasons.

To a considerable extent, the sudden winds of sit-down doctrine which spread the capital-labor deadlock all over the American scene reflected that faddism which is an American institution. Certainly the rise and decline of sit-down popularity resembled that of Mah Jong and Tom Thumb golf. It is, furthermore, a tactic resorted to mainly in industries that have been, or are, vigorously anti-union. There is, indeed, on the whole, a direct traceable "cause and effect" relation between the adoption of the sit-down method of protest by the worker and the degree of anti-union activity practiced by the employer. During the period previously mentioned, that from September 1, 1936, to June 1, 1937, which witnessed the greatest extent of sit-downing, motors—which had been historically open shop—had about a quarter of a million sitters; rubber, which for a generation has been a "No Man's Land" for unionism, had about forty-five thousand; and textiles, still a battleground for pro- and anti-union forces, had about twenty-five thousand. On the other hand, in coal mining, where the United Mine Workers is well established, there were only 270 workers who sought to use the sit-down, and none at all in the extremely well-organized men's clothing and women's wear trades.

The genesis of the sit-down is still in doubt. Some insist that the act itself bespeaks such resignation to Fate's decree that in its origins it must be more Levantine or Hindu than American. The attempt to trace it to its sources soon becomes the attempt to untangle the many-skeined and reciprocal interchange of ideas among the peoples of the world. For example, Mahatma Gandhi, foremost exponent of sit-down passivity, has time and again acknowledged his indebtedness to Henry D. Thoreau's measures for resisting the evils of society, while Thoreau in turn drew heavily upon the Hindu mystics, blending their doctrines with our own national propensity to flirt with anarchy.

One favorite interpretation, advanced by such an able labor authority as Louis Adamic, is that the movement originated in Akron, Ohio, sometime in the summer of 1934. It appears that two baseball teams comprising workers from two rubber plants refused to play a game on a Sunday afternoon when they discovered that the umpire was not a union man. Both nines, it is related, insisted that he step aside and let a union man call the game. To enforce this demand, both teams sat down on bases and on the grass of the diamond until a union umpire was summoned.

A few days later, the story continues, a dispute arose between a dozen workers and the superintendent of a division in a large Akron rubber factory. The superintendent made some offensive remarks which angered the workers, whereupon one of them allegedly said, "Let him go fly a kite; let's sit down." They did—crippling the flow in their own department and disorganizing five others. To the question "What's the matter?" raised all over the plant, the response, "Some guys have sat down, yeah, like in the ball game," went quickly up and down the plant's assembly lines to give American paternity to this strike technique.*

Probably the first sit-down type of strike on record in this country occurred early in December, 1906, at the General Electric plant in Schenectady, New York. It was inspired by Wobblies (I.W.W.) who as an experiment wanted to vary their usual strike strategy by the tactics of a stay-in. At a given signal picked groups of mechanics and machinists in key departments literally folded their arms and stood gazing at their tools and worktables. They remained indoors, refusing to budge, for sixty-five hours; and were joined by many of the 3,000 employees at the plant, 250 of whom formed picket lines outside it to protect the men in the interior, and also furnished them with food and drink. Demands for more pay were quickly granted.

Despite the efficacy of this procedure, it was hardly imitated at all in the United States—mainly because its sponsors, the I.W.W., were syndicalists, with Marxist trimmings, and their revolutionary appeals on the whole did more to repel than to beguile the American worker.

* At least ten months before this occurrence, however, 2,500 employees of the Hormel Packing Corporation in Austin, Wisconsin, sat down for three days and achieved improved wages and hours and a slowing up of their machines.

In fact the hasty and superficial comparisons of the American sit-down cycle (1936-37) with the occupation of Italian factories by union groups just before Mussolini's "March on Rome" reveal a lack of logic on the part of too many of our public-affairs commentators. For in Italy the intent was revolutionary. The workers hoped to take over all manufacturing and run it themselves. But in the United States the sit-downs are at most revolutionary only in implication, not in objective. The workers may "hold" a plant, true enough, but their purpose is the redress of immediate grievances, not the inauguration of some future collectivist state.

The American sit-down, in short, affirms not the right to the factory (which is not operated but kept in a state of quiescence) but the right to the job, a "vested interest" in it, and the attempt to protect this work territory against the invasion of others, strikebreakers, pending the settlement of differences between labor and management.*

In 1915 the United States Commission on Industrial

* The rubber workers of Akron, Ohio, are adepts in the use of the sit-down, indulging in more of them than any other labor group in the United States. Their views on this subject have been expressed as follows by Sherman H. Dalrymple, president of the United Rubber Workers of America, one of the most capable and courageous C.I.O. leaders, who was twice beaten nearly to death by vigilantes for his union sympathies:

"Sit-downs do not occur in plants where true collective bargaining exists. Where management does not attempt to destroy unionism by financing company unions, by the formation of vigilante groups, and by placing other obstacles in the path of legitimate union growth, there is such a spirit of coöperation between the union and management that cessations of work do not occur.

"Recent sit-downs in Akron have occurred because management either did not enter into fair negotiations on certain grievances or deliberately post-poned decisions until resentment of the workers grew so keen that they resorted to sit-downs as a last resort.

"The fact that these grievances were settled satisfactorily immediately after the sit-downs definitely indicates that they could have been settled just as easily before if management had negotiated fairly with the union committee in their efforts to secure peaceful settlement of the issues involved.

"It is our contention that the only way these sit-downs can be avoided in the future is through the proper application of all the rules of true collective bargaining in a spirit of fair play."

Relations recommended the "worker's right to the job" as an approach made almost mandatory by modern methods of manufacture. And more recently, Leon Green, Dean of the University of Wisconsin Law School, writing in *The New Republic*, has affirmed that the sit-down does not violate laws of trespass and seizure and is legal. He points out that workers, as participants in the processes of production, have a definite stake and interest in the industrial relation thus engendered; and that they "sit to negotiate some affair pertinent to their relation to industry." He states, further, that sit-downs involve economic matters which, in their totality of relationships, are beyond the authority of courts, and that properly their resolution should be left to other agencies of government and to the opposing sides. It is his opinion that the courts, when they assume jurisdiction over points incidental to the main source of conflict, tend to "prejudice" all the issues in the entire dispute. He concludes, therefore, that "occupation in good faith and peacefully of a plant . . . awaiting the adjustment of grievances growing out of the industrial relation is but an incident of the industrial relation and in no sense unlawful."

In any event, the sit-down does not challenge ownership of productive equipment; but it does challenge the privilege of the "employer," whether corporation or individual, to retain within his (or its) own hands the enormous powers over employees that result from the fact that most families of wage earners live from hand to mouth, through no fault of their own, and often are but a few days removed from starvation.*

* "Who has the better human and natural right to call the Fisher plant his," asked Robert Morss Lovett, a General Motors stockholder writing in *The Nation* at the height of the Flint sit-downs, "I, whose connection with General Motors is determined by the price recorded on the New York Stock Exchange, or the worker whose life and livelihood are bound up in the operation of making cars? I bought my shares at long odds and probably have already collected the purchase price in dividends. When I place a winning bet in a horse race I do not claim a share in ownership of the horse. I know

In another sense the sit-down may be an effort to recover at least a measure of that control over tools lost among the mutations of the Industrial Revolution. In times of discord, this aim can be more effectively accomplished by physical possession of plant than by any other withdrawal of labor energy.

Comfort is greater than when pickets tramp in the snow or rain or under a hot sun. The sitters are supplied with food from a central commissary set up by the union, a fact which serves to intensify the feelings of solidarity previously mentioned as among the most important attributes of the sit-down. It further places the responsibility for violence, for "starting something," squarely upon the shoulders of management and whatever armed forces it can summon to its assistance. The sit-down imposes and benefits from its own spartan disciplines. The property held is in most cases cared for; floors are kept clean and machinery furbished like a ship's brass. Rules of proper sanitation are rigidly enforced. No liquor, no smoking, no hell-raising, no entertainment save clog-dancing, music, or playing games like casino and checkers, is permitted. The plant general committee, which is the local government for the duration, observes its duties diligently. It holds its own court and metes out punishment to violators of such regulations as those against littering the premises or leaving them without an official pass or shirking "patrol" assignments.

From the mists and fogs of emotion-charged words marking the discussion of the sit-down one clear question emerges: Is purely legal title to a producing property the only right that should be recognized in the American de-

---

from my political economy that my position is the result of labor and sacrifice. Whose? Not mine. Obviously the enormous mass of wealth represented by the capitalization of General Motors, repeatedly enlarged by split-ups and stock dividends, is the surplus resulting from the toil of millions of workers over many years. Obviously they have not shared fairly in the wealth they have produced."

mocracy? The answer of the United Automobile Workers was put by its "in-and-out" vice-president, Wyndham Mortimer, when he inquired:

Is it wrong for a worker to stay at his job? The laws of state and nation, in a hundred ways, recognize that the worker has a definite claim upon his job; more fundamentally . . . every workman has a moral right to continue on his job unless some definite misconduct justifies his discharge. These sit-down strikers [i.e., in Flint and elsewhere] are staying at their workplaces; no one has a better right to be there than these men themselves. . . . The sit-down strikers have performed valuable services in those factories; General Motors and the public alike have profited. . . . To call them trespassers now, and to deny their right as human beings to remain with their jobs . . . is manifestly unjust.

In Flint, Michigan, the power of General Motors was arrayed against the implications of this view in a community where, out of 165,000 inhabitants, 50,000 depended directly upon the company for livelihoods gained from Buick, Chevrolet, and Fisher Body Plants. Anti-sit-down sentiment, after the first days of the strike, was crystallized by an organization called the Flint Alliance. It was in theory composed of "loyal employees" most of whom somehow contrived to resemble bar-flies and poolroom toughs from nearby Detroit. The Alliance also contained a sprinkling of General Motors executives and subadministrators and people from its technical and commercial divisions, some local businessmen, and almost all the vigilante-minded personalities in the vicinity, the kind of men, and there are many of them, who in their perpetual adolescence come fully alive only when they can have "adventure" by doing physical injury to others. The Alliance's propaganda was fabricated by the high-pressure, high-priced Floyd E. Williamson who, himself an "outsider" imported from Manhattan for his special purpose, amusingly enough based a large part of his anti-union blasts upon the "un-American activities" of "outside" organizers. The chairman of the Alliance was George E. Boysen, former paymaster in a Buick factory, and latterly himself the owner of a spark-plug concern. As the sit-down progressed, Alliance spokesmen grew daily more vociferous in their demands for violence, some of them promising that soon law and order committees of indignant citizenry would forcibly evict the sit-downers who by the thousand had "dug-in" for a long siege.

To oust the strikers, General Motors had secured from Judge Edward Black an injunction which commanded them to vacate company property and also forbade picketing. Although he owned nearly $200,000 worth of General Motors stock, Judge Black considered himself sufficiently impartial to issue his edict, a belief not entirely in accord with the more commendable traditions of the American bench. When Sheriff Wolcott delivered the Black document to the sit-downers he was jeered and good-naturedly told to go home. Meantime, company officials, both local and national, and U.A.W. and C.I.O. leaders were busy fencing, mustering all their skill for parry and riposte, all of them with an eye on the public gallery.

On January 12, the company shut off the heat in Fisher Body Plant No. 2 and its own gray-uniformed police, reinforced by regulars from the local Flint force, were instructed to prevent the shipment of food into the building. It was hoped that this "diet of cold and hunger" would break the morale of the sit-downers.

Inside the plant, the men missed their lunch, shivered, and grew restive at the prospect of being also deprived of their dinner. Shortly before seven o'clock that evening, a United Automobile Workers sound truck rolled up before the great rectangle of Fisher No. 2, with Victor Reuther, a top-notch organizer for the union, at the microphone. At first he politely asked the police, both public and private, for permission to have food sent in to the sit-downers from the union's kitchen. The metallic lungs of the amplifier lifted his voice high above the sounds of the street until everyone within a half-mile radius could hear his plea. The officers, both the gray and the blue, were mute. Reuther tried another tack. He appealed to them as workers, urging the necessity for coöperation among all kinds and degrees of labor. There was no response, save the cheers of the sit-downers. He then became more aggressive, assuring the officers that strikers outside the plant would get food to the sitters. Some fifteen minutes later a group of pickets carrying pails of coffee and cartons of buns, like an oversized backfield, starting on an end run, bowled over the police guarding the door to the plant and brought food to their famished friends.

At 8:45 some sixty policemen set upon pickets stationed at plant entrances, clubbed them with night-sticks, and drove them inside the building. A sergeant smashed a glass pane in one of the doors and thrust the nozzle of a tear-gas gun through the jagged space, pumping shells into the vast interior. Other officers fired buckshot into pickets and men clustered near the door, wounding fourteen who were later removed to the hospital.

The sit-downers replied to this attack with literally everything they had: coffee-mugs, pop-bottles, and steel automobile hinges weighing two pounds each. At the beginning of the battle, a clarion voice from the sound truck cried: "We wanted peace. General Motors chose war. Give it to 'em!" In the road strikers formed a phalanx around the sound truck, repelled all efforts of police to dismantle it, and overturned three police cars and another belonging to the sheriff.

At midnight the policemen closed in their ranks and, with guns cracking, tried to rush the main entrance, only to be met by a devastating stream of water from a big fire hose which, along with the steel-hinge missiles, compelled them to retreat and finally to abandon their assault. This affair was promptly named "The Battle of the Running Bulls."

The bloodshed of that night, and the fears of more violence to come, resulted in the appearance of 1,500 of Michigan's National Guardsmen in Flint. Acting under instructions from the cool-headed, humanitarian Governor Murphy who was valiantly seeking to settle the strike by pacific means, they managed on the whole to preserve order almost impartially, though various commanders chafed at the restraints placed on them and would have preferred to try out their new machine guns, howitzers, and knowledge of the "how to quell" riots sections of military manuals on the sit-downers, in response to the beseechings of the Flint Alliance that the requirements of patriotism be fulfilled.*

Meantime—after the strikers by a ruse had captured the crucial Chevrolet motor assembly plant No. 4, and John L. Lewis had called on President Roosevelt to intercede for them against the "economic royalists represented by General Motors and the Du Ponts," who had opposed his reëlection with the same fervor that the auto workers had supported it; and also after Washington conferences between Secretary of Labor Frances Perkins and Alfred P. Sloan, president, and William S. Knudsen, vice-president of the company, had produced mutual recriminations— General Motors obtained from Circuit Judge Paul V. Gadola a significant and sweeping court order. It directed the sit-downers to evacuate company-owned plants under penalty of imprisonment for contempt of court and a fine of $15,000,000, the estimated value of the invested properties. Again Sheriff Wolcott served to mocking and derisive groups of determined men the order that set

* One major in particular confessed his bitter disappointment that he was unable to test the value of his pet idea, shooting vomiting gas into the sit-downers via the plants' ventilating systems.

3 P.M. on February 3 as the deadline for leaving the struck plants.

In reply the sit-downers sent telegrams to Governor Murphy, who was still exerting almost superhuman patience and persuasion to bring both sides into agreement. The message from Fisher Body Plant No. 1 read in part:

We the workers . . . have carried on a stay-in strike over a month in order to make General Motors Corporation obey the law* and engage in collective bargaining. . . . Unarmed as we are, the introduction of the militia, sheriffs, or police with murderous weapons will mean a blood-bath of unarmed workers. . . . We have decided to stay. . . . We have no illusions about the sacrifices which this decision will entail. We fully expect that if a violent effort to oust us is made many of us will be killed, and we take this means of making it known to our wives, our children, to the people of the state of Michigan and the country that if this result follows from the attempt to eject us, you are the one who must be held responsible for our deaths.

The night before the "zero hour" day of February 3, the sit-downers, pallid under blazing arc-lights, listened grimly to their radios, or played cards or parcheesi or checkers or dominoes, or tried to lose themselves in newspapers or magazines, or talked in subdued tones. Many were convinced that the morrow meant massacre. For defense against expected machine guns, inadequate clubs dangled from their belts. An air of almost Oriental passivity, as of men who wait in resignation for the beat of destiny's drum, hung over them. Their faces were stern and thoughtful, and few slept.

In the morning roads leading into Flint were filled with cars and trucks carrying union sympathizers from Akron, Lansing, Detroit, and Toledo who by the thousand swarmed over the town and had to take over the direction of traffic themselves, for no policemen were in sight. The

* The National Labor Relations Act.

visitors moved toward the various sit-down plants, and only the women's emergency brigades, with their red and green berets, brought color to a somber procession that for weapons held pokers, broom handles, and pieces of pipe.

While Flint's clocks ticked on toward the showdown hour of three in the afternoon, Governor Murphy in Detroit finally succeeded in arranging a conference between William S. Knudsen for the company and John L. Lewis for the United Automobile Workers. To Sheriff Wolcott, who had the duty of enforcing the Gadola eviction order, Governor Murphy wired that everything should be held in abeyance during the Knudsen-Lewis conversations; and the Sheriff, more than pleased to oblige, suddenly discovered that he lacked proper legal sanction, anyway, along with a sufficient force to carry out the Gadola edict, although the Flint Alliance and the company's legal staff in Flint assured him that they could together remedy both deficiencies.

When this turn of events was made known, sit-downers, pickets, and unionists from other cities made high holiday. Their violins, saxophones, banjos, cornets struck up hill-billy airs and square-dance tunes, and men and women swung partners joyously over the frozen lawns surrounding the various plants.

Next day the company complied with President Roosevelt's request that in the public interest its representatives should again meet with spokesmen of the strikers. A wearing week of conferences ensued between William S. Knudsen, G. Donaldson Brown, and John Thomas Smith for General Motors, and John L. Lewis, Lee Pressman (general counsel for the C.I.O.), Homer Martin, and Wyndham Mortimer for the strikers. Time after time only the moral strength and suasions of Governor Murphy, who presided over the negotiations, prevented their collapse, and cigarette and cigar ashes spilled over trays amid the temper-fraying clashes of strong wills and stronger wants.

Eight days later, the Governor, his face haggard with strain and lack of sleep, had the great personal triumph of seeing at long last a meeting of minds out of which came the agreement terminating one of the most important capital-labor disputes in recent times.

The contract signed by General Motors and the United Automobile Workers was a great step forward for unionism in motors and contained seven basic provisions: (1) recognition was to be granted to the U.A.W. for its members only, and not as sole collective bargaining agent; (2) straight seniority rules were to prevail after six months of service; (3) shop committees were to be set up to smooth out grievances on the job; (4) a survey of speed-up evils was to be made; (5) the forty-hour week was to continue in force; (6) time and a half for overtime was to prevail; (7) no discrimination was to be exercised against unionists, who could wear their union buttons and talk about their organization during lunch hours.

The union requests for a uniform minimum wage, affecting plants in all parts of the country, and for the thirty-hour week were both denied.

III

PRIMARILY as the result of its sit-downers' forty-four-day defiance of General Motors, the United Automobile Workers (late in 1938) has some 370,000 dues-paying members out of an industry-wide maximum potential of 450,000. It is thus the third largest among the C.I.O. unions. It has collective bargaining agreements with all of the independents and with two of the Big Three, General Motors and Chrysler. Currently it is trying to unionize Ford against an opposition as stubborn as a peasant's prejudice and as strong as a billion dollars.

The U.A.W. is doubly young—both in its short time of

existence as a union and in its membership, since the industry still places a premium upon speed and endurance in its workers, attributes most generally found in men and women under forty, even under thirty-five. The union's maverick sit-downs, condemned by motor magnates and (some of them) by Martin himself, have derived from a new sense of liberation from oppression; from flawed methods of adjusting "line" and departmental grievances; from foreman-worker antagonisms that had been piling up for years and were often aggravated by both the self-assertion of the new unionists and the desire of the straw boss to show them that he was still top-dog. Many of the pettier officials, indeed, still believe it their purpose in life to bring obloquy upon the union whenever possible;* and neither side has as yet been "educated up" to the patience and will to good will necessary for a harmonious management-union relationship.

* General Motors has discharged a superintendent who by "riding" unionists tried to provoke them into sit-down action.

Trouble Is the Word for Textiles:
The Textile Workers' Organizing Committee

ALONG the Appalachian foothills, eastward to the sea, starting south from Maine and spreading over all New England into New York, New Jersey, Pennsylvania, thence dipping down into Tennessee and through the Carolinas to Georgia and Alabama, 5,400 textile mills—92 per cent of the nation's total—sent peak-production smoke into a sky where new storm clouds gathered early in the spring of 1937. Elsewhere the weather vanes of 470 mills, scattered widely among eighteen other states, veered to the same signs of stress.

For, following the victory in motors and Big Steel, the C.I.O. was mobilizing for its big push on textiles while scare-headline writers and chambers of commerce and manufacturers' associations and particularly Southern senators all started to shout in syllables that seemed to portend at least some new kind of civil war. In this respect they were mistaken, if not disappointed. When C.I.O. legions began to invade textile territory, scarred by many years of industrial strife, their banners were inscribed less with slogans of battle than with those of even-tempered, constructive coöperation between ownership and unionism, and with the promise of helping to bring stability to an industry which, since its first boom in the War of 1812, has needed—in a phrase used by textile men—"a Moses, a Mussolini, or a Messiah."

The word "textiles" derives from the Latin "textilis," meaning woven. Today in America it stands for a diverse and complex and troubled industry with $7,000,000,000 total value in the production of cloth and fabrics: cotton, silk, rayon, woolens and worsteds, along with knit goods, carpets, bags, and hosiery and various related processes such as finishing and dyeing; and further connotes 10,000 officers and managers, 250,000 stockholders, 1,100,000 workers of whom 662,000 are men, 428,000 are women, and 110,000 are children from the ages of ten to seventeen.*

In 1789 Samuel Slater, the "Father of Cotton Manufacture in America," brought Great Britain's Industrial Revolution to the United States. An overseer in an English mill which had pioneered in the use of the Arkwright machinery, he was allured by the premiums and opportunity offered by various American bodies, such as the Philadelphia Society for the Encouragement of Manufactures, to anyone who could "construct or introduce" in this country the Arkwright type of water frame for cotton cloth.†

To evade English laws forbidding the emigration of artisans familiar with the Arkwright and ancillary methods of manufacture, Slater sailed secretly to America; and a few months after his arrival in New York learned of the efforts in Providence of the shrewd Quaker, Moses Brown, who was "desirous" that "the business of cotton manufacture be useful to the country" and patriotism thus be linked with his own fortunes. After an exchange of mutually subtle letters, Brown induced Slater to come to Providence and improve the inadequate and balky jennies and other equipment he had acquired at considerable cost from Bridgewater and Beverly.

Within a year, and entirely from memory, Slater had built two efficient carding machines and a water frame of twenty-four spindles; and by 1791 he had set up a mill at a choice water site. His achievement was publicized by the

* The Federal Wages and Hours Act, when it begins to operate, will prohibit the employment of minors under sixteen years of age.

† Whereas woolens were woven in the United States, at this time, by crude machines, and Hamilton had hailed the first Hartford woolen factory as "a precious embryo," it was not until a generation later that factory production of woolen cloth began really to come into its own.

following advertisement which appeared in the Providence *Gazette*:

Cotton Manufactory
To be Sold By
Almy and Brown

At their Store, opposite the Baptist Meeting House, by Wholesale and Retail, A Variety of Cotton Goods, manufactured in this Town, among which are, Cords of various Sorts, rib and plain Thicksett, Stockinet, rib and plain Denim, Jeans, Jeanets, Fustians &c. &c. . . . Also, Cotton Yarn of various Sizes, spun by Water, suitable for Warps or Stockings, superior in Quality to any spun by Hand, or upon Jennies. Those who are engaged in manufacturing Cotton, either in Factories or in Families, are invited to make Trial of its Quality, and those who wish to encourage the Manufactures of their Country, to lend their Aid to establish in it this useful business, by wearing cloth of its own Manufacture. . . . They have also for Sale a few barrels and Half Barrels of Pork and Beef, with a Variety of other Articles. . . . They want a Quantity of Tow Cloth, for which they will exchange Cotton, Flax, Wool &c.

N.B. Cotton, and Cotton and Linen Goods, of All Kinds are dyed and finished at their Dye House by an experienced workman from Europe.

Other Yankees besides Brown and his partners Almy and the naturalized Slater were quick to see the tremendous potentialities of this new kind of factory. Funds accumulated from whaling, fishing, and foreign and "the Orient" trade were used to finance new establishments at Providence and Pawtucket and in the old seaport towns of Salem and Portsmouth and Newburyport.

In 1813, Francis Cabot Lowell, scion of a prosperous mercantile family, founded the Boston Manufacturing Company with a paid-in capital of $300,000, a prodigious sum for that time; and a year later, together with the machinist Paul Moody, he had perfected a power loom that gave great impetus to the whole industry as imitators opened mills not only in New England but also in New York and New Jersey.

The labor supply for such forerunners of the factory system was recruited mainly from women and children; despite their "inferior strength" they were considered hardy enough to be "the little fingers . . . of the gigantic automatons"—the more especially since they were willing, or compelled, to sell their services for less than either adolescent or adult males who were attracted by the agricultural and commercial opportunities of an expanding economy. Accustomed to weaving and spinning at home, women found it easy enough to transfer this activity from the hearth to the factory; and to achieve the independence of nondomestic service, cooks, seamstresses, wax-workers entered the mills and were soon followed by teachers and daughters of clergymen and farmers, some seeking freedom from household drudgery, others wishing to help support their families, until in Massachusetts in 1815 more than 80 per cent of the cotton-mill operatives were girls and women.

Since Slater had observed that English millowners profited greatly from the very cheap labor of children, he copied the custom here. He discovered, however, that in this country there were too few poorhouses to permit the transfer of children, by wholesale, from the supervision of charity to that of the overseer. He therefore instituted the procedure of hiring the whole family, a practice soon generally adopted and which had a double advantage. In the first place, the waterfalls needed to provide power for the looms were usually located in out-of-the-way areas requiring the manufacturer to establish not only his factory but also his own population adjacent to it, to insure a stable labor force. He had to put up houses for his help; and he found that families were more likely to stay rooted to the same spot than single men and women, and that the former's progeny could also often be employed. Thus, in the Providence *Manufacturers' and Farmers' Journal* of January 14, 1828, a typical notice read: "Families wanted—Ten or Twelve good respectable families consisting of four or five children each, from nine to sixteen years of age, are wanted to work in a cotton mill, in the vicinity of Providence."

The contract signed between Dennis Rier and the proprietor of a cotton mill in Lancaster, Massachusetts, illustrates the beginnings of this family arrangement which still prevails in a large section of the textile industry. The faded entry, written in a fine hand on a yellowed ledger, reads thus:

1815, Jan. 27, Dennis Rier of Newberry Port, has this day engaged to come with his family, to work in our factory on the following conditions. He is to be here about the 20th of next month, and is to have the following [weekly] wages for work:

Himself	$5.00
His son, Robt. Rier, 10 years of age . . .	.83
Daughter, Nancy, 12 years of age . . .	1.25
Son William, 13 years of age	1.50
Son Michael, 16 years of age	2.00
	———
	10.58
His sister, Abigail Smith	2.33
Her daughter, Sally, 8 years of age . . .	.75
Son Samuel, 13 years of age	1.50
	———
	4.58

House rent to be from $20 to $30. Wood cut up, $2 per cord.

It was thought that, as still another advantage flowing from this state of affairs, parents would relieve overseers from the responsibility of correcting the waywardness of children, a process usually accomplished in the whipping rooms, an almost inevitable appendage of New England's cotton mills.*

When Slater himself had begun operations, his first nine employees consisted of seven boys and two girls, all of them between the ages of seven and twelve. Yet he was regarded as a benefactor, not as a monster. The sanguine Hamilton expressed prevailing opinion when he declared that "women and children are rendered more useful, and the latter more early useful by manufacturing establishments than they would otherwise be." In accord with this view of work as the means to righteousness, children would receive both vocational and moral benefits from being molded in their plastic years to habits of industry. Yet when, in 1801, Josiah Quincy visited a Slater mill, he was moved to protest that while his guide was "very eloquent on the usefulness of this manufacture and employment it supplied for many poor children . . . an eloquence was exerted on the other side more commanding than his, which called us to pity these little children, plying in a contracted room, among flyers and coggs, at an age when nature requires for them air, space and sports."

The pursuit of profits among the cotton and later the woolen manufacturing entrepreneurs, the Lowells, the Appletons, the Browns, and the Walthams, blended with the Puritan conviction that idleness is a temptation to vice, created a factory system which, from its infancy, was marked by a dollar-and-Deity paternalism, with results happier in its earlier years from 1792 to 1845 than from the mid-nineteenth century onwards.

To dispel the widespread view that factory work was degrading—an impression fostered by stories of the English mills with their drabs and doxies—New England's new industrialists decided that it was at once a duty and necessity

* It is an interesting commentary upon the mores of the time that certain Massachusetts "reformers" berated Rhode Island millowners for using the strap instead of sprinkling water on the children to keep them awake during their eleven- to fourteen-hour shifts.

to keep the morals of their operatives' environment at a high level. They therefore discharged girls and women for profanity, for indolence, for non-attendance at divine worship, for dancing, for immodesty; and blacklisted them for such frailties as prostitution, which was broadly interpreted, and for inability to tend their looms with proper diligence.

In many of the new mill communities the companies provided boarding-house accommodations for their women workers, and the keepers of such institutions had to be certified as persons of probity and sobriety who could be depended on to maintain an atmosphere equivalent to that of a Ladies' Seminary or nunnery. Doors were locked at 10 P.M.; and anything remotely resembling the improper was reported to the factory overseer at once. He, in turn, was usually married, a pillar of the church, selected quite as much for his seemly conduct as for his supervisory talents. In 1836, for example, the Lowell Manufacturing Company affirmed that it would not "continue to employ any person who shall be wanting in proper respect to the females employed by the company, or who shall smoke within the company's premises, or be guilty of inebriety."

In this milieu at Lowell, for instance, the "females" seemed contented enough on the whole. They tacked biblical quotations and elevating verse on their looms to memorize "ennobling sentiments" while they worked. They had French and German study clubs, and a debating society, and a publication known as the *Lowell Offering* which contained from-farm-to-palace romances in which the pure and honorable young woman always captured the millowner's handsome and elegant son, only after, of course, a nip-and-tuck race against the blandishments of some siren (most often a widow) who didn't attend church with proper humility, and flaunted her frills and furbelows and probably wasn't any better than she should be. The *Offering* also featured such revelatory versifying as:

> In plain words,
> I am a schoolma'am in the summer time
> As now I am a Lady of the Loom.
> . . . inside these factory walls
> The daughters of our honest yeomanry.
> Children of tradesmen, teachers, clergymen,
> Their own condition make in spinning;

and rapturously reported the lecture of the great Mr. Emerson at the local Lyceum, "crammed nigh to bursting" by millworkers to whom the tenets of Transcendentalism were at once daring and beautiful.

Many girls were attracted to Lowell, Waltham, and similar centers by the chance to combine a measure of education with earning some money, often to show that, with the gradual breakdown of home industry, they were able to make their way in the world. Their turnover rate was very rapid, however; for after a year or two in the mills, with its adventuresome new contacts with people and culture, they would return home—especially in slack times—to marry, or to go on with their schooling, or become simply "home-bodies" until "Mr. Right" came along.

Chiefly of Revolutionary stock, they had been brought up on tales of Bunker Hill, of Lexington and Concord, and when in Lowell during the fall of 1834 the management tried to cut their wages they turned to the strike. Under big hand-lettered proclamations reading, "As our fathers resisted unto blood, the lordly avarice of the British ministry, so we, their daughters, never will wear the yoke which has been prepared for us," they marched through the streets of the gaping town, singing:

> Oh, isn't it a pity that such a pretty girl as I
> Should be sent to the factory to pine away and die?
> Oh! I cannot be a slave,
> For I'm so fond of liberty . . .

Yet both proclamation and song were somewhat hyperbolic; for by the standards of their own epoch they were generally treated with consideration and made fairly comfortable. Today's tendency of the labor historian to weep over their twelve-hour day simply wrenches the reality of their existence from its social context. The from-dawn-to-darkness working schedule had been unconsciously taken over by commerce and industry from agriculture; and the farmer, the clerk, the lawyer all put in about the same amount of time as did the millworker; nor were the tempo and intensity of the factory routine any faster than those in other spheres during this period.

A dozen years later, however, this industrial garland had begun to fade, what with the "Great West open for our girls away there, and all this clamor for teachers, missionaries, and wives," and the first big wave of Irish immigration, result of the great famine of 1846, which enabled employers to acquire weavers and the like at wages spurned by the native New Englanders who were, in any case, being drawn off to other and better occupations. At the same time, moreover, the character of the millowners themselves had also begun to change. The strait-laced founders of the early factories, who had personally supervised their establishments, and who, for all the excesses of their piety, still definitely showed a sense of obligation for the welfare of their operatives, were being more and more supplanted by the managers appointed by absentee stockholders who desired dividends more than celestial grace and who deplored any fuss and feathers about the well-being of people who made dividends possible.

During the next five decades, immigration kept increasing and coincided with the ever-widening separation between ownership and personal administration (not only in textiles but elsewhere), until in 1900 from 70 to 90 per cent of all operatives in New England mills were foreign born; and the practice of ignoring their claims upon the conscience of either the individual or the community was already encrusted with tradition.

In 1912 in the city of Lawrence, Massachusetts, this dual development reached what was perhaps its Northern apogee. For in January of that year, more than 25,000 wage earners of Austrian, Belgian, English, French-Canadian, Irish, Jewish, Lithuanian, Polish, Portuguese, Russian, and Syrian descent rebelled against the "Woolen Trust" as represented chiefly by the American Woolen Company with four of its thirty-four mills located in Lawrence.

The immediate stimulus to their uprising seemed on the surface inconsequential enough. The state legislature in its autumn session in 1911 had passed a law, effective January 1, 1912, which reduced the hours of work for women and minors under sixteen from fifty-six to fifty-four a week. In Lawrence, mill managers extended this provision to male adults who comprised about 48 per cent of the labor force and who, along with all other operatives, were surprised to discover, on the first payday after this ruling had gone into effect, that their earnings had been cut about 3½ per cent, or two hours' worth. Whereas this diminution of income in most instances amounted to only 25 or 30 cents a week, it was serious enough to people who in the busiest times had an average wage of $8.76.*

Despite this destitution level of wages, however, the "few of loaves of bread" taken away would not have impelled the Lawrence workers to risk a strike if it had not seemed to them a crowning indignity. For years they had been forced to live in slums, in ramshackle run-down tenements, with as many as seventeen people to five rooms; 172 out of every 1,000 of their offspring died before reaching their first birthday; their children who survived had rickets and the diseases of malnutrition. They worked under a premium plan devised to extract their last reserves

* In the dyehouse, spinning, and winding divisions of American Woolen Company mills, wages ranged from $5.10 to $6.05 to $7.15 and $7.55 per week.

of energy by paying them a bonus only if they maintained a high rate of output over a month, without a single absence—a source of great nervous strain and tension. They were the "untouchables" insofar as the A. F. of L. was concerned; for the Federation, while organizing a few of the skilled among them, paid no attention to the vast unskilled majority.

On the other hand, the Lawrence English branch of the Industrial Workers of the World alone offered them encouragement in resisting oppression, and gave them leadership and hope. It had early in the month written to the Boston headquarters of the American Woolen Company asking for a conference between a millworkers' committee and the corporation's executives. The letter was never acknowledged. After a week of anxious waiting the walkout urged by the local I.W.W. began on January 11, on payday, when Polish women weavers left their looms with the curt "Not enough money," in reply to overseers' expostulations at the Everett mill. Next day their example was emulated at the Washington and Wood mills; and within sixty hours about 10,500 of Lawrence's "mill-hand furriners" were on strike. After a noisy meeting at the Franco-Belgian hall, they voted to invite Joseph Ettor of the I.W.W. national Executive Board to come to Lawrence and generally take charge.

The choice of Ettor was doubly significant. Among the 25,000 workers at the Lawrence woolen mills, only a gross of the more expert had been chartered by the A. F. of L. as a local of the United Textile Workers of America, and a few dozen more, banded together in the crafts forming the American Labor Union, had also received Federation blessing; but more than a thousand of the more plebeian workers had been enlisted by the Lawrence affiliate of the Industrial Workers of the World, which was a revolutionary union and very dramatic and candid about its aims, and which had been born but seven years before at a secret meeting in Chicago, on January 2, 1905. It was in large measure the creation of William Dudley ("Big Bill") Haywood, a tempestuous, Bull of Bashan kind of man, hard as the stone of the Rockies where he was raised, and a leader of the Western Federation of Miners, the tough, scrappy organization of the gold, silver, copper, and coal miners of the West.

An unconscious disciple of Sorel's "violence" as the means to emancipation of the wage earner from his "capitalist chains," Haywood embodied all the fierce "don't tread on me" psychology of the frontier with its reliance upon direct action. He was a Socialist with syndicalist trimmings who wanted his creed to prevail not in some distant future but tomorrow or the day after. His contempt for gradualism, for parliamentary methods of making haste slowly in terms of social change, was matched only by his contempt for the A. F. of L. and its officialdom which he denounced as "labor fakers from Gompers and Mitchell down."

In his opening speech to the secret Chicago conference which laid the groundwork for the I.W.W., and which was attended by Eugene Debs, Daniel DeLeon, and Mother Jones, together with railroad, brewery, and mining unionists and others interested in building a national federation for socialist-minded labor, Haywood declared: "Fellow workers: . . . The . . . objects of this organization [the projected I.W.W.] shall be to put the working class in possession of the economic power, the means of life, in control of the machinery of production and distribution, without regard to capitalist masters."

Six months later, 186 delegates from 34 extremely diverse labor alignments responded to the rap of his gavel at a new meeting in Chicago and officially voted into being the Industrial Workers of the World. It was launched as a "One Big Union" movement, and proposed to adopt the general lines of Knights of Labor structure, exchanging its ritualism and its ambiguous "uplift" for purposes described in the preamble of the I.W.W.'s constitution as follows:

The working class and the employing class have nothing in common. There can be no peace so long as hunger and want are found among millions of working people, and the few, who make up the employing class, have all the good things of life.

Between the two classes a struggle must go on until the workers of the world organize as a class, take possession of the earth . . . and abolish the wage system.

Instead of the conservative motto "A fair day's wages for a fair day's work," we must inscribe on our banner the revolutionary watchword "Abolition of the wage system."

It is the historic mission of the working class to do away with capitalism. The army of production must be organized not only for the everyday struggle with capitalists, but also to carry on production when capitalism shall have been overthrown. . . .

Despite the pleas of many delegates, Haywood himself refused the presidency of the society since he had been recently reëlected to the post of secretary-treasurer of the Western Federation of Miners, and the office went instead to the Socialist politico, Charles O. Sherman, who soon discovered that he headed a mob, not a movement. In addition to the regular trade unions like the United Brotherhood of Railway Employees which, feeble as it was, still was transformed into the I.W.W.'s "Transportation Department"; the United Brewery Workmen, which had joined up mainly because it had quarreled with the A. F. of L. over jurisdictional rights; an American Branch of the Amalgamated Society of Engineers of Great Britain which, of all things, was a benevolent and fraternal order; and the Western Federation of Miners (Mining Department), the Industrial Workers of the World was a catch-all for Anarchists, opportunists, crackpots, idealists, Socialists, parliamentarians, and "to hell with the Constitution" elements.

They were all adepts in factional discord. Marxists like Daniel DeLeon wanted to turn the organization into an adjunct of his own "economic" Trade and Labor Council and his "political" Socialist Labor party, both of which existed chiefly on paper and in his own wishful thinking. On the other hand, Haywood's bloc, consisting of some of the men who had literally shot and blasted scabs out of possession of the Smuggler-Union mines, and who had an abiding faith in the efficacy of force, scorned the "betrayals of the ballot" and looked toward the great General Strike which somehow, someday, would enable the workers to take over the country, and run it, in one fell and final swoop.

In 1908 this "direct-action" group was in the saddle, and attracted to the I.W.W. elements hitherto unreached by unionism, especially the hobo "bundle stiffs," the rough migrant labor of Oregon lumber and logging camps, of San Francisco docks, of fruit orchards in the San Joaquin valley. Along with the relatively more stable miners in Nevada, Colorado, and Montana, they formed the "eye for an eye" mainstay of the I.W.W. They had scant respect for the courts, for constituted authority. If a police nightstick cracked an I.W.W. skull, a policeman received identical treatment. And whatever the logical defects of their philosophy, they had courage. They clawed and slugged a seventy-five-cent daily raise in wages for sawmill workers of Portland. In 1909, in McKeesport Rocks, Pennsylvania, they brought out 8,000 employees of the Pressed Steel Car Company on a summer-long strike; and stood up against the State Constabulary, the most brutal and efficient anti-labor military in the United States. They had assured the officers of the Constabulary, called the Pennsylvania Cossacks, that for every striker killed or injured, a "Cossack" would meet the same fate. The I.W.W. kept their word. When a striker was shot through the temple, they picked off a trooper in exactly the same way. And in a

William Dudley Haywood.

pitched battle with the Constabulary, they killed twelve and wounded fifty of their foes, losing about the same number on their own side but winning the strike.

Immediately thereafter, however, national officers of the I.W.W. decided to forego the missiles of force for fervid organizing tactics that would give them "force of numbers" and thus allay the fears and hostility that their very name aroused.* It was a decision arrived at largely through the influence of such I.W.W. leaders as Elizabeth Gurley Flynn, New Hampshire born of Irish parents, an excellent organizer, lecturer, and called the Joan of Arc of labor; Arturo Giovannitti, Abruzzi born poet who, after coming to the United States, was by turns a clerk, a minter, and an editor of a small radical Italian sheet in New York City; and Joseph Ettor, who in 1906 had been jailed in San Francisco for trying to organize the debris workers after the city's famous earthquake and fire.

When, therefore, Ettor answered the request of the Lawrence strikers to guide them, he proceeded to lay out a program indistinguishable from that of any other intelligent and resourceful strike commander. He kept the flaming promises of the New Day for his stirring, morale-building speeches, and otherwise devoted himself to the practical business of setting up a Strike Committee, with himself as its head and two local leaders as secretary and treasurer; and of drawing up a quartet of demands: (1) a 15 per cent raise in wages on a fifty-four-hour week; (2) double pay for overtime; (3) elimination of the premium and stretch-out plan; (4) no discharge or demotion for strikers if and when they returned to their jobs.

But the reputation of the I.W.W. for militancy had preceded his appearance; and after his arrival, 250 militiamen from a local company patrolled mill areas and were soon reinforced by more guardsmen and state police called

* Sabotage (literally from the French *sabot*, or shoe thrown into cog or cylinder) as an I.W.W. method, with the exception of a few scattered strikes, was not extensively used until after the World War.

out by the Governor of Massachusetts at the request of
Lawrence's frenzied Mayor, John Scanlon.

On January 19, when it looked as if the strike would
paralyze every mill in Lawrence, President Wood of the
American Woolen Company made an interesting discovery which he relayed to his employees by means of an open
letter:

Last Friday many of you left our mills and have since remained away. This action was wholly a surprise to me. You
sent no notice of what you were intending to do and you
stated no grievances. I learn from the newspapers that the
reason for your staying away is that the company paid you for
only 54 hours' work; but you know that your wages are paid
by the hour or by the piece, and as you work only 54 hours
you could be paid for only 54 hours work. . . . I have consulted . . . with the directors . . . and regretfully we have
come to the conclusion that it is impossible . . . to grant at
this time any increase in wages.

In reply to this remarkable display of ignorance as to
what was happening in mills owned by the corporation of
which Mr. Wood was president, the Strike Committee
explained that:

On Thursday morning, January 3rd, 1912, a committee
called upon the agents of the Ayer, Wood and Washington
mills [all three were owned by the American Woolen Com-
pany] and endeavored to hold a conference . . . and so come
to a peaceful understanding. Two of the agents refused to have
dealings with the committee, while the other advised . . . to
write or to consult with you at your Boston office. . . . The
committee sent a letter to your address containing the demands
of the workers, but . . . the letter was not answered. . . .

The day after this exchange of letters, the inevitable
"dynamite plot" was uncovered and sticks of this explosive
materialized, among other places, at the cobbler's next door
to a printing shop where Ettor was known to "hang out"
a lot, and where he collected his mail. It was an amateurish

performance and some time later John C. Breen, a local undertaker, confessed that he had planted it, at the behest of company and police officials, to discredit the strikers, an objective it achieved to some extent since the nation's press was almost unanimously sure that the dynamite was evidence of Ettor's diabolical machinations. Shortly after the "dynamite plot" was revealed in two-inch type, a Citizens' Committee of company officials, local lawyers, merchants, and politicians was formed to denounce the strike as an evil of anarchism; and thugs were hired to derail street cars and smash their windows in order to accuse the strikers of "un-American violence."

The Strike Committee, reinforced by the presence of Arturo Giovannitti of the I.W.W. Executive Board, was unable to give very much attention to any of these incidents. It was too busy with its main problem: feeding the 50,000 strikers and their dependents. Soup kitchens and food stations were established along racial lines to facilitate their functioning, and supplies were purchased from funds contributed by labor and liberal groups throughout the country. As the days dragged on, negotiations at the Boston headquarters of the American Woolen Company were carried on by the Strike Committee and President Wood and reached a series of stalemates.

Then in the dusk of a winter evening, January 29, Anna Lo Pizzo, an Italian weaver on strike, was killed by a bullet presumably fired by a police officer. Her death was the "break" that local authorities had been waiting for. They arrested Ettor and the recently arrived Giovannitti, despite the fact that neither of them had been anywhere near the scene of the fatality. They were charged with being accessories to the murder on the grounds that before it had been committed ". . . Joseph J. Ettor and Antonio(?) Giovannitti did incite, procure, and counsel or command the . . . person whose name is not known . . . to com-

mit the . . . murder . . . against the peace of the Commonwealth."

Seven days later they were denied freedom on reasonable bail; and Big Bill Haywood, along with other I.W.W.
officers, including Elizabeth Gurley Flynn and William
Trautman, the organization's ablest pamphleteer, hastened
to Lawrence to assume direction of the Strike Committee
and assist their "comrades" in their trial.

Martial law was promptly clamped down over Lawrence. The city swarmed with troops. Picket lines were
everywhere shattered. Strikers were arrested in the early
hours of the morning, and dragged, sleep-drunk, from their
beds to court; and two sisters, fifteen and eighteen respectively, were roused from sleep at midnight to face charges
of "intimidating."

To discourage the strikers, who composed more than
90 per cent of the textile labor force in Lawrence, company
managers set the wheels turning in various factories, but
a New York *Times* reporter who made a personal inspection of the Washington mill discovered that "in the
spinning room every belt was in motion, the whirr of machinery resounded on every side, yet not a single operative
was at work and not a single machine carried a spool of
yarn. Outside the gates, a large force of infantry kept the
strikers away." His experience confirmed Ettor's observation that "bayonets cannot weave cloth."

Meantime, the A. F. of L. crafts in Lawrence, the Central Labor Union and the United Textile Workers, endorsed the strike, after it had been going for three weeks,
but their sympathy with it was more theory than fact.
They submitted their own list of demands to company
officials and received courteous treatment; and on the
promise of receiving "every consideration" for themselves,
they refused relief* to anyone who failed to follow their

---

* Their conduct in this regard was denounced by Mary K. Sullivan, first
woman organizer for the A. F. of L., who complained that "nothing was so

own "back to work" movement, and later put themselves forward as bargaining agents for people whom they would not help and certainly did not represent.

In order to ease the burden of feeding the strikers and their families, the Strike Committee, on February 5, adopted a procedure frequently used in France, Italy, and Belgium. It proposed to export the children of strikers to other cities and towns where they would be taken care of by other workers, by sympathizers. The announcement of this undertaking in the Socialist New York *Call* elicited within three days offers from four hundred people who guaranteed to board and lodge one or more of the children in their homes until the strike ended.

Hence on February 10, 119 children from the ages of four to fourteen, accompanied by two trained nurses and two guardians, embarked for New York City where they were welcomed at Grand Central station by cheering crowds of workers and the notes of the "Marseillaise" and the "Internationale."

The millowners, the New England press, and public authorities excoriated this maneuver as "exiling" and "exploiting" innocent children merely to publicize the strike, and accused the Strike Committee of tearing them from tender family bosoms to place them in surroundings that would lead them toward an idle, immoral, and dissolute life.

The Strike Committee retorted that, in every case, the parents' consent was obtained in writing; that the temporary homes were carefully investigated before children

---

conducive to organization by the Industrial Workers of the World as the methods used by the . . . branches of the American Federation of Labor. . . . Catholics, Jews, Protestants, and unbelievers—men and women of many races and languages—were working together as human beings with a common cause. The American Federation of Labor alone refused to cooperate. As a consequence, the strikers came to look upon the federation as a force almost as dangerous to their success as the employers themselves. . . . The operatives have more respect for the mill owners themselves than the leaders of this antagonistic element within their own ranks. . . ."

were sent to them; that the children would get better nourishment and lodging in such places than they were in the habit of having; and that the "exploitation" of children in the mills was far more harmful than their alleged exploitation for a purpose described by John Golden of the A. F. of L. Textile Workers as merely an attempt to "keep up the agitation and further the propaganda of the I.W.W."

To prevent the shipment of such ambassadors for the strikers' cause, Colonel Sweetser, militia commander, forbade any more "exportations" unless he personally was certain that the parents had consented; and the marshal of Lawrence went even further and flatly ordained that no trainloads of the strikers' children could henceforth leave the city.

The Strike Committee defied this prohibition, and on February 24 sought to send forty children to Philadelphia; children, guardians, and mothers gathered at the Lawrence station were clubbed by the police with a ferocity usually reserved for criminals, turning a crowd assembled to smile and weep farewells into a panic-stricken shambles. A pregnant woman, Bertha F. Crouse, was beaten around the abdomen by policemen until she fell to the ground unconscious; and sometime later the bleeding pulp of a dead infant was removed from her womb at the local hospital. More than thirty arrests were made on an "anti-congregation" ordinance; and fourteen of the children were sentenced to the city farm, an institution for delinquents, by local Judge Rowell in juvenile court.

The nation was horrified, and its editors outraged, by the vision of defenceless women and children battered and bruised by officers of the law. The House of Representatives called for an investigation. The protests of a nationally aroused social conscience whipped about the heads of the mill operators until they were frightened by the repercussions of the barbarity they themselves had fostered.

Gradually they began to weaken. Early in March they retreated step by step in a chastened, even a conciliatory mood, until on March 12 the American Woolen Company granted all of the strikers' demands, and its lead was promptly followed by others.

After nine and a half weeks the strikers had gained one of the few unequivocal victories in the annals of American labor's striving toward a better life. In Lawrence, membership in the I.W.W. bounded to 14,000 as the Strike Committee was dissolved and Local No. 20 of the National Industrial Textile Workers' Union set up in its place.

In Big Bill Haywood's opinion, however, the strikers' triumph was but a "preliminary skirmish" of a continuous battle that would end only "when the working class has overthrown the capitalist class, and has secured undisputed possession of the earth and all that is in it and on it."

The alarm and uneasiness which his words aroused—they were delivered as a curtain speech for the disbanding Strike Committee—were carried over into the trial of Ettor and Giovannitti which, after several postponements, opened on September 30 in Salem, Massachusetts. The prosecution, led by District Attorney Atwill, had meantime dug up a new "accomplice" named Joseph Caruso, a Lawrence spinner. Caruso, it was alleged, had assisted still another and mysterious "man in a brown overcoat," who was never found, in the shooting of Anna Lo Pizzo, an act "instigated" by the incendiary speeches and behavior of Ettor and Giovannitti.

During the late spring and summer which preceded the trial, both Ettor and Giovannitti had warned the workers of Lawrence against mass demonstrations in their behalf, lest such protests antagonize a public already inimical enough. Despite the adjuration of the prisoners, however, the new Local No. 20 of the National Industrial Textile Workers' Union in Lawrence called out 15,000 workers for twenty-four hours. This successful "political" or pressure strike inspired textile workers in Lowell, Haverhill, Lynn, and other Massachusetts textile centers to declare that they too would go out on strike if "anything went wrong" at the trial of Ettor and Giovannitti.

To scotch this "anarchist" tendency at its source, all the more important members of the Ettor-Giovannitti Defense Committee, which boasted legal and financial and publicity departments and which had raised $60,000, were indicted and released on bail, for alleged conspiracy to intimidate textile workers in Lawrence and elsewhere.

Similarly coercive methods were used at the trial itself. Yet the evidence presented by the state was so flimsy, so much the handiwork of minds still influenced by the more lurid tales of intrigue and detection, that the obvious "frame-up" against Ettor and Giovannitti daily became more apparent. When the prosecution's case bogged down, the Attorney-General and his aides tried Ettor and Giovannitti, not on the charge of complicity in the murder of Anna Lo Pizzo, but rather on their doctrines of political economy. Neither did anything to tone down his views, or disguise his profound opposition to the status quo, or otherwise draw upon that discretion which is the better part of valor. Both made closing speeches to the jury that revealed them to be stiff-necked, unyielding zealots in what they felt was a holy cause. "Let me tell you," said Giovannitti, "that the first strike that breaks again in this Commonwealth or any other place in America where the work and help and intelligence of Joseph J. Ettor and Arturo Giovannitti will be needed . . . there we shall go again, regardless of any . . . threat. We shall return again . . . obscure, unknown, misunderstood soldiers of this mighty army of the working class of the world, which, out of the shadows and the darkness of the past, is striving towards . . . the emancipation of human kind. . . ."

After fifty-eight days of a trial marked by strong international protests, by calls upon the government of the

United States to intervene and thwart "repugnant injustice," by boycotts of American woolen products in Italy and Sweden, the jury on November 26 returned a verdict of not guilty; and when the defendants appeared a few days later at a giant rally in Lawrence they were hailed as liberators of labor, as its saviors, amid the hosannas and thanksgiving of a melting-pot multitude.

The I.W.W. of course was more interested in winning converts for the revolution than in building a day-to-day collective bargaining agency. It therefore failed in Lawrence, as it failed a year later among the silk workers in Paterson, New Jersey, to leave in its wake any solid and permanent organization. By temperament and conviction I.W.W. leaders were crusaders for times of crisis. They could stir and guide workers over the exciting stretch of a strike whether it lasted three days or three months. And in arranging settlements and in negotiations they could be amazingly cool-headed and astute. Basically, however, they were by the logic of their own creed forced to repudiate their own achievements. Compromise with the employer, the implacable foe, was in their view anathema; and any pact that improved wages, hours, conditions—all the desiderata of trade, as against revolutionary unionism—was worthwhile to them first as its accomplishment might have aroused workers to a sense of their "historic mission," namely, the abolition of capitalism, and only secondarily as it might make things easier for men and women at looms, in orchards, in the pit.

A dozen years after its most important triumph, the Lawrence strike, and the benefits flowing from it, the I.W.W. had all but disappeared, its leadership disrupted by the knight-errant individualism of its component parts; its morale undermined by persecution under the criminal-syndicalist laws during the World War, and its aftermath of labor-baiting; and its human mainspring, Big Bill Haywood, dying as a fugitive from American justice in

Russia where he was buried with the pomp befitting a working-class hero; while other I.W.W. chieftains, including the up-and-coming organizer William Z. Foster, joined the American Communist party.

During this time, moreover, the inability of the I.W.W. to establish a sober management-union relationship, intrinsically a compromise phenomenon, compelled the workers in Lawrence and elsewhere to shift their allegiance to bread-and-butter unions, if any, in order to consolidate and retain gains already won. The chief beneficiary of this trend was the United Textile Workers which, despite its policy of craft exclusiveness, had 105,000 members in 1920 and was the dominant union in the industry. Three years later it was joined by the Federation of Full Fashioned Hosiery Workers and by other independent groups and seemed on the highroad to stability. Within twelve months, however, it had lost 75,000 members, chiefly the unskilled, a circumstance due in part to Japan's capture of Chinese, Indian, and South American cotton-goods markets from United States manufacturers; in part to the high mortality of war-baby firms which, born in the boom of 1916-18, were unable to survive the rigors of "normal" competition; and in part to the apathy and inefficiency of U.T.W. leadership.

The rows of red ink on the ledger of textiles, sometimes valid, sometimes faked to justify "lowering labor costs," resulted in a wage-cutting program that turned the period from 1924 to 1933 into a decade of strikes as workers in both the North and the South tried to arrest the downward sweep of their incomes. In 1924 in Paterson, for example, a local union, the Associated Silk Workers; in 1926 in Passaic, the Communist National Textile Workers Union, captained by the economic theorist, Albert Weisbord; in 1928 in New Bedford (Massachusetts) the U.T.W. in conjunction with the independent American Federation of Textile Operatives—to mention only a few—all conducted strikes from six days to twenty-six weeks in duration, which were largely futile.

In the South, in 1929 at Elizabethtown, Tennessee, and in Marion, North Carolina, the U.T.W., called in to direct a spontaneous uprising of rayon workers, had no better luck. And in Gastonia, North Carolina, the National Textile Workers Union, guided by Fred E. Beal, rammed head-on into a collision with all the prejudices of Dixie. The front page of the Gastonia *Daily Gazette* carried a cartoon in which the American flag was threatened by a snake coiled for its spring, captioned: "Communism in the South. Kill it." Banner headlines of the same paper declared, "Red Russianism Lifts Its Gory Hands Right Here in Gastonia." The N.T.W.U.'s admission of Negroes on a basis of equality provoked a hail of pamphlets and handbills asking, "Would you belong to a union which opposes White Supremacy?"

The shooting of unarmed strikers and pickets by company-hired and official deputies; the kidnaping and flogging of union organizers by bands of night-riders; the murder by vigilantes of the widow Mrs. Ella May Wiggins, composer of "home-made" strike songs and the mother of five children; the killing of Police Chief Alderholt, shot either by one of his own policemen or by a Loray mill striker when trying to invade the tent colony of the union at the outskirts of the town; the subsequent trial of Beal and others charged with complicity in Alderholt's death were combined with events at Elizabethtown and Marion to plant the first sturdy seeds of textile unionism in the South, but at great cost, with bitterness and blood, and with few immediately visible gains.

Indeed, despite 5,910 textile strikes during the past fifty years no big stable union had emerged until recently from all this turbulence, a circumstance rooted in the industry's ruthless and anarchical competition, domestic and foreign, and intensified by the fact that wool fights cotton and both war on silk for a larger share of the consumer's dollar. As in the garment trades, the relatively small amount of capital required to enter the business, and its possibility of quick and ample profits, still encourage shoestring enterprisers to invade the field with a few looms in a foul loft.

Textiles as an industry is also hyper-sensitive to style changes, with a short skirt fad, for example, depressing woolen sales to an appalling extent; and the distribution system remains in large part early nineteenth century. It hasn't as yet developed any simple and direct marketing methods. Instead there is a maze of criss-crossing lines from mill to wholesaler to broker to converter to jobber. The "commission agents," hangovers of the old English practice of "factoring," confound confusion all the more, once prompting Ethelbert Stewart, former U.S. Commissioner of Labor Statistics, to say:

"Goods are manufactured and turned over to a commission man for sale and he gets a commission on that sale whether he sells at a price below the cost of production or not. . . . His object is sales, not profits to the manufacturer . . . and when he sells below cost the difference . . . flows from the capital invested in the factory into the pockets of the commission man. Thus we find scores of mills . . . owned by the commission men."

From its beginning a "family" industry, wherein the efforts of mother, father, sons and daughters permitted group subsistence as an alternative to individual starvation, its labor supply has been historically the cheapest of any in the country, with a national annual wage in 1937 of $850.00, or $300.00 less than the overall $1,150.00 average for all American industries.

Hence, acting upon the assumption that low wages anywhere make for low wages everywhere, the Committee for Industrial Organization, early in 1937, began to organize weavers, spinners, quillers, tenders, lap-carriers, can-boys, and all the rest into a vast vertical union, hoping to succeed where many others had failed before.

The conduct of the campaign, among the most difficult ever undertaken, was turned over to Sidney Hillman, president of the Amalgamated Clothing Workers, treasurer of the C.I.O., and a moving spirit in Labor's Non-Partisan League and New York State's American Labor party. He was named chairman of the C.I.O.-sponsored Textile Workers' Organizing Committee which, for all practical purposes, "took over" the United Textile Workers under a special agreement by which, as soon as the unionizing of textiles has been achieved in thoroughgoing fashion, more permanent organization will be established.

Nominally, in accord with usual union practice, the assignment would have gone to Francis J. Gorman, the hard-working, conscientious president of the U.T.W. He was willing to "step down" for the duration of the campaign, not because he lacked ability but because Hillman's name carried more weight with the manufacturers in general and also with certain sections of labor in the textile field.

On September 6, 1934, began the famous textile walkout to protest the maintenance of low wages by NRA's Cotton Code Authority in the face of rising profits for the mill operators who, in their new prosperity, not only refused to raise pay but also discharged and discriminated against adherents of the United Textile Workers which, impelled by Section 7a, was waging a vigorous membership drive.

The strike, involving more workers than any other in American history, had been called under the auspices of the United Textile Workers, with Gorman, then vice-president, acting as chairman of the General Strike Council. He was a field marshal without adequate supplies. Whereas various American labor groups, notably in the needle trades, contributed generously to the U.T.W.'s war chest, funds were insufficient for a sustained campaign of such tremendous scope. Despite brilliant publicity, and an excellent use of "Flying Squadrons" of organizers, swinging from town to town like old-time revivalists on the "Moody and Sankey" circuit, and despite the 500,000 textile workers who "went out" either for direct causes or in sympathy with their fellow workers, attempts to raise pay and get union recognition were almost entirely abortive.

When therefore on September 17, 1934, the Winant Board, appointed by President Roosevelt to mediate the issue, recommended in its report a new and objective study of wages, hours, and stretch-out; the acceptance of collective bargaining, at least in principle; and the creation of a Textile Labor Relations Board to deal with complaints in a juster spirit than that displayed by Cotton Code Authority, Gorman called off the strike. His friends defended this action, as a strategic retreat, pending a more propitious day. His opponents denounced him for what they termed a "dishonorable surrender." They cited the thousands of workers who were not rehired because of their union activity, and pointed to the many dead and injured in clashes between police and pickets. In any event, Gorman's record had been marred by a dubious victory and his popularity among many textile operatives, especially in the South, had suffered as a result.

On the other hand, Hillman had never lost a major engagement. He had retreated, bided his time, but over the long pull always had won.

Less colorful, less dynamic, less eloquent than John L. Lewis, he remains the former's equal, if not his superior in questions of administration and strategy. Certainly C.I.O. helmsmen tack in no new direction until Hillman has helped to chart the course. In appearance, he seems more the social theorist or philosopher than the efficient executive and prudent tactician. He is trim and compactly built and of medium height; his nose is big and fleshy, his chin strong, and his shock of wiry black hair touched with gray at the temples. Behind steel-rimmed glasses, his eyes are grayish-blue with a marble-hard keen look that contradicts first impressions of the purely contemplative personality. His exterior of a calm, even cold, *savoir faire* conceals a nervous intensity, an *élan vital* that enables him to work eighteen hours a day over long intervals. His humor is wry and ironic, deriving from a sharp intellect often impatient with the comparative slowness of other minds.

Lesser lights in the Amalgamated, his own union, complain that he is too peremptory by far, even arrogant and high-handed; various rank and filers assert that in recent years, with his increasing prominence in labor and political affairs, his head has become too big for his hat. His partisans, on the other hand, hail him as a genius.

He was born of Jewish parents in 1887, in Zagare, Lithuania, the son of a wool merchant. At twelve he was sent to the town's Talmudic seminary where he was taught Jewish history and "the law" as expounded by Jewry's great ethicists, Rabbis Akiba and Eleazar, and their countless heirs and assigns. Like most bright youngsters in his milieu, Hillman soon began to read the secular literature forbidden not by statute but by custom. He was attracted to the sciences, both "social" and "physical," and at fifteen quit school to take a job as laboratory assistant in a local chemical concern.

He joined the "underground" trade-union movement for a brief period at the time of the Revolution of 1905 and at twenty he emigrated to the United States, landing in Chicago where he got a job as an apprentice cutter in a Hart, Schaffner, and Marx clothing factory, working twelve hours a day for $7.00 a week. He lived at Jane Addams' Hull House, studying at night, steeping himself in economics—Smith, Ricardo, Sismondi, Mill, Marx, and Engels—and learning the English which he still speaks with a slight accent.

He still reads voraciously in government and political economy and is something of an authority on labor and social-security legislation, both here and abroad. He is the father of the Impartial Arbitration Plan, forerunner of others throughout American industry, and adopted by Hart, Schaffner, and Marx in 1911 as an aftermath of the 1910 strike of spongers, pressers, tailors and trimmers, and makers of coats and pants in which Hillman was a ringleader. Here, indeed, he earned his first stripes as a labor leader. Despite his youth, Hillman at twenty-three had managed to coalesce a concrete list of grievances from all the diffused discontent of Turks, Albanians, Greeks, Poles, Bohemians, Bulgarians, and Jews who knew only that they were being exploited, that thousands of them were paid from $2.50 to $4.00 for a week ranging from 60 to 70 hours, and who, foreign to the American scene and alien to each other, must needs distrust anyone seeking to rescue them from the Promised Land's perdition.

Although this 1910 strike was lost, the drive toward a genuine rank-and-file union in men's clothing had at last begun. At that time, the single existing union in the industry was the United Garment Workers. Hillman's devotion to the idea of industrial unionism dates, in fact, from his many clashes with the U.G.W. officials, a craft-conscious clique more concerned with dues and jurisdiction than with the general welfare of workers in men's apparel.

In January, 1911, Hillman was chosen to represent the clothing workers at a Palmer House meeting with Hart, Schaffner, and Marx executives; and three years later he was elected president of the Amalgamated Clothing Workers, a post he has occupied continuously for twenty-four years. Almost from the beginning he departed from orthodox precedents of pure and simple unionism, urging Amalgamated adherents to make their organization more than a vehicle for collective bargaining and to share with their employers the problems and responsibilities of improving quality, increasing output, abolishing waste, and reducing overhead.

"We help the employers," he declared in 1923, "for one excellent reason. The clothing workers must make their living out of the clothing industry—just as their employers. Until now labor has fought mainly from a sense of outrage against exploitation. Henceforth it will fight more and more from a sense of social and industrial responsibility."

To make this approach an actuality, the Amalgamated has often loaned large sums from its own treasury to clothing manufacturers to tide them over hard times and to maintain employment for its members. Similarly its first-rate statisticians and research staff often have conducted costly surveys into the clothing market, from sheep-shearing to retail sales. They then turn over their findings to union employers to guide them toward greater profits, and, as a corollary, to preserve the high wage scales the Amalgamated demands.

When, therefore, at the 1937 Golden Jubilee dinner given by the officers of Hart, Schaffner, and Marx to celebrate the fiftieth anniversary of their firm's founding, Hillman as a guest speaker stated that "for fully 25 years the Amalgamated Clothing Workers and Hart, Schaffner and Marx have coöperated in a labor-management movement that has not only been steady and unbroken, but also mutually beneficial," he was not indulging merely in post-prandial politeness.

Today he is the outstanding example of "constructive coöperation" between industrialist and wage earner; and the policy of the Amalgamated reflects that "class collaboration" which pristine Marxists abhor.* It has, by using its

---

* Like other unions, notably the I.L.G.W.U., its policy also reflects the gulf separating its abstract philosophy and its day-to-day behavior. On December 28, 1914, when the Amalgamated Clothing Workers of America was born out of an internal row between a Hillman-led faction within the United

own special technique of mutual aid, wrung concession after concession from the clothing industry, organizing the men's apparel centers—New York, Chicago, Baltimore, Philadelphia, St. Louis, and Rochester, New York— to the tune of an average 87 per cent closed shop. It has also pioneered the two most successful ventures of American labor into banking and coöperative housing.

In the early 1920's a number of unions which had especially benefited from labor's wartime prosperity had been able to accumulate treasuries which exceeded current needs. Such surplus funds were deposited in banks at the usual low rates of interest for savings—a situation which dissatisfied various labor leaders, keenly aware of the higher returns the bankers were getting on union money. Among railroad, machinist, and men's clothing union officials, particularly, the idea developed that the rainy-day reserves of their own organizations could simultaneously be put to work and remain available for such union exigencies as a strike or the payment of benefits.

The question was, however, how to keep union funds profitably invested and immediately liquid at one and the same time. Labor banking was hailed as a practically perfect solution. It was furthermore widely argued, in effect, that:

Labor would mobilize the wage earner's savings in its own financial institutions and would unlock the door of open-shop industry with the golden key of credit. Nay, labor would go

Garment Workers of America convening at New York City's Webster Hall, the new union's constitution carried a preamble which, in part, declared:

"The economic organization of labor has been called into existence by the capitalist system of production, under which the division between the ruling class and the ruled class is based upon the ownership of the means of production. The class owning those means is the class that is ruling; the class that possesses nothing but its labor power, which is always on the market as a commodity is the one that is being ruled.

"A constant and increasing struggle is being waged between these two classes.

". . . Clear knowledge and class consciousness will put the organized working class in actual control of the system of production and the working class will then be ready to take possession of it."

much further; it would effect a total redirection of capitalism by emerging as a first rate financial power. Labor's struggle for its rights would be transferred from the picket lines, the Congressional lobby, and the courts to the stockholders' meetings of large corporations.*

A supplementary advantage of labor banking, its advocates affirmed, would be to curtail the pressure exerted by bankers upon industrialists to maintain the open shop as an avenue to higher profits. The labor bank, in the future, would extend credit to union firms, withhold it from open-shop employers. Moreover, when workers were made idle because of an employer's refusal to comply with union wage scales, the labor bank would loan money to some new rival, and otherwise carry out an imitation of business that in many respects would become identified with business. Hence by 1926 there were thirty-six labor banks, with a total paid-in capital of more than $13,000,000, and extravagant hopes. Within four years only fourteen of them had survived the debacle of 1929, most of them precariously, a condition due to incredible inefficiency in direction, a whole-hearted devotion to wild-cat stocks and the fancier forms of speculation and—in some cases—to sheer thievery.

The two banks founded by the Amalgamated Clothing Workers, however, one in Chicago in 1922 and another in New York City a year later, not only withstood the ravages of depression but still are flourishing. They rejected the belief that labor could gain control over jobs by means of control over credit, and instead stressed small personal services to their membership, loans, the transmission of funds to relatives and friends in foreign countries, and counsel for the small investor, the latter through the Amalgamated Securities Corporation in Chicago and the Amalgamated Investors, Inc., in Manhattan. Between them, the two Amalgamated banks currently record total

* Perlman and Taft, *History of Labor in the United States*, p. 572.

assets exceeding $15,000,000 and are managed with exceptional competency.

Similarly, the Amalgamated shares with the American Federation of Hosiery Workers in Philadelphia labor's most notable accomplishments in the field of coöperative housing. It has constructed a $3,500,000 group of coöperative dwellings in the Bronx (New York City), housing 2,500 persons at an average of $11.00 a room for airy and sunlit apartments, or about $5.25 a month less than the private cost for the same sort of thing. In addition to pleasant living quarters, the Amalgamated's apartments supply their tenants with a coöperative grocery, fruit market, and tea room, along with a coöperative laundry, milk, electric light and bus services. Their children attend a coöperative day nursery; and the parents themselves attend lectures and debates on current topics,* in addition to the concerts, dances, bridge parties, and the like held in the auditorium and recreation halls on the premises.

Since Hillman is neither a utopian nor an opportunist but a combination of both, and the Amalgamated is fashioned in his image, his supervision of the Textile Workers' Organizing Committee campaign has tended to carry forward the principles underlying the Amalgamated's own pragmatic idealism, in itself a part of that enlightened self-interest which, almost by reflex action, extends the helping hand to the underdog. The Amalgamated, which always "comes through" for unionism's causes in the conviction that in the long run its own well-being depends upon that of all labor, raised $500,000 to start the T.W.O.C. drive off in substantial style.†

Hillman mapped it out with all the plasticity of his chess-

---

* The extraordinary interest in public affairs displayed by members of the Amalgamated springs from the Socialist sympathies of a considerable portion of its membership and is at once stimulated and fed by the union's official monthly, *The Advance*. J. B. S. Hardman, its editor, is chief author and compiler of *American Labor Dynamics*, one of the few indispensable books for any student of the labor question in the United States.

† The I.L.G.W.U. and the United Mine Workers as the "great givers" of the C.I.O. also contributed hundreds of thousands of dollars.

player's mind, and all the resolution of a man who at fifty matches dimes against his own destiny; for the T.W.O.C. offensive which is still in progress, with considerable ground gained but more to capture, may well prove to be the most crucial and costly ever waged by the C.I.O.

Among the more difficult obstacles which the T.W.O.C. has had to face are the textile industry's 5,870 different producing units, owned by 3,400 separate companies. The trend toward consolidation has quickened, of course, during the past fifteen years. Today a syndicate of eight banks —Durpee Trust, Fall River; Rhode Island Hospital National, Providence; the National Shawmut and Old Colony in Boston; the National City in New York; the First National in Greenville, South Carolina; the Citizens and Southern in Atlanta; and the American Trust in Charlotte —control 150 corporations, accounting for 33 per cent of the nation's mill capacity, and including such famous firms as Amoskeag in Manchester, New Hampshire; the American Woolen Company with plants all over New England; the Pacific Mills of Lawrence; and Manville-Jenckes with its mills in Rhode Island and in Gastonia and High Shoals, North Carolina.

Outside of this single great interlocking directorate there is no other concentration of control in textiles comparable to Carnegie-Illinois in steel, to General Motors Corporation in automobiles; and this diffusion has necessitated extra conversions, extra journeyings, extra negotiations, and extra expense in general for the four hundred T.W.O.C. organizers working out of central headquarters in New York City and regional offices in Boston, Passaic, Philadelphia, Chicago, Atlanta, and Rochester. Otherwise the relative smallness of textile producing units and their economic set-up has redounded to the advantage of the T.W.O.C. since it is usually easier to pit union strength against a small or medium-sized manufacturer than against a big one supported by a great bank with all its direct and indirect influences. Sometimes, however, the reverse is true, wherever strong trade associations exist.

Below the Mason-Dixon line T.W.O.C. missionaries encountered a double hardship. They have had to confront an employing opposition that in general looks upon the open shop as the life and the redemption. The extreme of this anti-union attitude was expressed by B. W. Baldwin, president of the Marion Manufacturing Company in Georgia. At 7 P.M. on October 1, 1929, six strikers were killed and eighteen wounded when deputy sheriffs fired three volleys into a crowd of 250 demonstrating before the factory gates. The next day, interviewed by a reporter for the Asheville *Citizen*, Mr. Baldwin declared:

"I understand sixty or seventy shots were fired in Wednesday's fight. If this is true, there are thirty or thirty-five of the bullets accounted for. I think the officers are damned good marksmen. If I ever organize an army they can have jobs with me. I read that the death of each soldier in the World War consumed more than five tons of lead. Here we have less than five pounds and these casualties. . . ."

Although the majority of manufacturers in the South do not necessarily share Mr. Baldwin's interest in this branch of ballistics, per se, their views were dramatized by the action of Governor Eugene Talmadge of Georgia when in 1934 he placed hundreds of striking mill girls behind the barbed wire of concentration camps, under strict military guards.

In addition to facing such strong anti-union feeling among employers, T.W.O.C. organizers have also had to try to convert upwards of 450,000 workers most of whom a generation ago left a scraggly upland farm or a cotton patch "down below" to stand at a spindle, and to exchange simple barter for the bright wonder of money. They were and still are ignorant, ornery, clannish. They are anti-foreign, anti-Catholic, anti-Yankee. They distrust anyone who doesn't go to church, or opens the windows to night air, or is educated beyond the three R's. Although they themselves were originally sons of the soil, other farmers look down upon them as "white trash," and so do the townsfolk. At the very bottom of Southern white society, they have taken refuge in a pride in their "pure American stock" which is about all they have left to be proud of. Their faces display a "mill pallor" similar to the gray-white appearance of people long confined in prison; it seems more than skin deep and is in large part due to their diet of sow-belly and hominy grits, with green vegetables a rarity. They look always tired, inert, docile. They work amid a whir and bob and crash of machinery that is at once dazing and deafening, that prevents any companionable chattiness, and that deepens their taciturn traits. Many succumb to pellagra, the disease of poverty's malnutrition. Tuberculosis and other respiratory ailments are frequent, as the dust and acid-charged air of many ill-ventilated mills eat away their lungs. Until the passage of the national wages and hours bill which put a ceiling on hours at forty-four per week, the whole family (and textiles is after 150 years still a family industry) labored in the mills from ten to twelve hours a day, or night, and often longer.

More than 70 per cent of these people (as against about 20 per cent in Massachusetts) live in company-owned villages of a type which a former textile worker described in 1936 as follows:

Here we find unpaved streets of red mud and black cinders with no sidewalks . . . houses all exactly alike . . . in long rows up and down the mountain side. Some . . . are painted very ugly colors . . . others have no paint at all. Lots of them are built on stilts so high you could easily park a car . . . under them. They are exactly like a box, with four partitions dividing it into four and six rooms. These . . . are very small and there are usually two open fireplaces to each house. . . . In the back lot between every two houses you would find one toilet, to serve two families . . . open toilets, a pit being only a few feet deep. . . . About every four or six houses you will find an open pump on one side of the street. About four to six families from the other side of the street also get water from this pump. . . . Here the cows, chickens and children are all watered together.

On down the road is the mill itself . . . a large brick structure with a tall smokestack from which the smoke pours daily . . . to settle on . . . the little homes of the workers. The company store is directly in front of the mill with a public highway between. The workers get paid sometimes in scrip and this is redeemable in merchandise only at the company store. There are also two churches in the village, one Methodist, and one Baptist, owned and partly controlled by the company.

On a hill overlooking the village is quite a different scene. Here is a nice little village apart from the workers, nice winding lanes . . . shade trees, pretty gardens, paved streets and sidewalks . . . nicely painted houses. These . . . have sun parlors, sleeping porches, heating systems, water systems and lights. These are the bossmen's houses and this section is known as "bossmen's row."

As in the coal-mining community of a somewhat earlier day, the "company" sees, hears, knows, and owns all, is able to evict the complaining from its property, and to limit the rental of its houses exclusively to its own workers, often on the condition that all able-bodied members of the family will remain at the mill and not seek employment elsewhere. This is especially difficult to enforce since the family can bundle up its worldly goods in an hour or two, put them into a single dray or battered car, and roll off in search of some better place. The population of Southern textile mills, indeed, is incessantly shifting, since workers confuse their discomfort with the dispensations of a particular mill rather than with the general system of textile labor relations in Dixie. The labor turnover in

Southern mills is 189.5 as compared with 94.9 in the North, or actually double.

The Southern mill hand, "settin'" at home during his few hours of leisure, exudes grievances in his own lackadaisical fashion; and the introduction of labor-saving devices (textiles, as the first of our industries to be mechanized, has been for years the happy hunting ground of the efficiency engineer), bringing the speed-up and the stretch-out in which a weaver, for example, has to watch forty-eight instead of twenty-four looms, comes in for hours of lamentation. Yet when "Southern labor stirs," as it often has, it is almost as easy to organize into a fighting force as its Northern fellows, but more difficult to hold in unions. For Southern management has few compunctions when it comes to discharging a man for union affiliation, fewer indeed than similar executives in the North, and if a union does get a toe-hold in its mill "seizes the first trade slackness as an excuse for a shut-down, and after a time starts up with non-union operatives."

The Southern manufacturer, however, is on the whole very touchy when either his own employees or an outsider suggests that conditions might be bettered for his employees. He regards himself as a benefactor; and in one sense he is perhaps right. Many of the superior mill villages like that of the Bibb Manufacturing Company in Porterdale, Georgia, provide hospitals, swimming pools, community houses, nurseries, and kindergartens.* Compared with the dreadful poverty of "the hills" and of tenant farming, the millworkers are perhaps better off for leaving the farm for the factory.

On the other hand an astute observer like Frank Tannenbaum insists:

One gets the feeling when he sees these long, emaciated figures, wan and sleepy-looking and without any vividness or

* In the upper grades, however, the mill-run school is always inferior in every respect to the state's brand of elementary education.

interest, that it were far better if they had remained on the farm and scratched the soil with their nails . . . better they had starved on bitter roots, killed one another in long family feuds, that their children had lived in ignorance and had gone barefoot . . . and hunted wild cats, some going to the mad house, some making moonshine, some escaping barefoot into a mountain or valley school. A few would have gone to the legislature or become teachers, or perhaps bitter relentless persecutors of other people. Now and then there would have been a poet or a preacher. There was some escape. The adventure of living was not at an end. . . .

Yet the millowner believes, often sincerely, that his kind of paternalism is just what the situation requires. He tends to regard his employees as somewhat weak-minded children who need his care. His picture of himself as philanthropist harks back to the Reconstruction days of a shattered Confederacy. When the first textile operators built their mills, they helped to restore economic and moral solvency to a moribund social order. In pre-Civil War times, moreover, the wealthy were accustomed to "looking out for the poor," and the desire to help the underprivileged has remained less a duty than an impulse, but always for charity's sake, not in recognition of the right to work as means to personal independence. Since in the South traditions die slowly, the Southern millowner or mill manager (Northern investors usually retain in charge a native who knows conditions) occupies somewhat the position held by planters of a bygone day and feels sure that the exercise of his kind of *noblesse oblige* is both humanly and economically sound.

Hence when T.W.O.C. emissaries entered this region of "cheap and contented" and "100 per cent American labor" boosted by Chambers of Commerce—and forming the chief reason why in 1927 alone $60,000,000 of New England's cotton capital migrated southward, and why profits are about 6 per cent higher in the South than in the North—they found employers wary and antagonistic, and workers still suspicious of "imported" saviors.

The T.W.O.C. was, however, prepared for this. In the first place, employers were offered a technique for regularizing labor costs, and thus bringing a measure of rationale and equilibrium into the confused price and wage structure of textiles. In the second place, T.W.O.C. organizers were selected with great care, and only those able literally and figuratively to "speak the language" were sent out to distribute the cogent, simply written literature, and otherwise put across the C.I.O.'s lesson of "Be Wise, Organize." In the Chattanooga area, for instance, only "100%, native white Anglo-Saxon American Protestants of mountaineer stock" were allowed to carry T.W.O.C. gospel and become prophets honored in their own counties. Many of the T.W.O.C. organizers are women, since their sex comprises 39 per cent of the industry's work force and is traditionally hard to unionize, and it is believed that women might respond more readily to a union sales-talk if delivered with feminine understanding. Perhaps a majority of the women operatives in textiles either regard their jobs as transitory, or accept the notion of "pin-money" whereby the husband is the chief breadwinner and his wife's wage is but supplementary. Or perhaps they simply do not question the social arrangements and cultural lags—"woman's place is in the home," etc.— which have made them "cheap help" for 150 years of factory life in the United States.

As a whole both men and women organizers are chosen for their resourcefulness and "nice" appearance; and among newer recruits attractive, college-bred people are preferred. Certainly one of the most significant aspects of the C.I.O. is that, with the depression's restriction of business opportunity, university and professional-school graduates who, ten years ago, would have been seeking to carve out careers as business executives, now look to the C.I.O.

as the framework for their own futures, thus infusing the movement with some of the best brains and talents in the country. Degrees have proved especially valuable in unionizing new areas; the white-collar respectability and "tone" they imply do much to undermine the widespread belief that to belong to a union is a sign of inferior social status, an outlook especially endemic among women workers who cling to the popular magazine glorification of "the shabby genteel" mores.

Every detail of the T.W.O.C. drive has been planned with diligence, discussed, and whenever possible tested by the "controlled experiment" methods of the laboratory insofar as they can be applied to the unpredictables of human behavior. A research staff surveys the earnings and financial structure of every textile enterprise in the United States. Indeed, the T.W.O.C. campaign marks American labor's first use of statistics on the really grand scale.

At its beginning, the brainy and expert Solomon Barkin was persuaded to resign his post as chief of staff of the Labor Division of Industrial Economics in the United States Department of Commerce in order to direct T.W.O.C. collection of pertinent data. A former instructor of economics at C.C.N.Y., and then Director of Research for New York State's Old Age Security Commission, and Assistant Director of the NRA's Labor Advisory Board, he is the author of *Old Age Security* and *The Older Worker in Industry*. His files bulge with information on textile companies, their business history, their creditors, their sales outlets, their personnel, their wage scales as compared with the whole industry's and with similar mills in the North or South. In accord with his belief that research is a tool of unionism too long neglected, comparative studies are conducted into a mill's output by way of its type of spindles, into its labor force by way of its sociological status.

Along with his chief, Hillman, Barkin is convinced that

the success of the T.W.O.C. undertaking to a great extent hinges upon an intimate, systemized, and cross-indexed knowledge of the industry, a knowledge that must be instantly available in order to lay the basis for both the immediate and long-range program for labor in textiles.

These data have been used mainly to buttress Hillman's argument that the best way to bring order into the industry is for management to accept voluntary collective bargaining, as an alternative to more stringent government intervention, and to make wages as uniform as possible.

In the North and the Middle and Far West, the T.W.O.C. has, of course, found the sledding easier and has achieved substantial gains in virtually all branches of the industry. It has signed collective bargaining contracts with hundreds of firms such as, for example, the Monument Mills at Housatonic, Massachusetts, which makes bedspreads and coverlets and has 450 workers; the Columbia Products Company in Brooklyn, which turns out plushes with a force of 50; the Klearfax Linen Looms at Duluth, Minnesota, which manufactures linen carpet and has 200 workers; the Silkcraft Mills in Paterson, New Jersey, which produces silk Jacquards and has a labor force of 150; along with such "giants" as the American Woolen Company with its 34 mills and 28,000 workers, 13,000 of whom are T.W.O.C. members.

In Amsterdam, New York, carpet and rug center of the East, the T.W.O.C. in the spring of 1938 waged and won a seven-week strike against the Bigelow Sanford Carpet Company; it kept a double picket line of 8,000 people encircling the three-mile area occupied by this firm's mills; enlisted the boycott aid of the League of Women Shoppers, sponsored radio broadcasts which denounced the company's "nothing to arbitrate" stand as an anachronism; got teamsters and truck-drivers to refuse to move its goods from its warehouses or pick them up at railroad loading points in twenty-five cities from Boston to Seattle, from

Atlanta to San Francisco; and otherwise unleashed a social power of vast effect. In Amsterdam also the T.W.O.C. obtained a National Labor Relations Board* decision against the huge Mohawk Carpet Company which employs 4,000 workers and which was ordered to dissolve its company union and to reinstate with back pay two unionists discharged for T.W.O.C. activity. And even in the South, it has slowly and stubbornly advanced under the shrewd guidance of Emil Rieve, president of the Hosiery Workers, R. R. Lawrence, Regional Director for the Deep South, and John A. Peel, ace organizer among the 120 that the T.W.O.C. has placed in the South with instructions to "last just a day longer than the most recalcitrant employer."

In compliance with this order, the organizers have already recorded several notable successes. In the Pacific Mills in Columbia, South Carolina, which with a work force of 2,500 turns out print cloth, shirtings, and broadcloth, the T.W.O.C. secured an agreement which recognized it as sole bargaining agent, granted full seniority and the forty-hour week, accepted arbitration as the only *modus operandi* for settling disputes, and established similar gains which, even a few years ago, were regarded as visionary.

Moreover, the chartering of locals in West Durham, Gastonia, and Erwin, North Carolina, in "the heart of the open shop," and the forty-hour, five-day week passed by South Carolina's legislature in response to the pressure of textile workers politically directed by the T.W.O.C. would seem to justify the effectiveness of Hillman's "statistical olive branch."

The T.W.O.C. currently has 450,000 members enrolled, or about 39 per cent of its maximum potential. Some 275,000 of them, mainly in the North, are under contract;

* In a five-month period, out of 125 NLRB elections to determine the bargaining agency for a plant's workers, and involving 79,000 people, the T.W.O.C. has won 96.

and about the same number regularly pay dues, the others being unable to do so by reason of unemployment (bankruptcies are still plentiful in textiles) or the excessively low wages of part-time jobs.

In general, contrary to the expectation that "when the government does it, the workers won't want a union," the Federal Wages and Hours Act* has helped rather than hindered the T.W.O.C. in its organizing. For the T.W.O.C. has made no secret of its strenuous efforts to lobby this enactment through Congress and it has therefore been able to exploit the advantages conferred by the law upon mill hands as (in part, at least) its own contribution to their welfare, and as a tribute to what a strong nation-wide union can do, and what in the future it must do. To many Southern workers especially, the idea that the union had influenced folks in Washington not only to recognize their existence but also to help them was an entrancing experience which inspired them with the desire to "get next" to this wonder-working organization.

The T.W.O.C. at present is urging the immediate creation of textile-industry boards under Wages and Hours Act provisions in the hope that they will put a floor of a national minimum $16.00-per-week wage in the industry. It is also urging employers to organize themselves more thoroughly into associations that will voluntarily police textiles, abolish chiseling and unfair trade practices, replace the methods of the jungle with those of reason, and otherwise coöperate with the T.W.O.C. in its self-defined mission of "helping to democratize America."

* The Act covers all textile employees except executives, supervisors, and technical staffs; and sets a first-year minimum for wages of 25 cents an hour, 30 cents for the next six years, and 40 cents or more thereafter, with latitude given to the Boards, which will be able to fix wages at the 30 and 40 cent rate if "so warranted." It further prohibits child labor under 16, and under 18 for the more hazardous tasks; and sets maximum hours of 44 per week for the first year of employment; 42 for the second; and 40 for the third.

Conclusion

I

IN 1900 the American Federation of Labor proudly counted its 548,321 members who, by their very dues-paying existence, seemed to vindicate its official policy as defined by Adolph Strasser, president of the Cigar Makers, when he had testified before the United States Senate Committee on Education and Labor in 1885.

"You are seeking to improve home matters first?" he was asked.

"Yes, sir," he replied, "I look first to the trade I represent; I look first to cigars, to the interests of the men who employ me to represent their interest."

The following exchange then took place:

Chairman: I was only asking you in regard to your ultimate ends.

Strasser: We have no ultimate ends. We are going on from day to day. We are fighting only for immediate objects—objects that can be realized in a few years.

Question (by Mr. Call): You want something better to eat and to wear and better houses to live in?

Chairman: I see that you are a little sensitive lest it should be thought that you are a mere theorizer. . . .

Strasser: Well, we say in our constitution that we are opposed to theorists, and I have to represent the organization here. We are all practical men.

Thirty-one years later, Samuel Gompers, on the witness stand before the United States Commission on Industrial Relations which in 1914 was conducting an inquiry into the "underlying causes" of what is often called "labor unrest," reaffirmed what were to him the impregnable values of this general approach.

Question (by Mr. Hillquit): . . . Inform me on this: In its practical work in the labor movement, is the A. F. of L. guided by a general social philosophy, or is it not?

Answer (by Mr. Gompers): It is guided by the history of the past, drawing its lessons from history. It knows the conditions by which the working people are surrounded. It works along the line of least resistance . . . to accomplish the best results in improving the condition of the working people, men, women and children, today and tomorrow, and each day making it a better day than the one that had gone before. . . .

Mr. Hillquit: Now, "the highest and best ideals of social justice," as applied to the distribution of wealth—wouldn't that be a system under which all the workers, manual, directive and executive, would together get the sum total of all the products of their toil?

Mr. Gompers: Really, a fish is caught by tempting bait; a mouse or rat is caught in a trap by tempting bait.* The intelligent common sense workmen prefer to deal with the problems of today, the problems with which they are bound to contend if they want to advance, rather than to deal with a picture and a dream which have never had, and I am sure never will have, any reality in the actual affairs of humanity, and which threaten, if they could be introduced, the worst system of circumscriptional effort . . . invented by the human mind.

Both Strasser and Gompers, along with the third co-founder of the A. F. of L., P. J. McGuire, had been Socialists of a mild kind; the first, influenced by Lassalle, acted as the Secretary of the Social Democratic Party of North America; Gompers studied German solely for the purpose of reading Karl Marx in the original; and McGuire in his salad days orated with fervor about a fuzzy and far-off "brotherhood of man." Yet when they were guiding the Federation through its contentious early years, they threw overboard all the canons of the coöperative commonwealth and embraced instead the doctrine of more pay, fewer hours, better working conditions. In this respect they re-

* This bit of moralizing derived from Gompers' ruling fear that he might be tricked into some assertion that would seem to show him to be in sympathy with Socialism which, in his later career, he abhorred.

flected the aspirations of their followers. The American
worker, of the kind drawn into the A. F. of L., was not
opposed to the capitalist economy and its wage system.
He wanted to get all he could out of existing arrangements, not to disturb their intrinsic profit purposes. He
wanted to make the best bargain he could in exchanging
his labor-power in the market, in the same way that the
businessman wanted to get the highest price possible for
his commodity; and neither was troubled overmuch by
"ultimates," by considerations of whether or not his actions promoted or detracted from the general welfare.
Hence the A. F. of L. quarrels with employers often have
expressed a *rebus sic stantibus* outlook, as if they were,
indeed, "inside" or even partnership affairs, disagreements
over a fair split in the returns of business activity in which
both sides had a rough equality of interest.*

From its beginnings, of course, the A. F. of L.'s central
aim has been to achieve for its members an "American
standard of living." When this maxim is crystallized a little, it is found to signify a number of tangible things, and
an equal number of imponderables quite as important. It
means first of all job-opportunity and job-security. It
means the chance to improve your economic status by the
exercise of mind and muscle or either or both; and the
reasonable assurance that after spending the best years of
your life at a particular vocation, you will not be deprived
of your right to work but will have a job in an environment and at a remuneration at least somewhat compatible
with your idea of yourself as a free and independent citizen. It means enough income to keep yourself and your
family in a moderate degree of comfort, to have meat on
the table a few times a week, to have butter on your bread,
fresh vegetables in your diet, and good milk for the baby.
It means housing where you have the privacy of your

* The first slogan of the Federation was a "fair day's pay for a fair day's
work."

own plumbing. It means the ability to pay for such extras as church donations, a vacation, wedding presents. It means a modicum of leisure that you can use in the way you want to use it, at a ball game or sitting at home with a pipe and a book. In recent years, of course, it has meant increasingly a trip to the movies, or listening to the radio, or taking a drive in your (usually) second-hand car. It means laying aside something in the bank against old age, and for educating your children, enabling them to rise in the world and wear white collars, enter the professions, or become business bosses.

In pursuit of such ends, the Federation—rooted in capitalist modes of production, and accepting its middle-class mores, and itself an offshoot of their reciprocal interaction—became far more cartel-minded than class-conscious: a view somewhat extremely exemplified by the International Typographical Union. Formed in 1851, and long before then marked by a high level of intelligence in the craft (Horace Greeley and Henry George were both "printing graduates"), the I.T.U. has managed to maintain a rigorous policy of job-control over large sections of its own work area.

It has, for instance, formulated an elaborate code of shop rules, known as "International Law," under which, among other things, the foreman is paid by the employer but is really responsible to the union. If the foreman permits any fracture of I.T.U. regulations, relating to apprenticeship, to hiring and firing, or to rotation of the available number of jobs, he may be fined or expelled by the I.T.U.; and expulsion, of course, means discharge, since to be a foreman he has to belong to the union in the first place. In case of disputes, when, say, a union typographer is discharged by this union foreman, the question may be referred to the Chapel, or plant unit, which in a body sits as judge; and if no satisfactory settlement is reached, the contestants may appeal to the union local and even to the Executive

Samuel Gompers.

Council of the I.T.U. itself. The controversy is thus re-
viewed only by union tribunals and the employer is excluded from any direct participation.*

On the other hand, when agreements between employers and I.T.U. locals are being drawn up, the employer
may make various stipulations; but the application of the
contract terms remains in the union's hands, under the
supervision of the I.T.U.'s national office. When the introduction of typesetting machines threatened I.T.U.
members with loss of their jobs, it quickly passed another
"International Law" to conserve their employment opportunities. "The International Typographical Union," this
statute declared, "directs in all offices in its jurisdiction"
that where typesetting machines are installed, "practical
union printers shall be employed to run them." It further
debarred apprentices, who had to serve five years, from
running the machines, permitting them, however, to learn
how to operate them during the last six months of their
novitiate. By this means the I.T.U. evaded or at least
cushioned, in the printing industry, the usually difficult
transition from hand to machine processes, and the hardships usually visited upon craftsmen when any such new
development occurs.†

* In 1900, President Lynch of the I.T.U. declared: "We do not expect that
the foreman shall represent the union. It is understood that he is engaged
by the office to protect its interests and to carry out its wishes and desires.
It must be remembered, however, that a union officer agrees to conduct the
composition room in accordance with union rules. If he [the foreman]
willingly violates a union law, or permits its violation without notifying
union authority, he should be prepared to accept the consequences."

† Its scrupulous attention to the well-being of its members has given it
great influence among the other eleven unions in paper manufacturing,
printing, and publishing, some of which have imitated the I.T.U. in its death
benefits and its Union Printers' Home for old or retired craftsmen. The
I.T.U., with its 75,000 members, the International Printing Pressmen and
Assistants Union with 39,000, the American Association of Photo-Engravers
with 8,700, the International Stereotypers and Electrotypers Union of North
America with 8,000, and the Brotherhood of Bookbinders with 890 are combined in the International Allied Printing Trades Association. Through its
board of governors, the Association issues and controls use of the union
label, and has tried to make it standard in the publication of textbooks and
religious periodicals but has been generally thwarted in this undertaking by
the anti-union attitudes of most school and church boards.

It is this desire of the union to own collectively the total number of employment opportunities within its own job-territory that forms the basis for the structure of the A. F. of L. and largely explains its strategy. From the first, it issued its charters to its various affiliates upon the assumption that the upper stratum of labor, by fusing the skills and abilities of a single occupation into a union, could maintain the maximum of market strength and a measure of job-monopoly. It wanted not only to grant every affiliate autonomy in internal affairs but also to safeguard its authority over existing and new or allied tasks within the confines of a particular trade. The ever-lengthening names of A. F. of L. unions, such as the International Association of Marble, Slate and Stone Polishers, Rubbers, Sawyers, Tile Setters and Terrazzo Helpers, illustrate the expansion of this principle which very early fostered that "bane of unionism," the jurisdictional row; for the use of new materials and the invention of new machines created many borderland procedures of production.*

In addition to this perpetual vexation over "who gets what" among craft groups, the Federation also set about organizing the unskilled to heed Gompers' prediction in 1899 that "the artisan of yesterday is the unskilled laborer of tomorrow," displaced "by the invention of new ma-

---

* Among the more celebrated jurisdictional quarrels not previously mentioned are those between the Brewery Workers and the Teamsters as to which should claim brewery wagon, and later, truck drivers; and the free-for-all still waged among the Flint Glass Workers, the Bottle Blowers, and the Electrical Workers as to which of them deserves the dues and allegiance of operatives who make neon products. Today in the construction of a modern apartment house or skyscraper the installation of elevators calls forth claims by the Elevator Constructors, who insist that the whole undertaking belongs to them, while various parts of the process are claimed by the Sheet-Metal Workers, the Electrical Workers, the Machinists, the Structural Iron Workers, and, inevitably, by the Carpenters. In 1902, Gompers warned that "the danger which above all others most threatens the success and the very existence of the American Federation of Labor is the question of jurisdiction. No combination of labor's enemies need cause us the apprehension which this fratricidal strife does in the claims made by the unions for the situation of their trade jurisdiction."

chines and the division and sub-division of labor." The A. F. of L. leadership therefore devised three more or less new unionist vehicles on which, it was hoped, the unskilled would climb and ride along toward that terminus of the blessed, "pure and simple unionism"; the phrase, as coined by Gompers, not only denoted wage- or business-consciousness but also contained the ingredients of social uplift, of a kind which is the more appealing for being kept nice and vague.

The Federation banded the unskilled together in "federal" unions which were granted the privilege of paying dues but could not vote.* These federal unions turned out to be catch-alls for the uncategorized, who were signed up in pell-mell fashion and then often picked off into the crafts whenever a claim could be made or imagined for their allegiance; this practice merely intensified the jurisdictional conflicts. Again, the unskilled were admitted directly into various craft unions, as helpers; and a few were placed in "Internationals," or full-fledged unions of their own, such as the Hod-Carriers and the Building Laborers.

In unionizing the unskilled, however, the Federation has never been notably successful. The aristocrats of skill had little fellow-feeling for the lower-paid groups, the immigrants, the women, the Negroes, who without organization and without special aptitude were forced to take what they could get and therefore tended to depress employment standards generally.

It was not that the A. F. of L. unionists were cruel or callous. They had "their own troubles." They feared the competition of cheap help and wanted to preserve their own provinces against encroachment by others. A certain snobbery played its part, of course; for in addition to this urgency to protect the interests of the higher skills from

---

* That is, they were allowed only *one* vote for the entire union as against the per capita representation of the national and international unions.

the menace of "any wage, any amount of time," the A. F. of L. membership tended to look upon the immigrant as someone different from themselves, with his strange speech and strange customs. It looked upon woman as having her rightful place in the home, a view reinforced by age-old delusions concerning the superiority of the male in all except household functions. It looked upon the Negro as belonging to a pariah race by reason of his color, his alleged mental incapacity, indolence and ignorance, and his historic association with the most menial and poorly paid tasks.

From the decade of the 1880's especially, when the Protestants of the American Know Nothings began their "keep them out" agitation against "Romish" Catholics, religious and racial and linguistic differences and prejudices have hindered unionizing of every form in every American industry. Until recent years, the gulf separating the skilled from the unskilled more often than not coincided with that separating the native from the foreign-born. And to assure themselves of a "pliable," unorganizable labor force, American employers have not been over-fastidious in trying to foment Old World antagonisms and play them off against each other, often consciously mixing the Wop, the Bohunk, the Canuck, and the Squarehead to thwart communication that might lead to sympathy and mutual aid in a common cause.

Although, as early as 1880, the 2,647,000 women workers comprised 15.2 per cent of the nation's gainfully employed, they then as now functioned chiefly in the unskilled or semi-skilled trades.* The A. F. of L., while it sponsored legislation to limit their hours, provide sanitary

---

* The World War immeasurably quickened the influx of women into industry; by 1930 10,571,300 of them constituted 22.1 per cent of the gainfully employed; and among this number, 29.6 per cent were engaged in either domestic or personal service occupations; 18.5 in office and clerical work; 17.5 in manufacturing and mechanical pursuits; 14.2 in the professions (mainly teaching); 9.0 in trade; 8.5 in agriculture, forestry, and fishing; and 2.6 in transportation and communication.

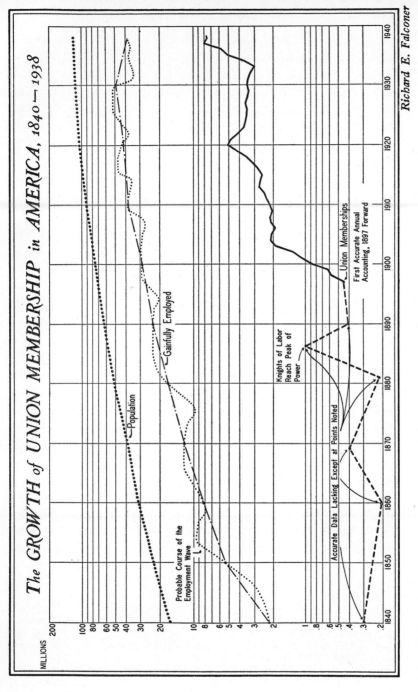

The GROWTH of UNION MEMBERSHIP in AMERICA, 1840 — 1938

MILLIONS

Population

Gainfully Employed

Probable Course of the Employment Wave

Knights of Labor Reach Peak of Power

Accurate Data Lacking Except at Points Noted

Union Memberships

First Accurate Annual Accounting, 1897 Forward

Richard E. Falconer

Unionism and the Business Cycle.

conditions, and the like, never enrolled them in appreciable numbers. Its attitude toward this problem was indeed never clear-cut. On the one hand, it believed that it should obey the dictates of masculine chivalry and protect them as the weaker sex, a view still as vigorously denounced by the feminists of the National Woman's party as it is defended by various welfare and philanthropic organizations. On the other hand, the A. F. of L. was afraid that women in time would become serious rivals for the jobs of the "normal bread-winners"; and amid this confusion of counsels nothing very much has been accomplished.*

Even more neglected than the immigrant and the woman, the Negro until very recently has been almost as outside the pale of unionism, both locally and nationally, as in the South he has been outside the pale of Civil Liberties. During the World War he came into his industrial own, nearly two million Negroes moving North, congregating mainly in the "black belts" of New York, Chicago, Pittsburgh, St. Louis, Detroit, Buffalo, and Philadelphia. He automatically received the lower-wage jobs, "the work that white men won't do, such as common labor, the heavy, hot and dirty work" in steel mills, in motor factories, in municipal departments of sanitation. He also tended to move into so-called "blind-alley" jobs, the "leavings" of employment that others have vacated in the search for something at once more remunerative and more "dignified."

Whereas the Knights of Labor honestly tried to organize the Negro, in accord with its "all for one, one for all" preachments, the A. F. of L., as the antithesis of the Noble Order, excluded him, tacitly or definitely, to a very

* At the Federation's 1937 convention, Elizabeth Christman, president of the National Woman's Trade Union League, accused A. F. of L. officers of neglecting the question of the woman in industry, and recommended that she be treated not as a "female of the species" but first and foremost as a worker. "Why not," she inquired, "open the door without further delay and let women work shoulder to shoulder with men [i.e., in unions] in the making of labor policies as they do in the making of goods and earning of a livelihood?"

great extent, despite constant pressure by both white and black groups to live up to its pledge of unionizing all labor, regardless of "creed, color or previous condition of servitude." A handful of Negro locals were chartered, through the years, and other Negro unions formed as "independents."

By far the most important of all Negro unions, at present, is the Brotherhood of Sleeping Car Porters, developed after a dozen years of sacrificial effort by A. Philip Randolph, its president. The son of a Negro Methodist minister in Crescent City, Florida, he traveled North after finishing high school in Jacksonville. While a porter for the Consolidated Edison Company, he studied political science, history, and economics at the College of the City of New York. In 1917 he was a co-founder of *The Messenger*, "radical" Negro monthly which rejected all the implications of Jim Crowism for his race and sought to substitute political and economic equality for philanthropy. When he began to unionize the Sleeping Car Porters, he was assailed for his Socialist views by Negro preachers, and more than 450 of the first group of porters he had converted were discharged by the Pullman Company for their union activity. By 1934, however, he and his chief aide, A. L. Totten, had performed the almost incredible feat of enrolling enough members to win a National Mediation Board election which established the Brotherhood as collective bargaining agency over its rival, the Pullman Porters Benefit Association of America, part of an "employee representation plan" fostered by the Pullman Company. In the same year the Brotherhood signed a contract with the Pullman Company and ten months later was the first Negro union to be given an International charter by the A. F. of L.

The porters and maids drawn into the Brotherhood, who made beds and shined shoes and carried luggage, not only represented the lower reaches in the sphere of the unskilled but also, in the opinion of the veteran unionist, were among those "impossible to organize." The very fact, therefore, that they had created their own Brotherhood, under the leadership of an "educated" Negro, an intellectual, was at once a symbol and a portent of drastic changes in our society that were soon to challenge the policies and the personnel of the American Federation of Labor.

II

To the hour of his death in San Antonio, Texas, on December 12, 1924, Samuel Gompers, eighty years old, and nearly blind, had never deviated from the essentials of union doctrine which he himself had largely shaped during the last two decades of the nineteenth century. During his thirty-seven years as president of the A. F. of L. (he was defeated only once for reëlection—in 1894) he often deplored the deficient gumption of the unskilled, saying with deep conviction that "their lack of organization stands out clearly as due wholly to their lack of courage, lack of persistence, lack of vision." Certainly his concern with the personal elements, the human equation, seemed often to crowd out any acute perception of the interplay of external social, political, and economic forces. He tended to think of unions in terms of people; men rolling cigars in a shop of the kind from which he himself had been graduated, carpenters unpacking their tools at a building site, barbers stropping their razors. He by temperament distrusted abstractions and intellectuals whom he had often heard hairsplit the hours of many false dawns. In his opinion they were doctrinaire and unrealistic, carrying around in their heads images of what they wanted labor to be, not what it really was.

He was himself a person of considerable mental energy and capacity which he expended to serve labor's own high caste. Although he considered himself the spokesman for all American labor, it was often doubtful whether he really represented his rank and file. He was rather the mouthpiece for union officialdom, and its model. He was a good speaker even if inclined to be pontifical and to reveal the obvious with all the solemn cadences of a Bishop intoning the Lord's Prayer. He was an astute politician, distributing his patronage of "headquarters" jobs in a manner to keep the good will of his fellow officials. He could remember to tell the visiting delegate that he hoped his wife had recuperated nicely from her operation. He could "mix with the boys" yet retain just the proper tone of aloofness befitting the dignity of his station. He was a bureaucrat who kept the press, the funds, and the whole machinery of organization under his eye. He could talk, with endurance, about the nobility of toil. He had, within the limits of his creed, undeniable gifts for "industrial statesmanship" and could negotiate with the most hardbitten employer with all the shrewdness of a man to whom the manipulation of people is a way of life.

He was extremely ambitious, yearning after power and acclaim. But he wanted both power and acclaim only as a leader of labor. He consistently refused the high government and business posts which other union officials often sought and secured. Thick-set in build, with strong jaws and a chin cleft by a dimple, he was coarse of skin, and his broad brow was surmounted by a shock of curly and unruly hair. His rimless pince-nez were always polished till they glittered, imparting a sparkle to his dark eyes and helping to lend to his appearance a combativeness that was perhaps his basic trait. His manners could be gracious; and financiers and industrialists and statesmen often referred to him as "very much of a gentleman." He was susceptible to their praise.

He was impeccably honest in money matters, dying a poor man and bequeathing to his widow such slim resources that in 1937 she had to apply for a W.P.A. position. Certainly he never "sold out" in the sense that he accepted cash-on-the-line for treachery to his cause. Yet the more or less subtle pressures of that social lobby which lives in Washington and is fed by interested groups often influenced him to override the preferences of his own adherents.*

Few men have stamped their own ideas more indelibly upon a movement. His ghost still haunts A. F. of L. conventions. His behavior is still imitated, and his practical wisdom still extolled by orators who like to look back upon a past which seems less vexing and clamorous than the present. In 1936, for example, at the Federation's annual convention, Daniel J. Tobin, hard-boiled and autocratic president of the Teamsters, wound up an attack upon industrial unionism by declaiming: "To us was given a charter . . . and Gompers . . . and the others said 'Upon the rocks of trades autonomy, craft trades, you shall build the church of the labor movement and the gates of hell nor . . . industrial unionism shall not prevail against it.' "

* Before America entered the World War, for example, the sentiments of the A. F. of L. membership were distinctly pacific. Many of its officials belonged to the National Peace Council, the Friends of Peace, and kindred groups. By means of flattery, however, Ralph Easely, executive secretary of the National Civic Federation, a capital-labor "let's all be friends" society, persuaded Gompers to undermine "dangerous" peace movements among American workers. In the press, Easely described Gompers as that "great statesman"; in his correspondence with him he denounced "the mushy nonsense emanating from the sentimentalists about peace with a capital P," "young college men with half-baked ideas absorbed from their *socialistic* professors [*touché!*]," and the "dishonorable" attitudes of the American League to Limit Armaments, the American Neutrality League, and Labor's National Peace Council. In December of 1915 Gompers, upon whom Sir Gilbert Parker, chief British agent of propaganda, had also "gone to work," put his hand to the composition of a National Civic Federation statement which asked even at this early date that a Council of National Defense be created against future "emergencies." Despite the anti-English sentiment of the many Irish in the A. F. of L., and the anti-Allied sentiment of its many Germans, and the general anti-militarist, anti-war feelings of the socialist part of its membership, Gompers soon was saying that "human nature" made certain wars necessary, and left no doubt that it was the belligerent human nature of the Teutons and the Turks to which he referred. His devotion to the "preparedness" crusade conducted by the National Security League and the American Defense Society and similar organizations prompted him to "influence" the resignation of A. F. of L. officials from one peace group after another.

During the very time, of course, that Gompers was bottle-feeding the infant Federation, he had seen the last of labor's experiments in the coöperative workshop bogging down largely because everybody, with the American's get-ahead-fast preoccupation, wanted to be boss. He had seen the Knights of Labor crumble from its inability to cope with the unwieldy heterogeneous masses attracted by its grand promises of brotherhood, and from too much bureaucracy at the top and not enough farther down the scale. He had seen the anathema visited upon the anarchists and Governor Altgeld's pardons after the hurling of the Haymarket bomb. He had seen the Sherman Anti-Trust Law converted into an anti-labor bludgeon by the courts and the Federal government. He had seen labor affix itself as the tail to the kite of agrarian politics, the Populists and Greenbackers and all the other anti-monopoly campaigners of three decades, and get nothing for its pains except an exhilarating ride. In New York City he had seen various "protest" parades of Socialists dispersed with a cracking of skulls while horses of the mounted police trampled women and children. He perceived that any reform save the mildest, any hint of drastic modification of private ownership would arouse against unionism the maledictions and hostility of the more articulate portions of a public still property-loving and property-conscious, still convinced that the "making of money out of men" was an end in itself, an expression of virtue quite as much as the result of proficiency in a vocation.

It was to evade any such hindrances to a stable unionism that he developed the cardinal points of the A. F. of L.'s body of doctrine. First and foremost was "voluntarism," by which workers animated by identity or similarity of trade interests were of their own free will to join together into unions for collective bargaining. They were to depend upon their economic strength alone. They were to avoid as the plague government influence or intervention in labor affairs. They were to refrain from forming any partisan, or independent, or third, or "class" political party as the Socialists were constantly urging them to do. Nor were they to pay any special attention even to the emblems of the great, established, major parties.

They were to vote instead for either Republican or Democratic candidates upon the basis of "Reward your friends, punish your enemies." At the same time, the Federation, whenever possible, was to get both factions to sponsor legislation that, for example, would effectuate the eight-hour day, prevent the immigration of Chinese and other "cheap Asiatic" workers, stamp out or at least curtail the use of convict and sweat-shop labor, extend employer liability for industrial accidents, provide government funds for vocational training in the schools, abolish the hiring of "armed bodies of men" by private persons or corporations during a strike, eliminate the "abuse and perversion of the writ of injunction" in capital-labor disputes, and otherwise supplement collective bargaining within the framework of the status quo.

From its early days the Federation carried out such precepts diligently enough; and in its administration reflected the preachments of that pragmatism which is merely opportunism with a college degree. Gompers kept the top leadership flexible and always ready to compromise and coöperate with the heads of the strong Internationals, who were granted the widest possible latitude and who, indeed, in their relation to the central authority resembled feudal chiefs. In return for benefits received from affiliation with the A. F. of L. they exchanged a certain measure of loyalty expressed in the payment of per capita dues and the support of a policy uniform only in its lack of uniformity. Yet like the barons of medieval times they not only fought among themselves, the one coveting the other's domain, but also tried to dominate the sovereign power which they themselves had set up to be their ruler and judge.

In accord with its earnest desire for industrial peace, the A. F. of L. supported the strikes of its member unions as rarely as possible, and then only as a last resort. It placed great faith in the efficacy of the union label,* a mark affixed to a product to signify its manufacture by unionists, and in the boycott, a device borrowed from the businessman's boycott of a rival and his blacklisting of labor "agitators" and "malcontents." The only difference was, however, that employers were able to invoke the boycott secretly whereas labor had to do it out in the open if it was to be effective.† Immediately the A. F. of L. was assailed as a trust and under the Sherman Anti-Trust Laws its use of the boycott was countered with injunctions issued wholesale and on the basis of "conspiracy to obstruct commerce among the several states."

In mid-August, 1906, for example, some workers in the nickel department of Buck's Stove and Range Company in St. Louis, Missouri, were discharged for refusing to put in more than nine hours a day. Their union, a branch of the International Metal Polishers, Buffers, Platers, Brass Moulders, and Brass and Silver Workers of North America, interceded for them, asked for their reinstatement,

---

* The Federation's Union Label Department, founded in 1909, advanced, among others, the following claims: "The union label is powerful because it accomplishes by peaceful means, with absolute certainty and at little cost, that which the strike and boycott seek to accomplish, always at great cost and sacrifice." "The workers who strike in protest against their wrongs may be defeated, but the public protest registered in the demand for the union label is invincible." "The union label enlists and arms in labor's cause those elements which determine the issue in every cause in civilized society— namely, the women and children. . . . It organizes the purchasing power . . . against those conditions which destroy the health and morality of the producer and endanger the well-being of the purchaser."

† "It is important," says Norman J. Ware in his *Labor in Modern Industrial Society*, "to define a boycott as an attempt to aid the workers involved in the dispute and not as an attempt to injure the employer. As in a strike, the primary purpose is not to injure the employer. The injury . . . is secondary, though nearly all definitions of boycott put it first and thus by definition give it an illegal aspect. The courts have been great offenders here. Their standards have been subjective, covering intent or motive, which the courts have held as intent to injure another, rather than intent to help oneself."

and called a strike when the company let it be known that "no union" could "dictate" its policy. The strike was endorsed by the St. Louis Trades and Labor Council and by the American Federation of Labor itself, meeting in convention six weeks later. Samuel Gompers personally tried to negotiate with James Van Cleave, who was not only president of Buck's concern but also one of the three most ardent and implacable anti-union employers in the United States. He was head of the Stove Founders National Defense Association, president of the National Association of Manufacturers, and a director of the National Founders Association, all of which were raising funds and sending out field representatives to mobilize businessmen against the "tyranny" of unions and for the establishment of an industrial community that by means of an open shop could end their "un-American oppression."

When Gompers' own deft suasions failed, in May, 1907, Buck's was placed on the "unfair to labor"–"We Don't Patronize" list published in the monthly *Federationist*, the A. F. of L.'s official organ edited by Gompers, who fancied he had quite a literary flair. Circulars were broadcast to A. F. of L. locals, advising them to "call on business men in your respective communities, urge their sympathetic coöperation, and ask them to write to Buck's Stove and Range Company . . . to make an honorable adjustment of its relations with organized labor. . . ."

The response was nation-wide and surprising to Gompers himself. Within a few months Buck's sales of stoves and ranges had dipped down from a million a year to an estimated 150,000 as local dealers informed Van Cleave, who was "fit to be tied," that the boycott made it impossible for them to move his firm's products "off the floor."

The Buck's Company thereupon in December, 1907, obtained from Justice A. M. Gould of the Supreme Court in the District of Columbia an injunction for "cessation of concerted action" against A. F. of L. officials which, among other things, restrained them from

interfering in any manner with the sale of the products of the plaintiff, and from declaring or threatening any boycott against the complainant, or printing or distributing through the mails any paper which contained any reference . . . to the complainant . . . in connection with the term "Unfair" . . . or any other word of similar import, or from . . . circulating, whether in writing or orally, any statement . . . calling attention of the complainant's customers, or of dealers, or of tradesmen, or the public, to any boycott against the complainant. . . .

Gompers, however, along with other A. F. of L. leaders who took their cue from him, kept repeating often and loudly that "the injunction cannot compel union men and their friends to buy Buck's stoves and ranges."* He also kept asking why "isn't the Sherman Act enforced against the capitalistic trusts whose improper, anti-social doings have provoked its passage?" and "Why is it used to curb labor when it was originally intended to curb capitalistic trusts?" He received a shattering reply to both queries; for in December, 1908, he was charged by Judge Wright with contempt of court and was sentenced to a year in prison while John Mitchell, president of the United Mine Workers and vice-president of the A. F. of L., was given nine months and Frank Morrison, secretary-treasurer of the Federation, was handed a six months' term.

Gompers was stunned, indignant, and felt a man betrayed. It had been understandable that Olney in 1894 could send a Gene Debs, a natural-born agitator, to jail and enjoin his heretical American Railway Union, which was outside the reservation of the A. F. of L. and the Rail-

* The A. F. of L. publications thereupon announced:
It is unlawful to
**BOYCOTT BUCK'S
STOVES AND RANGES**

road Brotherhoods alike. It had been equally understandable that the roughneck radicals of the Western Federation of Miners had had injunctions and jail terms imposed upon them almost as weekly occurrences. But the A. F. of L. was respectable. It "belonged." It had burned its joss sticks before all the proper gods. Its officials were solid citizens and men of standing. Gompers was a friend of McKinley's; Mitchell was close both to Teddy Roosevelt and Mark Hanna; and Frank Morrison with his patrician manners was liked by everybody who was anybody, from August Belmont down.

The case against the A. F. of L.'s triumvirate was kicked along in the courts for months and was upheld on appeal in November, 1909. While it moved, argument by argument, up toward the heights of the Supreme Court, James Van Cleave died. His less adamant successor settled quickly with the union which had started the whole battle; and he also—to the immense relief of Gompers and the others— withdrew the injunction. The Supreme Court therefore on May 15, 1911, dismissed the contempt proceedings on the ground that the primary issue, namely the injunction, no longer existed.*

Meantime, another *cause célèbre*, the Danbury Hatters case, had in 1903 begun its progress along the tortuous pathways of the law. It was the outcome of a campaign by the United Hatters of America to unionize their industry in which small or medium-sized establishments and skilled craftsmen predominated. In 1902 the Hatters, who had developed the use of the boycott to a minor art, conducted one against D. E. Loewe and Company in Danbury, Connecticut, and caught a Tartar for their pains. Like Van Cleave, D. E. Loewe was a die-hard open-shopper, and aided by such lawyers of the Anti-Boycott Association

---

* Still other attempts were made by lawyers for the Anti-Boycott Association and the National Association of Manufacturers to jail Gompers, Mitchell, and Morrison on contempt complaints which, conceded in the lower courts, were discarded by the Supreme Court.

as Daniel Davenport, he retaliated with vigor and ingenuity. He and his attorneys invoked the Sherman Anti-
Trust Law for a novel purpose. Instead of seeking to restrain the union from its boycott, per se, they sued 250
of its local members who had also gone on strike for
$240,000—an amount equal to the triple damages allowed
by Section 7 of the Act to anyone whose interests had
been impaired by its violation.

After thirteen years of litigation, the verdicts of the
lower courts—all of which were in favor of Loewe and
Company—were sustained by the Supreme Court amid
labor's lamentations. And within twenty-three months
the A. F. of L. and the United Hatters between them had
been forced to collect the money to pay for all damages.
They raised $234,000 by voluntary subscription and this
sum was accepted by the receivers for the then bankrupt
Loewe and Company in lieu of the $310,000, including
interest, technically due.

Of course, the tremendous significance of this event to
all American labor was less monetary than juristic and
derived from two principles which the Supreme Court's
decision for the first time proclaimed. In brief, members
of a union had been sued as individuals and solely because
they belonged to a union which was trying to exercise its
presumably inalienable rights to boycott and to strike.
Their homes, their savings accounts, and other property
had been attached by court order. Moreover, the Supreme
Court had, from their point of view, reversed the issue.
It had based its opinion on the ground that the union's
primary purpose was not to organize Loewe and Company
but rather to interfere with the employer's business, an
intervention which in the nature of the situation was necessarily incidental to the main objective. Hence by ascribing
the intent and motive of injury and interference to the
union, the court by implication pronounced every union
an illegal combination in restraint of trade. Quite mani-

festly the effort to change conditions, to raise wages, or shorten hours in a firm which sent its products beyond state-wide boundaries could by the assumptions of this same brand of logic be construed as interference with interstate commerce and therefore subject to the provisions of the Sherman Act.

Curiously enough this whole case in many respects paralleled the famous Taff-Vale decision in England when in 1901 the House of Lords held that the Amalgamated Society of Railroad Engineers, a labor union, was liable for damages inflicted by its officers in calling a strike. It was an opinion which in England not only gave great impetus to British labor to build its own political party but also, four years later, prompted the passage of the British Trades Disputes Act which completely reversed the Taff-Vale decision and established the rule that no union could be sued for any action stemming from the reasons for its existence.

In this country the net effect of the Buck's and the Danbury Hatters cases was to wean the A. F. of L. away from its fairly close coöperation with the Republican party in national affairs, since almost all the judges who had proved to be inimical were G.O.P. appointees. It even flirted for a while with the idea of independent political action;* but this promise was never fulfilled, for the Demo-

* In March, 1906, it had drafted its Bill of Grievances for submission to the President, the Senate, and the House, which, upon presentation, was conspicuously ignored. It complained chiefly that the national government had not enforced the eight-hour law on Federal employment; had not sufficiently safeguarded American workers against the menace of both Oriental and European immigration; had not effectively prohibited the sale of goods produced by convict labor; and had abused the anti-trust laws by making labor their victim rather than their beneficiary. It furthermore offered a reform program which included sanitary inspections of mines and factories; elimination of sweat-shops; curtailment of the injunction in labor disputes; one day's rest in seven; and an extension of employers' liability for injury or death resulting from the existence of industrial hazards. It also demanded the enactment of child labor laws in the various states; free text books in the schools; more parks and playgrounds; votes for women; national ownership of the telephone and telegraph; municipal ownership of public utilities;

crats in their 1908 platform deflected the tendency by incorporating various "labor" planks. Gompers personally opposed Taft, the "father of injunctions"; and after the elections of 1912 he became closely associated with Woodrow Wilson.*

His reward was a lovely phrase in the new anti-trust law, the Clayton Act, passed in 1914, which in its Section 6 affirmed that "the labor of a human being is not a commodity or an article of commerce." This line so enchanted the word-conscious Gompers that he neglected to see that, in essentials, the Act was not at all that "Magna Carta upon which the working people will rear their constitution of industrial freedom" which he declared it to be. It was quite the opposite, for prior to its enactment, only the Federal government could secure injunctions, and even then there had usually to be an anti-labor Attorney General to swing the job. Under Section 16 of the Clayton Act, however, injunctions could be obtained by any private person or organization; and until the enactment of the Norris-LaGuardia Anti-Injunction Act in 1932 such federal writs, like hail-storms, drummed relentlessly down upon labor's fields, ruining many of its harvests and destroying many of its most hopeful crops.†

and endorsed the initiative, referendum, and recall. The Bill of Grievances implied that the A. F. of L. might be compelled to revise its non-partisan practice if its demands went unheeded; and the Bill's ending was explicit enough, reading in part: "Labor brings these, its grievances, to your attention because you are the representatives responsible for legislation and for [its] failure. . . . Labor now appeals to you, and we trust that it may not be in vain. But if perchance you may not heed us, we shall appeal to the conscience and support of our fellow citizens."

* Despite this shift in allegiance, however, the Federation still maintained that its political policy was non-partisan, as, indeed, in congressional and state elections it generally was within the meaning of "Reward your friends and punish your enemies."

† In commenting on the Clayton Act the distinguished lawyer, Thomas Reed Powell, pointed out in 1928 that "Congress has thus far acquiesced in the decision that the Clayton Act, with all its specifics, restrained the federal courts from nothing that was previously proper. A statute full of words that seemed a balm to labor turned out upon interpretation to be chiefly a bane and Congress has since kept still. The future of labor injunctions bids fair

III

IN 1920 the American Federation of Labor was at the pinnacle of its power and prestige. It had 4,078,740 members; and a treasury of $1,121,746,000 from per capita dues. The entrance of the United States into the World War had given it a commanding position in national affairs. Its full coöperation with both industry and government was urgently required to meet wartime production needs. It had never subscribed to the view that it was a separate world in the American cosmos; and amid the mingling of national energies for the task of making the world safe for democracy it was pridefully patriotic, even to excess. It assured the friendly Wilson of the "New Freedom" of 1912 that it would be faithful to the Administration's war aims, and in return its leaders received a measure of "recognition." They served on the War Labor Board (branch of the War Industries Board) and on various other commissions; their service was limited, however, to agencies which dealt with industrial disputes, and the A. F. of L. was not represented on boards which let contracts. They spoke at Liberty Bond rallies; they went to foreign lands on "labor missions." Gompers particularly was a considerable power and in a state of bliss. He was consulted on every hand; and he devoted himself to removing, insofar as he was able, management-union frictions that might have impeded the efficient meshings of all the cogs in the great machine dedicated to death. He was active in the so-called President's Mediation Commission which, in the copper mines of Arizona, the oil fields of California, the meat-packing plants in Chicago, and elsewhere, did a great deal to adjust industrial disputes by encouraging unionism whenever possible. Indeed, in accord with Gompers' for-

---

to be judge-made law, like so much of the law of the past—judge-made by five to four decisions often years after the practical issue has been settled. . . ."

mula, labor really had exchanged its right to strike for protection against lockout and discrimination and thus, amid a world at war, was able to pursue its organizing peacefully, backed by all the force of government sanction. And while the opportunity for organization was greater than the A. F. of L. was equipped to embrace, it did emerge from the war not only stronger numerically but also with something else for which it had consistently striven: recognition and acceptance as an integer in the American equation.

Yet soon after the Armistice it faced Armageddon. The postwar boom collapsed, as usual; and in December of 1920 more than two million workers were out on the street. The war days of labor shortage were over; in August, 1921, 5,735,000 workers were idle. Employers were opposing the wartime union prerogatives, and with the dismantling of government labor boards they undertook the most vigorous and successful open-shop campaign in American annals. The National Association of Manufacturers, that hardy perennial of pre-war anti-union activity, blossomed forth with an Industrial Relations department that was to help manufacturers keep labor as "contented" as Carnation Milk cows. The League for Industrial Rights, the National Metal Trades Association, the American Plan League joined with the National Association of Manufacturers in "going after the unions" with hammer and tongs and corps of propagandists, many of whom had been trained in veracity by George Creel, head of the Bureau of Public Information during the war. "Personnel" managers were hired by the score, on the theory that "employee representation" plans, which gave the worker the right to do anything that management wanted him to do, would supplant any desire to join a union and speak for himself. Simultaneously, various scandals in the building trades wherein corrupt labor leaders were maneuvered into "taking the rap" for equally corrupt politicians and contractors, strengthened the view that "unions were a racket," while the adroit publicity of the National Association of Manufacturers reinforced this attitude on every side.

To offset the triple threat of "unemployment, reaction and Bolshevism" the A. F. of L. tried creating its own publicity bureau which conducted a clumsy campaign against profiteering and aroused more resentment than it allayed. It also joined the witch-hunt for "reds"; and yet to the dismay of its leaders found itself catalogued with the hare instead of the hounds. The dissatisfaction generated by this combination of events stirred up some insurgent trends within the A. F. of L. as radicals of varying hue prodded it toward the political solution of its problems. Then in 1922 the railroad unions, opposed to the Esch-Cummins bill, started a movement for a new and liberal political alignment which, two years later, culminated in the Conference for Progressive Political Action. This assembled in Cleveland on July 4, 1924. It was attended by some six hundred delegates from the A. F. of L.'s international unions; city centrals and state federations; coöperative associations; the Republican party of Wisconsin; the Socialist party; the Committee of Forty-Eight; the Women's Committee on Political Action, along with assorted third-party, educational, and agrarian groups. It nominated Senator Robert Marion LaFollette for the presidency; and shortly thereafter named Senator Burton K. Wheeler, Democrat of Montana, as his running mate. The platform called for the smashing of monopoly and for the re-affirmation of civil liberties on a real, as against a paper, basis. It asked the repeal of high tariff duties, the establishment of a government marketing corporation for farm products, the abolition of child labor, and the use of injunctions in labor disputes. It condemned the sycophancy of the courts toward capitalists and urged more public control over money and credit. It denounced the Versailles

Treaty and asked for its revision. It recommended the nationalization of railroads and electric light and power utilities, and government conservation and control of natural resources.

While Conference delegates were polishing this platform, the conservative-minded Executive Council of the A. F. of L. was approaching both Republicans and Democrats with a list of what, in its own opinion, labor wanted. Its ambassadors were virtually shown the door by the G.O.P. bosses in the backroom who were rigging the Republican convention to nominate Calvin Coolidge of Massachusetts who had been credited with putting down a strike of policemen in Boston. The campaign managers for the Morgan lawyer, John W. Davis, were more courteous but quite as definite in repulsing the Executive Council's program. It therefore endorsed LaFollette and Wheeler, as a last alternative, stressing the point that both candidates were tried and true friends of labor. It hastened to explain, however, that the "coöperation hereby urged is not a pledge of identification with an independent party movement, or a third party, nor can it be construed as support for such a party, group or movement, except as such action accords with our non-partisan political policy. We do not accept government as the solution to the problems of life. . . ."

The A. F. of L., partly because of this left-handed approval, was able to collect only a paltry $25,000 for election purposes. Many of its stalwarts, indeed, were busy elsewhere. John L. Lewis of the Miners, William Hutcheson of the Carpenters, Terence O'Connor of the Longshoremen, and many others supported the Republican party with varying degrees of enthusiasm; George L. Berry of the Printing Pressmen underwent a last-minute conversion, reversed his pledge to aid the LaFollette-Wheeler ticket, and plumped for the Democrats instead.

In the election the Progressive Independents polled

4,826,382 votes, or 16.5 per cent of the total. They captured only thirteen electoral votes, however, and these in Wisconsin which to the last was loyal to its greatest statesman. And at its 1924 convention in December, the Executive Council by a 7 to 1 vote again ratified the A. F. of L.'s non-partisan policy as the only sane and sensible course.

IV

ON December 19, 1924, two days after the Grand Old Man of Labor had been buried in the Sleepy Hollow Cemetery in Tarrytown (N. Y.), William Green—round, cherubic-looking and very affable—received the dead king's crown and sceptre, scrolls and signet-ring from the hands of John L. Lewis. The chief of the United Mine Workers, who controlled the largest single bloc of votes within the Federation, was in this affair doubly delighted to play the role of Warwick. In the first place he had for some time wanted one of his own kind, an industrial unionist, to occupy the seat of Federation authority; and Green, as secretary-treasurer of the United Mine Workers, was among the most eloquent exponents of his own union's vertical form of organization* as against the "crafts first, last and always" emphasis of the building trades unions which, together with the teamsters and Gompers, had dominated the A. F. of L. for a quarter of a century.

In the second place, the selection of Green enabled Lewis to pay off an old score against Matthew Woll, head both of the Photo-Engravers and the profitable Union Labor Life Insurance Company. In 1921 it had been Woll who, as Gompers' right-hand man, had scotched Lewis' own bid for the presidency of the A. F. of L., largely by

* In 1917 Green had often affirmed that "the organization of men by industry rather than by craft brings about a more perfect organization, closer cooperation. . . . The causes of jurisdictional disputes are considerably decreased, and in many industries can be eliminated altogether. . . . It is becoming more and more evident that if unskilled workers are forced to work long hours and for low wages, the interests of the skilled are constantly menaced thereby."

Daniel Tobin and William Green.

implanting in the minds of other Federation leaders the idea that Lewis was by nature so dictatorial that once in the saddle he would strip them of their prerogatives and impose his own will. It is said that Woll was so persuasive that three years later Lewis, widely respected and admired though he was, did not dare risk another try himself; his choice of Green therefore marked an approximation of his own innermost desire.

The new president of the A. F. of L. had been born in Coshocton, Ohio, in 1873, the son of Welsh immigrants. His father was a miner and at sixteen he himself went into the pit and soon joined the United Mine Workers union. He was a very "nice" young man. He taught Sunday School at the local Baptist church, as a compensation, perhaps, for his financial inability to prepare himself for the pulpit, the chief ambition of his earlier years. He was amiable and well liked by his associates; but he never drank beer with the boys, or smoked, or chewed. He concentrated on that respectability which spells salvation, and on success in politics, not only in union circles but also in public affairs. In 1900 he was chosen sub-district president of his union; and six years later, by diligent devotion to reports and resolutions and other dreary minutiae, he had plodded his way to the captaincy of the United Mine Workers for the entire Ohio district. In 1913 he was elected as a Democrat to the State Senate, where he drafted and put through the legislature some very creditable "reform" bills. One shortened the work week for women in industry; and another compelled operators to pay miners for their coal on the basis of the "mine run" or as it came out of the pit, and not after "screening," which cut down their tonnage and their compensation.

In recognition of such services to labor in coal, he was awarded the post of secretary-treasurer of the United Mine Workers. This event opened up new and larger vistas. He moved to Indianapolis; and since he was a "jiner," he often visited the local lodges of the Elks, the Oddfellows, and the Masons, to all of which he still belongs. A good family man (he had married at twenty-one), he applied himself steadily to his job. He was soon promoted, for in 1914 a vacancy occurred in the A. F. of L.'s Executive Council, leaving the United Mine Workers without a representative on that body which combines the functions of both cabinet and supreme court in the Federation's system of government. Gompers offered John P. White, then head of the miners, the position of seventh vice-president, which, like all such offices, carried with it a place on the Council. White scorned this post as being "too far down," and took the offer as an insult to himself and to his great union. The issue hung fire for a time; and Gompers appointed someone else. He realized, however, that if the United Mine Workers were too long denied a voice in Council sessions, it would violate the whole hierarchy of A. F. of L. representation. As a way out of this predicament, and as balm to United Mine Workers' slights, he named William Green the eighth vice-president of the Federation. Green accepted with alacrity; and ten years later the death of five predecessors had enabled him to move up, funeral by funeral, so to speak, to the third vice-presidency, where he could anticipate even greater honors in the future.

When, somewhat unexpectedly, he was given high command of the A. F. of L., the United States had entered upon its "new era" of prosperity which promised to be as perpetual as the instalment-payments on the cars and vacuum cleaners that were the new insignia of the "second industrial revolution." Although in "sick" industries, such as coal and textiles, wages remained at low levels, elsewhere they rose appreciably during the 1924–29 period, especially in sectors already unionized.

In Wall Street the speculative boom paralleled an apparently irresistible trend toward greater concentration of

control over American finance, industry, and commerce.
By 1929, less than 8.5 per cent of the corporations in the
United States employed 71 per cent of its wage earners.
The holding company—vertical, horizontal, and spiral—
flourished like the green bay tree. Mergers in public utilities
moved side by side with the consolidation of great banking houses, the formation of new cartels in food, steel,
and oil, and the sweep of chain stores across the nation.
And although the participation of the wage earner and
common man in this mad dance of the dollar has been
vastly exaggerated, even the onlookers were imbued with
the hope that their day also would soon come, and cheered
the call for louder music and stronger wine.

Contrary to all expectations, however, the A. F. of L.
failed to prosper in accord with that "law of the growth
of labor" which Gompers had formulated in 1904. His
premises had been historically correct enough—namely,
that from "the formation of the first bona fide trade union
movement in modern times, it [unionization] has grown
with each era of industrial activity, and receded to some
degree with each industrial depression, but with each recurring revival in industry, the degree of growth has been
greater, and with each recurring period of depression it
has receded to a lesser degree than its immediate predecessors."

Of the 105 international unions in the A. F. of L. during
the 1925–29 interval, 36 lost strength, 25 remained stationary, and only 44 expanded at all, mainly in the building, printing, and amusement trades. The income of the
Federation dwindled; it curtailed its activities to a considerable extent. In addition to other obstacles, indigenous
to both *tempora et mores*, it faced a new dilemma in the
manufacturers' dual program for maintaining a stable and
satisfied labor force, on the one hand, and combating
unionization on the other. Personnel managers of the day
were ingenious and effective in promoting friendly rela-

tions between the worker and his boss. Acting upon the advice of such experts, employers, to enlarge output and prevent "labor unrest," offered financial incentives to "loyal" employees, either through cash bonuses, or stock in the company, or other profit-sharing schemes, which did much to give their recipients a sense of being part of the enterprise, having a vested interest in its success. The "one big happy family" spirit was fostered by plant outings, picnics, card parties, dances, and other social events; and by intra-departmental baseball teams, and intra-industry leagues.

To enable employees while on the job to obtain wholesome food cheaply and conveniently, many plants set up company lunch-rooms and cafeterias which served good meals on a non-profit basis. Low-price lodging was frequently supplied by company real-estate developments; company buses furnished free transportation. Questions of workers' health and safety received a new attention; and the plant dispensary, hospital, nurses, doctors, and dental and optical clinics, along with the various "safety" committees, accomplished a great deal in extending competent medical care to the worker and his family and in reducing accidents. By 1926, moreover, nearly five million workers were covered by company-sponsored group-insurance plans which totaled about five and one-half billion dollars and did much to supplant the death and disability benefits paid by the unions, traditionally one of their chief attractions.

In short, American workers in many sections of industry were being "treated like human beings." They were not as a whole displeased, or disturbed by the fact that even in the most enlightened "employee representation" schemes they had at best "collective discussion" instead of collective bargaining, since the ultimate decision of disputed points remained in the hands of the employer who could, if he wished, scrap the whole program.

"The assertion may be boldly made," announced S. B. Peck, Chairman of the Open Shop Committee of the National Association of Manufacturers, "that the decreasing membership in most of the unions and the great difficulty they are experiencing in holding their members together, is due to the fact that the employers—notably the once so-called 'soulless corporations'—are doing more for the welfare of the workers than the unions themselves."

While his enthusiasm may be discounted, his contention was true enough to cause the Federation great concern. At its 1927 convention it reiterated on paper the truism that new conditions required new outlook and new methods. It recommended management-union coöperation on the assumption that the new era's industrial relations had moved from the plane of conflict to that of collaboration. It argued that unionists, secure in their fair wages and working rules, should be allowed to assist management in devising and applying more efficient methods of production. It urged the adoption of the social wage principle whereby wages should be kept in sliding-scale ratio to the per capita increase of output and thus achieve a dynamic adjustment between increasing productivity and the workers' purchasing power. It tried to stimulate research activities to lay the groundwork for more extensive inquiry into the causes of booms and slumps. It endorsed the five-day week. It suggested that labor unions either start or modernize insurance plans to fight the allurements of the employer's variety.

While in theory the A. F. of L., by formulating such new ideas, had broken new ground, in practice its officials tended to validate the French adage that "the more things change, the more they are the same." The habits and behavior-patterns of the Gompers tradition were too strongly ingrained to be effectively overcome by a series of resolutions, no matter how up-to-date or intelligent. The debacle of Black October, 1929, therefore found the

Federation as baffled and bewildered and shaken as most other groups in the country; and like almost everyone else, its leaders anticipated an early return to prosperity. They conferred with President Hoover in his "organize against panic" meetings which merely spread the contagion they were designed to cure. Moreover, in the same way that every time Hoover adjured "Be confident" stocks tumbled, every time William Green warned against cutting wages, they were drastically reduced, while employee-welfare plans were jettisoned as excess cargo on the foundering ship of industry. By 1932, when even the most sanguine were admitting that the depression had set in for an unpredictable length of time, the A. F. of L. at the suggestion of some noted economists again broke drastically, but again by way of resolutions, with the precepts of its past and came out for a national economic council to stabilize employment by means of advance planning; for a thoroughgoing study of the displacement of men by machines; for a large-scale program of public works; and for a Federal system of unemployment insurance, a proposal fought for by John L. Lewis and supported even by such Gompers disciples as William Green and Matthew Woll. Beyond this repudiation of "voluntarism"—as heretical as it was purely verbal—the Federation did little, and in 1933 its membership dropped to a new low of 2,126,796.

V

THE passage of the National Industrial Recovery Act, with its celebrated Section 7a* which guaranteed to labor

* "Every code of fair competition, agreement and license approved, or issued under this title shall contain the following conditions; (1) that employees shall have the right to organize and bargain collectively through representatives of their own choosing, and shall be free from the interference, coercion, or restraint of employers of labor or their agents, in the designation of such representatives or in self-organization or in other concerted activities for the purpose of collective bargaining or other mutual aid or protection; (2) that no employee and no one seeking employment shall be required as a condition of employment to join any company union or to refrain from joining, organizing or assisting a labor organization of

the right to bargain through representatives of its own choosing, stirred American labor to a frenzy of organizing, and thousands sought to identify themselves with the A. F. of L. which, in the face of this great scoring opportunity, constantly fumbled the ball. The partitioning of new recruits into separate crafts and the lack of funds to maintain competent field organizers on the scene until growing unions were firmly on their feet combined to cool the ardor to be a "union man." Yet this problem of new eager thousands clamoring for admission into the A. F. of L. prompted long debates on the floor of the Federation's 1934 convention in San Francisco. The result was another resolution which approved industrial unionism in the "automotive, cement, aluminum and such other mass-production and miscellaneous industries"; and which empowered the Executive Council to grant charters wherever necessary to "meet the situation" and further imposed on it the duty "at the earliest possible date" to "inaugurate, manage, promote and conduct a campaign of organization in the iron and steel industry." Despite such pledges of swift action, the Executive Council once more embodied the law of the conservation of energy, issued no new industrial charters, and allowed the crafts to continue to absorb whatever new members joined the federal unions.

Hence in Atlantic City, on the eighth day of its convention in the fall of 1935, the subject of craft-versus-industrial unions transcended all others. Among the fourteen A. F. of L. officials on the important resolutions committee, six pressed and eight opposed the total of twenty-one different proposals to organize mass-production workers by mill, plant, field, or factory instead of by "skill." The minority report was presented by Charles P. Howard, the calm, ailing, precisionist president of the International

---

his own choosing; and (3) that employers shall comply with the maximum hours of labor, minimum rates of pay, and other conditions of employment approved or prescribed by the President."

Typographical Union. It affirmed that after fifty-five years of experience the A. F. of L. had at best 3,500,000 adherents out of a maximum potential of some 39,000,000, an indication of some profound lack.

We declare the time has arrived when common sense demands that the organization policies of the A. F. of L. must be moulded to meet present-day needs. In the great mass-production industries and those in which the workers are composite mechanics, specialized and engaged upon classes of work which do not qualify them for craft-union membership, industrial organization is the only solution. . . . Jurisdictional claims over small groups of workers in these industries prevent organization by breeding a fear that, when once organized, the workers in these plants will be separated, unity of action and their economic power destroyed by requiring various groups to transfer to international and national unions organized upon craft lines. . . .

It is not the intention of this declaration of policy to permit the taking away from national or international craft unions any part of their present membership, or potential membership, in establishments where the dominant factor is skilled craftsmen. . . .

In his speech supporting his view, Howard reminded the audience that the International Typographical Union, for which he was spokesman, contained a large number of the most highly skilled and highly paid members of the Federation who yet realized that in the long run their welfare was inextricably linked with that of all labor.

In an eloquent address John L. Lewis took up the refrain of this argument, asking the assembly to "heed this cry from Macedonia, and organize the unorganized. . . ."

"A year ago," he said, ". . . I was beguiled into believing that the Executive Council would honestly interpret and administer . . . the policy of issuing charters to industrial unions. . . . I know better now. At San Francisco, they seduced me with fair words. . . . Now, I am enraged. . . .

"Miners on strike," he continued, "in the captive mines of the Tennessee Coal and Iron Company are suffering tonight by the fact that the A. F. of L. has failed, after all these years, to organize the iron and steel workers."

He paused for a moment, a brooding hulk of a man, with a graying mane of hair, gazing at his audience out of deep-set eyes. In a resonant, sacerdotal voice, he posed the larger inferences of the craft-industrial debate:

What of the future of our country? Who among us that does not know the hazards of the present moment? The teaching of false prophets falling upon the ears of a population that is frightened and discouraged, depressed and disturbed, the attempts of interests to form a philosophy . . . of the Communists on one hand . . . of the Nazis on the other hand, equally repugnant and distasteful to the man of labor. . . . How much more security we would have for our form of government if we had a virile labor movement that represented not a mere cross-section of skilled workers but the men who work in our great industries, regardless of trade or calling. . . .

If we fail . . . the workers will believe and know that the A. F. of L. cannot and will not make a contribution toward the obvious need of our present . . . conditions. . . . We will be compelled to carry on as best we can in the mining industry, knowing that our terrible adversary, the steel industry, having tasted blood, may at any time open up and attempt to destroy us. . . . We will accept that [adverse] decision sadly for despair will prevail where hope now exists. The enemies of labor will be encouraged and high wassail will prevail at the banquet tables of the mighty if the A. F. of L. refuses to grant the petition of these . . . who are fighting for the objectives of labor and to defend the right of mankind.

After an adjournment of a few hours, debate was resumed. John P. Frey, who had led the majority anti-industrial faction on the resolutions committee, again sought to justify the majority report previously submitted which had in part declared: "We consider it our duty . . .

to protect the jurisdiction rights of all trade unions organized upon craft lines. . . . The American Federation of Labor could not have been organized upon any other basis of relationship."

A tall, white-haired man, very erect for his sixty-eight years, Mr. Frey is head of the Metal Trades Department, guardian of several craft unions including the Moulders whose journal he used to edit. He is known as the Federation's scholar, and he has indeed a turn of mind well suited for researches into heraldry. In a lengthy peroration, he implied that industrial unions were virtually identical with (a) company unions, (b) Fascist Labor Confederations, (c) Nazi Labor Front Councils, and (d) Communist Labor Soviets. He traced the origins and development of the A. F. of L. and cited the fate of the Knights of Labor, the American Railway Union, the I.W.W., and other embodiments and approximations of the industrial idea as a warning of what would happen to the Federation if it fully accepted the Howard-Lewis program. His views were endorsed by craft stalwarts like Arthur O. Wharton, lean and mistrustful and part Cherokee, who, as chieftain of the 70,000 Machinists scattered among metal-working and railroad shops, shipyards and motor and steel plants, was afraid that his organization would be "torn to pieces." William Hutcheson of the Carpenters, Daniel J. Tobin of the Teamsters, Daniel Tracy of the Electricians, John Coefield of the Plumbers felt very much the same way about it. In addition to any philosophic differences, they had built their unions as men build a business and they were uneager to relinquish or endanger their positions and prerogatives, even though they had been assured that the adoption of the industrial policy would not jeopardize their supremacy. They suspected that any change in this direction would for them be on the debit side.

The fear of the union official that, with his specialized training, he may lose his job with no alternatives in sight is genuine enough, and almost all-pervasive. The very attributes which have brought him to leadership, his ability to handle people, to speak effectively, to negotiate successfully with employers, to keep abreast of new developments within his own trade, and to maintain harmony in internal affairs, all have a low market value elsewhere. Unlike the business executive or the professional man, he has a very meager list of employment possibilities. If he knows copper mining inside and out, he is still virtually of no use to unions in printing or the needle trades. He can rarely return to the tools of his youth, he has lost the knack, or hasn't the physical strength. He is too old to embark upon a political career. And whereas in some cases an employer may hire him as an industrial relations adviser, such posts are scarce. He therefore often tends to become somewhat of a bureaucrat, centralizing authority in his own hands, controlling the union's finances and sub-officers and the like to preserve the status quo and "keep his seat at the pie-counter." On the other hand, he must over the long haul produce results to satisfy the membership or he will be ousted. Frequently, of course, a superannuated and ineffectual union leader is allowed to keep his post because the members feel sentimentally and morally obliged to "take care of him" in acknowledgment of past services rendered.

William Green himself, who wanted to resolve the perplexity to please everyone, nevertheless lined up with the die-hards of the ruling crafts. During the 1920-33 period the ebbing strength of the United Mine Workers had caused him to rely increasingly upon the good will and support of the relatively more powerful building trades and other craft leaders since his reëlection to the presidency of the A. F. of L. depended upon their votes. Lacking the color and forcefulness of Gompers, Green also lacks his preceptor's talent for fashioning the kind of personal political machine which, by the horse-tradings of organization politics, can often change nominal power into a thing of substance. Although he owed his elevation to the presidency first of all to the United Mine Workers, he owed its continuation primarily to the support of Tobin, Hutcheson, Wharton, Tracy, et al., and with them he has remained.

When the balloting on the craft-industrial issue was tabulated at this historic convention the minority report was defeated by a vote of 18,024 to 10,933, cleaving the ranks of organized labor.

In protest against this outcome, John L. Lewis of the United Mine Workers, Charles P. Howard of the International Typographical Union, Thomas H. Brown of the Mine, Mill and Smelter Workers,* Thomas MacMahon of the United Textile Workers, along with Sidney Hillman of the Amalgamated Clothing Workers and David Dubinsky of the International Ladies' Garment Workers, gathered in Washington on October 9, 1935, and founded the Committee for Industrial Organization.† In an official statement they declared:

It is the purpose of the Committee to encourage and promote organization of the workers in the mass-production industries and the unorganized workers of the nation and their affiliation with the American Federation of Labor. Its functions will be educational and advisory and the Committee and its representatives will cooperate for the recognition and acceptance of modern collective bargaining in such industries.

Within three months, however, in January, 1936, the A. F. of L.'s Executive Council ordered the dissolution of the C.I.O. as a "dual" movement. The "secessionists" countered with a guarantee to raise one third of a $1,500,-000 war chest for unionizing steel if its own organizers could conduct the campaign. The Executive Council rejected this offer; and shortly thereafter the C.I.O. began

---

* An outgrowth of the old Western Federation of Miners which helped to found, and later withdrew from, the I.W.W.

† Max Zaritsky of the Hatters attended the meeting but only as an individual.

its invasion of steel under the auspices of the Steel Workers Organizing Committee and the brilliant generalship of Philip Murray. The S.W.O.C. superseded the Amalgamated Association of Iron and Steel Workers, an A. F. of L. affiliate that had some ten thousand members out of a potential half million.

Murray radiates the quiet confidence of a man who for thirty years has been successful in difficult organizing assignments. From the outset of the S.W.O.C. drive he expressed the all-embracing character of the C.I.O.'s creed in a special appeal to the Negro in which he affirmed that "the Negro steel worker is doomed to economic degradation unless he seeks the protection of a great industrial union."*

By the time Murray had established S.W.O.C. headquarters in Pittsburgh's Grant Building, and while radio and auto and other workers were transferring their allegiance from the A. F. of L. to the C.I.O., the Executive Council in September, 1936, suspended the constituent unions of the insurgent group. In reply the C.I.O. took steps to form a more permanent body, and elected John L. Lewis president, John Brophy director, and Sidney Hillman treasurer of the new organization. When spasmodic peace negotiations failed, month after month, a bitter rivalry developed between the two great factions of American labor.

It has been a rivalry dramatized by the decisions of the National Labor Relations Board created under Section 3 of the National Labor Relations Act passed by Congress on July 5, 1935.† The Act derives its legal sanction from the power of Congress to regulate interstate commerce; and its primary aim is declared to be "to diminish the

---

* It is pertinent to recall, in this connection, that among the A. F. of L.'s affiliates, the mining and the needle trades unions have been almost alone hospitable to the Negro.

† Both Act and Board were the direct outgrowth of Section 7a of the NRA, modified, however, to avoid the errors and loopholes of 7a.

causes of labor disputes burdening or obstructing interstate and foreign commerce."* In economic terms it is
based on the theory that the bargaining power of the
employer and worker should be equalized—since lack of
balance in this sphere gives rise to the majority of industrial discords and, further, tends to depress rates of pay,
which in turn reduces the national purchasing power,
fosters and prolongs business depressions, and thwarts the
stabilization of wages and working conditions in various
industries. On the other hand, it is affirmed, the free exercise of the right to organize and bargain collectively
". . . safeguards commerce from injury, impairment and
interruption by removing certain recognized sources of
industrial strife and unrest, by encouraging practices fundamental to the friendly adjustment of industrial disputes
arising out of differences as to wages, hours, or other working conditions and by restoring equality of bargaining
power." From such postulates it therefore follows that the
government should remove all these possible obstructions
or ameliorate them by "encouraging the practice and procedure of collective bargaining and by protecting the exercise by workers of full freedom of association, self-organization, and the designation of representatives of their own
choosing, for the purpose of negotiating the terms and
conditions of employment or for other mutual aid and
protection."

Despite the request of Secretary of Labor Frances Perkins that the National Labor Relations Board become part
of the Department of Labor, it was established upon a
separate basis and is responsible alone to the President and
to Congress. The board is, of course, an administrative

* Section 1 of the Act states that "the denial by employers of the
employees' right to organize, and the refusal of the employer to accept the
procedure of collective bargaining, leads to strikes and other forms of industrial strife and unrest which burden or obstruct commerce by impairing
efficiency and safety of operation, interfering with the flow of goods or
with their prices, causing diminution of employment and wages in such
volume as to substantially affect the flow of goods in commerce."

agency similar in spirit to the Federal Trade Commission. Indeed, in signing the Act which brought the Board into existence, President Roosevelt carefully pointed out that it is "an independent quasi-judicial body. It should be clearly understood that it will not act as mediator or conciliator in labor disputes. The function of mediation remains, under this Act, the duty of the Secretary of Labor and of the Conciliation Service of the Department of Labor."

"It is important," he continued, "that the judicial function and the mediation function should not be confused. Compromise, the essence of mediation, has no place in the interpretation and enforcement of the law."

Nor does the board concern itself with regulating rates of pay or work conditions, all of which remain within the purview of the state governments and the recent federal wage and hour act. Unless an employer happens to be operating under a complete closed shop contract, the board cannot in any manner affect his right to hire or fire on the basis of efficiency, or race or religion or color or political creed or whatever else may determine his selection of a labor force. The only step that the board can stop him from taking is discharging an employee or discriminating against him because he belongs, or wants to belong, to a union of his own choice.

In short, the National Labor Relations Act is designed solely to safeguard the right of workers to organize themselves for collective bargaining with their employers, and the National Labor Relations Board exists solely to enforce that right. That is the board's only function. In that light alone can its defects and merits be honestly measured.

The board is composed of three members (J. Warren Madden, Chairman, and Edwin S. Smith and Donald Wakefield Smith are the present ones) who are appointed by the President with the advice and consent of the Senate. They are each paid $10,000 a year, may engage in no other vocation than their board jobs and may be removed for "neglect of duty, or malfeasance in office, but for no other cause." They are assisted by a variegated personnel of some eight hundred men and women including the board's general counsel, Charles Fahy; regional directors; field, review and litigation attorneys; field and trial examiners; and a research* and publicity staff.

The cases which come before the board fall into three general classifications and reflect its powers. First are the so-called "complaint" cases which involve "unfair labor practices" of management such as discharge for union activity.† Second are the "representation" cases arising from the board's selection of the "appropriate unit for collective bargaining," whether craft, plant, department or sub-division of all three, and the board's naming of the labor organization (A. F. of L., C.I.O., or independent union) that will most properly represent that unit's workers in dealing with the employer. The third category, that of the much-publicized "contracts," combines elements of both "unfair labor practice" and "representation"; for the board may declare existing contracts invalid if they were entered into with a company-controlled union, or if the events surrounding their execution embodied palpable favoritism shown by management to one union group as against another.

* David J. Saposs, an associate of the John R. Commons group of labor historians at the University of Wisconsin, and himself one of the most profound labor authorities in the United States, is director of research.

† Section 8 of the National Labor Relations Act defines such practices as follows:

"1. Interference, restraint or coercion of employees in the exercise of the rights guaranteed under Section 7.

"2. Domination or interference with the formation or administration of any labor organization or contribution of financial or other support to it.

"3. Discrimination in regard to hire or tenure of employment, designed to discourage membership in any labor organization.

"4. Discharge or other discrimination against any employee because he has filed charges or given testimony under the Act.

"5. Refusal of employer to bargain collectively with representatives of his employees' choosing."

A case which charges management with "unfair labor practices" is presented either to the National Board itself or to one of the seventeen regional sub-divisions it has established in twenty-one cities.* In either event, hearings are set within five days after the receipt of the complaint to which the employer may file an answer or appear in person alone or with his lawyers. The board may subpoena his presence, or that of his substitute, and it may also examine his records. Upon weighing the evidence submitted by both sides, the board may dismiss the whole case, as it does more often than the nation's press cares to admit (see below). It may, for instance, order a discharged employee to be reinstated, as in the Jones and Laughlin case where a crane operator, with a record of fifteen years of faithful service, was fired ostensibly for leaving a key on a bench (a frequent enough occurrence among cranemen) but inferentially, or actually, for his display of union zeal at the height of Jones and Laughlin's anti-S.W.O.C. campaign.

If the board decides the employer has been guilty of an unfair labor practice it may issue a cease-and-desist order.

If the board's ruling is ignored it may petition any federal circuit court of appeals for enforcement of the order, and may also institute contempt proceedings against recalcitrants. On his own part the employer is afforded protection against arbitrary action of the board since he has full and free access and recourse to the court and may ask it to alter the board's decision or throw it out altogether.†

---

* If the board's regional director for any reason believes that any complaint of an unfair labor practice is beyond his authority, the person or organization making it may refer directly to the National Board which has also been empowered to transfer to its own jurisdiction any case which, in its opinion, warrants this change.

† Contrary to an erroneous opinion which is held quite widely, no criminal penalties are provided under the Act for employers found guilty of unfair labor practices. Such penalties may be imposed, however, upon those who shall "willfully resist, prevent, impede or interfere" with the board itself or its agents. If, after a circuit court has sustained a board decision, the employer involved continues to ignore it, he may be cited for contempt of court and the usual penalties inflicted.

From the very introduction of the National Labor Relations Bill by Senator Wagner of New York, early in 1935, to its approval by the Supreme Court on April 19, 1937, and after that, the Act and its board have been steadily assailed on the grounds of constitutionality and fair play by employers and upon the ground of favoritism by both the A. F. of L. and the C.I.O. Late in 1937 the Federation sent a message to President Roosevelt urging him to correct the "deplorable, disruptive, and destructive" conditions allegedly fostered by the board's rulings. As if in response to the A. F. of L. contention, the C.I.O. through the Steel Workers Organizing Committee maintained that the board, swayed by Federation attacks, was becoming partial to the crafts.

Still under fire by employers and their powerful union, the National Association of Manufacturers, for its lack of objectivity; still denounced by the A. F. of L., often with a lunatic recklessness; and still not altogether pleasing to the C.I.O., the board has disposed of some 16,770 cases (affecting an estimated 3,981,052 employees) with an even-tempered honesty and reasonableness that recommend themselves to its detractors, and render it one of the most valuable public agencies in American society. The United States Supreme Court has upheld twelve out of twelve of the board's "test" decisions, a perfect score. In the circuit courts, the board has won thirty-four and lost fourteen cases and is expected to appeal five or six of these reverses. From October 17, 1935, date of the first board hearing, to July 1, 1938, some 16,000 cases of unfair labor practice complaints were brought before the board by unions and by unorganized workers. In this thirty-three-month interval, the board has disposed of about 77 per cent of these cases as follows: about 16 per cent, including the United Fruit Company and the Solvay Process Company, were dismissed because of lack of evidence or foundation in fact; about 25 per cent were withdrawn after proceedings had begun; and about 54 per cent, including the Postal Telegraph Company case, were settled by mutual consent of the contending parties. Only 5 per cent of the cases traveled the whole distance to formal hearings before a trial examiner. At such hearings, of course, the employer may summon his own witnesses, or cross examine the board's witnesses; and any labor union with a stake in the outcome may also participate.

Under the provisions of Section 9b of the National Labor Relations Act, the board is assigned the difficult and delicate task of determining the "appropriate unit" for collective bargaining. In arriving at this decision it must ask and answer such questions as these: In a specific shoe company, and in the shoe industry as a whole, is the dominant form of unionization craft or industrial? Should the cigar-making branch of a great tobacco plant which also manufactures cigarettes and pipe tobacco be considered as a separate establishment for the practical purposes of collective bargaining? Should the "live traffic" control experts in a radio communications company be marked off into a separate category, distinct from other workers, by virtue of their highly specialized training?

Once the "appropriate unit" is defined, the problem of certifying the union to represent that unit still remains; and it is here that the board has had to immerse itself in the roily waters of A. F. of L.–C.I.O. factionalism.

Despite the widespread impression that the board shows a pronounced C.I.O. bias, the record (as of July 1, 1938) reveals that in the forty-one most important cases in which the A. F. of L.–C.I.O. issue was basic, the board upheld the A. F. of L. twenty-one times and the C.I.O. only sixteen times.*

---

* From October 30, 1935, to July 1, 1938, the board has handled 112 cases which involved the A. F. of L.–C.I.O. dispute. In fifty-four of these, both sides were completely agreed as to what should comprise the appropriate unit; and again in seventeen other cases both sides agreed on all except secondary details. The remaining forty-one cases, however, contained the

Quite naturally the most vexatious part of the board's function in specifying the "appropriate unit" occurs where the A. F. of L. (which now also has many mixed unions of craft, semi-skilled, and "industrial" members) and the C.I.O. do not agree on what the appropriate unit is, or should be. In situations of this kind, all other things being equal, the board generally follows what is known as the Globe policy, named after its solution of one of its more "doubtful" borderline problems. This involved the Globe Machine and Stamping Company in Cleveland, Ohio, where the C.I.O. affiliate, the United Automobile Workers, was opposed to a group of A. F. of L. unions. The C.I.O. as usual wanted a vertical or plant-wide unit. The A. F. of L. insisted that two of the company's divisions, embracing certain definite skills, should be placed in the "crafts only" category. The board therefore "put it up to the men themselves." It conducted a separate election for each proposed unit, both the plant-wide and the craft type.*

Up to July 1, 1938, the board had scrutinized the terms and backgrounds of ninety-three existing management-"union" contracts presented to it as counterfeits of genuine collective bargaining. It voided thirty-five of them, twenty-eight because they violated the provision of the law which forbids the owners of an enterprise to sign an agreement with a company-dominated union. The other seven cases all involved the Federation and were invalidated because the A. F. of L. unions, according to charges placed with the board by the C.I.O. in six instances, and a Railroad Brotherhood in the seventh, had been in agreement with the employer to transform themselves into

crux of the conflict, for in them the board was called on to decide between "tool" or "vertical" units; between an all-inclusive unit to embrace several plants at once or a unit for each plant individually; and between units to be set up department by department or on a plant-wide scale.

* The C.I.O. won the elections in both of the craft-units claimed by the A. F. of L., as well as the rest of the plant.

company-controlled unions in everything but name. The most celebrated of these cases centered around the fight between the C.I.O.'s United Electrical and Radio Workers and the A. F. of L.'s International Brotherhood of Electrical Workers to gain recognition as the sole collective bargaining agency for workers in the National Electric Products Corporation. This company signed a closed-shop contract with the A. F. of L.'s "Brotherhood" just as the C.I.O.'s "United" was getting a strong organizing drive under way.

In its decision, which also called for an election to determine the issue, the board in part declared that the National Electric Products Corporation, by "persuading and warning its employees to join the Brotherhood [A. F. of L.] and to refrain from joining the United [C.I.O.] and by threatening them with discharge if they failed to comply," has "engaged and is engaging in unfair labor practices. . . ." The head of the Brotherhood, Dan Tracy, berated board members as ". . . puffed-up commissars, prejudicially minded muddiers of waters," and "men without scientific method or social vision. . . ." In spite of these remarks, the Brotherhood won the board election by a vote of 918 to 685. The United promptly accused the company of exerting undue pressure to achieve this result, but through its president, the youthful James Carey, it announced to the board and to the public that "in the interest of the labor movement and true collective bargaining we waive our right to file exception in this case, although we have sufficient grounds to do so."

In these ways of determining the "appropriate unit," as in disclosing unfair labor practices and voiding "imitation" contracts, the board has been granted broad discretionary powers. Its supporters assert that complex human equations of an equally complex industrial relation today demand that the board be allowed to retain a great measure of flexibility in its approach; the more particularly since the intangibles of human behavior elude codifying into statutes. The American Federation of Labor, however, and the National Association of Manufacturers alike want to curtail this exercise of an elastic discretion on the part of the board, but for entirely different reasons.

The A. F. of L., which originally sponsored the National Labor Relations Act by every means of law and lobbying, still officially regards the C.I.O. as a dual movement, an organization of insurgents who by unionizing mass-production workers in particular have deprived the Federation of many members and a good deal in dues. If the present A.F. of L.–C.I.O. war continues, the former will therefore probably seek to nullify, or to limit, the board's present right to void contracts; and will try to make mandatory the recognition of craft unions in units where workers want them, to allow management to side openly with one union or another, to inaugurate court review of board decisions naming a particular union as the bargaining agent, and perhaps even to divest the board of its judicial prerogatives and transfer them to some new government bureau. The National Association of Manufacturers has meantime proposed that any union which resorts to "violence" of any kind should be deprived of government protection of its rights to organize and bargain collectively; that to "equalize things" the employer should also be given the opportunity to submit charges of unfair practice against a union; and that coercion of employees should be redefined to include the persuasions of union organizers. All such recommendations, of course, deserve to be pondered, taking into consideration their source as well as their intention.

VI

IT was no accident that the labor leaders who eventually formed the C.I.O. were more favorable to government

regulation of economic problems than were the rest of
A. F. of L. officials. In debates over the years, the former
insisted that the Federation should be in the vanguard of
supporters of the kind of legislation that was finally embodied in the Social Security Act approved by the President on August 14, 1935.*

An omnibus measure, the Act was devised, in the phrase
of its board spokesmen, to "provide some safeguard against
the insecurity of modern life through coöperative action
by Federal and state governments, thus making possible
fullest consideration of the local economic and social problems existing within states while maintaining a national
unity of program and purpose." In brief it is the function
of the Social Security Board, which administers the Act,
to extend assistance to needy and crippled children and
the blind; to rehabilitate the vocationally "lost"; and to
amplify various public health and welfare services, including pensions to the needy aged, by means of grants-in-aid
to the states. All such activities, naturally, are nothing new
in principle; and under the board's aegis are new only in
the attempt to give them wider effectiveness and scope.

What is new, and startling to many, are the two extremely important innovations: unemployment compensation and old-age benefits. With the exception of the so-
called "annuity" part of the old-age benefits system, which
is exclusively a national plan, the Act was designed primarily to enable and guide the states to pass their own laws
to assist the unemployed and the aged, and to establish
their own agencies which, it was believed, were better
adapted to local needs and conditions. Hence, to apply

---

* "What do you think," William Green inquired in 1930, speaking about
the British Unemployment Act, "of the situation that would make it possible for the employment exchange in America to say to the workman 'Go
work in the non-union mass production industry where I found you a job
or lose your insurance?' The American workman, proud of his freedom and
his liberty, is not yet willing to make himself a ward of the state." A year
later, however, with A. F. of L. unions reporting 25 to 50 per cent of their
members idle, the Federation and Mr. Green officially reversed this position.

this principle in unemployment compensation, a payroll tax of 1 per cent of the total payrolls in 1936, 2 per cent in 1937, and 3 per cent beginning on January 1, 1938, and thereafter, is imposed upon those who employ eight or more persons over a period of twenty weeks. Funds thus collected go to the Federal treasury. Farming and domestic labor is excluded along with government employees, relatives of the employer, and people who work for religious, scientific, educational, cultural, and other non-profit organizations. Employers, however, may offset up to 90 per cent of the payroll tax, amounts contributed to an unemployment fund created by the state under any statute which meets with the board's approval. Moreover, the Federal government grants money for administrative purposes to states which conform with certain minimum requirements.*

In addition, accurate reports of all this activity must be kept constantly on file and the state must also establish an impartial body to hear any and all complaints. The states are further authorized to permit employers, as an alternative to contributing to an unemployment insurance fund, to adopt various methods that will guarantee steady work to their standing labor force for at least forty weeks a year, on the basis of the thirty-hour week.

The operation of the law as it affects old-age benefits resembles the unemployment-insurance provisions in several respects, and excludes, for example, pretty much the same groups of labor. In dealing with the question of old-age security, however, two drastically different methods

---

* Section 5 covering such minima is of special interest to unions since it stipulates that "compensation shall not be denied by such state to any otherwise eligible individual for refusing to accept new work under any of the following conditions: (a) If the position offered is vacant due directly to a strike, lockout or other labor dispute; (b) if the wages, hours, or other conditions of work offered are substantially less favorable to the individual than those prevailing for similar work in the locality; (c) if as a condition of being employed the individual would be required to join a company union or to resign from or refrain from joining any *bona fide* labor organization."

are used: the one to satisfy immediate need, and the other to confirm an earned and cumulative right. In the first case, the basis of need, the states receive from the Federal government one-half of all sums paid to persons over sixty-five years of age under their own old-age pension laws, an amount limited to a monthly top of $15 per pensioner, plus $5 to reimburse the state for expenses incurred in looking after him.

In the second case, the basis of right, an annuity system—borrowed from the actuarial techniques of private life-insurance companies—has been established, and the Federal government itself assumes complete responsibility for its administration. Under this arrangement, a tax is imposed upon every $3,000 of wages and payrolls up to $3,000 per worker, with both employer and employee contributing at the following rates:

Calendar Year	Per Cent of Wages Received by Employee	Per Cent of Payroll	Total
1937-1939	1	1	2
1940-1942	1½	1½	3
1943-1945	2	2	4
1946-1948	2½	2½	5
1949 and thereafter	3	3	6

Significantly enough, the money thus collected is paid into the Federal treasury, not as a separate item, but as a part of general revenue. To meet necessary outlays, however, Congress is to appropriate annually for an Old Age Reserve Account a sum which must be "sufficient as an annual premium to provide for the payments required" as well as to serve the purpose of establishing a reserve, the interest on which will defray the deficit in later years when annual taxes do not meet annual benefit claims. The major distribution of earned benefits is scheduled to begin on January 1, 1942, on the basis of wages received and paid out since December 31, 1936; for, as the preceding table shows, both employer and worker contribute an equal share. From this Old Age Reserve Account, monthly payments will be made to all properly qualified persons. When, for example, a worker reaches the age of 65 on January 1, 1948, after earning $3,000 a year from December 31, 1936, onwards, he is entitled to monthly "dividends" calculated on graduated percentages as follows:

½ of 1 per cent for the first $3,000, or $15;
¹⁄₁₂ of 1 per cent for the remaining $30,000, or $25;

adding up to $40 a month or $480 a year. This will hardly enable him to wallow in that sybaritic luxury which conservative opponents of the measure feared would undermine American self-reliance. The possibility would seem even more remote when it is recalled that $3,000 a year is an income enjoyed by relatively few wage and salary workers and that the average is nearer to half that amount annually, so that anyone who earns, say, $1,500 a year would have to work for twenty-four years to receive $480 annually in pensions.*

The necessity to accumulate and freeze vast reserves to meet premium payments; the placing of the major burden upon the younger workers by calling upon them to support the previously employed aged who have contributed only for comparatively short periods; the failure of the government to specify precisely the degree of its own participation and to tap wealth in the higher brackets to help pay for this plan; the fact that the tax on employers virtually exempts them since it is passed on to consumers in the form of higher prices or taken out of labor in the form of lower wages—these are but few among many of the Act's features which have been assailed by its critics. Abraham Epstein, perhaps the outstanding authority on the social security question in the United States, and the author of *Insecurity: A Challenge to America* and many

---

* It is also provided that upon the death of a worker before he reaches 65 years of age, his heirs shall receive 3½ per cent of his total wages upon which taxes have been paid.

other treatises on the subject, has arraigned the Act as a hodge-podge of deficiencies, as unsound in its insurance principles and wrong in its social and economic thinking; as, indeed, a "Social Insecurity Act."

Despite all this, the C.I.O. has approved the measure as at least a beginning, a "step in the right direction"—the direction of government responsibility for the welfare of the worker and recognition of his claim upon society as the recipient of a right, not as an object of charity.

The A. F. of L. approved it also, but negatively, and with misgivings. Yet it is not the principle of government aid to the worker which disturbs the Federation quite as much as it is the kind and extent of aid implicit in this newer type of legislation. The A. F. of L. has been traditionally labor's embodiment of the laissez-faire doctrine that "that government is best which governs least." It has wanted to be left alone to pursue its own ends, primarily by non-legislative means—an approach exactly opposite to that usually advocated by the "theorists" who provoked Gompers into saying that "not one school of political economy in any era of our industrial and commercial life has advanced the wage-earners one jot in their material interests." It has wanted to stand on its own feet, and its suspicion of the Social Security Act reflects the fear of its elders, like John P. Frey and Matthew Woll, that the extension of state authority, even when "humane," is something evil in itself, tending to curb personal independence. It still subscribes, on the whole, to the belief that "economics" and "politics," instead of being Siamese twins, are merely quarrelsome third cousins better kept apart.

Despite its distrust of government intervention, the A. F. of L. has always been in politics, twenty-four hours a day, seeking its own sort of laws to promote its own sort of economics. Its Legislative Committee of three, appointed by the Executive Council, has been for years among the effective and diligent lobbying groups in the nation's capital. The committee's task is to observe, classify, and analyze proposed legislation and to influence Senators "for or ag'in" on the basis of whether or not the passage of pending bills would hurt or help the Federation and its affiliates. In the expectation of favors already received or to come, the Legislative Committee—assisted by a staff of lawyers—has often coöperated with other pressure groups; in 1927, for example, it joined with various farmers' alliances to support the McNary-Haugen bill. Ever since 1925, moreover, the A. F. of L.'s Non-Partisan Political Campaign Committee, consisting of William Green and five members of the Executive Council, has submitted to the platform-makers of both Republican and Democratic parties the Federation's own set of planks; and then has mailed out a pamphlet to the local unions to indicate to what extent its recommendations have been recognized or rejected. The Federation also examines and lists the labor records of presidential nominees but only as a comparative study, not as a guide to balloting. Congressional candidates, however, are subjected to a close scrutiny of their stand on labor issues, and local union committees are urged to endorse or oppose them by statements to the press and in other ways. This method, like the lobbying of the Legislative Committee, has been frequently successful and certainly did much to pave the way for the Norris-LaGuardia Act which, passed in 1932, was designed to curb the indiscriminate use of the injunction as an anti-labor weapon in industrial disputes.

The Federation asserts that its non-partisan policy avoids all the pitfalls of quarrels within the union over "politics" and that instead of "partisanship to a party" it develops "partisanship to principles."* It would seem, however,

* Other advantages usually cited are that the non-partisan method gets results at very small cost; that, indeed, only $57,000 for the whole decade of 1920-30 was spent by national headquarters for political purposes, half of

that in reality this non-partisan practice is, in effect, bi-partisan and divides the workers at the polls with great regularity. In 1932 the labor bureau of the Republican party was managed by William Hutcheson of the Carpenters; the labor division of the Democratic party was managed by Daniel Tobin of the Teamsters, both members of the Executive Council; while the labor section of the Socialist party was managed by Emil Rieve, president of the Full Fashioned Hosiery Workers.

Devotion to the non-partisan tactic has also tended to make A. F. of L. unions and their leaders the associates of municipal and state political machines. The city centrals or labor councils which combine all the unions in a community on a "let's get together" basis, and the state federations which combine the city centrals for the same purpose, are the instruments through which unions are linked to ruling local and state political cliques. The official of the city central or the state federation is often paid next to nothing or only on a part-time basis, and he is inclined to seek a political appointment as a means of earning a living. He holds his job as president or secretary or whatever only so long as he can furnish favors to the unions which elect him and pay his salary, which is secondary to the honor of an office that makes an excellent springboard into a political career. In the city, "political pull" can often mean winning or losing a strike, since policemen can be ordered either to leave pickets fairly alone or to molest them and arrest them wholesale. In both city and state, "drag with the administration" can restrict work on public projects to contractors who will employ only union labor. In either case, by standing in with the right people the council or federation official can help to determine the results. In return, of course, he promises and as a rule actually delivers a certain bloc of labor votes

which was for the LaFollette campaign in 1924; and that it avoids the danger of diverting union energies from "strictly business" affairs.

for the machine's standard-bearers; and usually is able to acquire and distribute some patronage for himself and his friends.

The basic distinction, however, between the political views of the A. F. of L. and the C.I.O. is that the former has wanted to enlist government assistance to serve the self-interest of a special stratum of labor which, with its job-monopoly, was in theory able to fend for itself and needed only particularized legislation here and there to do it. The C.I.O., on the other hand, with its millions of unskilled less well-entrenched in their control over whatever employment exists, seeks government intervention on a basis defined by John L. Lewis in October, 1937, in a statement not without overtones of autobiography:

Time was, before the depression, when the representative labor leader would have said "Guarantee labor the right to organize and we shall do the rest." Now he knows that modern mass production industry—not only natural resources industries but the manufacturing and mechanical industries as well—are uncoordinated, uncorrelated and overcapacitated. With the guarantee of the "right to organize," such industries may be unionized, but, on the other hand, better living standards, shorter working hours and improved employment conditions for their members cannot be hoped for unless legislative or other provisions be made for economic planning and for price, production and profit controls. Because of these fundamental conditions, it is obvious to industrial workers that the labor movement must organize and exert itself not only in the economic field but also in the political arena. . . .

In accord with the implications of this view, the C.I.O. as early as 1936 formed Labor's Non-Partisan League* as its political arm, while the United Mine Workers contributed a half-million dollars to reëlect President Roosevelt and to further the New Deal, and only incidentally to aid

* George L. Berry of the Printing Pressmen was named first president of the League, and Sidney Hillman its treasurer; John L. Lewis was chairman of its Executive Board, and E. L. Oliver was elected executive secretary.

the Democratic party. The same year, in New York State, the American Labor party, sponsored by the League, rolled up a quarter of a million votes for President Roosevelt and Governor Herbert H. Lehman. In 1937, in the New York City elections, more than 480,000 people voted the American Labor party ticket to help reëlect LaGuardia Mayor and to place the crusading Thomas E. Dewey in the office of District Attorney. In Pennsylvania the League in 1938 joined Senator Guffey in an attempt to acquire control of the Democratic party, but missed by a fairly wide margin; yet it has kept branching out into other states and, with success in some, and defeat in others, it has established nuclei for the future, allying itself firmly with various agrarian groups in the mid- and north-west.

In Detroit in 1937 the League aided the United Automobile Workers, C.I.O. affiliate, in its maiden effort to elect a city administration. It gathered 154,000 votes, and would have made a better showing if it had had the assistance of the A. F. of L. and, even more importantly, if it had stressed union issues less and the public welfare more.*

Certainly this latter mistake has been avoided by the American Labor party which, managed by a shrewd tactician, Alex Rose, its State Secretary, has been thus far the most successful of the League's ventures into politics. It aims to unite various progressive-minded elements in the community on a broad program to benefit not only the wage earner but also the farmer, the smaller businessman, and salaried and professional people. In this respect its strategy of coöperation with like-thinking Republican,

---

* The active opposition of the A. F. of L. to C.I.O. candidates in Detroit was significant not only in itself but also as a contrast to a contrary trend displayed elsewhere. In the State of Washington, for example, the 1937 convention of the liberal Commonwealth Federation was attended by 104 C.I.O. delegates and 103 A. F. of L. delegates who worked in unison, despite the Carpenters-Woodworkers row that turned the state into a labor battleground, and also despite the promise of Dave Beck, Pacific Coast lord of the Teamsters, that the C.I.O. would be "pushed into the ocean."

Democratic, "Social-Democratic," church, civic, and grange groups would seem to be a forerunner of the C.I.O.'s political intentions: not to build a strictly "labor" party but rather to guide the creation of a new farmer–white-collar–worker party which, in its egalitarian emphasis upon the common interests of the common man, will perhaps duplicate the pattern of the Jacksonian uprising of more than a hundred years before in order to meet the new needs of today's vastly changed conditions.*

* Whether this trend will manifest itself in the attempt to build a completely new national party or to capture the Democratic party will be difficult to determine until late 1939 or early in 1940. It is quite probable, however, that the latter course may be pursued, thus retaining the traditional two-party system but arraying liberal and conservative forces against each other with a sharper realism than has prevailed in recent years. The more immediate aims of Labor's Non-Partisan League are implicit in the legislative program adopted by three hundred C.I.O. leaders meeting in Atlantic City, in October, 1937. The eight points of this program proposed to limit the authority of the courts in handing down labor injunctions; to curb the use of private detectives, police, and guards by employers; to establish State Labor Relations Boards modeled after the N.L.R.B., to prohibit the eviction of the unemployed when involved in an industrial dispute; to protect and enlarge civil liberties by erasing local ordinances which, as in Mayor Hague's Jersey City, prevent the exercise of freedom of speech and of assembly; to incorporate collective bargaining provisions in all state contracts for public work; to curtail the indiscriminate swearing in of deputy sheriffs and their payment by private corporations; to safeguard wages against default by employers.

In addition, a set of resolutions dealing with somewhat more generalized topics was unanimously passed. It called for an extension of the Social Security Act to cover the four and a half million agricultural workers, the six million personal and domestic service employees, and the 300,000 maritime workers now excluded. It asked that the Act be further enlarged to include permanently disabled workers and that provisions on health and medical care be added. It recommended the Federal licensing of corporations engaged in interstate commerce, by which they would comply with a code that guaranteed to labor its full rights under the National Labor Relations Act and related legislation. It urged that labor's "right to work" be preserved by larger W.P.A. and P.W.A. appropriations to take up the slack of unemployment when willing workers have been deprived of their jobs through no fault of their own. It recommended special grants to promote the education of youth. It urged the prompt creation of state housing authorities under the Wagner-Steagall Act to stimulate employment in the building trades, A. F. of L. stronghold. It cited "the community of economic interest between industrial workers and farmers" and pledged its aid in efforts to stabilize farm prices on a cost-of-production basis. It denounced the undemocratic control over the radio allegedly exercised by communications

This emphasis upon partisan political action has given a special fillip to Mr. John P. Frey's charges at the windmills of "Communism" as identical with the C.I.O. It may, indeed, be categorically asserted that any similarity between the C.I.O.'s political program and the current Communist party "line" is purely accidental. Since, however, in the minds of many people the cry Communist is per se damaging, employers who hate unions and journalists who thrive on that hatred, along with some of the A. F. of L.'s more irresponsible old-timers, have yelled Communist at the C.I.O. for their own ulterior motives; in the hope, no doubt, that in accord with the advertising precept that "repetition is reputation" they may injure their adversary. Yet Communist influence within the C.I.O. is chiefly confined to the hysteria of its antagonists of one sort or another; and to the wish-fulfilment articles and class-angled news stories in the *Daily Worker* and the *New Masses* and other Communist party publications. On the other hand, in various C.I.O. unions there are Communists of one faction or another in positions of trust,* perhaps as many as one to every twenty-five thousand members of the C.I.O. Moreover, Communists directly control a number

---

companies and urged the Federal Communications Commission to investigate their lobby. It assured employers of its complete coöperation in living up to the letter and spirit of contracts covering wages, hours, and the like. It condemned the American Newspaper Publishers Association for using "freedom of the press" slogans to becloud the anti-union drive of its members against their employees.

* The future and stability of the United Automobile Workers were for eighteen months menaced by internal squabbles between the Stalinite Communists and the Lovestonite Communists. This dispute was in the main an officers' quarrel over the union program, and power and place for themselves. It was an especially pointless conflict since it had virtually nothing to do with the needs of the rank and file. Nevertheless, the Progressive or Lovestonite group, led by President Homer Martin, and the Unity or Stalinite group, led by Wyndham Mortimer, locked themselves in a bitter combat for supremacy. To prevent them from rending the union, which contains less than a thousand Marxists of any kind out of a membership of three hundred and fifty thousand, John L. Lewis dispatched Sidney Hillman and Philip Murray to arrange a truce, which was accepted by the warring factions at least for a time.

of unions, notably the vigorous International Fur Workers (27,500), the United Office and Professional Workers with a dubious 7,500, and the Federation of Architects, Engineers and Chemists with their even more dubious 5,900 members—the last two, indeed, being more nominal than real in their existence. Communists also dominate the United Cannery, Agricultural, Packing and Allied Workers where their claim of an enrollment of over 100,000 is pure fantasy; and their authority in the International Woodworkers of America (75,000), while once important, is now declining. The ratio of their influence in unionism is somewhat higher than their ratio of 75,000 Communist party ("official-Stalinite") members to the 67,000,000 (potential) voters in the United States, since they are usually intelligent and willing to work hard. The majority of Communists belong to the Stalinite school and their activity in the American labor movement reflects the shifting needs of the Soviet Union in its international relations. They therefore have been compelled to alter their tactics with all the surprise and dexterity of the old-time vaudeville comedian ripping off layer after layer of fancy colored vests. During the past twenty years they have tried, in regard to American unions, (1) to coöperate with revolutionary groups such as the I.W.W.; (2) to "bore from within" existing unions, as in their attempt to capture control of the International Ladies' Garment Workers' Union; (3) to create new, separate, or "dual" organizations within trade or industry, as in the National Textile Workers; and (4) latterly to join with any and all organized labor on a new "popular front" against Fascism and for democracy. This last policy, like its predecessors, not only is "subject to change without notice" but also is completely non-revolutionary in character; to such an extent, indeed, that the "party" line at the moment is on the surface as mildly liberal and reformist as the New Deal itself.

The leaders of the C.I.O. tend to distrust the Communists, not because they hold, or have held, unpopular views, but because they place the welfare of the party above the welfare of the union. At times when the party line, again by the exigencies of the Soviet occasion, has happened to coincide with American unionism's own programs, Communists have been excellent organizers. They are disciplined and devout, and almost without exception have the high courage which is a characteristic of political as well as of religious fanaticism. Over the long pull, however, their loyalty to a particular union is always suspect; they must obey the party first, and if a collision of interests between party and union should arise, they must seek to change or even destroy the union.

Paradoxical as it may seem, moreover, if a Communist—and this holds as true for the Stalinite as for the Trotskyite and Lovestonite and the other offshoots of our everdissolving Marxist factions—were to seek union office on the understanding that to choose him would be to endorse his brand of Communism, he would almost never be elected.

Consider, for instance, the case of Harry Bridges, the slight, sardonic, long-nosed, and tireless leader of the Pacific Coast's Longshoremen. Born in Melbourne as Alfred Renton Bridges, the son of a well-to-do real estate agent, and with an accent more London cockney than Australian, he has said, "I neither affirm nor deny that I am a Communist"; and for the time being anyway the dock-wallopers along San Francisco's Embarcadero do not care whether he is or not. He has done a lot for them; and they respect him and refer to him affectionately as "Limo." Sharp-eyed and tight-lipped, he is an immensely able unionist. He ousted the "gorillas" of Joseph P. Ryan, president of the International Longshoremen's Association, who often boasted of the manner in which his strong-arm squad kept the membership "in line." He captained the Pacific Coast longshoremen in the successful strike of

1934, wringing many concessions from the shipowners, notably permission to keep a union dispatcher at hiring-halls, the thirty-hour week, and more or less uniform coast-wide agreements in which wages were raised. He has helped to eliminate the speed-up whereby gangs, in stop-watch competition with each other, were forced to load more and more cargo every hour. He is addicted to the "class struggle" thesis; he has accepted aid from the Communist party; and it was at his suggestion that the Communist-edited *Waterfront Worker* was adopted as the Longshoremen's official organ. Yet, despite all this, it is still more likely than not that he retains his place of authority primarily because of his personal qualities as a union chieftain who gets results, and not because of his Marxist devotion, an indulgence which most of his followers will condone only as long as he continues to better their conditions of work.

The very fact, of course, that the old red-baiting slogans still are effective in the hands of unionism's foes may in large measure be assigned to the neglect of both the A. F. of L. and the C.I.O. to develop press and publicity services which would tell their side of the story and interpret the aspirations of the labor movement not only to the general public but also to their own followers. In regard to the usual methods of publicity, releases, special features, and the like, the union leader is inclined to believe that the general press, owned by people who must cater to the preferences of advertisers, would rarely give his cause a decent break in any case. He has seen too many headlines doctored and distorted to lay the blame for strike or violence upon the union when it really belonged to the employers. He tends to be equally mistrustful of the radio's handling of labor news and comments. A certain parochialism among labor's leadership, a tendency to think only in terms of labor wants, has underscored this disregard of the advantages, even the necessity, of molding a public opinion which, if not favorable, at least would be more neutral and informed in its attitude toward unionism in many a strike situation.

The National Association of Manufacturers, and its 31,000 manufacturers who are banded together under the National Industrial Council, cannot be charged with the same apathy toward the good will of the phantom public. In a recent letter sent to members, its headquarters staff declared:

Now, more than ever before, strikes are being won or lost in the newspapers and over the radio. The swing of public opinion has always been a major factor in labor disputes, but with the settlement of strikes being thrown more and more into the laps of public officials the question of public opinion becomes of greater importance. For it is public opinion—what the voters think—that moves those elected to action along one course or another. . . . Machinery should be set up in every community to cope with the issue of unscrupulous unionism and radicalism, both in its immediate aspects and long-range possibilities. . . .

During 1937 alone the National Association of Manufacturers raised and spent $793,043.06* on its "public information" program which, according to Alfred Hirsch, in a recent issue of the *Forum*, "depicts industry as the knight in shining armor, imbued with the idea of chivalry, entering any and all tournaments on behalf of the oppressed, with Closed Shop, Racketeering Labor Organizers, and even New Deal government as the black villains who threaten all Americans, rich and poor, employer and employed."

The National Association of Manufacturers devotes

* That this expenditure does not begin to represent the extent of N.A.M. publicity was indicated by the fact that Outdoor Advertising, Inc., in 1937 donated 60,000 billboards, or about $1,250,000 worth of space, to the N.A.M.'s "The American Way" campaign; that 270 radio stations donated a million dollars' worth of time for N.A.M. propagandists, and that newspapers in varying localities similarly donated 2,000 full pages, which at current advertising rates would have cost another million to buy outright. Thus the actual cash value of N.A.M. publicity in 1937 was closer to $4,000,000 than to the $793,043.06 collected from its subsidiaries.

most of its anti-union zeal to the C.I.O., helping to distribute a pamphlet entitled, "Join the C.I.O. and Help Build a Soviet America," a forgery so blatant that its distributors must be disappointed in it. Nor is the A. F. of L. excluded from the N.A.M.'s list of the unredeemed.

"We are not opposed to good unionism," affirmed *American Industries*, an N.A.M. publication, in 1937. ". . . The American Federation of Labor brand of unionism, however, is un-American, illegal and indecent."

The better to promote such views, the N.A.M. late in 1937 and throughout 1938 has been distributing two electrically transcribed radio broadcasts, the one called "American Family Robinson," which exalts "rugged individualism" and has been used by 268 stations; and the other consisting of talks by George Sokolsky, New York *Herald Tribune* commentator, and used by 260 stations. A movie in similar vein, called "Let's Go, America," was shown, free of charge to the exhibitor, in 2,812 theaters. The N.A.M.'s Industrial Press Service reported that its "canned" news stories, features, and editorial analysis have been printed in 6,252 weekly and daily papers in the United States, mainly in the smaller communities.

In addition to all this constant and more or less subtle defamation of unionism and all it stands for, the N.A.M. is quite generally credited with starting all the present clamor for the incorporation of unions and their compulsory registration, and other legislation by which the government would strictly regulate their conduct. The procedure is recommended to (*a*) rid them of racketeers and (*b*) make them more "responsible." Of the N.A.M.'s sincerity in pursuing such objectives there can be no doubt; it is the purity of its motives which is in question.

In the first place, with the exception of the trucking and building trades, cleaning and dyeing services, and wholesale and retail food supply, all of which by their peculiar marketing methods and competitive conditions lend themselves to racketeering, virtually none exists among American unions; or if it exists it has been so microscopic as to evade the diligent researches of many competent and interested investigators.* In the second place, existing state and Federal statutes, namely, criminal laws and the Federal anti-trust acts when racketeering has an effect upon inter-state commerce, are more than adequate to safeguard the employer, the public and labor unions against this evil—as the convictions obtained by Thomas E. Dewey against labor racketeers in New York restaurants amply attest. In the third place, despite the stories of anti-union columnists about the fabulous tribute exacted by leaders from their rank and file, high union officials are paid from three to seven thousand dollars a year, on the average, depending usually upon the size of their union, while the heads of locals average from $40.00 to $75.00 per week.† Moreover, union funds—to an overwhelming extent—are audited regularly by certified public accountants, and receipts and expenditures reported to the membership, usually through publication in the union's paper. In recent years, indeed, the most celebrated case of a union official who absconded with the treasury turned out to be a Pinkerton agent hired by the Fruehauf Trailer Company to act as a stool-pigeon among its workers. Finally, the financial integrity and

---

* "Nor is racketeering in any proper sense typical of the labor movement," says the City Club of New York in its *Report on Certain Aspects of Labor Union Responsibility and Control.* "On the contrary, it is merely an invasion of that movement by a relatively negligible element. It is only in a few large cities that one hears of racketeers. Moreover, racketeering by and large has been and is being eradicated. The number of prosecutions and convictions are impressive. Indeed, there appears to be a tendency to exaggerate the problem in order to lend weight to proposals for union regulation. This is not to say that no problem exists. But that problem is not one of remedies which are ample; it is one of enforcement."

† John L. Lewis receives $25,000 a year as president of his 600,000 United Mine Workers, and nothing for his chairmanship of the C.I.O.; William Green gets $12,000 a year as head of the A. F. of L.; Sidney Hillman is paid $7,500 a year as president of the Amalgamated Clothing Workers and nothing for his chairmanship of the Textile Workers Organizing Committee. In addition, like most labor leaders, they are given expense accounts for traveling and the like.

business sense of the union officials may be favorably compared with their counterparts among business executives.

As far as responsibility is concerned, unions which have been able to exist over a few years' time observe their contracts. In fact, less than one-half of one per cent of the contracts between American unions and their employers have been violated over a period of thirty-six years. With courts constantly crowded with suits between business firms arising from breach of contract, this record of American unionism's 99½ per cent fidelity to its pledges is perhaps a point to be pondered.*

In the rare instances in which unions fail to live up to their pacts, employers may readily resort to court action. As indicated in the Danbury Hatters case, individual union members may be sued for injury or damages inflicted by their organization, a decision which is still a precedent at law and which would seem to puncture the widely fostered illusion that unions have no legal liability. Under their present status, indeed, they have far more liability than if they were compelled to incorporate; the more particularly since the basic purpose of incorporation is to escape or to limit the liability of the individuals involved in any enterprise.

In an editorial in *Advance*, organ of the Amalgamated Clothing Workers, Mr. J. B. S. Hardman observed:

Incorporation would give the courts . . . a free entry for meddling in all and every legitimate union activity each time unions contemplate strike action or anything else that may not suit a powerful and juridically well-connected employer.

Labor has had ample experience with injunction judges to justify lack of confidence in the impartiality of the dispens-

* When Tom Girdler of Republic Steel refused to sign a written agreement with the Steel Workers Organizing Committee, he explained his action upon the ground that C.I.O. unions were not "responsible." Yet the underlying reason why he and other employers will not give a union a contract, although this device governs their other business relations, is that an agreement, "signed, sealed and delivered," increases the union's prestige; it testifies to its complete recognition.

ers of justice in the thousand and one jurisdictions of the courts. . . . Incorporation of unions would make it particularly easy for anti-union employers to have union funds tied up interminably and thus to cripple union activity. This they would do through lawsuits for damages caused by strikes or less conspicuous breaches of contract initiated by their undercover agents, disguised as union members and acting contrary to union advice and interest.

The extent to which anti-union employers will go in such practices has been brought to light by recent senatorial investigations. . . . Deliberate union-wrecking activities . . . are not quite so easy . . . under the present manner of union functioning.

Since in the act of incorporation one goes to the state and asks for the right to be legally born, the granting and revoking of charters to unions might well become a political football, with an opposed administration restricting and a friendly administration expanding the scope and kind of activity allowed. It is interesting to observe that employers who urge incorporation as just what the unions need have failed to urge that their own associations be subjected to the same sort of government supervision. Likewise, in proposing various legal curbs upon the right of unions to contribute to the campaign funds of a political party, employers have neglected to request that the owners of vast fortunes and the officers of great corporations and the members of such trade societies as the National Association of Manufacturers be prevented from doing the same thing.

To offset the reiteration of "racketeering," "radicalism," "irresponsibility," and companion calls for corrective legislation, both A. F. of L. and C.I.O. have been, and still mainly are, inadequately equipped. In addition to their joint lack of up-to-date publicity techniques through the radio and general newspapers and magazines, the union press (as distinguished from the labor press) is with few exceptions in rather bad shape. The majority of union journals, of course, whether weekly or monthly, are simply "house organs"; prepared for a special membership either present or future, given to the use of anything that comes free in the mail, and maddeningly dull. They frequently contain the efforts of newswriting or literary hopefuls who have hardly learned to spell and who are inclined to the belief that to announce the arrival of a bouncing ten-pound boy to Mr. and Mrs. Patrick McCarthy (congratulations, Pat!) is to ascend to new heights of journalism.

The single service that such publications perform—giving information on affairs within the union—is rendered in a very expensive fashion; for in addition to supplying such details the pages are usually a hodge-podge of union gossip, reprints from as many other union papers as the book will hold, routine syndicated features, aphorisms from Bartlett's *Familiar Quotations*, and jokes from magazines that even dentists have discarded. Since subscriptions to the union paper are as a rule allocated from dues payments, its circulation is no real index of "reader-interest." Often it is a sounding board for the pet dogma of the man in charge, whether the Single Tax or Vegetarianism. Its editors are roughly divided into three types: the busy official who can't spare the time to do more than hurl copy frantically gathered at the last minute at the head of the printer; the man who has failed in every other phase of union endeavor. ("In the prevailing number of cases," according to J. B. S. Hardman, "the job of getting up a union paper is considered one that could be done by anybody who can do nothing else. 'Lame ducks.' . . . Some editors of union publications take their readers for granted. Others feel equally certain that the members won't read their press, no matter how well . . . edited.") In the third and select category are the well-trained and full-time union publicists and editors who really try to educate and inform and inspire their readers; who can make up their pages with typographical attractiveness; and who write with fluency and understanding of larger social and political issues, despite the "house organ" character of the periodical and its tendency to become a claque in print, a mouthpiece of the administration, glorifying the wisdom and good works of prevailing personnel and policies.

Outside of the *United Mine Workers' Journal*, the *Journal of Locomotive Engineers*, the *Advance* of the clothing workers, the *Justice* of the garment workers, the A. F. of L.'s official organ, *The Federationist*, and perhaps a few others, the strictly union press in this country fails to interpret labor to itself or to clarify in the minds of its readers their own relationship as citizens, as unionists, as consumers to their economic environment.

The more general labor press, as against the union press, per se, is on the whole considerably better in content, even when likely to be the vehicle of some special political doctrine. The *New Leader*, published at the Rand School in New York City, is perhaps the outstanding weekly in the entire field. It has lately tempered its socialist slant and handles foreign and domestic labor news and comment with accuracy and with a flair for the human-interest story. *Labor*, the organ of various railroad unions, published in Washington, is also among the more informed and readable of the labor weeklies. Three years ago the *People's Press* was launched as an experiment in fusing the material of a general labor paper with regular intra-union news and has been quite successful. It too is a weekly, which in format and presentation has adopted some of the sensational appeal of the tabloid.* The *Daily Worker* is owned by the Communist party, and its dispatches and editorials are "angled" to conform rigidly with the party line.

* A union in subscribing to the *People's Press* supplies the editors with its own local copy which is printed separately on slip-sheets that are inserted between the pages carrying general material.

There are several news services which provide labor journalists with information in much the same way that the Associated Press and the United Press serve the regular newspapers. The *Federated Press*, for example, an independent enterprise, with branches in New York, Washington, and Chicago, and with correspondents in all parts of the country and several in Europe and the Orient, has in recent years done a good deal to improve the standards of labor journalism by supplying union editors with interesting and significant data. Both the A. F. of L. *International Labor News Service* and the C.I.O. *Union News Service* are clip sheets sent out from Washington and containing more or less officially sponsored releases. The recently created C.I.O. *News*, a small weekly, has made at least a good start toward becoming a general labor paper and may soon father still another more "popular" publication modeled after *Collier's* or the *Saturday Evening Post.**

Among many arguments favoring unity between the A. F. of L. and the C.I.O., the view has been often cited that a fusion of forces would make it easier to create an effective national newspaper, and national radio and research and educational and propaganda agencies which the whole American labor movement needs badly. There is of course nothing in the objective political and economic situation that stands in the way of A. F. of L.–C.I.O. peace. Outside of the clash of personal ambitions and rivalries, and the desire to retain old or to achieve new prerogatives of power and place, there are no genuine obstacles to harmony that could not be overcome if the will to peace itself prevailed. It is silly to think that leaders of both sides, many of them men who have conducted some of the most far-reaching and complex negotiations, covering contin-

---

* The Marxists, of course, Communists and Socialists of many kinds, still publish a vast literature such as *Workers Age*, the *Socialist Appeal*, and *Living Marxism*, to mention three among several hundred; but all of them, in their discussion of labor problems, are too esoteric and elaborate in their phraseology to have any meaning for the majority of American workers.

gencies that shaped the welfare of thousands of workers in vast industries, could not—by pooling their experience and their knowledge—devise formulae that would lay the ghost of jurisdictional disputes. The principle of industrial unionism, moreover, has been vindicated. It is no longer an abstraction to be debated; it is a *fait accompli*. It exists in many mass-production spheres hitherto untouched by unionism. It is also daily more evident that the common interests of A. F. of L. and C.I.O. members transcend the differences between craft or industrial forms of occupation or organization. Whether in factory, mine, mill, in a truck, or on a train; whether at a building site and next to a crucible, or in a store or office, they work with income-producing property that belongs to someone else, to the employer, whether "he" is a single or collective "person." They work under the direction of his foremen, managers, supervisors; and with his tools and machinery and materials; and their only claim to the net product of their labor is liquidated by the wage or salary they receive.

At its 1938 convention in Pittsburgh, however, the action of the C.I.O. in changing its name to the Congress of Industrial Organizations and building a more permanent structure upon the basis of a broad Constitution which reiterated the industrial unionist faith, seemed to indicate that the A. F. of L.–C.I.O. controversy might continue for a considerable time.

The 591 delegates, representing a claimed four million members divided among 32 national unions, 23 state councils, 115 city councils, and 130 industrial locals (similar to the A. F. of L.'s federal unions), were predominantly young men in their twenties and thirties. They had been conditioned by the social forces of the post-crash epoch. And they were inclined to be skeptical when not contemptuous of the "old fogeyism" of the A. F. of L. leaders.

Amid scenes more like the nomination of a presidential candidate than a labor convention, these delegates elected John L. Lewis president; Philip Murray and Sidney Hillman vice presidents; and James Carey secretary of the new Congress of Industrial Organizations. This choice of three veteran generals and a promising young subaltern was said to reflect the preference of the C.I.O. membership for a going-it-alone policy. Certainly its four officers have been notably unwilling to "compromise" any precepts of the industrial idea. They have been more or less committed to the belief that, in the A. F. of L.–C.I.O. conflict, a strong offensive not only is the best defense but, in the long run, may tend to create a more "honorable peace" between the fifty-seven-year-old Federation and the recent "Congress."

But conspicuously absent from the C.I.O. convention was the powerful International Ladies' Garment Workers' Union whose General Executive Board took the view that the very establishment of the Congress of Industrial Organizations endangered both immediate and eventual prospects for peace. At least for the present, the International is remaining independent of both the C.I.O. and the A. F. of L. In the opinion of the International's high command, this position alone could enable it to continue its efforts to promote harmony between labor's warring factions, thus laying the groundwork for overcoming the setbacks to labor's political aims embodied in the defeat of Governors Murphy in Michigan, LaFollette in Wisconsin, and Benson in Minnesota, in the 1938 elections. It is a position which seeks to arrest the spread of public antagonism toward unions which has been fostered by the C.I.O.–A. F. of L. dispute and which became explicit in the stringent anti-strike, anti-picketing measure approved by Oregon voters in the fall of 1938; and it would otherwise further the implications of President Roosevelt's plea to both the A. F. of L. and the C.I.O. that they take steps to "prevent the continued dissension which can only lead to loss of influence and prestige in all labor."

Despite the accusations of Mr. Frey, "Communism" is not an issue preventing labor peace. Indeed, as a "historian" of American unionism he should know better. By and large the apostles of any Marxist creed have been compelled to operate on the fringes and not in the center of the American labor movement, and the reasons are not far to seek.

In the *Communist Manifesto* of 1848, Karl Marx and his collaborator, Friedrich Engels, both German revolutionaries "exiled" in England, outlined the five cardinal points that Marx was to develop at greater length in *Das Kapital*: namely, the economic interpretation of history; the theory of class warfare; the concept that under private ownership of the means of production concentration of control would proceed at an ever-quickening rate; the theory that the depressions of the capitalist cycle were due to "overproduction"; and the doctrine of surplus-value.

Marx affirmed that in any given society the way men and women feed, clothe, house, and procreate themselves and seek to satisfy derivative desires determines the social, moral, religious, political, and cultural institutions of that society. He contended, further, that in all civilized history there has been a struggle between the oppressors and the oppressed, between master and slave, baron and serf; and that in more modern times employer and wage earner were but different manifestations of this relationship. He declared, in the *Communist Manifesto*, that the mutations of capitalist modes of production would result in "splitting society more and more into two great hostile classes . . . bourgeoisie and proletariat. . . ." In accord with the axioms of the Hegelian dialectic, both of these classes were always in opposition and would remain in that condition until one of them supplanted the other as the ruling class. The middle groups, the tradesmen and shopkeepers, would be absorbed into one or the other of the two chief classes; and in a final conflict between bourgeoisie and proletariat, the latter as the "rising" and most numerous and significant class would strike off its chains of exploitation, dispossess the capitalists of their command over industry, and establish an ultimate classless society in which instruments of production and distribution would be owned and administered by the state. Marx regarded this unfolding of future events as more or less preordained, although the triumph of the proletariat might be swift or gradual, and its consummation violent or peaceful, the latter a possibility in nations where workers could vote.

It is quite reasonable to regard Marx as a great seminal genius without assuming as do some of his more devout disciples that he was infallible, that he knew, saw, and predicted all. Certainly one of the fundaments in his philosophy, the thesis of the "class struggle," has thus far, at least, failed to take hold in the United States, despite the zealotry of Marxists in this country from Civil War days.

In the first place, in the United States, as in other industrial nations, the development of capitalism did not divide society into "two great hostile classes." Instead it created a vast and powerful middle class,* itself divided into lower, middle, and upper groups, with strong pro-capitalist lean-

* Classes may be defined by sex, nationality, occupation, income, or attitude. "If," as Alfred Bingham points out in his provocative *Insurgent America*, one follows the Marxists and "chooses to classify as to general economic status in relationship to the means of production—that is, workers and owners, one must accept the limitations of such a classification. It is rough, vague, and bears no necessary relation to mental attitudes or political effectiveness. There may be . . . as bitter conflict between groups of capitalists, over world markets, for instance, or between groups of workers, over religion or union leadership . . . as ever between employers and workers. . . . The Iowa corn-hog farmer does not consider himself in the same class with the Negro share-cropper and the Yankee train conductor may feel no solidarity with the 'Hunkie.' . . . Race, language, standard of living, type of work may all serve to divide 'worker' from 'worker' or 'owner' from 'owner' far more than 'worker' from 'owner.'" For the sake of clarity in this discussion, however, the seven million farmers who own their own farms, the seven million professional people, doctors, dentists, lawyers, teachers, chemists, architects, technicians, accountants, engineers, artists, research scientists, and the like; the eight million white-collar workers, sales and advertising and credit men; clerks, stenographers, and bookkeepers, and government employees; and the two and a half million small business proprietors, factory supervisors, department-store managers, morticians and the like are somewhat arbitrarily assigned to the colloquial category of "middle class."

ings, and which in standards and behavior has dominated, and today still largely dominates, American psychology.

In the United States, moreover, the proletarian failed to emerge in any significant or long-lasting numbers as a *homo Americanus*. The factory and mine laborers whom Marx had observed in England and on the Continent occupied a status that was virtually permanent. They had to sell their labor power for wages that gave them no more than a sub-subsistence. Whatever reserves they might have accumulated were too scanty to allow for the purchase of either real or productive property. They could not return to the land; their ancestors had been driven from the land into mine and factory. They had no escape from endless toil, endless trouble, and endless insecurity. Like their forebears on the estates of duke, count, or margrave, they were born into a caste apart from which, for most of them, there was no release except emigration or death. They could not pass the line of scarcity living, nor rise to a higher station in life. They were surrounded with the vestigial remains of a feudal past, an atmosphere in which the new merchants, industrialists, and bankers had retained all the class distinctions of the older aristocracy but had discarded its *noblesse oblige*.

In this country, however, feudalism and its remnants had been largely left behind by the time Washington took his oath as first President of the United States. Nor could "an aristocracy rise in the face of the forests." For roughly a hundred years, say from 1790 to 1890, in America, more people had more access to economic opportunity than any people ever before in the history of the world. The American worker, even though he had arrived in this country as an indentured servant, had at least a chance to rise in the world when his term of service expired. He had the chance to improve his economic condition. He had alternatives, the mobility that inhered in a growing land of boundless resources. If he didn't like his job, he could "go west" as millions did, draining industry of its potential proletarians. He had a voice in the government; he could even try his hand at politics himself. No stigma of a leisure-class outlook was affixed to his desire to "make something of himself," to "grow with the country," to be "a big man." The fluidity of the social circulation further tended to make class lines meet, waver, blur. The worker who was "getting along all right" saw men below him climbing toward his own "middle" position; he saw men above him climbing higher than he perhaps could aspire—but not higher maybe than his son John who was third assistant cashier in the bank. If he became in fact a pioneer, his own worth and his own ability were what counted, not who his father was.

When toward the close of the nineteenth century Werner Sombart, the great economist, made a survey of American labor, he published a book entitled *Why There Is No Socialism in the United States*. He had discovered, he said, that in creature comforts the standards of the American worker were two to three times higher than those of his European counterparts. "He is well-fed," Sombart noted, "and knows nothing of the discomforts of life when one's diet is a combination of potatoes and alcohol. . . . On the reefs of roast beef and apple pie socialistic Utopias of every sort are sent to their doom."

If he had come at a later date, say in 1930, Sombart might have pointed out that the use of soap, safety-razors, and bathtubs had dissociated "labor" from its traditional grime; that $5.00 rayon imitations of Worth originals selling for $500 in Paris; 25,000,000 savings accounts, and 65,000,000 life insurance policies of which 20 per cent had been taken out by industrial workers; and 26,000,000 automobiles were all contributing to that middle-class consciousness which is the only class consciousness that American labor has ever had, at least to any appreciable extent.

Any such observations, of course, need to be qualified;

there have always been groups of extremely poor and ruthlessly exploited labor in this country; and obscene contrasts between splendor and squalor, opulence and misery. Yet even in poverty, the American worker—super-saturated with success-story injections pumped into him by what he read and what he heard—has tended to hold to the hope that he would some day get a break, as others had; and ascribed his own difficult plight less to the cupidity of the rich than to his own tough luck. It was part of a mental-set, an approach to living, that has consistently repulsed the ideology of the class struggle, rendering the Marxists much like Gnostic sects, unable to convert the true believer. In the presidential election of 1936, therefore, the Marxist parties, Socialist-Labor, Socialist, and Communist, all together polled 300,000 votes out of a total of 45,000,-000 cast.

But with nine black and bitter years of depression, the Marxists claim, labor and the middle classes alike have become "proletarianized." It would be perhaps more accurate to point out that it is labor's own middle-class aspirations which have been denied to it that have infused it with a new vitality, a new willingness to fight, not as a downtrodden, humiliated class rising in revolt, but as Americans deprived of their heritage, of the right to work and to participate in some of the good things of life.

Today, in the United States, as we know, only ten out of every hundred persons listed as gainfully employed own their own business; and among this number nearly 75 per cent are farmers who cannot boast of even a single hired hand, while 3 per cent are independent retailers.

". . . If you do not already own a business," Mr. George Soule has observed, "and want to engage in private enterprise, your choice is virtually limited nowadays to buying a farm or starting a retail shop, or setting up another filling station or garage or beauty parlor on still another corner."

So, if the land frontier closed at the century's turn, the business frontier seemed to have closed sometime after October, 1929, and its passing also marked the end of an era of optimism for American labor. Today, however, the grandchildren of pioneers are by the millions on relief rolls or in W.P.A. or P.W.A. projects or in C.C.C. camps or crowding factory gates or office doors applying for jobs which, once obtained, they worry about keeping.

Among hundreds of thousands of American youth the very ideals of success have changed from acquisition as an end in itself and a way of salvation to that deep craving for security which has already become a kind of national neurosis and is strange in the young. Yet it reflects a nation-wide and desperate search for some stable niche in an economy which seems to be contracting with terrifying speed, in exact reverse to the economy of their forebears which for about 125 years had been expanding with an exhilarating speed.

The precepts of self-reliance by which men could become independent by their own thrift and initiative are gone with the opportunity, and even the hope of opportunity, that gave them birth and being. The old idols of "business" and "bigness" are beginning to get clay feet; and their prophets, mumbling the old incantations to summon a past that can never be recaptured, are jeered in the street.

Meantime, the banal but very real paradox of poverty amid potential abundance has become a challenge to the American labor movement; a challenge definitely accepted by the C.I.O. and incipiently accepted by the A. F. of L. For with the pragmatism which in a different milieu marks a Lewis and a Green as well as a Gompers, the American labor movement has begun to ask some new and crucial questions. It inquires, in effect, why it is that in this country with its still ample natural resources, with its wonderfully proficient industrial equipment, its knowledge of the technical arts, and its vast reservoirs of man-power, a third of American families (the statistical family is 4.1) are compelled to subsist on $471.00 a year, 70 per cent of them not on relief. In stating this problem, and pondering its implications and its solutions, the American unionist is not becoming a "radical" in the usual sense of the term. He is rather indicating his ingrained American common sense and matter-of-factness, his desire to deal with a concrete situation in a concrete way.

He sees his material welfare, his human dignity, and his personal freedom menaced by a growing lack of economic opportunity and economic security. He wants to create them, or to re-create them; and with this new motivation American unionism has reached a more mature stage in its development. It has begun to discard its historically negative character and to assume a new and affirmative role. Its incentives up to the present have been mainly to defend and protect its job-interests; and while it has been able to improve conditions of work it has not previously been able to help create that work itself. It is toward this objective that it now is striving. Nor is it moving in this direction as a separate and self-sufficient class. It is rather displaying a deep fellow feeling for farmers and for middle-class groups, offering them its aid and coöperation in seeking to reëstimate and reëstablish the traditional American values of political and economic independence.

The very job-consciousness of the American unionist today prompts him more and more to insist that, if the depression continues, the government either introduce new price, profit, production, and wage controls in moribund industries or take them over and manage them itself.* Barring a war boom, he will keep pressing for this kind of action; not because he wants the socialization of industry but because some way, it seems to him, has to be found for

* The necessity for labor to achieve greater political power in order to inaugurate any such program is itself a strong force working toward unity between the A. F. of L. and the C.I.O.

employing the unemployed and increasing the national output of food and shelter and clothing. He has made up his
mind that the promise of life, liberty, and the pursuit of
happiness which is still the mainspring of his spiritual being
must be met in fuller measure/despite all the difficulties of
a day in which the tallow-candles are gone and the Cones-
toga wagons no longer rumble over the old Cumberland
road, westward to the prairie and again westward to the sea.

Bibliography

General

BEARD, CHARLES A., and MARY K. *The Rise of American Civilization*. Macmillan, New York, 1930.

BERLE, A. A., and MEANS, GARDINER C. *The Modern Corporation and Private Property*. Macmillan, New York, 1934.

BINGHAM, ALFRED M. *Insurgent America* (2d rev. ed.). W. W. Norton, New York, 1938.

BRIEFS, GOETZ A. *The Proletariat*. McGraw-Hill, New York, 1937.

CHASE, STUART. *Men and Machines*. Macmillan, New York, 1929.

—— *A New Deal*. Macmillan, New York, 1932.

COMMONS, JOHN R. *Institutional Economics*. Macmillan, New York, 1934.

COREY, LEWIS. *The Crisis of the Middle Class*. Covici-Friede, New York, 1935.

EZEKIEL, MORDECAI. *$2500 a Year*. Harcourt, Brace, New York, 1936.

HACKER, LOUIS M., and KENDRICK, BENJAMIN B. *The United States Since 1865*. F. S. Crofts & Co., New York, 1933.

KIRKLAND, EDWARD C. *A History of American Economic Life*. F. S. Crofts & Co., New York, 1934.

LAIDLER, HARRY W. *Concentration in American Industry*. Thomas Y. Crowell, New York, 1931.

LOEB, HAROLD, and associates. *The Chart of Plenty*. Viking Press, New York, 1935.

LYND, ROBERT S. and HELEN M. *Middletown, a Study in Contemporary American Culture*. Harcourt, Brace, New York, 1929.

——, and —— *Middletown in Transition, a Study in Cultural Conflicts*. Harcourt, Brace, New York, 1937.

ORTH, SAMUEL P. *The Armies of Labor*. Yale University Press, New Haven, 1921.

Ross, Edward Alsworth. *Roads to Social Peace*. University of North Carolina Press, Chapel Hill, 1930.

Veblen, Thorstein. *The Instinct of Workmanship*. B. W. Huebsch, New York, 1922.

—— *The Theory of Business Enterprise*. Charles Scribner's Sons, New York, 1923.

The Labor Movement

Adamic, Louis. *Dynamite*. Viking Press, New York, 1931.

Beard, Mary K. *A Short History of American Labor*. Workers' Bookshelf Series, New York, 1930.

Brooks, R. R. R. *When Labor Organizes*. Yale University Press, New Haven, 1937.

Carroll, Mollie Ray. *Labor and Politics*. Houghton Mifflin, Boston, 1923.

Catlin, Warren B. *The Labor Problem in the United States and Great Britain*. Harper & Brothers, New York, 1926.

Commons, John R., and associates. Documentary History of American Industrial Society, 10 vols. A. H. Clark. Cleveland, 1910. *History of Labour in the United States*. Macmillan, New York, 1926, 2 vols.

——, and Andrews, J. B. *Principles of Labor Legislation* (4th rev. ed.). Harper & Brothers, New York, 1936.

——, Editor. *Trade Unionism and Labor Problems*. Ginn & Co., Boston, 1905.

Daugherty, Carroll R. *Labor Problems in American Industry* (3d ed.). Houghton Mifflin, Boston, 1936.

Douglas, Paul H. *Real Wages in the United States, 1890-1926*. Houghton Mifflin, Boston, 1930.

Epstein, Abraham. *Insecurity: a Challenge to the United States* (3d rev. ed.). Random House, New York, 1938.

Fairchild, Henry Pratt. *Immigration*. Macmillan, New York, 1913.

Feldman, Herman. *Racial Factors in American Industry*. Harper & Brothers, New York, 1931.

Fine, Nathan. *Labor and Farmer Parties in the United States, 1828-1928*. Rand School of Social Science, New York, 1928.

FRANKFURTER, FELIX, and GREENE, NATHAN. *The Labor Injunction*. Macmillan, New York, 1930.

GOLDBERG, LOUIS P., and LEVENSON, ELENORE. *Lawless Judges*. Rand School of Social Science, New York, 1934.

GOMPERS, SAMUEL. *Seventy Years of Life and Labor, an Autobiography*. E. P. Dutton, New York, 1925.

GROAT, GEORGE GORHAM. *An Introduction to the Study of Organized Labor in America*. Macmillan, New York, 1919.

HARDMAN, J. B. S., and associates. *American Labor Dynamics*. Harcourt, Brace, New York, 1928.

HOXIE, R. F. *Trade Unionism in the United States*. D. Appleton, New York, 1917.

JEROME, HARRY. *Mechanization in Industry*. National Bureau of Economic Research, Inc., New York, 1934.

LESCOHIER, DON. D., and BRANDEIS, ELIZABETH. *History of Labor in the United States*, 1896–1933, Working Conditions and Labor Legislation. Macmillan, New York, 1935.

LORWIN, LEWIS W. *The American Federation of Labor*. Brookings Institution, Washington, 1934.

METCALF, HENRY C., *Editor*. *Collective Bargaining for Today and Tomorrow*. Harper & Brothers, New York, 1937.

MINTON, BRUCE, and STUART, JOHN. *Men Who Lead Labor*. Modern Age, New York, 1937.

MUSTE, A. J. *The Automobile Industry and Organized Labor* (pamphlet). League for Industrial Democracy, New York, 1937.

ONEAL, JAMES. *The Workers in American History*. Rand School of Social Science, New York, 1921.

PELL, ORLIE. *The Office Worker, Labor's Side of the Ledger* (pamphlet). League for Industrial Democracy, New York, 1937.

PERLMAN, SELIG. *A Theory of the Labor Movement*. Macmillan, New York, 1928.

—— *A History of Trade Unionism in the United States*. Macmillan, New York, 1929.

——, and TAFT, PHILIP. *History of Labor in the United States*, *1896-1932*. Vol. IV. Labor Movements.

SPERO, STERLING D., and HARRIS, ABRAM L. *The Black Worker*. Columbia University Press, New York, 1931.

WALSH, J. RAYMOND. *C.I.O. Industrial Unionism in Action.* W. W. Norton, New York, 1937.

WARE, NORMAN J. *The Labor Movement in the United States, 1860-1896.* D. Appleton-Century, New York, 1929.

—— *Labor in Modern Industrial Society.* D. C. Heath, Boston, 1935.

WOLMAN, LEO. *Ebb and Flow in Trade Unionism.* National Bureau of Economic Research, Inc., New York, 1936.

—— *The Growth of American Trade Unions.* National Bureau of Economic Research, Inc., New York, 1934.

YELLEN, SAMUEL. *American Labor Struggles.* Harcourt, Brace, New York, 1936.

United States Department of Labor, Bureau of Labor Statistics. *The Development of Minimum Wage Laws in the United States, 1912 to 1927.* Bulletin No. 61, Washington, 1928.

United States Department of Labor, Bureau of Labor Statistics. *Handbook of American Trade Unions.* Bulletin No. 618, Washington, 1936.

The United Mine Workers of America

CARNES, CECIL. *John L. Lewis, Leader of Labor.* Robert Speller, New York, 1936.

EVANS, CHRIS. *History of the United Mine Workers of America.* Official history published by the union, covering only the 1860–1900 period. Indianapolis, 1918. 2 vols.

GLUCK, ELSIE. *John Mitchell, Miner.* John Day, New York, 1929.

GOODRICH, CARTER. *The Miner's Freedom.* Marshall Jones, Boston, 1925.

GUYER, J. P. *Pennsylvania's Cossacks and the State's Police.* People's Publishing Co., Reading, Pa., 1924.

HAMILTON, WALTON H., and WRIGHT, HELEN. *The Case of Bituminous Coal.* Macmillan, New York, 1925.

HINRICHS, A. F. *The United Mine Workers of America and the Non-Union Coal Fields.* Longmans, Green, New York, 1923.

Lewis, John L. *The Miners' Fight for American Standards.* Bell Publishing Co., Indianapolis, 1925.

Lubin, Isador. *Miners' Wages and the Cost of Coal.* McGraw-Hill, New York, 1924.

Mitchell, John. *Organized Labor.* American Book and Bible House, Philadelphia, 1903.

Morris, H. L. *The Plight of the Coal Miner.* University of Pennsylvania Press, Philadelphia, 1936.

Rochester, Anna. *Labor and Coal.* International Publishers, New York, 1931.

Suffern, Arthur E. *The Coal Miners' Struggle for Industrial Status.* Macmillan, New York, 1924.

Van Kleek, Mary. *Miners and Management.* Russell Sage Foundation, New York, 1924.

Adamic, Louis. "John L. Lewis' Push to Power." *Forum*, March, 1937.

"The C.I.O. Controversy." International Juridical Association. Monthly Bulletin, August, 1936.

Gandy, Harry L. "Some Trends in the Bituminous Coal Industry." Annals of the American Academy of Political and Social Science, January, 1930.

Harrington, Daniel. "Safety in Coal Mining." Annals of the American Academy of Political and Social Science, January, 1926.

"John Llewellyn Lewis." *Fortune Magazine*, October, 1936.

Labor Research Association. Mining Notes. Monthly from January, 1932, to July, 1938.

Lauck, W. Jett. Combination in the Anthracite Industry. A survey prepared by the United Mine Workers of America for presentation to the United States Anthracite Coal Commission, 1920. Printed by the union.

—— "Coal Labor Legislation: A Case." Annals of the American Academy of Political and Social Science, March, 1936.

Roberts, Peter. "The Anthracite Coal Situation." *Yale Review*, November, 1902.

Rodman, Selden. "John L. Lewis, an Interview." *Common Sense*, January, 1936.

STOLBERG, BENJAMIN. "King Coal's Boss." *Independent*, July 11, 1925.

—— "John L. Lewis, Portrait of a Realist." *Nation*, August 1, 8, 15, 1936.

TIPPETT, TOM. "The Miners Fight Their Leaders." *American Mercury*, June, 1934.

WARNE, F. J. "The Real Cause of the Miners' Strike." *Outlook*, August 30, 1902.

Anthracite Coal Strike Commission. Report to the President on the Anthracite Coal Strike of May–October, 1902. Washington, 1903.

Committee for Industrial Organization. *Industrial Unionism* (pamphlet). Washington, 1935.

—— *Industrial Unions Mean Unity* (pamphlet). Washington, 1936.

—— *The Case for Industrial Organization* (pamphlet). Washington, 1936.

—— Address of John L. Lewis, at Conference of C.I.O. Unions, October, 1937, in Atlantic City. Washington, November, 1937.

—— Resolutions (mimeographed), Conference of C.I.O. Unions, Atlantic City, October, 1937. Washington, 1937.

United Mine Workers' Journal. SEARLES, ELLIS, *Editor*. Files from 1891 to 1938.

United Mine Workers of America. Convention Proceedings. Files from 1891 to 1938.

United States Bureau of Labor Statistics. *Hours and Earnings in Anthracite and Bituminous Coal Mining*, Bulletins Nos. 279, 316, 416, 454, 516.

United States Bureau of Mines. Annual Reports: Coal Mining Fatalities in the United States; Mineral Resources in the United States, from 1923 to 1938.

Supplementary

National Survey of Potential Product Capacity. Report published by the New York City Housing Authority. "Fuels and Energy" (chap. V), Walter N. Polakov. New York, 1936.

Technological Trends and National Policy. National Resources Committee. Sec. II: The Mineral Industries, Technology in Coal Mining. F. G. Tryon. Washington, 1937.

The United Brotherhood of Carpenters and Joiners

DEIBLER, F. S. *Amalgamated Wood Workers' International Union of America.* University of Wisconsin Press, 1912.

FOSTER, WILLIAM Z. *Misleaders of Labor.* Trade Union Educational League, New York, 1927.

HABER, WILLIAM. *Industrial Relations in the Building Industry.* Harvard University Press, Cambridge, 1930.

SEIDMAN, HAROLD. *Labor Czars.* Liveright, New York, 1938.

WHITNEY, N. R. *Jurisdiction in American Building Trades Unions.* Johns Hopkins Press, Baltimore, 1914.

"The Business Agent." *Iron Moulders Journal.* Unsigned article. November, 1900.

COMMONS, JOHN R. "The New York Building Trades." *Quarterly Journal of Economics,* XVIII, 1919.

CUMMINS, E. E. "Political and Social Philosophy of the Carpenters' Union." *Political Science Quarterly,* September, 1927.

—— "Jurisdictional Disputes of the Carpenters' Union." *Journal of Economics,* May, 1926.

Federated Press Dispatches. December 11 and 15, 1936.

The Carpenter ("Golden Jubilee" ed.). August, 1931.

LEVINSON, EDWARD. "Bill Hutcheson's Convention." *Nation,* January 2, 1937.

STEELE, JAMES. "The Decline of a Brotherhood." *New Republic.* March 14, 1934.

"This Is No Time for Experimenting with Hasty and Untried Theories" (Editorial). *Boilermakers' and Iron Shipbuilders' Journal.* November, 1922.

WOLL, MATTHEW. "The Story of the A. F. of L." International Labor News Service, Washington, 1923.

The Carpenter. Monthly organ of the U. B. C. J. A. Files from 1926 to July, 1938.

Constitution and By-Laws of the United Brotherhood of

Carpenters and Joiners of America. As amended in April, 1929.

General Executive Board of the United Brotherhood of Carpenters and Joiners of America vs. Local No. 1051. Philadelphia, 1933.

New York Times. September 4 to November 7, 1896; October 8 to November 9, 1900; January 16 and 26, 1936; August 2, 5, 6, and 14, 1936; September 7, October 16, November 28, 1936.

Proceedings of the conventions of the Building Trades Department of the American Federation of Labor, 1908-32.

Proceedings of the 1924 (21st), 1928 (22d), and 1936 (23d) general conventions of the United Brotherhood of Carpenters and Joiners of America.

Report of the National Survey of Potential Product Capacity. Harold Loeb, *Director.* Chap. X (Construction), Table III, Appendix, New York City Housing Authority, 1935.

The American Newspaper Guild

BROUN, HEYWOOD. "White Collar into Plume." *Nation*, April 10, 1935.

EDWARDS, ALBA M. "The 'White-Collar' Workers." *Monthly Labor Review*, March, 1934.

GRATTAN, HARTLEY C. "White-Collar Workers in Retreat." *American Spectator*, December, 1936.

KEATING, ISABELLE. "Reporters Become of Age." *Harper's*, April, 1935.

SPRINGER, GERTRUDE. "Ragged White Collars." *Survey*, November 15, 1931.

VOGEL, WILLIAM P., JR. "The Newspaper Guild." *Common Sense*, July, 1936.

WHITE, WILLIAM ALLEN. "How Free Is Our Press?" *Nation*, June 18, 1938.

The Guild Reporter. Files from January, 1937, to July, 1938.

International Labor Office (Geneva). *Conditions of Work and Life of Journalists.* Studies and Reports, Series L (Professional Workers), No. 2, P. S. King & Son, Ltd., London, 1928.

Reports of Convention Proceedings of the American Newspaper Guild, 1936, 1937, 1938.

The International Ladies' Garment Workers' Union

COMMONS, JOHN R. *Races and Immigrants in America.* Macmillan, New York, 1920.

COOMBS, WHITNEY. *The Wages of Unskilled Labor in the Manufacturing Industries of the United States,* 1900–1924. Columbia University Press, New York, 1930.

LEVINE, LOUIS. *The Women's Garment Workers.* A History of the International Ladies' Garment Workers' Union. B. W. Huebsch, New York, 1924.

ODENCRANTZ, LOUISE C. *Italian Women in Industry.* Russell Sage Foundation, New York, 1919.

ONEAL, JAMES. *A History of the Amalgamated Ladies' Garment Cutters' Union, Local No. 10.* The Cutters' Union No. 10, New York, 1927.

SAPOSS, DAVID J. *Left-Wing Unionism.* International Publishers, New York, 1929.

SOULE, GEORGE, and BUDISH, J. M. *The New Unionism in the Clothing Industry.* Harcourt, Brace, New York, 1920.

GORDON, HARRY A. "Conditions in the Cloak and Suit Industry in the City of New York" (pamphlet). Rand School of Social Science, New York, 1914.

International Ladies' Garment Workers' Union. Proceedings, 22d and 23d annual conventions, 1936 and 1937.

—— Publications of the Educational Department. *First Aid for Organizers* (mimeographed); *Handbook of Trade Union Methods* (pamphlet); *Manual for Trade Union Speakers* (pamphlet); *The Story of the ILGWU* (pamphlet); *You and Your Union* (pamphlet); *The Women's Garment Industry,* an economic analysis prepared by Lazare Teper (pamphlet); *Souvenir Journals.*

—— Publications (General). *Financial and Statistical Report, May 1, 1934 to March 31, 1937,* as submitted by David Dubinsky, President and General Secretary-Treasurer to the 23d convention, Atlantic City, May 3, 1937.

—— Publications of the Union Health Center. *The Union*

Dental Clinic (pamphlet); *Dental and Medical Clinic for Workers* (pamphlet); *Cooperative Health, Medical and Dental Service* (pamphlet).

Justice, monthly from January, 1936 to July, 1938.

MALKIEL, THERESA S. "The Diary of a Shirtwaist Striker." New York Cooperative Press, New York, 1910.

State of Illinois. Annual Report of the Factory Inspector of Illinois. Years ending December 15, 1902 and 1910, Springfield, Ill. State Document.

State of New York. Reports of the Factory Inspector. Years ending December 31, 1899, 1900, and 1901. State Document. Albany.

United States Bureau of Labor Statistics, Department of Labor. Bulletin No. 98; Conciliation and Arbitration and Sanitation in the Cloak, Suit and Skirt Industry of New York City. Washington, 1912.

— Bulletin No. 147; Wages and Regularity of Employment in the Cloak, Suit and Skirt Industry. With plans for apprenticeship of cutters and education of workers in the industry. 1915.

— Bulletin No. 183; Regularity of Employment in the Women's Ready to Wear Garment Industries. 1915.

United States House of Representatives, Report of Committee on Manufactures (Sweat Shop Investigation). Congressional Document, January 20, 1893. Washington.

Women's Wear Daily, January, 1936 to July, 1938.

The Railroad Brotherhoods (Big Four) and Other Railroad Unions

BING, ALEXANDER M. *War-Time Strikes and Their Adjustment*. E. P. Dutton, New York, 1921.

BURNS, W. F. *The Pullman Boycott: A Complete History of the Great R.R. Strike*. McGill Printing Co., St. Paul, 1894.

CARWARDINE, W. H. *The Pullman Strike*. Charles H. Kerr, Chicago, 1894.

COLEMAN, McALISTER. *Eugene V. Debs*. Greenberg Publisher, Inc., New York, 1931.

HINES, WALTER DONNER. *War History of American Railroads*. Yale University Press, New Haven, 1928.

HUNGERFORD, EDWARD. *The Story of the Baltimore and Ohio Railroad.* G. P. Putnam's Sons, New York, 1928.

JOSEPHSON, MATHEW. *The Robber Barons.* Harcourt, Brace, New York, 1935.

LAIDLER, HARRY W. *A Program for Modern America.* Thomas Y. Crowell, New York, 1936.

LEWIS, LEWIS, and SMITH, HENRY JUSTIN. *Chicago: The History of Its Reputation.* Harcourt, Brace, New York, 1929.

LOVESTONE, JAY. *The Government-Strikebreaker.* Published by the Workers' Party, New York, 1923.

McCALEB, WALTER F. *History of the Brotherhood of Railroad Trainmen.* Albert and Charles Boni, New York, 1936.

ROBBINS, E. C. *The Railway Conductors.* Columbia University Press, New York, 1914.

RUSSELL, CHARLES EDWARD. *Railroad Melons, Rates and Wages.* Charles H. Kerr, Chicago, 1922.

SOULE, GEORGE S. *Wage Arbitration, Selected Cases, 1920-24.* Macmillan, New York, 1928.

WOOD, LOUIS AUBREY. *Union Management Cooperation on the Railroads.* Yale University Press, New Haven, 1931.

Supplementary

Annals of the American Academy of Political and Social Science, September, 1936. Entire issue devoted to "Railroads and Government." Sec. 1: Railroad Services and Their Improvement; Sec. 2: Railroad Problems in the United States; Sec. 3: Government or Private Ownership and Operation.

BERMAN, EDWARD. *Labor and the Sherman Act.* Harper & Brothers, New York, 1931.

Constitutions and By-Laws of the Grand International Brotherhood of Locomotive Engineers; Brotherhood of Locomotive Firemen and Enginemen; Brotherhood of Railroad Trainmen; and Order of Railway Conductors.

CRAVEN, LESLIE. "A Plan for New Railroad Legislation." Appendix III, Report of the Federal Coordinator of Transportation to the Interstate Commerce Commission (mimeographed), December, 1933. Washington.

HARRISON, GEORGE M. "The Railway Labor Act." *American Federationist*, October, 1934.

STEVENS, F. W. *The Beginnings of the New York Central Railroad*. G. P. Putnam's Sons, New York, 1926.

Twentieth Century Fund, Inc., *Labor and the Government*. McGraw-Hill, New York, 1935.

United States Bureau of Labor Statistics. Bulletin No. 303, Use of Federal Power in Settlement of Railway Labor Disputes. Washington.

United States Senate, 73d Congress, 2d Session. Senate Document No. 119, Regulation of Railroads. Washington.

YELLEN, SAMUEL. *American Labor Struggles*. Harcourt, Brace, New York, 1936.

The United Automobile Workers of America

DUNN, ROBERT W. *Labor and Automobiles*. International Publishers, New York, 1929.

EPSTEIN, RALPH C. *The Automobile Industry*. McGraw-Hill, New York, 1928.

HOXIE, R. F. *Scientific Management and Labor*. D. Appleton, New York, 1915.

HUBERMAN, LEO. *The Labor Spy Racket*. Modern Age, New York, 1938.

TAYLOR, FREDERICK W. *Shop Management*. Harper & Brothers, New York, 1911.

Taylor Society, *Scientific Management in American Industry*. Harper & Brothers, New York, 1929.

ADAMIC, LOUIS. "Sit-Down." *Nation*, December 5 and 12, 1936.

Automobile Facts and Figures (pamphlet). Automobile Manufacturers Association, Inc., New York, 1936.

BISHOP, MERLIN D. Collective Bargaining, an Outline (mimeographed), publication of the United Automobile Workers of America. Detroit, 1936.

BLAKELY, PAUL L. "Property Rights in the Worker's Job." *America*, April 10, 1937.

BLIVEN, BRUCE. "Sitting Down in Flint." *New Republic*, January 27, 1937.

FITCH, JOHN A. "The Clash Over Industrial Unionism." *Survey Graphic*, January, 1936.

GREEN, LEON. "The Case for the Sit-Down Strike." *New Republic*, March 24, 1937.

HALL, HELEN. "When Detroit's Out of Gear." *Survey Graphic*, April, 1930.

HALLGREN, M. A. "Labor under the New Deal." *Current History*, September, 1935.

LEWIS, ALFRED BAKER. *Why the C.I.O.?* (pamphlet). League for Industrial Democracy, December, 1937.

LOVETT, ROBERT M. "A G.M. Stockholder Visits Flint." *Nation*, January 30, 1937.

"New Strategy in Labor War" (unsigned). *Business Week*, January 30, 1937.

RAUSHENBUSH, CARL. *Fordism* (pamphlet). League for Industrial Democracy, 1937.

RUTTER, JOHN T. "Sit-Down! Stay-In!" *Commerce*, Chicago, February, 1937.

SAPOSS, DAVID J. "Employe Representation as Labor Organization." Annals of the American Academy of Political and Social Science, March, 1935.

SEIDMAN, JOEL. *Sit-Down* (pamphlet). *New Frontiers Series*. League for Industrial Democracy, 1937.

"Sit-down vs. Sit-Tight." *Business Week*, January 9, 1937.

SOKOLSKY, GEORGE E. "The Law and Labor." *Atlantic Monthly*, April, 1937.

WHITEMAN, HOWARD. "France Stops Work." *Today*, August 1, 1936.

WILLIAMS, WHITING. "Sit-down—a Boomerang?" *American Machinist*, February 24, 1937.

"Why Did the Auto Workers Strike?" *Social Action*, national organ of the Council for Social Action, III, 4, February 15, 1937.

N.R.A., Research and Planning Division. Preliminary Report on the Study of Employment and Improvement of Labor Conditions in the Automobile Industry. Government Printing Office, Washington, 1935.

Supplementary

BINDER, PEARL. "The Strikes in Paris." *New Statesman* and *Nation*. London, June 11, 1936.

BOUISSOUNOUSSE, J. "Paris Sets a Strike Style." *Survey Graphic*, September, 1936.

KALTENBORN, H. V. "Backstage at a Sit-Down." *Commentator*, April, 1937.

PATCH, BUEL W. "Control of the Sit-down Strike." Editorial Research Reports, Washington, March 26, 1937.

"The Sit-Down Strike." *Employer-Employee Relations*, III, April 1, 1937.

"Sit-Down Strikes and the Law." Debate in the *United States News*, between Francis J. Gorman and James A. Emery, January 25, 1937.

WEINSTONE, WILLIAM. *The Great Sit-Down Strike* (pamphlet). Workers Library Publishers, New York, 1937.

Report of proceedings of the American Federation of Labor convention, 1927.

PART I

Textile Workers

ABBOT, EDITH. *Women in Industry*. D. Appleton, New York, 1910.

BRISSENDEN, PAUL F. *The I.W.W.: A Study of American Syndicalism*. Studies in History, Economics, and Public Law. Columbia University, New York, 1919.

COPELAND, M. T. *The Cotton Textile Industry*. Harvard Economic Studies, VIII, Harvard University, Cambridge, 1912.

DUNN, ROBERT W., and HARDY, JACK. *Labor and Textiles*. International Publishers, New York, 1931.

GAMBS, JOHN. *The Decline of the I.W.W.* Columbia University Press, New York, 1932.

HAYWOOD, W. D. *Bill Haywood's Book*. International Publishers, New York, 1929.

KIRKLAND, EDWARD C. *A History of American Economic Life*. Crofts American History Series, Dixon Ryan Fox, Editor. Chap. IX, The Formation of a Laboring Class. F. S. Crofts & Co., New York, 1934.

MACDONALD, LOIS. *Southern Mill Hills*. Hillman-Curl, Inc., New York, 1928.

MITCHELL, GEORGE S. *Textile Unionism in the South.* University of North Carolina Press, Chapel Hill, 1931.

RHYNE, JENNINGS. *Some Southern Cotton Mill Workers and Their Villages.* University of North Carolina Press, Chapel Hill, 1930.

ROBINSON, HARRIET. *Loom and Spindle.* Thomas Y. Crowell, New York, 1898.

TANNENBAUM, FRANK. *Darker Phases of the South.* G. P. Putnam's Sons, New York, 1924.

TIPPETT, TOM. *When Southern Labor Stirs.* Jonathan Cape and Harrison Smith, New York, 1930.

American Labor Year Book, 1920-21; 1928.

American Wool and Cotton Reporter. February through July, 1938.

BLANSHARD, PAUL. "One Hundred Per Cent Americans on Strike." *Nation,* May 8, 1929.

CARSTENS, C. C. "The Children's Exodus from Lawrence." *Survey,* April 6, 1912.

COLE, J. N. "The Issue at Lawrence," the Manufacturers' Point of View: A Reply. *Outlook,* February 24, 1912.

Daily News Record. January 10, 1938, to July 1, 1938 (pertinent clippings).

DAVENPORT, WALTER. "All Work and No Pay." *Collier's,* November 13, 1937.

EBERLING, E. J. "The Strikes among the Textile Workers in the Southern States." *Current History,* June, 1929.

GORMAN, FRANCIS J. "The Textile Situation." *Vital Speeches,* October 22, 1934.

HILLMAN, SIDNEY. *Labor in the United States* (pamphlet), 1929. Published by the Amalgamated Clothing Workers.

—— "The N.R.A., Labor and Recovery." Annals of the American Academy of Political and Social Science, March, 1934.

LAUCK, JETT W. "The Significance of the Situation at Lawrence." *Survey,* February 17, 1912.

MCMAHON, THOMAS F. *United Textile Workers of America* (pamphlet), Workers' Education Bureau, 1926.

MARSHALL, MARGARET. "Textiles, an N.R.A. Strike." *Nation,* September 19, 1934.

MATTHEWS, T. S. "Gastonia in Court." *New Republic*, September 18, 1929.

"The Meaning of the Textile Drive." Editorial, *New Republic*, September 26, 1934.

MITCHELL, JONATHAN. "Here Comes Gorman." *New Republic*, October 3, 1934.

National Industrial Conference Board, *Individual and Collective Bargaining under the N.R.A.* A report, 1934.

National News Letter, Textile Workers Organizing Committee. Weekly (mimeographed), New York City, 1938.

New York Times. January 7 to May 21; September 30 to November 27, 1912; from March 1, 1937, to July 1, 1938 (pertinent clippings).

O'SULLIVAN, MARY K. "The Labor War at Lawrence." *Survey*, April 6, 1912.

PALMER, GLADYS L. *Union Tactics and Economic Change: A Case Study of Three Philadelphia Textile Unions* (Wharton School of Finance and Commerce, Industrial Research Department Studies 19). University of Pennsylvania Press, 1932.

Southern Textile Bulletin, January 30, 1930. *The Southern Worker*, March, 1937. *Textile World*, February 4, 1922. *The Textile Worker*, November 1, 1929.

Textile Notes. Labor Research Association, New York, monthly from January, 1936, to July, 1938.

VORSE, MARY HEATON. "The Trouble at Lawrence." *Harper's Weekly*, March 16, 1912.

Report of World Conference on the Social and Economic Problems of the Textile Industry, Washington (D.C.), April 2–17, 1937. A supplement to *Labor Gazette*, Department of Labor, Ottawa, Canada, May, 1937.

United States Bureau of Labor Statistics. *Average hourly earnings in manufacturing*, 1933 to 1936 (pamphlet). Prepared by A. F. Hinrichs, Bulletin No. R. 542; reprint from *Monthly Labor Review*, April, 1937. Washington.

—— Bulletin No. 439. Washington, 1928.

United States Commissioner of Labor. Annual Report, No. 21. Washington, 1906.

United States Department of Labor (Women's Bureau). *Lost Time and Labor Turnover in Cotton Mills*. Bulletin No. 52. Washington, 1926.

United States House of Representatives. *The Strike at Lawrence, Mass.* Committee on Rules (Hearings). 62d Congress, 2d Session, House Document No. 671. Washington, 1912.

United States Senate. Report on Strike of Textile Workers in Lawrence, Mass., in 1912. 62d Congress, 2d Session, Senate Document No. 870, 1912.

PART II

Clothing Workers

BUDISH, J. M., and SOULE, GEORGE. *The New Unionism in the Clothing Industry*. Macmillan, New York, 1920.

Documentary History of the Amalgamated Clothing Workers of America. Vols. I (1914-16); III (1918-20); V (1924-26); VIII (1928-30), published by the Union.

HARDY, JACK. *The Clothing Workers*. International Publishers, New York, 1935.

PRINCETON UNIVERSITY, Department of Industrial Relations. *The Labor Banking Movement in the United States*. Princeton University Press, Princeton, 1929.

ZARETZ, CHARLES ELBERT. *The Amalgamated Clothing Workers of America* (A Study in Progressive Trades Unionism). Ancon Publishing Co., New York, 1934.

HARDMAN, J. B. S. Amalgamated Almanac (1925 ed.). Pamphlet published by the Union, New York.

SCHLOSSBERG, JOSEPH. *The Rise of the Clothing Workers*. Pamphlet published by the Union, New York, 1921.

SWING, RAYMOND GRAM. "Sidney Hillman Turns Architect." *Nation*, April 3, 1935.

United States Bureau of Foreign and Domestic Commerce. *The Men's Factory-Made Clothing Industry*. Report No. 33. Washington, 1916.

United States Department of Labor, Bureau of Labor Statistics. *Wages and Hours of Labor in the Men's Clothing In-*

dustry, from 1911 to 1930. Bulletin No. 329. Washington, 1932.

National Industrial Conference Board, *Representative Experiences with Trade Union Agreements in the Clothing Industries*. Report No. 38. New York, 1921.

INDEX

Adamic, Louis, 292
Agreements: auto workers, 303; carpenters (N.Y., 1916), 165, 166; Female Improvement Society, 37; garment workers, 212, 217 (1910), 209, "Voluntary Code" of, 217; mine workers, 113; Newspaper Guild, 186; textile workers, 348
Alcott, Bronson, 52
Allison, James, 54
Altgeld, Gov. John P., 91, 240, 241
Amalgamated Clothing Workers, 334-338, 390
Amalgamated Labor Union, 92
Amalgamated Trades & Labor Assembly, 83
American Federation of Labor, 92-95, 97, 113, 130, 139, 162-164, 169, 186, 193, 203, 204, 211, 224, 244, 249, 277-279, 281-284, 291, 315, 316, 322, 423-424
American Federation of Labor: aims and doctrines of, 353, 354, 365, 366; and women, 358, 360; attitude resultant from court actions, 372
American Federation of Labor: attitude toward strikes, 367; C.I.O., 422; C.I.O. factionalism, 397; Convention (Atlantic City, 1935), 385-390; federal unions, 357; fusion discussed, 423; and industrial unionism, 385-390; influence of Gompers' ideas, 364, 365; and jurisdictional disputes, 163; jurisdictional theory, 356; membership (1900), 351, 352, (1924-29) 381-384, (1933) 384; and Negro workers, 360-362; Non-Partisan Political Campaign Committee, 406; and N.R.A., 384, 385; orders C.I.O. dissolved, 390; and politics, 405-408; presidential election (1924), 377; and Social Security Act, 405; status in 1920, 374; suspends insurgents, 391; trade union, idea of, 356; under N.L.R. Act, 398-400;

unskilled labor, 356, 358, 362; and World War, 374, 375
American Federation of Railroad Workers, 249
American Federation of Textile Operatives, 328
American Industrial Association, 280
American Labor party, N.Y., 221, 409, 410
American Labor Union, 315
American Liberty League, 169
American Miners' Association, 102, 104, 105
American Newspaper Guild, 173-191
American Newspaper Publishers Association, 179, 180
American Railway Union, 233, 235-239, 245, 250
American Woolen Company, 319-325
Anarchists, Chicago, 82-91
Anthracite Board of Trade, 107
Anti-Boycott Association, 370
Anti-Monopoly Movements, 42-44
Anti-Sweating League (N.Y., 1886), 200
Anti-union activity, post-war, 375
Antonini, Luigi, 221
Arbeiter Verein, 199
Arbitration, 128; coal strike (1902), 129; garment workers, 210, 211; General Motors, U.A.W., 303; railroads, 252, 263; textiles, 332
Architects, Engineers & Chemists, Federation of, 412
Associated Automobile Workers of America, 284
Associated Press, 179, 180, 184, 186
Associated Press vs. National Labor Relations Board, 184
Associated Silk Workers, 328
Association of Mechanics & Manufacturers, 10
Automobile, Aircraft & Vehicle Workers, United (1918), 277, 278

Automobile Industrial Workers Association, 284
Automobile Labor Board, 282
Automobile Workers of America, International Union of, 267-304
Automobile Workers, United, beginnings of, 283-287; in effort to elect city administration, 409, 411

Baer, George F., 120, 121, 126
Banking control of textiles, 339
Barkin, Solomon, 346
Barondess, Joseph, 201
Bates, John, 102
Beal, Fred E., 329
Beast of Property, 203
Beck, Dave, 171
Bennett, Harry, 274, 276
Benson, Elmer A., 424
Berry, George L., 377
Bingham, Alfred M., 425
Bituminous Coal Code, 141, 142
Black, Edward, 298, 299
Black International, 82
Blacklist, 95
Blue Dale Dress Company case, 219
Boom (1924-29), 380, 381
Boycott, 367-369; Hatters, 370; Anthracite Strike (1902), 122; Pullman (1894), 238; Textile (1938), 347
Boysen, George E., 298
Brandeis, Louis Dembitz, 209, 210
Brewster, T. T., 133
Bridges, Harry, 413, 414
Brindell, Robert P., 154-157, 166
Brisbane, Albert, 52
Brook Farm, 52
Brophy, John, 137, 141, 287, 391
Brotherhood of the Footboard, 226
Brotherhood of Locomotive Firemen, 226
Brotherhood of Railroad Brakemen, 227
Brotherhood of Railroad Firemen, 227
Brotherhood of Railroad Trainmen, 227
Brotherhood of Signalmen, 249
Broun, Heywood, 173-178, 422
Brown, Moses, 306, 307
——, Thomas H., 390

Bryan, William Jennings, 161
Building Trades Council (N.Y.C., 1919), 154-156
Building Trades Employers' Association, N.Y.C., 155
Business agents, 152-154, 157, 158

Cameron, A. C., 68, 69
Cannery, Agricultural Packing & Allied Workers, 412
Carey, James, 399, 423-424
Carpenters, N.Y.C. strike (1833), 38
Carpenters & Joiners, United Brotherhood of, 93, 149-172
Carpenters' Society of Philadelphia, 5
Carriage & Wagon Workers, International Union of (1891), 277
Caruso, Joseph, 325
Carven, Leslie, 263
C.C.C., 428
Central Labor Union, 83
Channing, William E., 52
——, William F., 52
——, William H., 52
Check-Off, 97, 138
"Chicago Idea," 82
Chrysler Motors, 271, 303
Citizens Alliance, 123; Miners' Strike (1902), 126; Textile Strike (Lawrence, 1912), 321
City Central, 17, 18, 38
Civic Federation of New England, 209
Civil War, unionism after, 57-95
Clark, E. E., 128
Cleveland, Grover, 240, 241, 247
Cloak Manufacturers Association, 201
Coal Commission (1919), 134
Coal Labor Board, 142
Coefield, John, 388
Cohn, Fannia M., 222
Collective Agreements. *See* Agreements
Collective bargaining, theory of, 2
Committee of Fifty (1829), 30, 31, 33, 34, 35
Committee of Forty-Eight, 376
Committee for Industrial Organization (C.I.O.), 144, 145, 170-172, 186, 224, 225, 250, 283-291, 298, 302,

303, 305, 330, 331, 339, 345, 423-424; and Communism, 411-414; and Politics, 408-411; and Social Security Act, 405; organization and purposes of, 390, 396; steel campaign of, 391
Committee on Waste in Industry (1921), 151
Common law, definition of, 12
Communist International (1920), 211
Communist, *Manifesto*, 423-425
Communists, 211-213, 216, 280, 411-414
Company Unions, 281, 282
Conditions of Labor: automobiles, 269-277; garment industry, 198, 199; mining, 101, 114, 115; textiles, 311, 312, 314, 341, 343
Conference for Progressive Political Action (1924), 376, 377
Conspiracy, Criminal, 12-15, 109, 247, 326
Convention: C.I.O. (1938), 423-424; I.L.G.W.U. (1900), 193; I.L.G.W.U. (1910), Tenth Convention, 207; Newspaper Guild (1936), 189; U.M.W. (1902), 123; of Workingmen, National, 60
Coolidge, Calvin, 377
Coöperative Iron Founders Association, Troy, 70, 71
Coöperatives, 70-74
Cordwainers, Federal Society of Journeymen, 11
Corporations Auxiliary, 274
Creel, George, 176, 375
Crittenden Amendment, 61
Cummings, Samuel, 71
Cutters Union No. 10, 213, 215, 216

Danbury Hatters case (1903), 370, 371, 418
Danish, Max D., 220
Darrow, Clarence, 245
Davenport, Daniel, 371
Davis, John W., 377
Davis, William, 75
Davis-Kelly Act, 98, 140
Debs, Eugene Victor, 235-247, 316
DeCaux, Len, 178, 290
DeLeon, Daniel, 203, 316, 318
Dewey, Thomas E., 409, 417

Dillon, Francis J., 283, 284, 285
Dress & Cloak Makers (N.Y.C.), 201
Dressmakers Local No. 89, 221
Dubinsky, David, 213, 224, 390
Duffy, Frank, 168, 170

Earle, William H., 72
Eastman, Joseph B., 252
Eddy, Jonathan, 175, 179
Education: Garment Workers, 200; I.L.G.W.U., 222; labor's campaign for, 19, 20, 25, 26, 27
Eight Hour Association, 81
Eight-hour day, 66-68, 80, 251
Eight-hour strike (1886), 84
Emerson, Ralph W., 52
Employer Associations: Association of Railroad Executives, 258; Automobile Chamber of Commerce, 278; Building Trades, 155; Cloak Manufacturers, 201; General Managers Association, 238, 239, 241; Motor Mechanics of Boston (1867), 75; Michigan (1864), 74; National Association of Manufacturers, 375, 376, 383, 396, 400, 415, 416; National Industrial Council, 415; N.Y. Master Builders Association (1869), 75
Engel, George, 84, 90
Engels, Friedrich, 423
Epstein, Abraham, 404, 405
Ernst, Morris, 184
Espionage, 94, 95, 118, 274, 275, 276
Ettor, Joseph, 315-327
Evans, Chris, 113
——, George Henry, 33, 44-55, 67

Fahy, Charles, 394
Farrington, Frank, 138
Fashion Originators' Guild, 219
Federal Railroad Administration, 251, 252
Federal social security, legislation for, 401
Federal unions, 171, 281, 359
Federation of Organized Trades & Labor Unions, 80, 92
Female Improvement Society, Philadelphia, 37
Fielden, Samuel, 84, 88-91, 241
Filene, A. Lincoln, 209

Fincher, Jonathan, 62, 67
Firemen & Enginemen, Brotherhood of, 249
Fischer, Adolph, 84, 90
Flint Alliance, 297, 298, 302
Flynn, Elizabeth Gurley, 319, 322
Ford, Henry, 271, 274, 275-276, 278, 279-280, 303
Foster, William Z., 137, 211-213, 216
Fourier, François, 52
Frankensteen, Richard, 275
Freedom of the press, 180, 181
Free homesteads, 48-55
Frey, John P., 387, 388, 405, 411, 423
Fur Workers, National, 412

Gadola, Paul V., 300
Gandhi, Mahatma, 292
Garment Workers, United, 334
General Motors, 268, 271, 274, 278, 280, 285-288, 295-296, 297-304
"General Trades Union" (N.Y.C., 1833), 38, 39
General Trades Union (Philadelphia, 1831), 37
George, Henry, 46, 354
Giovannitti, Arturo, 319, 321, 325, 326, 327
Girdler, Tom, 418
Globe Machine & Stamping Company case, 398
"Globe" policy, N.L.R. Board, 398
Godwin, Parke, 52
Gompers, Samuel, 93, 94, 123, 125, 130, 205, 250, 253, 281, 351, 352, 356, 357, 362-366, 368-370, 374, 389, 429
Gorman, Francis J., 331, 332
Government Ownership of Railroads, 253
Gowan, Franklin P., 107, 118
Greeley, Horace, 48, 53, 54, 354
Green, Dean Leon, 295
——, William, 97, 134, 170, 250, 278, 283, 291, 378-380, 389, 390, 401, 406, 417, 429
Guffey-Snyder Act, 98, 142
Guffey-Vinson Act, 98, 142, 143
Guild, American Newspaper, 173-191

Hall, Helen, 267
Hanna, Mark, 121, 122, 128, 370

Hanson, Elisha, 179, 181
Hapgood, Powers, 137, 141
Harding, Warren G., 254, 260, 261
——, William, 68
Hardman, J. B. S., 418, 420
Harrison, Carter H., 87, 88
——, George, 265
Hart, Schaffner, and Marx, 333, 334-335
Hatters of America, United, 370, 371
Hayes, Rutherford B., 231
Haymarket, 86-90, 241, 365
Haywood, William Dudley, 316-328
Health Center, 222; I.L.G.W.U., 223
Hibernians, Ancient Order of, 115-119
Hillman, Sidney, 331-347, 390, 391, 411, 417, 423-424
Hirsch, Alfred, 415
Hochman, Julius, 222
Homestead Act, 48, 55
Homesteads, Free, 48-55
Hoover, Herbert, 260, 261, 384
Hopedale, 52
Hosiery Workers, American Federation of, 338
Hosiery Workers, Federation of Full-Fashioned, 328
Hours of work, automobile, 280; garment workers, 194, 201
Howard, Charles P., 385, 386, 390
——, George W., 237, 245
——, Roy, 177
Howarth, Charles, 72
Howatt, Alexander, 138
Hutcheson, William, 154, 164-172, 377, 388, 390, 407

"Immigrants' Strike," 201
Immigration, effect on textiles, 313; coal miners, 99; garment workers, 196-198, 204
Incorporation of Unions, 416-419
Industrial Revolution, 21-22
Industrial Unionism, 113, 114, 236, 277, 334, 385-390, 423
Industrial Workers of the World, 203, 204, 280, 293, 315-328
Ingalls, John J., 204
Injunction: against I.L.G.W.U. (1910), 209; United Miners (1919), 133; Buck Company vs. boycott,

368, 369; Conspiracy, 367; General Motors Strike, 298, 300; Pullman case, 232, 243; under Federal Legislation, 373

International Working People's Association, 82, 203

"Interstate Trade Agreement" (1886), 113

"Iron-Clad" Contracts, 111

Iron & Steel Workers, Amalgamated Association of, 92

"Jacksonville Agreement" (1927), 139

Jensen, Harry, 167

Jessup, William, 67

Jurisdiction, 356

Jurisdictional disputes between unions, 163, 171

Kellogism, 68, 69

Kirchwey, Frieda, 208

Knights of Industry, 92

Knights of Labor, 76-81, 89-95, 110-113, 201-204, 232, 316, 360, 365

Knights of St. Crispin, Order of, 71, 72

Knudsen, William S., 285, 286, 300, 302

Kriege, Herman, 50

Labor, defined, 4; history (early), 5-55; from the Civil War on, 57-95

Labor: housing, coöperative, 338; immigrant, miners (1910), 103, 104; immigration in the 1880's, 111; in railroads, type of, 249; in textiles, type of, 308, 309, 310, 341, 345; introduction to American, 1-5; labor movement defined, 17; Negro, 360, 361, 362; number of workers (1820, 1825), 17; skilled, carpenters, etc., number of, 149, miners, 100; unskilled, 9, organization of, 357, 358, 362

Labor, of women: in textiles, 345; proportion of, employed 1880-1930, 258; wages of (1834-36), 37

Labor banking, 336, 337

Labor legislation: Adamson Law (1916), 248, 251; Ash-Pan Act (1908), 248; Clayton Act (1914),

373; Commerce Act (1888), 248; Davis-Kelly bill, 98; early 8-hour laws, 67; eight-hour law (Pa., 1868), 106; Elkins Act (1903), 248; Emergency Railroad Transportation Act (1933), 248; Erdman Act (1898), 248; Federal Wages and Hours Act, 306, 349; General, 4, 36; Guffey-Snyder and Guffey-Vinson Acts, 98; National Labor Relations Act, 391-397; N.R.A., 384, 385; Norris-LaGuardia Anti-Injunction Act (1932), 373; Railway Boiler Inspection Act (1911), 248; Railway Hours of Service Act (1907), 248; Railway Labor Act (1926), 248, 262; Railway Labor Act Amendment (1934), 248, 262, 263; Railway-Safety Act (1893), 248; Railway Safety Appliance Act (1910), 248; Ten Hour Law (1847), 52; Transportation Act (1920), 248, 254, 255; Transportation of Explosives Act (1909), 248; Valuation Act (1913), 248; Wagner Labor Relations Act (1937), 4

Labor news services: Federated Press, 422; International Labor News Service (A.F.L.), 422; Union News Service (C.I.O.), 290, 422

Labor Press, 421; Advance, 418, 421; The Alarm, 83, 90; Budoucnost, 83; The Carpenter, 167, 168, 169; Chicagoer-Arbeiter-Zeitung, 83, 84, 86, 90; C.I.O. News, 178, 422; Daily Worker, 421; The Federationist, 368, 421; Fincher's Trades Review, 63, 64; Gerechtigkeit, 220; Giustizia, 220; Journal of Locomotive Engineers, 421; Justice, 220, 421; Labor, 254, 421; The Messenger, 361; National Labor Tribune, 73; New Leader, 421; New Post, 208; N.Y. Call, 208; People's Press, 421; U.M.W.'s Journal, 421; Vorwarts, 208; Workingman's Advocate, 33, 45, 47

Labor Reform Association (1864), 67

Labor's Non-Partisan League (C.I.O.), 331, 408-410
Labor stage, 222
Ladies' Garment Workers' Union, International, 170, 193-224, 338, 390, 424; membership, 220
LaFollette, Fola, 208
——, Philip F., 424
——, Robert M., 169, 376, 377
LaFollette Senate subcommittee, 274
LaGuardia, F. H., 409
Landis Award, 167
Lauck, W. Jett, 98, 256
Lawrence, R. R., 348
Leach, Joshua A., 227
League of Women Shoppers, 347
Legal Tender Acts, 62
Lehman, Herbert H., 409
Lehr und Wehr Verein, 83
Lever Act, 131, 132
Lewis, John L., 97, 98, 130-144, 169, 170, 250, 283, 287, 291, 300, 302, 332, 377-379, 386, 387, 390, 391, 408, 411, 417, 423-424
Lingg, Louis, 84, 90
Lloyd, Thomas, 102
Lockout, McCormick Reaper Works (1886), 85-86
Lockwood Committee, 157
Locomotive Engineers, Brotherhood of, 249, 250
Loewe, D. E., 370
Longshoremen, 413
Lo Pizzo, Anna, 321
Lovett, Robert Morss, 295
Lowell, Francis Cabot, 307

McCormick, Cyrus, 85
McGuire, P. J., 93, 160, 161
McKinley, William, 121, 127, 370
Machinists & Blacksmiths, International Union of, 62, 75
MacMahon, Thomas, 390
McParland, James, 118
Madden, J. Warren, 393
Martin, Homer S., 3, 284-287, 302, 304, 411
Marx, Karl, 50, 423-428
Marxism, 82
Masquerier, Lewis, 53
Mechanics Educational Society, 279
"Mechanics Union of Trade Associations," 17, 36

Mechanization of Auto Industry, 273
Mediation Commission, President's World War, 374
Merchant Capitalist, dominance of, 7-11
Metal Polishers, International, 367
Mine, Mill & Smelter Workers, 390
Miners Fight for American Standards, John L. Lewis, 138
Miners & Mine Laborers of the U.S., National Federation of (1885), 112, 113
Miners' National Association of the U.S.A. (1873), 108, 109, 110
Miners' Union, Progressive, 113
Mine Workers of America, United, 97, 148, 170, 206, 250, 338, 390, 408
Mitchell, John, 121-129, 369, 370
Moley, Raymond, 140
Molly Maguires, 115-119
Moody, Paul, 307
Moore, Ely, 38, 39
Morgan, House of, 120, 138
Morgan, J. P., 121, 127, 128
Morrison, Frank, 369, 370
Mortimer, Wyndham, 297, 302, 411
Most, Johann, 82, 89, 202, 203, 205
Moulders' International Union, 60, 69, 70, 71, 75
Murphy, Gov. Frank, 300-303, 424
Murray, Philip, 136, 287, 391, 411, 423-424
——, Walter, 173
Mutual Life Insurance Association, 226

Nagler, Isadore, 216
National Association of Manufacturers, 375, 376, 383, 396, 400, 415, 416
National Bituminous Coal Commission, 142, 143
National Coal Conservation Bill, 142
National Convention (Philadelphia, 1861), 60, 61
National Electric Products Corporation case, 399
National Industrial Council, 415
National Labor Congress (1866), 68
National Labor Relations Act, 179, 185, 301, 391-397, 400, 410
National Labor Relations Board, 180,

275, 410; explanatory, powers, purposes, history, 391-397; record of, 396-399; textiles, 348

National Labor Union, 68, 69

N.R.A., 3, 140-142, 216, 272, 282, 384-385; code, action, industrial, 280; cotton code, 331, 332; newspaper code, 178

National Railway Mediation Board, 248, 263, 264; Pullman election, 361

National Trades Union (1834), 39

Neebe, Oscar, 84, 90, 91, 241

"New Agrarianism," 44-55

New Deal, 98, 408

New Harmony, community of, 21-29

New Lanark, Owen Mills at, 22

"New Odessa," 197

Newspaper Guild, American, 173-191

N.Y. Cloak Joint Board, 216

Nihilism, 82, 202

Norris-LaGuardia Act, 373, 406

O'Connor, Terence, 377

Office & Professional Workers, United, 412

Old Age Benefits, Social Security Act, 401, 402, 403, 404

Olney, Attorney-General, 240, 242-243, 245, 247, 369

Order of Railway Conductors, 226, 249

Owen, Robert, 21, 22

——, Robert Dale, 20, 21, 24, 25, 34

Panic of 1857, 57

Parsons, Albert, 83, 88, 89, 90

Patrons of Husbandry, 71

Peel, John A., 348

Perkins, Frances, 300, 392

Petty, William, quoted, 8-9

Phillips, Thomas, 64, 72

——, Wendell, 67

Pier & Dock Carpenters' Union, 154

Pinkerton Agency, 94, 95, 274

Pinkerton detectives, 118

Pins and Needles, 222

Pioneers of Freedom, 199

Plumb, Glenn E., 253

Plumb Plan, 253, 254, 255, 265

Populist Movement, 247

Porter, Russell B., 183

Powderly, Terence V., 78, 79, 80, 91, 93, 94, 110-111

Powell, Thomas Reed, 373

"Preferential Shop," Newspaper Guild, 190

Pressman, Lee, 302

Price, Dr. George M., 223

Protocol of Peace, Garment Workers (1910), 209, 210-211

Progressive Independents, 377, 378

Propaganda, of employers in automobile strike, 297-298

Propaganda and Pressure Groups, 25

Property, definition of private, 4

Property rights in jobs, 294-295

P.W.A., 428

Publicity and Labor, 414-415, 416, 417, 418, 419

Pullman, George M., 232, 233, 234, 235

Racketeering in unions, 155, 416, 417

Railway Adjustment Boards, 252

Railway Conductors, Order of, 226, 249

Railway Labor Board under 1920 Act, 255, 256, 257, 258

Railway Mediation Board, National, 248, 263, 264

Railway unions, 225-265

Randolph, A. Philip, 361

Rand School, 421

Red Labor Union, 211

Rend, W. P., 111, 112, 113

Reuther, Victor, 298-299

——, Walter, 275

Rieve, Emil, 348, 407

Rights of Man to Property, Thomas Skidmore, 31

Rochdale coöperative system, 72

Roosevelt, Franklin D., 140, 282, 300, 302, 332, 393, 408, 409, 424

——, Theodore, 127, 128, 370

Rose, Alex, 409

Rosenberg, Abraham, 201, 208, 210

Saposs, David J., 394

Schilling, George A., 81

Schwab, Michael, 84, 90, 91, 241

Science of Revolutionary Warfare, 202

Seniority rights, 273
Sherman Anti-Trust Law, 369; Debs's conviction under, 245-246, 247; used against United Hatters, 365, 371
Sherman, Charles O., 317
Shop rules, 354
Siney, John, 107, 108, 109, 110
Single tax, 46
"Sit-down" strike, 288, 289, 290, 291, 292, 293, 294, 295, 296, 297
Skidmore, Thomas, 30, 31, 33, 34, 35, 44, 45, 46, 49
Slater, Samuel, 306, 307, 308, 310
Slavery, Labor's stand on, 59
Sleeping Car Porters, Brotherhood of, 361, 362
Sliding scale of wages, 107
Sloan, Alfred P., 300
"Slow-down," 289
Smith, Adam, 21
——, Donald Wakefield, 393
——, Edwin S., 393
——, Sidney, quoted, 16
Social Security Act (1935), 401-405
Socialist Labor party, 82, 199, 203, 205, 280
Socialists, 352
Sokolsky, George, 416
Sombart, Werner, 427
Soule, George, 428
Sovereigns of Industry, 71, 72, 73
"Speed-up," 270, 271, 272
Spies, August, 84, 86, 87, 88, 89, 90
Starr, Mark, 222
State guardianship, Owen plan of, 25, 26, 27
"Stay-in," 288
Steel, 222
Steel Workers' Organizing Committee, 287, 391, 395, 396, 418
Stephens, Uriah Smith, 76, 77, 78
Steward, Ira, 65, 66, 67, 80
Stone, Warren S., 253
Stove Founders National Defense Association, 368
Stove Manufacturers & Iron Founders Association, 69
Strasser, Adolph, 93, 351, 352
"Stretch-out," 272
Strikebreakers, 239, 260; Anthracite Strike (1902), 122

Strikes: Automobile—tool and die makers (1933), 279; Railway (1922), 258, 259, 260, 261; Boston carpenters (1825), 16; Buck's Stove & Range Co. (1906), 367, 368; carpenters (N.Y.C., 1833), 38; carpenters (N.Y., 1916), 166; Connellsville (Pa.) mine strike (1875), 106; eight-hour strike (1886), 84-85; first "organized," 11; first use of Federal troops, B & O Railway (1877), 230; Garment Workers (N.Y.C., 1883), 201, (1926), 216; General Motors sit-down (1936), 268; I.L.G.W.U. (1910), 207, 208; Lawrence textile (1912), 319, 320, 321, 322, 323, 324, 325; mine (Clearfield), 109; miners, Hocking Valley (Ohio, 1884), 111; miners (1902), 122, (Nov. 1, 1919), 133; Pullman Strike (1894), 232, 235, 237, 238, 239, 240, 241, 242; Railroads (1877), 230, 231, 239 (1882-84), 78; Sit-down-Automobile (1936) Fisher Body (Flint, Mich.), 286, 287, 297, 298, 299, 300, 301, 302, 303; Sit-down, first (1906), General Electric (Schenectady, N.Y.), 293; Steel (McKeesport Rocks, Pa., 1909), I.W.W., 318; Textile (1924-33), 328, 329; Textile walkout (1934), 331; Textile (Bigelow, 1938), 347; U.M.W. (1898), 97; use of Federal troops, Pullman, 240, 241
Sullivan, Mary K., 322
Supreme Court, 4, 216; Debs case, 246; Danbury Hatters case, 371
Sylvania, 52
Sylvis, William H., 60, 61, 68, 69, 70

Taff-Vale decision, 372
Talmadge, Eugene, 340
Tammany Hall, 156
Taylor, Frederick W., 269
Ten-hour day, 51, 52; carpenters (1825), 16
Textile Labor Relations Board, 332
Textile Workers of America, United, 315, 322, 328, 329, 331, 390
Textile Workers Union, Communist National, 328

Textile Workers' Union, National Industrial, 325
T.W.O.C., 305-349, 417
Trade Assembly, 65
Trevellick, R. F., 64
Tobin, Daniel J., 364, 388, 390, 407
Tocqueville, Alexis de, 39-40
Tracy, Daniel, 388, 390, 399
Trade union, definition and significance of, 2
Trade Union Educational League, 211
Trades & Labor Council, St. Louis, 368
Trainmen, Brotherhood of, 227, 249
Trautman, William, 322
Typographical Society, 28, 38
Typographical Union, International, 174, 354, 355, 390

Unemployment in 1890's, 204
Unemployment Compensation, in Social Security Act, 401, 402, 404
Union Coöperative Association, 72
Union Health Center, 222, 223
Unions: business agents, 152, 153, 154; effect of immigration on, 111; growth (1863-64), 63, 64; industrial vs. craft, garment workers, 206; jurisdiction, 356; jurisdictional disputes, 163, 171; label, 367; membership, carpenters, 158, I.L.G.W.U., 220, T.W.O.C., 348, 349, U.A.W. (1836 and 1895 compared), 38, 237 (1938), 303, miners, 97, 98, railway, 249; organizers, 345, 346; press, 419, 420, 421; under N.R.A., 385
U.S. Commission on Industrial Relations, 294, 295, 351
U.S. Steel Corporation, 144
Unity House, 223
Untermyer, Samuel, 157, 166

Wages: auto workers, 267, 268; carpenters (1833), 38; in the 1860's, 62, 63; garment workers, 194, 199, 201; miners, 107, (1884) 111,

(1927) 139, (1930) 141; mining, 131; mining, hard coal (1900), 120; newspaper employees, 179; railway, 252, 255, 256, 257, 258; railway Pullman workers, 233, 234; shoemakers (1799), 11, 12; "Sliding Scale," 107; textiles, 314, 330, 331, 349; women (1834-36), 37
Wagner Labor Relations Act, validation of, 4
Walker, Edwin, 242
War Labor Board, 131, 374
Walls, H. V., 75
Warrens, Henry, 98
Waterfront Worker, 414
Watson, Morris, 180, 184
Weaver, Daniel, 102
Weisbord, Albert, 328
Wexley, John, 222
Wiggins, Mrs. Ella May, 329
Wharton, Arthur O., 388
Wheeler, Burton K., 376, 377
White, John P., 130, 380
——, William Allen, 188
Whitney, A. F., 265
Williamson, Floyd E., 297-298
Wilson, Woodrow, 131, 132, 134, 251
Winant Board (textiles), 332
Wolman, Dr. Leo, 282
Woll, Matthew, 378, 379, 384, 405
Women's Committee on Political Action, 376
Women's Unions, 37
Woodworkers of America, International, 171, 412
W.P.A., 428
Woodworkers' Union, 162, 163
Workingmen's Benevolent Association of Schuylkill County, Pa., 107
Workingmen's party, beginnings of, 18
Workingmen's parties, development of, 29, 36, 45
Wright, Frances, 28, 29

Zaritsky, Max, 39

/c